ELIE ASSIS, Ph.D. (1999) in Biblical studies, Bar-Ilan University, Israel, is a lecturer of Bible at Bar-Ilan University. He has published on literary and theological aspects of biblical narrative including a study on the Book of Joshua: *From Moses to Joshua and From the Miraculous to the Ordinary* (Magnes, 2005, in Hebrew).

Self-Interest or Communal Interest

Supplements

to

Vetus Testamentum

Edited by the Board of the Quarterly

VOLUME 106

Self-Interest or Communal Interest

An Ideology of Leadership in the Gideon, Abimelech and Jephthah Narratives (Judg 6–12)

by

Elie Assis

BRILL

LEIDEN • BOSTON

2005

This book is printed on acid-free paper.

Translated by Stephanie Nakache

Library of Congress Cataloging-in-Publication Data

Assis, Eliyahu.
  Self-interest or communal interest : an ideology of leadership in the Gideon, Abimelech, and Jephthah narratives (Judg. 6–12) / by Elie Assis.
      p. cm. — (Supplements to Vetus Testamentum, ISSN 0083-5889 ; 106)
  Includes bibliographical references and index.
  ISBN 90-04-14354-8 (alk. paper)
    1. Bible. O.T. Judges VI–XII—Commentaries. 2. Leadership—Biblical teaching.
I. Title II. Series.

BS410.V452 vol. 106
[BS1305.6.L4]
222'.3206—dc22

                                                                                2005042197

ISSN 0083-5889
ISBN 90 04 14354 8

PRINTED IN THE NETHERLANDS

To my dear parents
(Proverbs 1:8–9)

CONTENTS

ACKNOWLEDGEMENTS

I thank the Almighty for enabling me to dedicate time to the study of scriptures so that I can fulfill ללמוד וללמד לשמור ולעשות.

I wish to thank my dear parents Yom Tov and Klara Assis. To my mother, for her devoted love and concern all these years. Her warmth has had a formative impact on my personality and my debt to her is immeasurable. My father is my mentor. I derive from him counsel and he is an inspiration for me in every way. His wisdom and understanding are for me a guiding light. It is difficult for me to express in words my appreciation for them, and for the way in which they are always there for me. May they be blessed with long life, and may they continue to derive joy and happiness from their children and grandchildren. It is to them that this book is dedicated with love and admiration.

Prof. Yair Zakovitch read an earlier version of this work and I thank him for his assistance. I wish to particularly thank him for his advice and encouragement over the years. In spite of the great burdens upon him, he has always found the time to offer me so generously his wise and expert advice. I wish to also thank my friends Dr. Jonathan Jacobs, who reviewed the Hebrew version of this book, and Dr. Joshua Berman for his skillful comments. Thanks go to Stephanie Nakache for her patience and diligence in translating the book.

Special appreciation is accorded to Bar-Ilan University for enabling me to invest my energies in that which I love doing more than anything else. Particularly, I would like to express my thanks to my colleagues and friends in the Department of Bible at Bar-Ilan, whose friendship has made our department such a pleasant place to work in.

I have no words to express my gratitude to Prof. André Lemaire, the general editor of Supplements to Vetus Testamentum. Prof. Lemaire was extremely supportive in the project's early stages. Without his encouragement, it is doubtful that the book would have appeared in its present form. I would also like to thank Mattie Kuiper and Kim Fiona Plas for their efforts in producing such a quality product in such an efficient manner.

I would like to acknowledge with gratitude the kind and generous support of "Beit Shalom"—Japan, that made this research possible.

Finally and most significantly, I would like to thank with deep love my wife Hanna and my children, Yom Tov and Shlomi, who grant profound meaning to all that is beautiful and exalted in Scripture.

Elie Assis
Adar I, 5765 – February 2005, Jerusalem

ABBREVIATIONS

AB = Anchor Bible
ABD = Anchor Bible Dictionary
BA = Biblical Archaeologist
BAIAS = Bulletin of Anglo-Israel Archaeological Society
BASOR = Bulletin of the American Schools of Oriental Research
BHS = Biblia Hebraica Stuttgartensia, Stuttgart 1984
CBC = Cambridge Bible Commentaries
CBQ = Catholic Biblical Quarterly
DCH = The Dictionary of Classical Hebrew, vols. 1–5, Sheffield 1993–
   2001
DJD = Discoveries in the Judaean Desert, IX, Oxford 1995
HALOT = The Hebrew and Aramaic Lexicon of the Old Testament, vols.
   1–5, Leiden 1994–2000
ICC = International Critical Commentary
JANES = The Journal of the Ancient Near Eastern Society
JBL = Journal of Biblical Literature
JJS = The Journal of Jewish Studies
JNES = Journal of Near Eastern Studies
JNSL = Journal of Northwest Semitic Languages
JPOS = Journal of the Palestine Oriental Society
JPS = *Tanakh: The New JPS Translations According to the Traditional
   Hebrew Text*, 1985
JTS = The Journal of Theological Studies
JSOPsup = Journal for the Study of The Pseudepigrapha, supple-
   ment series
JSOT = Journal for the Study of the Old Testament
JSOTsup = Journal for the Study of the Old Testament, supple-
   ment series
JSS = Journal of Semitic Studies
OTL = Old Testament Library
PEQ = Palestine Exploration Quarterly
RB = Revue Biblique
SBL = Society of Biblical Literature
SVT = Supplements to Vetus Testamentum

TZ = *Theologische Zeitschrift*
UF = *Ugarit-Forschungen*
USQR = *Union Seminary Quarterly Review*
VT = *Vetus Testamentum*

INTRODUCTION

The Book of Judges describes the period between the conquest of the land of Israel and the founding of the monarchy. Each of the judge deliverer accounts is made up of a four-stage cycle: the people transgress, practicing idolatry; God's punishes them through an enemy that oppresses Israel; the people lament to God; and a judge-deliverer appears to combat the enemy and deliver the people. This cycle appears in six accounts: Othniel (3:7–11), Ehud (3:12–30), Deborah (chap. 4), Gideon (chaps. 6–8), Jephthah (11:1–12:7) and Samson (chaps. 13–16). The main part of each of these accounts focuses on the description of the deliverance and of the figure of the judge-deliverer.[1]

The tribulations described in the book did not affect all the people of Israel, but smaller areas, and the judge leadership also seems to have been local and not over all the people. Avraham Malamat pointed out that the judge accounts are not repetitive; in each account the battle arena differs, the enemy differs and there are no two judges who came from the same tribe. He therefore concludes that the book presents different models of the types of oppressors and the different types of judges. In his opinion, the Book of Judges is a selective collection of accounts of wars from the pre-monarchic period in Israel.[2] There is evidence in the book itself of wars and

---

[1] The Hebrew word שפט has two distinctive meanings: 1. to rule (e.g.: 1 Sam 8:20; 2 Kings 15:5; Ps 2:10); 2. to judge in a juridical sense (e.g.: Deut 16:18). With the exception of Deborah (Judg 4:4–5), throughout the Book of Judges the meaning of the root שפט is to rule. On this topic see: O. Grether, "Die Bezeichnung 'Richter' für die charismatischen Helden der vorstaatlichen Zeit", *ZAW* 57 (1939), pp. 110–121; T. Ishida, "The Leaders of the Tribal Leagues: 'Israel' in the Pre-Monarchic Period", *RB* 80 (1973), pp. 514–530; M. Rosenberg, "The Šofᵉtim in the Bible", *Eretz Israel* 12 (1975), pp. 77–86; D. A. Mckenzie, "The Judge of Israel", *VT* 17 (1967), pp. 118–121. For an additional bibliography see: M. A. O'Brien, "Judges and the Deuteronomistic History", S. L. McKenzie and M. P. Graham (eds.), *The History of Israel's Traditions: The Heritage of Martin Noth* (JSOTsup, 182), Sheffield 1994, p. 236 n. 1.

[2] A. Malamat, *History of Biblical Israel: Major Problems and Minor Issues* (Culture and History of the Ancient Near East, vol. 7, Leiden 2001), pp. 153–154. Some think that it is no coincidence that the Book presents twelve judges. See S. Herrmann, *A History of Israel in Old Testament Times* (trans. J. Bowden), London 1975, p. 115.

events that were not included. In the introduction to the Jephthah
account, God reviews the period of the judges until that point,
describing how Israel returned to their transgression after He delivered them each time from another oppressor (Judg 10:11–12). This
review includes oppressors of whom there is no other mention in
the book of Judges, e.g.: the Maonites and the Zidonians; there is
also no account of deliverance from Ammon prior to this introduction. The most reasonable explanation of this lack of correspondence
between the list and the accounts in the Book of Judges is that the
book did not include all the events of the period and the list reflects
a historic reality of which there is no trace in the book in our possession.[3] The natural conclusion is that the book is merely a selection of accounts.

If indeed the Book of Judges presents only a representative sam-
ple of the events of the period, the question that follows is what the
considerations and criteria were for the inclusion in the book of the
specific accounts that do appear. What are the principles at the basis
of the structure of the book, and how did these considerations and
principles contribute to the shaping of the individual accounts? This
is the general question at the basis of this work in relation to the
Gideon, Abimelech and Jephthah accounts.

This work presents an analysis of three accounts in the Book of
Judges: the Gideon, Abimelech and Jephthah accounts. These three
accounts were selected because they deal above all with the same
subject: the extent to which the protagonist is suited to the role of
leader. In these three accounts the subject of their leadership appears
as a central part of the plot; such is not the case in the other judge
accounts. The people ask Gideon to rule over them, Abimelech actually rules. In the introduction to the Jephthah account, the princes
of Gilead propose that whosoever among them leads them in their
war will be head over all the inhabitants of Gilead. Subsequently

---

However, it is unlikely that it was intended to present a judge as a representative
for each tribe since there is not a judge for every tribe. Hermann's theory of
insufficient material is unconvincing. It should rather be assumed that there is no
editorial significance in the mention of twelve judges in the Book.

[3] The historical overview in 1 Sam 12:11 mentions the Judge "Bedan". It is
widely believed that this name refers to Samson. See BT, Rosh HaShana 25, 1.
Zakovitch suggested that Bedan is Jephthah, see: Y. Zakovitch, "יפתח=בדן", *VT* 22
(1972), pp. 123–125. However, it is possible that the verse in Samuel refers to a
judge who is not mentioned in the Book of Judges.

Jephthah agrees to deliver the people only after he is appointed head. What is unique in these three accounts is that they represent the negative aspect of the leadership. The climax in the extreme description of the negative trait of the personalities in the three accounts is in their savage slaughter of their fellow Israelites (8:14–17; 9:5, 40, 43–45, 49–52; 12:4–6). The three leaders kill their fellow Israelites in a situation of dispute and because they wish to protect their personal status. These are the only judges to act in this way. No other account in the Book of Judges deals so intensively with the subject of leadership. This is the reason for dedicating of a work specifically to these three accounts.

Critical study of the Book of Judges initially adopted the approach that the book is essentially a collection of J and E Pentateuch sources edited by the Deuteronomist.[4] While the scholars of this school were aware that the redaction of the Book adapted the accounts to a uniform pattern, their main concern was with criticism of the early sources, and far less with the late redaction of the accounts. Little attention was paid to the book in its final form, perhaps because the editors were not considered original authors, and because generally, scholars considered that most of the editorial material was limited to various connecting passages.[5]

The turning point came with Martin Noth's studies on the redaction of the Pentateuch and of the historical books. Noth asserted that the sources of the different judge accounts were not Pentateuchal but individual local accounts that were merged at an early stage, and subsequently the Deuteronomistic redaction unified the stories

---

[4] See e.g.: D. K. Budde, *Das Buch der Richter* (KHAT), Leipzig und Tübingen 1897, pp. xii–xv; G. F. Moore, *Judges* (ICC), Edinburgh 1895, pp. xxv ff.; C. F. Burney, *The Book of Judges*, London 1918, pp. xxxvii ff. A detailed source analysis of Judges is found in Simpson's monograph: C. A. Simpson, *The Composition of the Book of Judges*, Oxford 1957. The source analysis of the Book of Judges is not based on the typical vocabulary of J and E and not on stylistic characteristics. It is based principally on literary features such as inconsistencies, duplications and repetitions, but mainly on the assumptions that the Pentateuchal sources should be found in the Book. See Moore, *Judges*, p. xxv; C. F. Whitley, "The Sources of the Gideon Stories", *VT* 7 (1957), pp. 157–164. This approach is no longer adopted in scholarly works. For criticism on this approach see: S. P. Roberts, *Content and Form Within the Jephthah Narrative: A Literary-Historical Investigation*, Diss, The Southern Baptist Theological Seminary 1991, pp. 81–83.

[5] J. Barton, *Reading the Old Testament: Method in Biblical Study*[2], London 1996, pp. 45–46.

through introductions and conclusions.[6] There was a broad consensus in the research world around Noth's approach.

Noth, to a great extent, redirected research from the focus on the source of the individual accounts to the unifying redaction of the accounts. Barton correctly noted that the result of criticism of the redaction was that the more this criticism succeeded in showing the artistic work of the redaction, which combined various sources and created a coherent text from them, the less the importance that was attached to the different sources in the work's infrastructure.[7] As the redaction gained increasing importance, the borders became blurred between the stages of the composition and of the redaction.[8] In this way, diachronic Bible study was exhausted and the circumstances were created for application of new literary approaches.

The new critical approach known as 'New Criticism', evaluates the actual work separately from its historical background and the author's intentions. The work had to be studied on its own merits only. The new literary criticism was applied to large parts of the Bible and including also the Book of Judges.[9] In the new research into the Book of Judges, it was emphasized that the book is not an artificial work of stories that were combined in a primitive manner.[10] Increasingly scholars speak of a redaction that combines the accounts into a unified work.

---

[6] M. Noth, *The Deuteronomistic History*[2] (JSOTSup, 15), Sheffield 1991, p. 69. For a discussion on his approach and on the development of the research following Noth see: O'Brien, "Judges and the Deuteronomistic History", pp. 235–259; Roberts, *Content and Form Within the Jephthah Narrative*, pp. 119 ff.

[7] Barton, *Reading the Old Testament*, p. 57.

[8] Amit's study of the Book of Judges is an attempt to explain the editorial work of the Book, see her theoretical introduction: Y. Amit, *The Book of Judges: The Art of Editing* (Biblical Interpretation Series, 38, trans. J. Chipman), Leiden 1999, pp. 1–24.

[9] For a review of the literary criticism on the Book of Judges see: G. A. Yee (ed.), *Judges and Method: New Approaches in Biblical Studies*, Minneapolis 1995, pp. 1–14; J. C. Exum, "The Center Cannot Hold: Thematic and Textual Instabilities in Judges", *CBQ* 52 (1990), p. 410 n. 1; J. P. U. Lilley, "A Literary Appreciation of the Book of Judges", *Tyndale Bulletin* 18 (1967), pp. 94–102; B. G. Webb, *The Book of the Judges: An Integrated Reading* (JSOTsup, 46) Sheffield 1987, pp. 28–40; M. A. Powell, *The Bible and Modern Literary Criticism: A Critical Assessment and Annotated Bibliography*, New-York and London 1992, pp. 194–198. For rhetorical criticism of the Gideon, Abimelech and Jephthah accounts see: R. H. O'Connell, *The Rhetoric of the Book of Judges*, Leiden 1996, pp. 139–203. For a review of the research into the Book of Judges see: Webb, op. cit., pp. 19–36.

[10] R. G. Boling, *Judges* (AB), New York 1975, p. 29.

There are advantages and disadvantages in this approach. On one hand, a lack of distinction between the early and the later work can lead to misunderstanding of the passages. On the other hand, to the same extent distinctions between early and later writings, between composition and redaction, which are not accurate, will lead to baseless hypotheses.

Moreover, the distinction between author and editor is based principally on literary phenomena. However, a literary phenomenon can be explained at the literary level and not at the text composition level. Thus, for instance, 'repetition' constitutes a clear sign of combining of two sources, but 'repetition' plays a major role in shaping an account.[11] Hence, it is very difficult to decide whether to treat repetition as a sign of different sources or as a stylistic phenomenon that has meaning at the level of the initial composition of the work.

In this work, I will present a comprehensive literary study of the Gideon, Abimelech and Jephthah accounts. The basic hypothesis in the work is that the editor of the accounts collected the material, adapted it, added to it and gave it a new form. In my opinion, this editor should be seen as a kind of creative artist who left his imprint on his work and on his sources. My main assumption is that there is a synchronic logic in the text in our possession. We must not however ignore the fact that the Biblical text is not always homogenous.[12]

The main literary phenomena supporting diachronic analysis of a text are repetition and contradiction. Biblical scholars consider repetition and contradiction in a text to be unreasonable phenomena. Accordingly, scholars adopting a diachronic approach will base division of the text into its sources on the assumption that contradictions and repetitions are impossible in the original text, and the text analysis will leave several separate texts, each of which is harmonious

---

[11] M. Sternberg, *The Poetics of Biblical Narrative: Ideological Literature and the Drama of Reading*, Bloomington 1987, pp. 365–440.

[12] This approach is applied in other genres as well. Lord argues that the performer of an oral epic is an author in his own right, and that every performance is a new creation. See: A. B. Lord, *The Singer of Tales*, Cambridge Mass. 1960, pp. 101–102: "It should be clear from the foregoing that the author of an oral epic, that is, the text of a performance, is the performer, the singer before us. Given normal eyesight on the part of the spectator, he is not multiple, but single. The author of any of our texts, unless an editor has tampered with it, is the man who dictated, sang, chanted, or otherwise gave expression to it. A performance is unique; it is a creation, not a reproduction, and it can therefore have only one author".

in itself. The critical approach is based on the desire for harmony, if not in the present text, then at least in each of the sources at the basis of the text. Naturally, those who adopt the synchronic approach are also guided generally by the assumption that the text must be harmonious. This study will examine the possibility that there is significance in the inclusion of contradictions and tensions within a given text. An account does not have to be harmonious; it can include different points of view. The assumption of the work is that at times there are different voices in one text.[13]

The fact that the Gideon, Abimelech and Jephthah accounts deal with the subject of political and social leadership, shows that these accounts relate to a specific historical reality, and are not part of a literary composition that can be taken in isolation from a concrete political reality. This fact obligates a preliminary discussion of literature and history in the Book of Judges.

In the nineteenth century, literary study was subordinated to historic study; every literary work was examined in the context of its external factors: the author's life, the historical, social, cultural and economic conditions in which it was written. For the critic, the literary work was part of the author's biography. The New Criticism movement arose in response to this. The new literary criticism claimed that literature is a self-contained discipline, separate from the historic disciplines. The emphasis in literary criticism passed to the individual work, based on the view that every work has its own value as a work of art. This literary approach contradicted the prevalent approaches to the interpretation of a work based on historic and biographical knowledge.[14] The new literary criticism was of great benefit in that it freed literature from the fetters of the historic disciplines, and made it an independent discipline. However, as in most of the revolutions in the world, this revolution was also too extreme.

---

[13] See M. M. Bakhtin, *The Dialogic Imagination: Four Essays*, ed. M. Holquist, trans. C. Emerson and M. Holquist (University of Texas Press Slavic Series, 1), Austin 1981, pp. 259 ff. A comprehensive treatment of point of view as compositional device is found in B. Uspanski, *A Poetic of Composition: The Structure of the Artistic Text and Typology of a Compositional Form* (trans. V. Zavarin and S. Wittig), Berkley 1973. For the inclusion of different points of view for the presentation of a multi-dimensional truth in biblical narrative see: R. Alter, *The Art of Biblical Narrative*, New York 1981, pp. 131–154; A. Berlin, *Poetics and Interpretation of Biblical Narrative* (Bible and Literature Series, 9), Sheffield 1983, pp. 73–82.

[14] For a review of New Criticism see: R. Murfin and S. M. Ray, *The Bedford Glossary of Critical and Literary Terms*, Boston and New York 1997, pp. 237–238.

In response to the new literary approach, an approach called New Historicism arose. Those who profess this approach recognize the literary value of the text, but instead of relating to a work isolated from its historical context, they also relate to the historical and cultural conditions in which the work was written. However, this is not a return to the old literary approach, which saw the literary work as a reflection of the historic conditions in which it was written. The new historic approach insisted that the literary work is the result of the historic conditions but it also creates culture.[15]

In this work, the assumption is that the artistic work was not created in a vacuum, and certainly, the written work of art cannot be taken independently of time and place.[16] Art is not outside time. The relation between an artistic product and its cultural origin can be to different degrees. There are works that are fundamentally political, or works that deal with a specific social or economic problem. However, even in works that do not have a political, social or economic concern, their author generally was bounded by his time and place. The Gideon, Abimelech and Jephthah accounts deal intensively with the subject of leadership, and therefore in this case there is no possibility that they are artistic works outside a time frame. Hence, the obligatory conclusion is that their aim is to express a religious and moral attitude in relation to a political and social issue. It will be impossible to understand the significance of these accounts without the historical context in which they were written.

However, in a discussion of the historical period of the Judges, which is the setting of the book, it turns out that very little is clearly known. The historic value of the Book of Judges is uncertain. The book describes the period between the conquest of Canaan as described in the Book of Joshua and the period of Samuel and Saul and the founding of the monarchy as described in the Book of Samuel. From the historian's viewpoint, the most important fact is that we have no real evidence of this period outside the Bible. To this difficulty is added the fact that there is little material from Egypt and

---

[15] For a review of the New Historicism approach see: R. Murfin and S. M. Ray, *The Bedford Glossary of Critical and Literary Terms*, pp. 238–244.

[16] The correlation between the arts and politics has long been recognized. Clive Gray opens his book on politics and the arts in Britain with the statement: "The Arts have always been political". C. Gray, *The Politics of the Arts in Britain*, London 2000, p. 1.

Mesopotamia, which were in decline in the Iron Age I period. Therefore, study of this historical period can be based only on the Biblical source.[17]

The problem is that a comprehensive historical reconstruction of the period of the judges on the basis of the Book of Judges only is very difficult, given the avowed theological orientations of the book. The purpose of the Book of Judges is not to describe Israelite history in a given period but the theological model that transgression leads to Israel's failure, whereas Israel's return to God leads to prosperity.[18] We already saw that the material in the Book of Judges is a selection of stories, and the actual author knew other stories, and decided not to include them in his work. Clearly, the material that was included in the Book of Judges is the material that corresponded to the theological principles of the book. Material that was at variance with these principles or that did not serve the book's theological idea was not included. If so, to what extent is it possible to reconstruct Israelite history in this period faithfully in light of the selective and tendentious material that we have in our possession? Furthermore, it is not at all clear to what extent the theologian who collected the material intervened in the actual contents. Again, this matter is controversial in the research. Unfortunately, however, it seems that every scholar who has the pretension to express a certain position on the subject does not do so based on evidence, but based on his subjective and speculative knowledge of the editor's work.

In addition to the difficulty of reconstructing history in the period of the judges from the Biblical book, there is also doubt as regards the time of the book's composition, its formative stages, and the nature of its stories. Following rejection of the approach that postulates on the Book's sources, the widespread approach regarding the composition is that of Noth, according to which the Book of Judges is part of a homogenous Deuteronomistic work which includes the book of Deuteronomy and the historiographic books known as the early Prophets.[19] Scholars do not generally attach great historic

---

[17] See e.g. the historical reconstruction of Malamat, *History of Biblical Israel*, pp. 97–147. There is a mention of the actual presence of Israel in Palestine during the thirteenth century B.C.E. in the Merneptah Stela, but no other external significant evidence is available at present. See Also J. M. Miller and J. H. Hayes, *A History of Ancient Israel and Judah*, Philadelphia 1986, pp. 80–119.

[18] Noth, *The Deuteronomistic History*, p. 91.

[19] Noth, *The Deuteronomistic History*, pp. 15–44.

importance to the Deuteronomistic material because of its late period, and because of its preaching orientations. While Noth's approach is the accepted approach in contemporary research, there are a fair number of variations to the general approach, which raise further doubts regarding the possibility of providing a historic reconstruction of the period.[20] In Noth's opinion, this redaction dates from the mid sixth century B.C.E.; Cross maintains that there were two stages in the redaction, one in the period of Josiah as part of his reform for revival of the Davidic monarchy, and the second in the post-exilic period, with the purpose of updating the work for the benefit of the Judean exiles.[21] As against Noth's approach regarding the unity of the Deuteronomist's work, Greenspahn showed that the framework accounts are not always consistent, and that their theology is not Deuteronomistic.[22] Contradicting the prevalent attitude that the framework of the judge accounts is the result of the Deuteronomistic redaction, Brueggeman considers that the four stages of the judge account framework (transgression, punishment, lament and deliverance) are pre-Deuteronomistic, and are a compilation of two different sources.[23] Guest maintains that there is a great homogeneity in the Book of Judges and it is impossible to separate between the Deuteronomistic work and the sources of the book. His conclusion is that the book is a unified work that was published by another author who rewrote its sources, and the editor is the author.[24]

In relation to the actual judge accounts, the widespread opinion in current research is that these accounts are local and tribal dating from antiquity, and they were collected by a pre-Deuteronomistic

---

[20] For different opinions regarding the Deuteronomistic redaction, see: F. M. Cross, *Canaanite Myth and Hebrew Epic: Essays in the History of the Religion of Israel*, Cambridge Mass. 1973, pp. 274–289.

[21] Cross, *Canaanite Myth and Hebrew Epic*, pp. 287–289. See also: Boling, *Judges*, pp. 34–38.

[22] F. E. Greenspahn, "The Theology of the Framework of Judges", *VT* 36 (1986), pp. 385–396. Similarly already Boling, *Judges*, p. 36 indicated that the framework of the stories is pre-Deuteronomistic and belongs to the pre-monarchic period.

[23] W. Brueggemann, "Social Criticism and Social Vision in the Deuteronomistic Formula of the Judges", J. Jeremias and L. Perlitt (eds.), *Die Botschaft und die Boten: Festschrift für Hans Walter Wolff zum 70 Geburtstag*, Neukrichen 1981, pp. 101–114.

[24] See: P. D. Guest, "Can Judges Survive Without Sources?: Challenging the Consensus", *JSOT* 78 (1998), pp. 43–61. Van Seters already articulated this idea, see J. Van Seters, *In Search of History: Historiography in the Ancient World and the Origins of Biblical History*, New Haven and London 1983, pp. 342–347.

editor. A separate collection included anecdotes on the minor judges. The Deuteronomistic editor combined these two lists, adding to each account an introduction and a conclusion in order to arrange them into the Book of Judges as a consecutive account with a chronological continuity. Since the framework of the book is the result of the Deuteronomist's work, scholars suggested the possibility that the different judges did not succeed each other as presented in the book and there is no reason to think that some of the judges were not contemporaries.[25] Within the Deuteronomistic redaction, the judges were presented as national leaders, who assumed that office successively after intervals between the judges.[26] Scholars have generally accepted the authenticity of most of the accounts in the Book of Judges, but not the chronological framework. Consequently, we find two types of historic reconstructions. One type is of general descriptions of characteristics of the period: the social structure, the politics, in particular descriptions of the relations of the tribes with neighbouring peoples, and culture and religion.[27] The second type is a historical reconstruction of events based on the judge accounts on the basis of the contents of the Book of Judges, which are considered basically as authentic (without the chronological framework).[28]

---

[25] Noth, *The Deuteronomistic History*, pp. 69 ff. On the pre-Deuteronomistic collection of judge accounts see: W. Richter, *Traditionsgeschichtliche Untersuchungen zum Richterbuch* (Bonner Biblische Beiträge, 18), Bonn 1966, pp. 336 ff. On the Deuteronomistic redaction in the Book of Judges see: A. D. H. Mayes, *The Story of Israel Between Settlement and Exile: A Redactional Study of the Deuteronomistic History*, London 1983, pp. 58–80.

[26] Noth, *The Deuteronomistic History*, p. 72.

[27] M. Noth, *The History of Israel*[2], London 1960, pp. 147–163; J. Bright, *A History of Israel*[2], London 1972, pp. 154–160; R. de Vaux, *The Early History of Israel* (trans. D. Smith), Philadelphia 1978, p. 693; Miller and Hayes, *A History of Ancient Israel and Judah*, pp. 91–119; H. Reviv, "The Government of Shechem in the El-Amarna Period and in the Days of Abimelech", *IER* 16 (1966), pp. 252–257; H. Reviv, *From Clan to Monarchy: Israel in Biblical Period*[2], Jerusalem 1989, pp. 77–86 (Hebrew).

[28] Noth, *The History of Israel*, pp. 150–163; Bright, *A History of Israel*, pp. 156–159; Miller and Hayes (*A History of Ancient Israel and Judah*, pp. 90–91) claim that the period of the Judges cannot be reconstructed through the accounts in the Book, but that the accounts can easily be separated from the editorial additions, and represent early and reliable material. Similarly see de Vaux, *The Early History of Israel*, pp. 686–689. Boling, too, considers that that the judge accounts reflect the premonarchic period, see: Boling, *Judges*, pp. 35–36. This approach dominates the works of Avraham Malamat, see e.g. *History of Biblical Israel*, pp. 97–185. Mayes rejects Noth's view that Israel in the pre-monarchic period was formed as an Amphictyony. He attributes the notion of a central authority to the schematic framework of the Book. See: A. D. H. Mayes, *Israel in the Period of the Judges* (Studies in

Some scholars adopt an extreme sceptical approach and claim that the judge accounts do not reflect any historical reality and are merely tales.[29]

While I also feel that the chronology of the period of the Judges cannot be determined from the contents of the Book, I have to admit that we cannot completely negate the possibility that there is some support for the chronology presented there. Scholars generally consider that the judge accounts were formulated prior to the Deuteronomist's work, and in relation to this literary activity, there is no certitude in the research. The uncertainty in the distinction between the Deuteronomist's work and the earlier sources has already been discussed above.

On the other hand, while agreeing with the tendency of the research to consider the individual judge accounts authentic and the judges to be contemporaries, I cannot deny that we do not have tools to prove the authenticity of these accounts. We can neither corroborate nor negate the information. The doubts concerning the pre-Deuteronomistic editor are great, and there is no certainty in the research as to the period in which he lived, the nature of his work and his object. It is for good reason that the research calls this redaction pre-Deuteronomistic, without committing itself to a definite period.

Just as it is impossible to prove with certainty the authenticity of the individual accounts, it is also impossible to completely negate the authenticity of the Deuteronomistic sources in the book. Firstly, there is no certitude as regards the period of this redaction. We do not

Biblical Theology, 29), London 1974, pp. 84–105. However, throughout his book he ascribes historical value to the individual accounts. Reviv, *From Clan to Monarchy*, pp. 86–98.

[29] See N. P. Lemche, *Early Israel: Anthropological and Historical Studies on the Israelite Society before Monarchy* (SVT, 37), Leiden 1985, p. 379. According to these scholars, 'Ancient Israel' never existed and modern scholars invented Israel in their paraphrasing works of the Bible. See e.g. N. P. Lemche, *The Israelites in History and Tradition* (Library of Ancient Israel), London and Louisville 1998, e.g. 163–167. See also: P. Davies, *In Search of 'Ancient Israel'* (JSOTsup, 148), Sheffield 1992; T. L. Thompson, *Early History of the Israelite People: From the Written and Archaeological Sources* (Studies in the History of the Ancient Near East, IV), Leiden 1992, esp. 401–423. In a recent publication Finkelstein and Silberman cast doubt on the possibility of determining the authenticity of the accounts in the Book of Judges, see: I. Finkelstein and N. A. Silberman, *The Bible Unearthed: Archaeology's New Vision of Ancient Israel and the Origin of Its Sacred Texts*, New York 2001, pp. 120–122.

have real evidence regarding the work of the Deuteronomist, and it is impossible to determine the extent to which it was based on early historical sources. One of the reasons that the research calls into question the credibility of the Deuteronomist is the religious tendentiousness of this redaction. However, this religious orientation is not completely different from that of the first writers of the accounts or of the other redactions. What all have in common is their religious purpose.

The diversity of opinions regarding the historical value of the Book of Judges and the stages of its formulation and composition derive from the fact that the historical discussion is based almost exclusively on literary analysis of the Biblical source. It should be noted that there is no historical evidence for existence of the Deuteronomistic editor, and the assumption of his extensive activity in shaping parts of the Bible, which is a cornerstone in Biblical research, is based exclusively on literary analysis of the Biblical text. The historical reconstruction of the period of the Judges depends exclusively on interpretation of the Biblical source, and this depends on the basic fundamental position of the scholar of the period from the outset, whether or not he attaches credibility to the Biblical sources. Even if every scholar bases his historic reconstructions on scientific historical examples, one cannot but feel that the presuppositions of each scholar depend on subjective feelings in relation to the credibility of the Biblical historiography in general and the Book of Judges in particular.

Given all the doubts relating to the historical reconstruction of the period of the Judges, it is extremely difficult to receive a complete and exact picture of the period from the book. This situation contributed to the growing tendency in recent years to deal with the literary aspects of the book rather than the historical aspects. However, as already noted, a literary approach isolated from historic awareness distorts the intention of the work. This conclusion is correct particularly as regards the Gideon, Abimelech and Jephthah accounts, in which the political issue is prominent, in contrast to the Samson stories for instance, where it is not.

In this work, an attempt is made to adopt a safer policy, but at the price of a more minimalist goal. Firstly, I will undertake a literary analysis of the accounts, without basing myself on any hypothesis as regards the historical authenticity. Great progress has been made in the last few decades in implementation of literary study in the Bible. The structure of the account, the plot development, retrospection and anticipation, compression and expansion, Leitmotif, point of view, repetition, and many other literary tools have been studied intensively on the theoretical plane and applied in high quality literary studies. In this study, I intend to apply the attainments of literary research to three accounts in the Book of Judges. I will examine the structure of the accounts, the organization of the parts of the account within the whole, and I will effect a precise analysis of the stylistic formation and contents of the small units. Through this literary analysis, the intention and object of the work will be exposed, and the ideology on which it is based will be defined. Subsequently, rather than dealing with the history of the accounts, I will propose the historical conditions reflected in the ideological, political and social context of the accounts. The assumption of the work is that the book was not written in a vacuum but in the spirit of the period, or as in many cases in Biblical literature, as a confrontation with the reality in the context of which it was written.[30]

---

[30] Brettler adopted a similar approach: M. Z. Brettler, "The Book of Judges: Literature as Politics", *JBL* 108 (1989), pp. 395–418. In his article, Brettler described the separation of literary and historical disciplines in biblical research. He proposes to combine both disciplines and to uncover the historical factors behind the work of the editors of the Book. Because the historical reconstruction of the Book is doubtful, Brettler attempts to uncover its ideological aspects and a plausible historical background. This approach is refreshing in light of the historical character of the Book on the one hand, and the historical limitation on the other. Brettler suggests that the Book is a polemic against the kingship of Saul and northern worship established by the royal family. The main reservation as regards Brettler's methodology is that he attempted to uncover the message of the entire Book of Judges in a short presentation that does not and cannot devote adequate attention to all aspects of the Book. Subsequently, Brettler developed this article into a short book devoted to his approach and continuing his conclusions: M. Z. Brettler, *The Book of Judges* (Old Testament Readings), London and New York 2002. However, in this work he confined himself to only a few of the accounts (Ehud, Samson, Deborah and the Concubine at Gibeah). I believe that an accurate conclusion regarding the ideology of the book, designed to uncover its historical setting, should be based on a comprehensive and detailed investigation of each of the units of the Book.

CHAPTER ONE

THE GIDEON ACCOUNT (6–8)

1. *Introduction*

The Gideon account occupies a central place in the Book of Judges, both as regards its position in the centre of the book and as regards its length and its detailed descriptions. The Gideon account has one hundred verses and if we add to this the account of his son Abimelech, we will receive a narrative cycle of 157 verses, as opposed to 218 verses devoted to all the other judge accounts together. Most judge accounts deal with one or two main topics. For instance, the Ehud account deals principally with the assassination of Eglon, and the Deborah account mainly with Barak's appointment by Deborah and the killing of Sisera by Jael. The Samson stories are indeed long and detailed, but the Gideon stories, in contrast, are diversified and they detail almost every stage in the plot. The account includes the detailed description of the oppression, Gideon's appointment and his combating of the Baal worship. The organization of Gideon's army, his many doubts, his war against the Midianites, and the pursuit that he conducted after the battle are all described in very great detail. The account goes on to describe internal clashes, firstly with the Ephraimites and subsequently with the men of Succoth and of Penuel. The execution of the Midianite kings Zebah and Zalmunna is described exhaustively, after the execution of the Midianite captains Oreb and Zeeb had already been indicated. Unlike other accounts, the Gideon account does not end with the victory over the enemy. Here the story continues into the period after the victory, and describes how the people asked Gideon to rule over them, and how Gideon made the ephod, which led the people to transgress.

The diversified descriptions are also important in presentation of Gideon's character. The diversity of the stories and the presentation of Gideon's multifaceted character contrast sharply with the other judge accounts, which are far shorter. Gideon has the most round and multifaceted personality in the Book of Judges: He has doubts when initially appointed, but after a long process he leads the small

army confidently and he takes care of his people, but at the same
time he also enters into clashes with them. He combats the Baal,
but he sets up an ephod. The account closest to the Gideon account,
is that of Samson, which contains 97 verses. However, even in comparison with the Samson stories, the Gideon stories are more diversified
and Gideon's personality is complex. The Samson stories describe
how Samson was enticed by Philistine women, and the confrontations that followed this, with Samson smiting the Philistines severely.
Samson's personality is flat; throughout the account we discover his
great weakness for women and his great physical strength.

Clearly, the position of the Gideon stories in the centre of the
book is not incidental, and derives from the centrality of the Gideon
account in the Book of Judges. What are the intentions behind the
extensive and full descriptions in the Gideon stories?[1] In this chapter I will elucidate the significance of the Gideon account through
literary analysis; following this its place in the Book of Judges will
also become clear.[2]

2. *The Structure of the Gideon Stories*

The Gideon stories are divided into three parts according to the plot
development:[3]

---

[1] According to Boling the Gideon and Abimelech accounts were positioned at
the centre of the Book as part of a pro-Judean polemic against possible alternatives to Jerusalem. See: Boling, *Judges*, p. 185. For a pro-Davidic intention of the
Book of Judges see: Brettler, "The Book of Judges: Literature as Politics", pp.
395–418.

[2] The question of the origin of the Gideon story occupied the attention of scholars in the earlier stage of the research of the Book. In the nineteenth century and
until the middle of the twentieth century the scholastic trend was to seek Pentateuchal
sources in the account. See e.g. Moore, *Judges*, pp. 175–177; Burney, *The Book of
Judges*, e.g. pp. 176–184. Simpson, *The Composition of the Book of Judges*, pp. 25–40,
108–110, 125–126. For a summary of the various opinions on the Gideon narrative, see Amit, *The Book of Judges*, pp. 224–225 nn. 2–14. From the mid-twentieth
century this approach was replaced by the opinion that the Book is composed of
different traditions that are embodied in a Deuteronomistic framework. See: Noth,
The Deuteronomistic History, pp. 69–85. There are many variations to this approach,
see e.g. Soggin, *Judges*, pp. 103–105. Most scholars consider that the Gideon narrative is pre-deuteronomistic (e.g. Noth, *op. cit.* pp. 70, 73–75). Auld believes that
it is a later supplement to the Book A. G. Auld, "Gideon. Hacking and the Heart
of the Old Testament", *VT* 39 (1989), pp. 257–267.

[3] For different divisions see Soggin, *Judges*, pp. 108–109; Amit, *The Book of Judges*
pp. 224–232.

A. Before the war (the oppression, Gideon's appointment, and the forming of his army) 6:1–7, 15
   1. The transgression, the Midianite oppression and the lament (6:1–6)
   2. The Prophet's rebuke (6:7–10)
   3. Gideon's appointment as deliverer (6:11–24)
   4. Gideon destroys the altar of the Baal (6:25–32)
   5. Deployment by Midian and Gideon for battle, and Gideon's request
      for signs from God (6:33–40)
   6. Screening of Gideon's army (7:1–8)
   7. Gideon receives encouragement through the Midianite's dream
      (7:9–15)
B. The war, 7:16–8:21
   1. Gideon's battle in the Midianite camp (7:16–22)
   2. Gideon's pursuit of the Midianites (7:23–25)
   3. The clash with the Ephraimites (8:1–3)
   4. The clash with the men of Succoth and of Penuel (8:4–17)
   5. The execution of the Midianite kings (8:18–21)
C. After the war (the attempt to crown a king, and the setting up of
the ephod), 8:22–35
   1. Gideon's refusal of kingship (8:22–23)
   2. The setting up of the ephod in Ophrah (8:22–28)
   3. The House of Gideon and Gideon's death (8:29–35)

3. *The Transgression, the Midianite Oppression and the Lament (6:1–6)*

The story opening is characteristic "Then the Israelites did what was
offensive to the LORD" (3:7, 12; 4:1; 10: 6; 13:1).[4] As in the other
accounts, the next stage is the punishment (v. 1_2–6_1), which, as usual,
is followed by the lament to God stage (v. 6_b, compare: 3:9, 15; 4:3;
10:10). However, while the description of the transgression and the
lament resembles the other judge accounts, the description of the
oppression here is the longest and most detailed in comparison with
the other descriptions of oppression (3:8, 13–14; 4:2–3; 10:7–8). The
length of the description is certainly related to the extreme harshness of the Midianite oppression.[5] The Midianites seriously damaged

---

[4] This opening differs slightly from other expositions to the stories in the Book.
Apart from the first account (3:7), the other judge accounts commence: "The Israelites
again did what was offensive to the LORD" (3:12; 4:1; 10:6; 13:1). Compare
W. Bluedorn, *Yahweh Versus Baalism: A Theological Reading of the Gideon-Abimelech Narrative*
(JSOTsup, 329), Sheffield 2001, pp. 57–58. The wording gives the Gideon account
the nature of a new start, possibly because the redactor wished to underscore this
account and give it a central place in the Book.
[5] Malamat has shown that this story is a natural continuation of the Deborah

the Israelites' livelihood, destroying their crops and livestock, and preventing them from leading a normal existence (vv. 3–5). They also took lives and, in order to survive, the Israelites had to flee their homes and take refuge in hiding places in the mountains (vv. 2, 6).[6] The severity of the damage is expressed also in the description of the size of the area under Midianite control, extending to the west of the country: "they would attack them, destroy the produce of the land all the way to Gaza" (v. 4);[7] and in the fact that three nations joined together to attack Israel: "Midian, Amalek, and the Kedemites would come up and raid them" (v. 3).[8] The result was more grievous than in any of the other oppressions described in the Book of Judges: "Israel was reduced to utter misery by the Midianites" (v. 6).[9]

This grim description is inversely opposed to the relatively short duration of the oppression—only seven years as opposed to eighteen years under Eglon (3:14), eighteen years under Jabin (4:3), eighteen years under the Ammonites (10:8) and forty years under the Philistines (13:1).[10]

The difference between the Midianite oppression and the other oppressions in the Book of Judges is certainly related to the fact that the Midianites were nomads, and not an organized people with defined territory and long-term interests.[11] Oppressors usually wish

---

story, chs. 4–5. After the defeat of the Canaanite forces in the valley of Jezreel, the land was subjected to nomadic invasions from the east, as recorded in chapters 6–8. See: A. Malamat, "The War of Gideon and Midian", ed. J. Liver, *The Military History of the Land of Israel in Biblical Times*, Jerusalem 1964, p. 110 (Hebrew).

[6] Israel's oppression by the Philistines (1 Sam 13:6) is similar to the Midianite oppression, but less severe.

[7] Burney considers this statement to be an exaggeration since in the remainder of the narrative the Midianites appear in central Palestine. He therefore concludes that v. 4 is a late addition. See: Burney, *The Book of Judges*, p. 185.

[8] According to Boling (*Judges*, p. 125) Kedemites (lit. children of the east) is a term that includes the Midianites and the Amalekites.

[9] The repetition of 'Midian' five times in this passage is designed to emphasize the severity of the Midianite oppression. P. E. McMillion, *Judges 6–8 and the Study of Premonarchial Israel*, Diss., Vanderbilt University 1985, p. 175.

[10] McMillion (*Judges 6–8*, p. 175) claimed that the number 7 here symbolizes completeness. However, it is doubtful if this is the meaning, taking into account the comparison of this period with the longer oppressions in the other accounts in the Book.

[11] For further information on the Midianites see: Malamat, "The War of Gideon and Midian", pp. 110–111; G. E. Mendenhall, *The Tenth Generation: The Origins of the Biblical Tradition*, Baltimore and London 1973, pp. 163–173. On the changing relations between Israel and Midian see: Soggin, *Judges*, p. 107.

to impose heavy taxes on the peoples under their rule, and it is therefore in their interests to ensure the prosperity of the conquered territories. History, moreover, shows that conquering peoples invest in infrastructures in the lands that they occupy in order to develop the local economy. Since the Midianites were nomads with no defined territory or developed bureaucracy, they could not have any developed, well-established taxation system. It would therefore seem that they exploited the occupied area to extract from it all that they could, causing grievous damage both to the agricultural infrastructures and to the people, without having any long-term perspective.[12]

Unlike other oppressions in the Book of Judges, which are not described in detail, in the description of the Midianite oppression the author provides sufficient data to give a vivid impression of the conditions. The Midianites had a propensity for destroying and killing ("Thus they would invade the land and ravage it", v. 5). They were able to do so because of their overwhelming numbers ("For they would come up with their livestock and their tents, swarming as thick as locusts; they and their camels were innumerable", v. 5). They severely impaired the Israelites' possibilities of sustenance, destroying the agricultural produce in extensive areas ("they would attack them, destroy the produce of the land all the way to Gaza", v. 4). They also destroyed the livestock which constituted an important element in the Israelite economy ("not a sheep or an ox or an ass", v. 4). By these actions, the Midianites depleted the sources of sustenance ("and leave no means of sustenance in Israel", v. 4). The hardship of the Israelites is further underscored in an exceptional manner in our story. The verses describe the Israelite attempts, in the midst of adversity, to find new sources of sustenance, only to have the Midianites immediately sabotage these efforts ("For whenever the Israelites had sown, Midian came up, and Amalek, and the Kedemites would come up against them", v. 3). Not only did the Midianites destroy the Israelite economy, they also killed indiscriminately. The narrative does not give the reader an exact description of these acts, but they resulted in the flight by the people from their homes to seek refuge in mountains and caves ("The hand of the Midianites prevailed over Israel; and because of Midian, the Israelites

---

[12] Y. Kaufmann, *Sefer Shoftim*, Jerusalem 1961 (Hebrew), p. 155; Amit, *The Book of Judges*, p. 248.

provided themselves with refuges in the caves and strongholds of the mountains", v. 2). There is no parallel to such a description elsewhere in the Book of Judges. These attacks on the Israelite population and livelihood reduced the Israelites to utter misery (וידל ישראל מאד מפני מדין, v. 6).[13]

Verses 3–4 underscore the Midianite supremacy as against Israel's subordination by two overlapping expressions: ועלו עליו ("would come up against them") (v. 3), and ויחנו עליהם ("They would encamp against them") (v. 4). This emphasis also emerges through the use of the root עלה (came up) twice in this verse "For whenever the Israelites had sown, Midian came up, and Amalek, and the Kedemites would come up against them"[14] and by the fact that the root appears again in v. 5: "For they would come up with their livestock". The absolute contrast between the fortunes of Israel and Midian emerges in the comparison between the opening sentence describing the hardship (v. 2ₐ) and the closing sentence (v. 6ₐ). The former sentence describes the rise of Midian over Israel, and the latter, Israel's impoverishment before Midian. The verb used to describe the increased power of the Midianites is ותעז ("prevailed"), and the verb used as contrast—וידל ("reduced to utter misery") describes Israel's enfeeblement. The two sentences have the same meaning, but one describes Midian's supremacy over Israel, and the other Israel's subjugation to Midian. In this way, the contrast in the situation between the Midianites and Israel is highlighted. This contrast is expressed also in the reversed structure of the two sentences:

---

[13] The Hebrew word וידל has two meanings: 1. to become poor, 2. to become little. Thus Boling (*Judges*, p. 124) translates: "Israel became utterly destitute" as the first meaning, and the second is reflected in Moore's (*Judges*, p. 179) translation: "Israel was greatly reduced". In v. 6 the word may include the two meanings, namely that Israel became poor and reduced in number as a result of Midian's hostile activities. Any English translation must select one of these two meanings, thus suppressing the ambiguity of the Hebrew verse.

[14] In a fragment of this text found in Qumran designated as 4QJudges^a the words ועלו עליו are missing. See: *Discoveries in the Judaean Desert*, IX, Oxford 1995, p. 162.

The severity of the oppression has been explained in light of the Midianites' nomadic lifestyle, but does this severity explain the extensive details given in the description of the oppression in the account? In other words, what is the function of this comprehensive account for the story development?[15]

An answer will be given after study of the following passages, including the next exceptional unit in the story—the prophet's rebuke.

4. *The Prophet's Rebuke (6:7–10)*

In the other judge accounts, the lament to God is immediately followed by the story of the deliverance or the appointment of the judge. This is not the case in the Gideon account. Before the appearance of God's angel to appoint Gideon as deliverer (6:11–24), a prophet is sent to Israel to rebuke them for having strayed from God and adopted worship of the Canaanite gods. The appearance of the prophet at this point is particularly exceptional, in that it seems to be a result of the lament to God ("When the Israelites cried to the LORD on account of Midian, the LORD sent a prophet to the Israelites", vv. 7–8), whereas normally the reaction to the lament is the appearance of the deliverer. The elaboration "When the Israelites cried to the LORD" (v. 7) using the same words as at the end of the previous verse (v. 6): "and the Israelites cried to the LORD", is a literary means used by the author to emphasize the prophet's words that come here immediately after the lament instead of God's anticipated reaction, sending of a deliverer. The censuring of Israel for idol worship is not exceptional in the Book of Judges (2:1–5; 10:11–14).[16] However, its position here after Israel's lament

---

[15] Amit (*The Book of Judges*, pp. 247–248) holds that the object of the detailed description of the punishment in the exposition to the Gideon account is to stress the seriousness of the Midianite oppression in order to enhance the magnitude of the divine deliverance. This rationale does not explain why the editor did not apply this technique to other accounts in the Book, which are also meant to enhance the greatness of God's salvation.

[16] A repetition such as the one between v. 7 and v. 6 is called by Rofé *related expansion* and it indicates a late addition. See A. Rofé, *"The Book of Balaam" (Numbers 22:2–24:25): A study in Methods of Criticism and the History of Biblical Literature and Religion*, Jerusalem 1979, pp. 55–57 (Hebrew). For other examples of the phenomenon see *op. cit.* p. 56 and n. 108, and Y. Zakovitch, "Review on: A. Rofé, *"The Book of Balaam" (Numbers 22:2–24:25): A study in Methods of Criticism and the History of Biblical*

to God and prior to the appearance of the deliverer is unique in comparison with the other judge accounts.[17] In order to explain it, we will first study the structure and contents of the prophet's rebuke.

The rebuke is constructed in the form of a covenant in which each of the two sides has a commitment towards the other:

Literature and Religion, Jerusalem 1979, *Kiryat Sefer* 54 (1979), p. 788 (Hebrew). There is no simple answer to the question of whether the repetition in verses 6 and 7 is an indication of an additional insertion to the text or a literary device designed to highlight the prophets words and to indicate the surprise that his rebuke comes at a point where God's salvation through the actions of a deliverer is expected by the reader.

[17] One explanation is at the textual level. Many scholars believe that vv. 7–10 are a late interpolation. Some ascribe these verses to E (see e.g.: Burney, *The Book of Judges*, p. 177, Boling, *Judges*, p. 125), while others attribute them to the Deuteronomist (e.g. Soggin, *Judges*, p. 112). This conclusion is drawn from the fact that Gideon's ignorance in v. 13 of the reason for Israel's misfortune is provided by the unnamed prophet in vv. 7–10 (see: Burney, op. cit.; Soggin, op. cit. p. 118). However, I will show subsequently in this work that there is a strong connection between Gideon's complaint to the Angel of God and the prophecy in vv. 7–10. This connection proves that one author is responsible for the two passages vv. 7–10 and 11–13. These verses are missing in a fragment (4QJudges^a) found at Qumran. In this text, immediately after the description of the oppression by Midian, it is said: ויזעקו בני ישראל אל ה׳. This is followed by the encounter of the angel of God with Gideon ויבא מלאך.... This version, according, to Trebolle, constitutes evidence that vv. 7–10 in the Masoretic Version are a late addition not present in the Qumran version. See: J. Trebolle Barrera, "4QJudg^a", *DJD* XIV, Oxford 1995, p. 162; J. Trebolle Barrera, "Textual Variations in 4QJudg^a and Editorial History of the Book of Judges", *Revue de Qumran* 54 (1989), p. 238. Against this conclusion from the Qumran source see: R. S. Hess, Richard, "The Dead Sea Scrolls and Higher Criticism of the Hebrew Bible: The Case of 4QJudg^a", S. E. Porter and C. A. Evans (eds.), *The Scrolls and the Scriptures: Qumran after Fifty Years*, (JSOPsup, 26) Sheffield 1997, pp 122–128; O'Connell, *The Rhetoric of the Book of Judges*, p. 147 n. 178. Another explanation for the inclusion of the prophet's rebuke is at the literary level. Webb explains the departure from the normal pattern, in which God sends a deliverer immediately after Israel's lament to him, as the beginning of God's frustration. The prophecy is meant to warn against the assumption that every lament and repentance automatically changes Israel's fortune. See Webb, *The Book of Judges*, p. 145. Nonetheless, this explanation does not accord with the Book of Judges, which repeatedly shows how the lament to God does change Israel's situation. According to Klein and Exum, the appearance of the prophet creates an expectation that the pattern of the prophetess Deborah will be repeated. This expectation, however, is not met and the prophet suddenly disappears. L. R. Klein, *The Triumph in the Book of Judges* (Bible and Literature Series, 14), Sheffield 1988, p. 50; Exum, "The Center Cannot Hold", p. 416. Amit explains that verses 7–10 are an elaboration of the lament stage and they postpone the appearance of the deliverer. This elaboration is meant to explain the atmosphere of disappointment among the people and Gideon's scepticism towards God expressed in the next stage. Amit also speculates that since the cry to God was followed by rebuke rather than delivery, Israel continued to worship the Baal. Amit, *The Book of Judges*, p. 251.

God's acts (vv. 8–9): I *brought you* up out of Egypt and *freed you* from the house of slavery. I *rescued you* from the hand of the Egyptians and from the hand of all your oppressors; I *drove them* out before you, and *gave you* their land.

Israel's acts (v. 10): And I said to you, 'I am the LORD your God. *You must not worship* the gods of the Amorites in whose land you dwell'. But you did not obey Me.

God's acts for Israel are cited first, and they include delivering Israel from Egypt and giving them the Land of Israel, and in return it is expected that they will not worship other gods. This structure gives Israel's transgression the status of betrayal and breach of a covenant. Moreover, the description of God's acts for Israel, using five different verbs, is designed to show how intensive and comprehensive were God's acts for His people. Israel, however, did not live up to the expectations from them, and they did not refrain from only one act: "*You must not worship* the gods of the Amorites". The contrast between the five actions that God performed for Israel and the one thing that Israel did not refrain from doing underscores the censure and the disappointment over Israel's ingratitude towards God.

The prophet's harsh censure of Israel emerges through an analogy of the exhortation in the first two of the Ten Commandments:

Judges (6:8–10)	Exodus 20:2–3
I brought you up out of Egypt and freed you from the house of slavery. I rescued you from the hand of the Egyptians and from the hand of all your oppressors; I drove them out before you, and gave you their land. And I said to you,	*I am the LORD your God, who brought you out of the land of Egypt, out of the house of slavery*;
'*I am the LORD your God* *You must not worship the gods* of the Amorites in whose land you dwell'. But you did not obey Me.	*I am the LORD your God* *you must have no other gods* before me.

As in the Ten Commandments, so in the prophet's rebuke, it is God who is speaking, and this increases the seriousness of the rebuke. This analogy underscores the gravity of Israel's transgression. Beyond this, however, its aim is to indicate that they did not meet the fundamental condition at the basis of their relationship with God.

The gravity of the transgression emerges also from the analogy between the prophet's rebuke and the description of Israel's transgression and punishment in verses 1–6. The prophet says that the Lord delivered Israel: "I rescued you from *the hand of* the Egyptians and from *the hand of* all your oppressors" (v. 9); as against this, the Midianite oppression reverses this situation: "and the LORD gave them into *the hands of* the Midianites for seven years. *The hand of* the Midianites prevailed over Israel" (vv. 1–2). The prophet says that after God delivered Israel, He gave them their land: "and *gave* (ואתנה) you their land" (v. 9); as against this, because Israel transgressed, the punishment is: "*gave* (ויתנם) them into the hands of the Midianites" (v. 1). God brought Israel up from Egypt "I *brought you up* (העליתי) out of Egypt" (v. 8); because Israel sinned their punishment is that the Midianites 'came up' against them: "Midian *came up* (ועלה), and Amalek, and the Kedemites would *come up* (ועלו) against them" (v. 3). All this came about because Israel committed idolatry: "And I said to you, . . . You must not worship the gods of the Amorites . . . But you did not obey Me". (v. 10). The sin of idolatry is presented by the verb ירא (literally: "feared"). As against this, Israel feared the Midianites and fled from them to refuges, caves and strongholds (v. 2). The prophet says that God drove out Israel's enemies before them: "I drove them out before you" (v. 9); now Israel are fleeing before Midian.[18]

Let us now look again at the question of the position of this rebuke in the framework of the Gideon stories. If God had not sent a judge-deliverer, the object of the rebuke could have been understood in light of its gravity. However, this is not the situation. Why then was the rebuke included here whereas there are no rebukes of this kind in the other judge accounts?

The prophet's words here are similar to the words of the angel of the Lord who rebukes Israel at Bochim, 2:1–5;[19] comparison of the two rebukes can provide an answer to our question.

---

[18] Compare: McMillion, *Judges 6–8*, pp. 178–180.

[19] Rofé discussed the analogy between these two sources, considering that both belong to the E source. A. Rofé, "The Belief in Angels in the Bible and in Early Israel", Ph.D. The Hebrew University of Jerusalem, Jerusalem 1979, pp. 305–312.

Judges 2:1–5	Judges (6:8–10)
Now the *angel* of the LORD went up from Gilgal to Bochim, and said, *I brought you up out of Egypt,*	the LORD sent a *prophet* to the Israelites who said to them, . . . *I brought you up out of Egypt* and freed you from the house of slavery . . .
and brought you into the land that I had promised to your ancestors. I said, I will never break my covenant with you. *Do not make a covenant with the inhabitants of this land; tear down their altars.* *But you did not obey Me* See what you have done	I drove them out before you, *and gave you their land.* And I said to you, I am the LORD your God. *You must not worship the gods of the Amorites in whose land you dwell.* *But you did not obey Me*

The connection between the two rebukes is evident. The contents and the structure are similar. Both begin with the fact that God delivered Israel from Egypt and gave them their land, and both rebuke Israel for having strayed after other gods. Both use the same expressions and a similar vocabulary, and the speaker in both is God ("I brought you up out of", 2:1; 6:8). Notwithstanding, there is a significant difference between these rebukes. In response to the words of the angel at Bochim it is said that the people responded by weeping and making a sacrifice to the Lord. This response indicates acceptance of the rebuke: "When the angel of the LORD spoke these words to all the Israelites, the people lifted up their voices and wept. So they named that place Bochim, and there they sacrificed to the LORD" (2:4–5). In light of the similarity of the two passages, the people's failure to react to the prophet's rebuke in the Gideon account is blatant.[20] What is the explanation?

The sudden conclusion of the prophet's words with a direct appeal to the people and with the forceful determination "But you did not obey Me" (6:10) further dramatizes the prophet's words and increases the surprise at the people's failure to respond. This lack of response

---

[20] A widely held explanation for the sudden ending of the Prophet's rebuke is that this passage is secondary in the text, and when it was inserted its ending was omitted, see: Moore, *Judges*, p. 181; Soggin, *Judges*, pp. 112–113. Kaufmann claimed that the passage is not incomplete, but his explanation is not convincing, Kaufmann, *Sefer Shoftim*, p. 156. McMillion suggested that the sudden ending of v. 10 is meant to create an expectation in the reader as regards the next part of the account, McMillion, *Judges 6–8*, p. 177.

is significant in understanding the matter, and is intended, it seems, to show the people's indifference to the prophet's words. They do not agree or object; the narrator's intention is to show their complete apathy.

The object of the inclusion of the prophet's words in the account, therefore, seems to be in order to demonstrate the serious spiritual situation of the people, who had lost their faith and no longer had any hope of delivery by God. There are two known responses in the Bible to rebukes by prophets: acceptance of the prophet's words (e.g. Judg 2:1–5; Hag 1:12–13) or rejection and even dispute or confrontation with the prophet (e.g. the confrontation of the priests and prophets with Jeremiah over his prophecy of the destruction of Jerusalem, Jer 26). The possibility of the people not reacting to the prophet and of indifference to his words is the most serious. This is the situation described here.[21]

We will now understand the reason for the detailed description of the Midianite oppression in verses 1–6. The acute despair that gripped the people is a result of the harsh oppression of the Midianites. Even though this period was of relatively short duration, the severity of the oppression was particularly exceptional and the expectation that God would save the people had not been fulfilled. Instead, there was despair expressed in failure to respond to the prophet's rebuke.

Thus, the object of the two detailed descriptions at the beginning of the Gideon account, the description of the oppression (vv. 1–6) and the prophet's rebuke (vv. 7–10), is to show the unique religious problem present in Gideon's period. There follows the question of how it would be possible to surmount this religious problem, and how God's anticipated deliverance would restore the people to their religious faith.

---

[21] According to Bertheau, the prophets' words are a response to Gideon's question in v. 13: "is the LORD with us, then why has all this befallen us?". Because Gideon's question had remained unanswered, the editor inserted the prophet's words as a reply. E. Bertheau, *Das Buch der Richter und Ruth* (Kurzgefasstes exegetisches Handbuch zum Alten Testament), Leipzig 1883, p. 135. However, Gideon's question, in my opinion, is answered. The angel of God replies to him: "Go in this strength of yours and deliver Israel from the Midianites. I herewith make you My messenger (v. 14)". The meaning of this answer is that God did not abandon his people, and He will now deliver Israel through the commissioning of Gideon.

5. *Gideon's Appointment as Deliverer (6:11–24)*

The entire section (vv. 11–24) deals with Gideon's appointment as leader.[22] In other judge accounts, this stage is described briefly: "the LORD raised up a deliverer for the Israelites" (See for instance: 3:9; 3:15; in the Jephthah account the appointment is also described at length, as will be discussed below). Why is the account of Gideon's appointment developed at such length, in comparison with the Ehud and Deborah accounts, where the emphasis is on the judge's acts of deliverance and not on his appointment? This question will be answered through the detailed analysis of this section.

> An angel of the LORD came and sat under the terebinth at Ophrah, which belonged to Joash the Abiezrite. His son Gideon was then beating out wheat inside a winepress in order to keep it safe from the Midianites (6:11).

The first part of this verse seems insignificant in relation to the next part of the account, since immediately in the next verse the angel is revealed to Gideon: "The angel of the LORD appeared to him and said to him" (v. 12). What then is the significance of the report of the arrival of the angel in verse 11 if immediately afterwards we find that the angel appeared before Gideon?[23] The strange description of the angel of the Lord sitting under the terebinth in Ophrah also appears in this verse. Why is the angel sitting there and what

---

[22] This unit is considered by some to be made up of two separate parallel sources, one that dealt with the establishment of the sanctuary with an altar under a terebinth (vv. 11ₐ, 18–24), and the other describing the commissioning of Gideon (vv. 11ᵦ–17). Both sources were combined by the Deuteronomistic redactor. See e.g. J. D. Martin, *The Book of Judges* (CBC), Cambridge 1975, p. 83; Soggin, *Judges*, p. 117. Whitley, "The Sources of the Gideon Stories", p. 158. However, I believe that the verses should be assumed to comprise one continuous account. Indeed, there are other stories of building of an altar following an encounter with the deity as found here, see e.g.: Gen 12:7–9; 13:14–18. It should be noted that the separation of the verses is highly speculative, and Soggin admits that reconstruction of the original sources must be perspicacious because they were combined skilfully, and because none of the sources presents a complete account.

[23] Indeed, the opening of Gideon's dialogue with the angel is unique in comparison with parallel sources, see e.g.: Gen 18:1: "The LORD appeared to Abraham by the oaks of Mamre, as he sat at the entrance of his tent in the heat of the day"; Gen 26:2: "The LORD appeared to Isaac and said, "Do not go down to Egypt; settle in the land that I shall show you"; Gen 26:24: "And that very night the LORD appeared to him and said, "I am the God of your father Abraham".

is the significance of this report? How does it contribute to the next part of the dialogue between Gideon and the angel?[24]

The fact that the angel came and sat under the terebinth belonging to Joash is described in order to show Gideon's disregard of the angel at this stage. The verse is divided into two parts; the first part deals with the angel and the second part with Gideon. There is tension between the two parts of the verse. The first part describes the angel's arrival, but in the second part Gideon ignores the angel and continues with his aforementioned occupation, beating out wheat. The contrast between the angel and Gideon emerges from the syntactic structure of the second part of verse 11: וגדעון בנו חבט חטים בגת ("His son Gideon was then beating out wheat inside a winepress"). If the verse was referring to two separate pictures, the syntactic structure should have been ויחבט גדעון חטים בגת ("and Gideon was beating out wheat in the winepress"). The reversal of the subject and the predicate וגדעון בנו חבט is designed to contrast between the angel's action and Gideon's action. The meaning of the verse is therefore: While the angel was sitting under the terebinth, Gideon was beating out wheat.[25] Instead of drawing near to the angel, Gideon continued with his occupations. This picture symbolizes Gideon's remoteness from the angel and his tidings; it is a preliminary intimation of Gideon's feeling of alienation from God, which is the main point of the passage. Since Gideon ignored the angel, in the next verse, the angel will reveal himself to Gideon.

The two actions of Gideon and the angel are placed in contrast in the same verse. Gideon's beating of the wheat demonstrates Israel's critical situation. Gideon is beating the wheat in the winepress, which is where grapes are trodden, rather than on the threshing-floor, in order to hide his activity from the Midianites.[26] The harshness of

---

[24] According to those who separate the passage into two different sources (see above n. 22), verses 11 and 12 do not belong to the same source.

[25] On presentation of simultaneous events in Biblical narrative see: S. Talmon, "The Presentation of Synchronicity and Simultaneity in Biblical Narrative", J. Heinemann and S. Werses (eds.), *Studies in Hebrew Narrative Art throughout the Ages* (Scripta Hierosylimitana, 27), Jerusalem 1978, pp. 9–26.

[26] Most commentaries believe that גת means winepress, however, some have suggested that in Ugaritit and Biblical Hebrew it actually means "farm". See e.g.: A. Lemaire, in *Les inscriptions hébraïques I, Les ostraca*, Paris 1977, p. 58; A. Lemaire, "La tablette Ougaritique alphabétique UF 29, 826 replacée dans son contexte", *UF* 30 (1998), pp. 461–465; G. Del Olmo Lete and J. Sanmartín, *A Dictionary of the Ugaritic Language in the Alphabetic Tradition*, I, Leiden 2003, pp. 310–313.

the oppression emerges here, but the difference is still conspicuous between Gideon who nonetheless is able to continue with his agricultural occupation, and those who were obliged to flee their homes and hide. What is the significance in the fact of the angel sitting under the terebinth? This will be seen below.

> The angel of the LORD appeared to him and said to him, 'The LORD is with you, mighty man of valour!' Gideon said to him, 'Please, my lord, if the LORD is with us, why has all this befallen us? Where are all His wondrous deeds about which our fathers told us, saying, Truly, the LORD brought us up from Egypt? Now the LORD has abandoned us and delivered us into the hands of Midian! (6:12–13).

The way in which the angel addresses Gideon—עמך ה' ("the Lord is with you")—is merely a greeting at the beginning of the conversation, like Boaz's greeting of his reapers (Ruth 2:4).[27] The term "mighty man of valour" (גבור חיל) has two meanings, one in a military context,[28] and the other in relation to men of economic status,[29] and in the broader meaning—distinguished men, people of standing. It is unclear, whether the angel, in using this expression, is speaking of military strength or of standing.[30] However, the combination of this expression with the greeting ה' עמך attests that the appellation is part of the greeting and an expression of respect, perhaps like the modern expression 'good day, dear sir'. If we consider that the angel's address to Gideon "The LORD is with you, mighty man of valour" is a greeting, Gideon's reply is surprising. He reacts harshly, and through a rhetorical question contradicts the determination that God is with them. He bases his words on a comparison between the people's current critical situation from which God has

---

[27] G. Fohrer, *Introduction to the Old Testament* (Trans. D. Green), London 1970, p. 75; J. Gray, *Joshua, Judges, Ruth* (NCB), Grand Rapids 1967, p. 297. Reventlow considers the angel's words to be a prophecy of salvation. H. G. Reventlow, *Liturgie und Prophetisches Ich bei Jeremia*, Gütersloh 1963, p. 49. For the meaning of the term "the Lord is with you", see: Richter, *Traditionsgeschichtliche Untersuchungen zum Richterbuch*, pp. 147–148.

[28] See, for instance, the soldiers of the two and a half transjordanian tribes (Josh 1:14); the Jericho fighters (Josh 6:2); Jephthah (Judg 11:1); Jeroboam (1 Kings 11:28); Naaman (2 Kings 24:14).

[29] See e.g. 1 Sam 9:1; Ruth 2:1; 2 Kings 15:20; 24:14.

[30] Priests and Levites (only in Ezra and Nehemiah): 1 Kings 11:28; 26:6; Neh 11:14; 1 Chr 9:13. For the meaning of the term see: E. Eising, "*Chayil*", *Theological Dictionary of the Old Testament*, IV, Grand Rapids 1980, pp. 350–351.

not delivered them and the events in the past in which God delivered them from adversity.[31] He concludes that God has abandoned
His People and therefore he protests the angel's greeting: "The LORD
is with you". The fact that this greeting was not to be taken literally but was merely the preamble to the conversation shows the
extent to which Gideon was inflamed by this subject. Even though
this was only a greeting, Gideon was unable to remain indifferent
to hearing "the Lord is with you" and reacted harshly, expressing
his opinion that the Lord was not with Israel.[32]

Gideon's rhetoric indicates his great disappointment that God had
not delivered His people.

> A. (1) Is the LORD with us, then why has all this befallen us?
> (2) Where are all His wondrous deeds about which our fathers told
> us, saying,
> B. (2) 'Did not the LORD bring us up from Egypt'?
> (1) Now the LORD has abandoned us and delivered us into the
> hands of Midian!

Gideon's words are divided into two parts. The first part (A) contains two sentences, the first of which refers to the present ("then
why has all this befallen us?") and the second to the past ("Where
are all His wondrous deeds about which our fathers told us". The
second part (B) also contains two sentences, resembling the arguments in the first part, but in a reverse order. The first sentence in
the second part is that God delivered his people in the past ("Did

---

[31] In such situations, Israel expected direct divine intervention, possibly in a miraculous form, based on different traditions that they had about wonders and miracles that God had performed for them in the past, as indicated in Ps 44:1 ff.;
78:3 ff. Elsewhere I have demonstrated how the conquest narrative in the Book of
Joshua deals with the transition between the wilderness period, which can be identified
with God's miraculous intervention, and the period in which Israel dwells in the
Land and lives a normal and natural life. On this topic see: E. Assis, *The Literary
Structure of the Conquest Narrative in the Book of Joshua (Chs. 1–11) and its Meaning*, Ph.D.
Diss. Bar-Ilan University, Ramat-Gan 1999, pp. 49–62.

[32] See also Amit, *The Book of Judges*, pp. 252–253. Because of Gideon's trenchant
reply, Soggin adopted Reventlow's interpretation (see above n. 26) that the words
of the Angel "The LORD is with you" are an oracle of salvation. Soggin, *Judges*, p.
118. However, the simple understanding is that the angel's words are a common
greeting, as I have explained above. Gideon's harsh reply to the common greeting
is designed to present Gideon's attitude towards God. Kaufmann's opinion (*Sefer
Shoftim*, p. 159) that Gideon' reply is an expression of his yearning for God's rev-
elation and salvation is implausible.

not the LORD bring us up from Egypt'?") and the second sentence again refers to the present ("Now the LORD has abandoned us and delivered us into the hands of Midian!"). The object of the duplication in Gideon's words is to emphasize his allegations. The reversal of the order underscores the current critical situation. He opens with the present situation: "Is the LORD with us?", and concludes with the present: "Now the LORD has abandoned us and delivered us into the hands of Midian!" However, there is a further significance in this structure. The three sentences commence with interrogatives: "is", "where", "did not". This possibly indicates that Gideon has doubts about the matter and may be prepared to hear an explanation from the angel that will make it clear to him why deliverance tarries, like the words of the prophet in verses 7–10. However, the reader immediately realizes that Gideon's questions are completely rhetorical and the use of the style only reinforces his rigid determination. Therefore, he concludes with an unequivocal statement: "Now the LORD has abandoned us and delivered us into the hands of Midian!" Moreover, Gideon directly blames God, when he compares God's intervention in the past to deliver Israel with God's failure to deliver Israel in the present.

God's name is cited in the two parallel situations:

> Did not the *LORD* bring us up from Egypt?
> Now the *LORD* has abandoned us.

Instead of saying in short "Did not the LORD bring us up from Egypt, but now he has abandoned us", Gideon repeats God's name in the second allegation in order to blame Him directly and emphatically for the present situation.[33]

Gideon's outcry against God emerges all the more forcefully in the analogy between his words and the prophet's rebuke that precedes this passage:

---

[33] In a Qumran version of this verse (4QJudges[a]) God is referred to as **אלהים** instead of the tetragrammaton in the MS, see: Trebolle, 4QJudg[a], *DJD* XIV, p. 162.

Judges 6:8–10	Judges 6:13
The LORD sent a prophet to the Israelites who said to them, . . .	Gideon said to him, Please, my lord,
I brought you up out of Egypt and freed you from the house of slavery.	is the LORD with us, then why has all this befallen us?
I rescued you from the hand of the Egyptians and from the hand of all your oppressors;	*Where are all His wondrous deeds* about which our fathers told us, saying,
I drove them out before you, and gave you their land . . .	*Did not the LORD bring us up from Egypt?*
But you did not obey Me.	Now the LORD has abandoned us and delivered us into the hands of Midian!"

As in the angel's rebuke, Gideon relates to God's wondrous works for Israel when he brought them out of Egypt. However, Gideon's use of this precedent is the contrary of the prophet's. For the prophet, failure to obey God after He delivered them from Egypt is Israel's betrayal of God. On the other hand, according to Gideon, God's failure to deliver His people now as he delivered them from Egypt means that God has abandoned His people. Using the precedent of Egypt, the prophet blames Israel for forsaking God, whereas Gideon uses this precedent to blame God for abandoning His people. The angel commences with the deliverance from Egypt and ends with the allegation against Israel: "But you did not obey Me" (v. 10). Gideon commences with the deliverance from Egypt and ends with the allegation against God: "Now the LORD has abandoned us and delivered us into the hands of Midian!" (v. 13).

Gideon's words are the complete opposite of those of the prophet and they are another layer in presenting the religious problem existing in this account. The sharp contrast between the prophet's words and those of Gideon shows the extent of Israel's alienation from God. We have already seen that the absence of reaction to the prophet's words was designed to show the people's apathy to God's prophet and his rebuke, and in this way the tremendous spiritual crisis of the people in wake of the harsh Midianite oppression is illustrated.[34] Here we see a debate and a direct confrontation between

---

[34] Gideon's failure to relate to the prophet's words does not prove different sources as maintained by some scholars (above, n. 16). This failure to relate to the prophet's words and the literary link between the prophet's and Gideon's words show that

the prophet and Gideon. Gideon displays a sceptical approach to the God of Israel and reproaches Him. The description of the critical spiritual situation creates anticipation: how will the distance between the people and their God be bridged? Gideon's harsh words against God also raise the question of how the designated judge-deliverer will succeed in restoring the people to belief in God. For all these reasons, it is difficult to understand why Gideon, whose faith in God was uncertain, was commissioned by God to deliver Israel.

Immediately after Gideon's words of defiance, it is said (v. 14):

> The LORD turned to him and said, 'Go in this strength of yours and deliver Israel from the Midianites. I herewith make you My messenger'.

Until now it is the angel who spoke to Gideon. Even after this sentence, it is still the angel who speaks and Gideon discovers only at the end of this meeting that this was the angel of the Lord. Therefore, it is clear that it was not God who was speaking to him, but still the angel who appeared to Gideon in human guise. It is therefore interesting that the angel is called here by the Lord's name, and this precisely after Gideon's words of defiance.

What is Gideon's strength with which he is commanded to deliver Israel? The most reasonable explanation is that "this" strength of his relates to Gideon's words to the angel. Although Gideon defies God in his words, it emerges that Gideon is deeply concerned for his people. The angel greeted him in the singular ה׳ עמך ("The LORD is with *you*"). Gideon replied in the plural and as the people's representative: "is the LORD with *us*". Now it is clear that the source of his revolt against God is nothing other than concern for his people. In his reaction to the angel's greeting "The LORD is with you" Gideon uses the plural form seven times: "is the LORD *with us*, then why has all this *befallen us*? Where are all His wondrous deeds about which *our fathers told us*, saying, Did not the LORD *bring us* up from Egypt? Now the LORD has *abandoned us* and *delivered us* into the hands of Midian!" (v. 13). Gideon's intensive use of the plural in his wording is designed to present Gideon as someone whose main

---

the author's intention was to place Gideon in confrontation with the prophet and to characterize him as opposing the prophecy, and the understanding that God is behind the current events. Similarly see: Amit, *The Book of Judges*, pp. 250–251.

concern is the plight of his people.[35] It might reasonably be explained that when the angel says to him "Go in this strength of yours and deliver Israel" (v. 14) he means the strength of Gideon's concern for his people.[36] Gideon was chosen to deliver the people because of his concern for the people. This attribute is of the greatest importance in selection of an Israelite leader, as will be discussed in greater detail below.

Although Gideon reveals here an important attribute for the Israelite leader it may be assumed that he will undergo some spiritual change in order to be an effective representative of God and to restore the people to worship of God. This transition occupies a central place in the first part of the Gideon stories, as will be discussed below.

Gideon's suitable leadership attributes appear in his diffident reaction to his appointment, v. 15: "Please, my lord, how can I deliver Israel? Why, my clan is the humblest in Manasseh, and I am the youngest in my father's household". Gideon refuses the role of deliverer, considering himself unworthy and noting that he cannot be a leader because he is young and from a humble clan. This evasion resembles that of Moses (Exod 3:11–4:17) and Saul when he is appointed king (1 Sam 9:21). It transpires that Gideon's clan is not

---

[35] For a different explanation of Gideon's use of the plural form in his response to the angel's greeting in the singular form, see: Klein, *The Triumph in the Book of Judges*, p. 53.

[36] This idea was first raised in Midrash Tanhuma: "Since merit was found in Gideon who taught their [the Israelites'] merit, the Angel immediately appeared to him, as it is said: 'And the Angel of the Lord came to him and said to him: Go in this strength of yours'—with the strength of the merit that you taught of my children. 'and judge the people righteously', that they will teach the righteousness of the generation" (Tanhuma, printed version, *Šoftim*, 4, p. 111a). This interpretation is adopted by Rashi; Rabbi Don Isaac ben Judah Abravanel, *Piruš 'al nevi'im rišonim*, Jerusalem 1957; Kaufmann, *Sefer Shoftim*, p. 159. Others consider the meaning of the sentence to be that now God gave Gideon additional strength (Kimchi; Gersonides), or that He is referring to physical strength that Gideon already possesses (Kara; Isaiah di Trani). Soggin (*Judges*, p. 119) also raises these last two possibilities. Gray understood the Angel to be referring to Gideon's strength in beating out the wheat, or to his strength of character in his encounter with the Angel, Gray, *Joshua, Judges, Ruth*, p. 298. Schneider posits that the nature of the strength mentioned by the Angel is unclear to Gideon as it is unclear to the reader, and this is why Gideon continues to ask how he will save Israel. See: T. J. Schneider, *Judges* (Berit Olam), Collegeville 2000, pp. 104–105. Gros Louis believes that Gideon is selected at random, in order to demonstrate God's power. K. R. R. Gros Louis, "The Book of Judges", K. R. R. Gros Louis, J. S. Ackerman and T. S. Warshaw (eds.), *Literary Interpretations of Biblical Narratives*, Nashville and New York, p. 153.

humble, and his words derive from modesty,[37] coinciding with the stories of other appointments in the Bible.[38] The element of refusal of the role constitutes a kind of qualification for the role, and shows that he is indeed the right candidate. It shows that he has no personal motivations or egocentric interests when he assumes the commission. This refusal, which shows that Gideon has no personal motivation, complements Gideon's expression of concern for his people. Gideon is shown as someone who only has his people's plight before his eyes. Therefore, he is the right person to deal with the people's problems.

God answers Gideon, encourages him, and promises to be with him, v. 16: "The LORD said to him, I will be with you, and you shall defeat Midian to a man".[39] In light of God's answer, Gideon concludes that, despite his weakness, the fact that God is with him will give him additional strength, and he will therefore be able to defeat the Midianites. In God's words, there is also an answer to Gideon's initial doubt: "is the LORD with us, then why has all this befallen us?" (v. 13): God answers him in the same wording: "The LORD said to him, 'I will be with you'" (v. 16). In response to Gideon's allegation that God has abandoned his people, "Now the LORD has abandoned us and delivered us into the hands of Midian!" (v. 13), God says to him: "and you shall defeat Midian to a man" (v. 16).

However, even after hearing God's words of encouragement, telling Gideon that He will be with him, Gideon still does not accept the commission, and expresses doubt that it is indeed God who is speaking to him: "And he said to Him, If I have gained Your favor, give me a sign that it is You who are speaking to me" (v. 17). Gideon's

---

[37] Moore, *Judges*, p. 186; Burney, *The Book of Judges*, p. 189.

[38] N. Habel, "The Form and Significance of the Call Narrative", *ZAW* 77 (1965), p. 300.

[39] Some commentators consider that it is still the Angel speaking in this verse, see Gersonides; G. A. Cooke, *The Book of Judges* (The Cambridge Bible for Schools and Colleges), Cambridge 1918, p. 74. Boling and Kaufmann consider that it is God speaking here; earlier the Angel spoke to him, but at this point the Lord intervened. Boling, *Judges*, p. 131; Kaufmann, *Sefer Shoftim*, p. 159. This interpretation is already found in Rashi's commentary. Burney suggested that in the original text God Himself spoke to Gideon, the text was modified by introducing the Angel conversing with Gideon, but this modification was not fully carried out. Burney, *The Book of Judges*, p. 189. I cannot agree with Burney's supposition, since I find it difficult to explain why this modification would not have been completed.

doubt now focuses on the actual question of whether it is God who is speaking with him. In Habel's opinion, the sign for Gideon is one of the characteristic elements of the commissioning model.[40] However, apart from the fact that giving of a sign does not appear in every commissioning,[41] this element in the Gideon account is unique, in that it is Gideon who asks for a sign since he doubts that it is God who is speaking with him, whereas in the other cases the sign is given on God's initiative (as in the commissioning of Moses (Exod 3:12; 4:2–9). Truth to tell, there is no other case of commissioning in which the person commissioned asks for a sign.[42] This doubt expressed by Gideon is thus apposite for the account under study, in which the subject of spiritual doubt is a central motif.[43]

After Gideon asks for the sign, he makes a further request:

> Do not leave this place until I come back to You and bring out my offering and place it before You'. And He answered, 'I will stay until you return'. So Gideon came in and prepared a kid, and baked unleavened bread from an ephah of flour. He put the meat in a basket and poured the broth into a pot, and he brought them out to Him under the terebinth, and he presented them (vv. 18–19).

Why does Gideon prepare this offering for the figure standing before him? The offering proposed is to be understood through a comparison with a parallel story describing a meeting between an angel of the Lord and Manoah and his wife. Initially, when Manoah pro-

---

[40] Habel, "The Form and Significance of the Call Narrative", pp. 297–323.

[41] See for instance the commissioning of Isaiah (see: Habel, *op. cit.* p. 312), Deutero-Isaiah (Habel, *op. cit.* p. 316) and Ezekiel (*op. cit.*). In the commissioning of Jeremiah, it is not certain whether the touching of God's hand on Jeremiah's mouth is a sign as asserted by Habel (*op. cit.* p. 309). The giving of a sign is not included in the commissioning model according to U. Simon, *Reading Prophetic Narratives* (The Biblical Encyclopaedia Library, 15), Jerusalem and Ramat-Gan 1997, pp. 60–62 (Hebrew).

[42] Amit is therefore right when she asserts that the author is free to decide which of the various motifs associated with a specific story-type he will use, Amit, *The Book of Judges*, p. 254.

[43] For this reason the opinion of Webb and Dishon, that the commissioning of Gideon is parallel to that of Moses, in order to show Gideon to be devout like Moses should be rejected. J. Dishon, "Gideon and the Beginnings of Monarchy in Israel", *Tarbiz* 41 (1972), p. 257 (Hebrew); Webb, *The Book of the Judges*, pp. 150–151. Given the emphasis in the account on Gideon's scepticism, it is impossible to view Gideon positively. For criticism of Webb's view see: Exum, "The Center Cannot Hold", p. 417. For the affinity between the calls of Gideon and Moses, see: Klein, *The Triumph of Irony in the Book of Judges*, p. 51; Bluedorn, *Yahweh Versus Baalism*, pp. 75–77.

poses an offering to the figure standing before him, the impression is that he wishes to offer him refreshment, either as hospitality or because of a feeling of obligation towards someone who has promised them a good future (13:15, 17). Only after the angel tells them to give the offering not to him but to God, do they sacrifice the offering to God. Gideon's presentation of the offering also seems like hospitality and honouring of a person speaking in God's name.[44] However, the ritual context of the offering is evident through the use of the words: מנחה (offering), וינש (and presented), איפת קמח (ephah of flour) (Num 8:15; 1 Sam 1:24).[45] The ambiguity between a ritual offering and a human present seems to be intentional both here and in the episode of Manoah and his wife.[46] What makes the two stories unique is that both Gideon and Manoah have doubts about the identity of the figure standing before them.[47] The author illustrates this doubt through a situation that can be interpreted both at the secular and at the ritual level. The object of this passage is to present Gideon as alienated from God and his request for the sign expresses this alienation, already shown in his outcry against God "is the LORD with us".[48] However, Gideon's doubt is more significant than Manoah's. Gideon's cultic association is not worship of God, but idolatrous worship: "and he brought them out to Him *under the terebinth*, and he presented them" (v. 19).[49] The place where the offering is presented is cited here for good reason. Through reference to the terebinth,

---

[44] According to Burney in the original text the purpose was hospitality, and late additions gave the text a meaning of sacrifice. Burney, *The Book of Judges*, p. 191.

[45] Amit asserts that Gideon offered food not as an act of hospitality but as a means of ascertaining the identity of the guest. If he eats the offering then it is a sign that he is human, if he does not then it will point to his miraculous nature. Amit, *The Book of Judges*, p. 255. I doubt whether such a sophisticated act or knowledgeable understanding of miraculous beings may be attributed to Gideon. His ignorance as regards theophany is apparent when be recognizes that the guest is an angel and fears that he will die because he has seen God.

[46] Thus, Soggin's assertion that the offering is solely cultic is mistaken, in light of the clear motifs of hospitality. Soggin, *Judges*, p. 121.

[47] On this matter see my forthcoming article: "The Meaning of Samson's Birth Account (Judg 13)", *Shnaton: An Annual for Biblical and Ancient Near Eastern Studies* 15 (2004).

[48] Soggin, on the other hand, holds that the Old Testament does not view the asking God for proof of identity as illegitimate. He supports his assertion from Isa 7:10–25.

[49] In many instances the terebinth is associated with idol worship: e.g.: Gen 35:4; Ezek 6:13; Hos 4:13.

the idolatrous context is underscored. This element is a preliminary indication of the Baal worship that will come in the next section of the account. However, the use of the idolatrous associations in Gideon's action indicates the extent of Gideon's alienation from God, and even Gideon's involvement in idolatry.

The sign will be given in the offering presented by Gideon to the angel. The angel does not eat the offering and instead he instructs Gideon to lay the unleavened bread and the meat on the rock and to pour the broth over them, an act which will make it harder to set the food alight.[50] Yet, when the angel touches the offering with the end of the staff in his hand, fire comes up out of the rock and burns it (vv. 20–21).[51] This action shows the wondrous might of the man standing before Gideon. However, the spectacle that certainly greatly influences Gideon is the angel's miraculous disappearance: "And the angel of the LORD vanished from his sight".

The angel's disappearance brings Gideon for the first time to the realization: "that it was an angel of the LORD" (v. 22). When Gideon understands ultimately that it is indeed God who spoke with him and commissioned him to deliver Israel, he is stricken by fear that he will die since he has seen the angel of the Lord: "and Gideon said, 'Alas, O Lord GOD! For I have seen an angel of the LORD face to face'" (v. 22).[52] God immediately appears to him and calms him, telling him that he will not die (v. 23). This dialogue recalls Manoah's fears that he will die when he understands that he has seen God (13:22).[53] However, there it is clear that Manoah's reaction shows his ignorance and insignificance as compared with his wife, who with wisdom and logic explains to him: "If the LORD had meant to kill us, he would not have accepted a burnt offering and a grain offering at our hands, or shown us all these things, or now announced to us such things as these". (13:23). Manoah is shown

---

[50] Similarly, Elijah pours water over the sacrifice in order to increase the wonder: 1 Kings 18:34–35.

[51] Supernatural fire symbolizes divine acceptance, see: Lev 9:24; 1 Kings 18:23–39; 1 Chr 21:26; 2 Chr 7:1.

[52] This corresponds to the conception that whoever sees God dies, see: Exod 33:20; Isa 6:5. Hearing God's voice may also have the same consequences, see: Deut 4:33; 5:21–25.

[53] For the analogies between the two stories see: Y. Zakovitch, "Assimilation in Biblical Narratives", J. H. Tigay (ed.), *Empirical Models for Biblical Criticism*, Philadelphia 1985, pp. 192–196.

there ironically in light of his wife's wise conclusion. Thus, Gideon is also presented as ignorant and a novice when he passes from doubts on the identity of the figure before him to an opposite extreme of fear of death since he has seen the angel of the Lord. Gideon does not reach the simple understanding of Manoah's wife by himself; in this he resembles Manoah. However, the expectations from Gideon, the future deliverer of Israel, are greater than the expectations from Manoah. Apart from these two cases, whenever God's appearance is related, there is no reaction of fear of death following the appearance. Thus for instance the angel of the Lord appears to Hagar (Gen 16:7–11; 21:17), to Abraham (Gen 22: 11, 15), to Moses (Exod 3:2 ff.), to Balaam (Num 22:31), to Joshua (Josh 5:14), David (2 Sam 24:17), Elijah (2 Kings 19:7; 2 Kings 1:15–16), etc.

After God tells Gideon that he will not die, Gideon finally arrives at a balanced and correct perception of his encounter with the angel, and he builds an altar to God:[54] "So Gideon built there an altar to the LORD and called it Adonai-shalom. To this day it stands in Ophrah of the Abiezrites" (v. 24). This action recalls the action of the Patriarchs when they expressed their respect and their faith after God spoke to them, through building of an altar (see: Gen 12:7, 18; 26:25; 28:18; 33:20). However, as opposed to other cases, Gideon undergoes a lengthy process before his recognition of the theophany. What is the significance of the name that Gideon calls the altar: "Adonai-shalom"? The meaning of the word "shalom" is wholeness, success, health and peace.[55] It is difficult to determine the precise meaning of the word in this context. However it seems that Gideon calls the altar "Adonai Shalom" on the basis of what God said to him in reaction to his fear that he would die: "But the LORD said to him, *Peace be to you* (שלום לך); have no fear, you shall not die".

---

[54] How is it possible that after the Angel of God went from his sight God continues to converse with Gideon? Burney suggested that vv. 22–24 were added by another author. Burney, *The Book of Judges*, p. 193. Some of the Jewish Medieval commentators explained that now the voice came from heaven, see: Kimchi; Gersonides. Amit, too, understands that it is God Himself who is talking to Gideon. In her opinion, this is another sign given to him. Amit, *The Book of Judges*, p. 256.

[55] For the meanings of the word שלום see: *HALOT*, vol. 4, pp. 1506–1510. Regarding this word von Rad indicated: "Seldom do we find in the OT a word which to the same degree as SALOM can bear a common use and yet can also be filled with a concentrated religious content far above the level of average conception". G. von Rad, "שלום in the OT", *Theological Dictionary of the New Testament*, vol. 2, Grand Rapids, p. 402.

God promised "shalom" (peace) to Gideon and against this Gideon calls the altar "Adonai-shalom".[56]

The theme of the account of Gideon's commission is the lengthy process undergone by Gideon until he recognizes that it is God who is addressing him. At the beginning of the passage, the alienation between the angel and Gideon is emphasized. The angel comes to sit under the terebinth on the land of Gideon's family ("which belonged to Joash *the Abiezrite*") and Gideon continues with his occupations without paying attention to the guest (v. 11). At the end of the passage, the location is still "To this day it stands in Ophrah of *the Abiezrites*", but here the relation between Gideon and God is described through the building of the altar rather than reference to the "terebinth" with the idolatrous connotation of the beginning of the passage, and through calling the altar "Adonai-shalom" (v. 24). Since Gideon did not turn to the angel, the angel appears to Gideon and addresses him with the greeting "The LORD is with you" (v. 12). Gideon immediately reacts harshly to the greeting and negates the possibility that God is with Israel (v. 13). Here begins the intricate process in which Gideon draws near to the angel and to God's message. Towards the end of the passage, the angel again conveys a greeting of peace to Gideon: "the LORD said to him, *Peace* (שלום) be to you" (v. 23). This time this greeting leads Gideon to build an altar, to call it after the blessing that he now received "Adonai-*shalom*" (v. 24).

As already noted, the detailed description of Gideon's commission is exceptional in the Book of Judges. From study of the meaning of the commission, we learn that the object of this detailed description is to underscore Gideon's lack of faith and the process that he undergoes until he succeeds in recognizing that the figure standing before him is none other than an angel of the Lord who has come to commission him to deliver Israel.[57] The fact that Gideon is the only judge with whom God speaks emphasizes the problematic nature of

---

[56] Marais maintains that the calling of the altar "the Lord is peace" is ironic since Gideon is about to fight against the Baal and Midian. J. Marais, *Representation in Old Testament Narrative Texts* (Biblical Interpretation, 36), Leiden, Boston and Köln 1998, p. 110. I do not believe there is any irony at this point, since the intention of the Angel of God is that Gideon will recognize God, and act upon this by fighting against the Baal and saving Israel from her oppressor.

[57] See also: Klein, *The Triumph of Irony in the Book of Judges*, pp. 52–53.

Gideon's communications with God. The object of the great emphasis on this meeting is to underscore the tremendous spiritual crisis in Israel in wake of the Midianite oppression, and in this aspect this unit is a direct continuation of the description of the oppression and of the description of the angel's words prior to Gideon's appointment. In most of the judge accounts, the stages of transgression, punishment and appearance of the judge are part of the exposition of the story. In the Gideon account, these stages are part of the plot, and they describe the serious spiritual situation with which Gideon is faced when he comes to deliver Israel and to restore Israel to divine worship. At this stage the reader may wonder even more how the Israelites will surmount their difficult spiritual situation, and how Gideon will be able to faithfully represent God who has commissioned him, as Ehud and Deborah did, and how he will restore the people to divine worship.[58]

6. *Gideon Destroys the Altar of the Baal (6:25–32)*

In the other judge accounts, the commissioning or raising up of the deliverer is immediately followed by the account of the deliverance. Here too, the Gideon account differs. This is the only account in the book in which the judge is commanded to combat idolatry: "the LORD said to him: '... pull down the altar of Baal which belongs to your father'" (v. 25).[59] How is this commandment to Gideon to be explained in light of its uniqueness in the judge accounts?[60]

---

[58] According to Marais, God's effort to bring Gideon to act and to overcome his fear represents a degeneration in the Book. Initially the problem was a military one with an external enemy, now the struggle is with Israel and on religious grounds. Marais, *Representation in Old Testament Narrative Texts*, p. 108. Amit rightly understood that the commissioning of Gideon is exceptional in comparison with the other deliverers. She explained the uniqueness of this story as part of the editorial theme of signs, which in her opinion expresses the idea that God is responsible for Israel's salvation. Amit, *The Book of Judges*, pp. 251–252. This explanation is too generalized and does not deal with the specific intention of the Gideon account.

[59] According to Zakovitch this account is the source of later stories of struggle against Idols, See: Y. Zakovitch, "The Story of Yair and the Fiery Furnace: A Study of Pseudo-Philo Chapter 38", S. Japhet (ed.), *The Bible in Light of Its Interpreters: Sarah Kamin Memorial Volume*, Jerusalem 1994, pp. 141–156 (Hebrew).

[60] Scholars of the source criticism school believe that vv. 25–32 belong to E and describe a polemic against Baal worship, and the building of an altar to God. Vv. 11–24 belong to J and deal with Gideon's appointment; they are connected with

According to Amit, this account illustrates the doing of what was offensive to God in the period of the Judges: in Gideon's house, there is idolatry that serves the people of the city. Therefore, before Gideon is sent to deliver Israel from the Midianites, he must cleanse Israel of idolatry. The deliverance depends on prior eradication of the Baal worship by Gideon.[61] However, the main point of this passage is not the destruction of the Baal only, which is the subject of verses 25–27. The second half of the passage, which is longer than the first, deals with the fanatical response of the Baalist men of Ophrah, in their search for the transgressor who harmed the Baal and in their eagerness to punish Gideon. In fact, it is not the war against the Baal that the passage emphasizes, but precisely the corruption of the men of Ophrah in their Baal worship. An exhaustive study of the contents and structure of the passage will duly clarify the matter.

The structure of this unit dealing with the destruction of the Baal shows its function. The unit is divided into two parts:

> Vv. 25–27 – God's order to Gideon to destroy the altar of Baal and the sacred post and to build there an altar to God and to sacrifice on it a sacrifice that was intended for the Baal.
> Vv. 28–32 – The struggle of the men of Ophrah against Gideon.

The first part describes the struggle of Gideon against the Baal, and the second the struggle of the men of Ophrah against Gideon in response to his attack on the Baal. This fact in itself shows that the main point of the passage is not Gideon's struggle against the Baal, but the confrontation between Gideon and the Baalists. The object of the passage is to illustrate the critical spiritual situation existing before Gideon began to act as deliverer. In the other judge accounts

---

the altar in Ophrah. See: Burney, *The Book of Judges*, pp. 177–178. For a variation on this, see: Martin, *The Book of Judges*, pp. 77–78, 87–88. Martin divides the text into two separate stories, but does not ascribe them to the Pentateuchal sources. Others rightly claim that the two passages form a continuous sequence. See Boling, *Judges*, p. 130. On this matter see: B. Lindars, "Gideon and Kingship", *JTS* 16 (1965), pp. 315–326. Soggin holds that vv. 25–32 were inserted into the story of Gideon's appointment in order to establish a symmetry between his two tasks. In the former passage he is called to fight against the external enemies, and in vv. 25–32 he is to fight against the internal enemy. See Soggin, *Judges*, p. 128.

[61] See: Kaufmann, *Sefer Shoftim*, p. 165.

the deliverer is supported or favoured by the people; Gideon here goes against his family and the men of his town.

The passage shows that the men of Ophrah had the upper hand. The first part (vv. 25–27), which describes Gideon's actions, ends in a frame that opens and closes with the motif of 'night'. At the beginning of the passage: "*That night the* LORD *said to him*". (v. 25), and at the end: "but as he was afraid to do it by day, . . . *he did it by night*" (v. 27). On the other hand, the second part, which describes the struggle of the men of Ophrah against Gideon, finishes with the motif of 'day'; at the beginning of the passage: "When the townspeople *rose* early in the *morning*, the altar of Baal was broken down" (v. 28), and at the end: "Whoever fights his battles shall be dead by *morning*! . . . That *day* they named him Jerubbaal" (vv. 31–32).

These motifs combine well with the meaning of the passage. Gideon fears the men of the city; he is apparently beset by doubts, and therefore acts at night. On the other hand, the men of Ophrah act resolutely and confidently; accordingly their acts are carried out in the context of the 'day' motif. The men of Ophrah react forcibly to the destruction of the Baal, but in the second part Gideon is completely passive in face of their rage. The men of Ophrah accuse him, and demand that his father bring him out to be killed, and in the entire relation of this act, no reaction is heard from Gideon. Gideon's failure to react in the daytime reflects his internal state, and he acts at night.

Let us now analyze the text. The emphasis in the verse on the expression "belonging to your father" shows Gideon's difficult situation, in that he must challenge his father: "That night the LORD said to him: "Take the young bull *belonging to your father* and another bull seven years old; pull down the altar of Baal *which belongs to your father*, and cut down the sacred post which is beside it" (v. 25). It is somewhat ironic that Gideon will destroy his father's altar of Baal using the bullock that belongs to his father; this is a kind of metaphor of the fact that it is Joash's son, Gideon, who will oppose his father.

In place of the destroyed altar, Gideon is ordered to build an altar there to God: "Then build an altar to the LORD your God, on the level ground on top of this stronghold. Take the other bull and offer it as a burnt offering, using the wood of the sacred post that you have cut down" (v. 26). This action is designed to express Gideon's belief in God. However, this action is to a great extent declarative. Gideon builds an altar on the site of the altar of Baal. On this altar, he offers up to God a sacrifice that was intended initially to be offered up to the Baal. This sacrifice is a choice, fat seven-year old bullock.[62] However, he does something more serious. He sets up the divine worship on the ruins of the Baal worship. The Asherah tree (sacred post) which symbolizes the Asherah goddess, who is of special importance in Canaanite mythology, is merely burning material with which Gideon will offer the sacrifice to the Lord, and this shows the lack of substance of the Asherah.[63] This act expresses the insignificance of the Baal and the Asherah and of their worship, and in the same place Gideon establishes divine worship.

Such a serious action taken against Baal worship and the direct clash with his father were certainly no easy matter for Gideon. Gideon indeed feared to carry out this action in daytime and performed it in secret at night. God gave Gideon the order at night and Gideon intended to carry out the action in the morning: "So Gideon took ten of his servants and did as the LORD had told him" (v. 27$_a$). However, out of fear he went back on this intention: "but as he was afraid to do it by day, on account of his father's household and the townspeople, he did it by night" (v. 27$_b$). The passage emphasizes Gideon's intention to destroy the Baal altar in daytime, in order to show ultimately his fear of doing so. Gideon's fear serves the account at two levels. Firstly, it shows the difficult confrontation faced by

---

[62] The simple understanding of the term שׁבע שׁנים is that the second bull is 7 years old, and thus it is fat and good as a sacrifice. With the first bull he destroyed the altar of the Baal. This is the understanding of the Septuagint. Bluedorn suggested that the omission of the words שׁנה+בן is intentional, in order to draw attention to the Midianite oppression (6:1, שׁבע שׁנים). See: Bluedorn, *Yahweh Versus Baalism*, p. 94. For a discussion on the syntax of the verse and the various explanations for the term הפר השׁני see: G. R. Driver, "Problems in Judges Newly Discussed", *The Annual of Leeds University Oriental Society*, IV (1962–1963), p. 12; J. A. Emerton, "'The Second Bull'' in Judges 6, 25–28', *Eretz Israel* 14 (1978), pp. 52–55. Guillaume suggested a reading הפר השׁני which he interprets according to Arabic as a full grown animal. A. Guillaume, "A Note on 'happar hassenī', Judges VI. 25, 26, 28", *JTS* 50 (1949), pp. 52–53. Burney thinks that the word שׁני should be omitted. Burney, *The Book of Judges*, pp. 194–195. However, it is unlikely that the word was mistakenly inserted in the text three times. For another suggestion see: W. Rudolph, "Textkritische Anmerkungen zum Richterbuch", J. Fück (ed.), *Festschrift Otto Eissfeldt zum 60 Geburtstag*, Halle 1947, p. 200. For a summary of opinions see: Bluedorn, *op. cit.* pp. 91–93.

[63] The worship of Asherah is forbidden in Deut 16:21. It is debatable whether the Asherah was a tree or a wooden object. On this matter and on the Asherah cult see: Burney, *The Book of Judges*, pp. 195–198; J. Day, "Asherah", *ABD*, vol. 1, 1992, pp. 483–487.

Gideon before going out to deliver Israel as commissioned by God; he has no support even in his father's house, where Baal worship prevails and not belief in God. This fear therefore continues the apostasy that appeared until now in the story. Here, though, there is a deeper and more serious aspect in this problem. Now it emerges that not only are the people disbelievers or apathetic, as was seen above in the account, but that they are apostates and idol worshippers. The fact that the bullock intended for sacrifice to the Baal was seven years old, as the number of years of the Midianite oppression, is designed to show that they were steeped in Baal worship. This fact also constitutes a background to Gideon's natural habitat. The Baal worship situation as reflected here gives a broader context to Gideon's words of defiance against God. This is not merely a man who expresses doubts about the God of Israel; God has already been abandoned and Baal worship adopted in his home. This leads the reader to a second level in Gideon's fear. Gideon's fear may also reflect his doubt about the new path forced upon him on the previous day; the doubt about worshipping the God of Israel increases and prevents him from raising his head as God's representative against the Baal. He therefore prefers to act at night, in a far less affirmative way. Given the expectation that Gideon will stand and openly make a statement about the non-existence of the Baal and the belief in the God of Israel in daylight, his night action must be seen as a retreat from the recognition to which he has arrived. Here again the question arises of how a man full of spiritual doubts concerning the God of Israel, and facing serious opposition from his Baalist relatives, will succeed in restoring the people to divine worship.

Gideon's fear of taking a position supporting the God of Israel and against the Baal is understood in light of the energetic activity of the men of Ophrah the next morning to find the identity of the person who has harmed the Baal (vv. 28–32).

V. 28: "When the townspeople rose early in the morning, the altar of Baal was broken down and the sacred post beside it had been cut down, and the second bull had been offered on the newly built altar". The fact that the men of Ophrah rise early in the morning and go immediately to the Baal's altar shows the centrality of the Baal in their lives. Unlike Gideon who postpones the destruction of the altar to the night, the men of Ophrah act directly on the same day. Immediately the sight that meets their eyes is related: the destruction of the Baal's altar, the cutting down of the sacred

post, the sacrifice of the bullock on the new altar. These details
already appeared in God's command, but are not found in Gideon's
action. However, they are repeated again in the description of the
sight that meets the eyes of the men of Ophrah. The absence of
details in Gideon's action shows that it is to some extent defective.[64]
However, this description is again given in detail from the viewpoint
of the men of Ophrah. The details from their point of view, even
though the actual information has already been given, are designed
to underscore their serious attitude towards the act. They react immediately and energetically, seeking out the transgressor:

> They said to one another, 'Who did this thing?'
> They enquired and asked, and said
> 'Gideon son of Joash did this thing!' (v. 29).

The question "Who *did this thing?*" at the beginning of the verse is
answered rapidly and already in the same breath the reader discovers: "Gideon son of Joash *did this thing!*" The repetition of the
same words in the question and the answer in the same verse shows
how quickly they discover Gideon. Their determination to find the
transgressor emerges from the use of the list of verbs: וידרשו ויבקשו
ויאמרו ("they enquired and asked, and said").[65] The action is initiated by the men of the city "They said to one another", and they
also carry out the enquiry and the investigation. This determination
to find the transgressor and the rapid discovery of Gideon show the
zeal of the men of Ophrah in their Baal worship. Their devoutness
is also expressed in their determined and unanimous decision: Then
the townspeople said to Joash: "Bring out your son, that he may
die; because he has broken down the altar of Baal, and because he
has cut down the sacred post that was by it". The passage thus contrasts Gideon's delay and indecision with the immediate and energetic action of the men of Ophrah.

The men of Ophrah present their request to Joash, Gideon's father,
apparently because of Joash's high status in the city leadership, or

---

[64] This stands in contrast to cases were the implementation is immediately repeated
after the command. Such a repetition is meant to convey the idea that the command was fully executed. For this device see n. 130.

[65] For a similar phenomenon see e.g.: Gen 25:34. Marais' opinion that the details
of the action of the people of Ophrah is meant to heighten the effect of the confusion that gripped them is unlikely. Marais, *Representation in Old Testament Narrative
Texts*, p. 111.

because he conducts the Baal worship.[66] His status emerges explicitly in v. 25: "the altar of Baal which belongs to your father", and from the fact that the men of the city demand that Joash carry out the death sentence.[67]

Gideon's sentence depends on his father Joash. The narrator shows Joash as facing a great crowd that vehemently and decisively demands Gideon's death: "Joash said to all who had risen against him" (v. 31). Even if the father wishes to defend the son, seemingly this would not be simple given the resoluteness and inflexibility of the men of Ophrah who seek Gideon's death. Joash answers them: "Do you have to contend for Baal? Do you have to vindicate him? Whoever fights his battles shall be dead by morning! If he is a god, let him fight his own battles, since it is his altar that has been torn down!" (v. 31).[68] According to Joash, the zeal of the townspeople for the Baal is in fact heresy; if they execute Gideon, this means that they do not believe in the Baal's ability to punish those who transgressed against him. Further, according to Joash, anyone killing Gideon will be subject to an immediate death sentence, since he denies the Baal's ability to do this: "Whoever fights his battles shall be dead by morning!". Joash's words show his agreement that his son deserves a death sentence, but his determination that the Baal himself must be allowed to carry out the sentence, if indeed he is a god: "If he is a god, let him fight his own battles, since it is his altar that has been torn down!" Joash's belief in the Baal is thus more extreme than the stance of the men of Ophrah, and it is precisely this radicalization that averts Gideon's immediate execution.[69] At the same time, the

---

[66] Altman thinks that this story indicates the failure of the tribal leadership to deal with internal affairs. A. Altman, "The Development of the Office of 'Judge' in Pre-Monarchic Israel", *Proceedings of the Seventh World Congress of Jewish Studies* 7, 2 (1981), p. 17 (Hebrew). However, such a conclusion cannot be derived from this account if, as we assume, Joash occupied a high position. Moore asserts that the people of Ophrah approach Gideon's father in order to prevent a confrontation with Joash's family. Moore, *Judges*, p. 194. Kaufman opines that the custom in the patriarchal society was that the father was a Judge in his house; therefore, it was impossible to prosecute the son without Joash's consent. Kaufman, *Sefer Shoftim*, p. 167.

[67] There is an irony in the name Joash, which is a theophoric name, but yet he has an altar for the Baal. See: Schneider, *Judges*, p. 103.

[68] Rashi; Kimchi; Kara.

[69] It is unclear whether Joash believes in what he says or whether his reply is a sophisticated stratagem to save his son. However, Zakovitch's opinion that Joash's

phraseology of Joash's words, "If he is a god", is a reminder that the question on the agenda is who is God. The death sentence still hangs over Gideon, but is not carried out because of the men's absolute faith in the Baal. Now they expect a calamity to befall Gideon and this will be interpreted by them as Gideon's punishment by the Baal.[70]

This explains the intention behind Gideon's throwing down of the Baal. After this event, the dispute between the Baalists and those loyal to God becomes extremely intense. From this time onwards, it is impossible to remain uncommitted and indifferent to events. Following the imminent war, the truth will become clear as to who the real God is. Gideon will wage war against Midian in order to deliver Israel from their enemies in God's name. If Gideon wins this war, he will prove that he was indeed commissioned by God and that the Lord God of Israel is the true God. However, if he loses the war, it will be proved that the Baal has taken vengeance on Gideon because he destroyed his altar. In other words, any result of the battle will prove two things simultaneously. If Gideon wins, it will be proved that God sent him and that the Lord is the true God, and on a parallel the Baal's powerlessness will be proved since the Baal has not taken vengeance on Gideon for striking out against Baal worship. If Gideon loses, it will be proved that God has not sent him and that the Baal is the true god who has taken vengeance on Gideon for the attack.[71] In the act of destroying the Baal Gideon

---

answer is sarcastic is unlikely since the people of Ophrah continue to insist on Gideon's immediate execution. If Joash's words were meant to offend the Baal, a second confrontation would have been expected. See: Y. Zakovitch, "A Study of Precise and Partial Derivations in Biblical Etymology", *JSOT* 15 (1980), p. 32.

[70] According to Zakovitch the name Jerubbaal has two different derivations in Joash's words: the first in v. 31: "let him strive for himself" (ירב לו); and the second in v. 32: "Let Baal strive against him" (ירב בו הבעל). Zakovitch, "A Study of Precise and Partial Derivations in Biblical Etymology", pp. 32–33. I doubt that the verses contain two separate derivations. The only derivation appears in verse 32, because only in this verse the full derivation exists with the word Baal, and it is only here that the name ירבעל is given in the derivation. V. 31 reads ירב לו not as a separate derivation but in the wording of Joash's rhetorical question and as a continuation to it: האתם תריבון לבעל אם אתם תושיעון אותו אשר יריב לו יומת עד הבקר אם אלהים הוא ירב לו.

[71] Webb, on the other hand, considers that it was proved immediately that the Baal is powerless, since at that point nothing happened. In his opinion the people of Ophrah were impressed by this and Gideon became a hero in there eyes. Thus he is reborn and given a new name. Webb, *The Book of the Judges*, p. 149. For a

takes the confrontation between the belief in the Baal and the belief in God to a decisive stage, following which it will be impossible to remain indifferent to the religious significance of the events. As already shown, the subject of faith was extremely problematic in the wake of the Midianite oppression; already above the doubt was raised of how it would be possible to restore the people to belief in God. The attack on the Baal was supposed to be a solution to this problem. However, the solution is not in the fact of the war against the Baal but in the popular interpretation that will be given to Gideon's victory or defeat following the destruction of the Baal.[72]

Now the meaning of the two names, Gideon and Jerubbaal, will also be understood. Jerubbaal, the name given to Gideon by Joash, expresses the faith and hope of the Baalist men of Ophrah that the Baal will take vengeance on him: ירב בו הבעל (v. 32), ירב from the root ריב (contend).[73] The name Gideon, from the root נדע (to cut down) reflects the actions of the destruction of the Baal's altar and the sacred post.[74] Both names correspond to both parts of the unit.

---

variant of this approach, see Klein, *The Triumph of Irony in the Book of Judges*, p. 54. There is no basis, however, for this theory. There is no indication that the people were impressed. The new name is not because Gideon was accepted by the people of Ophrah, on the contrary, it expresses their hope for his downfall: "That day they named him Jerubbaal, meaning "Let Baal contend with him, since he tore down his altar" (v. 32).

[72] For the struggle of monotheism against Canaanite paganism in the context of the Gideon story, see: W. F. Albright, *Yahweh and the Gods of Canaan: A Historical Analysis of Two Contrasting Faiths*, Winona Lake 1968, pp. 168 ff.; U. Oldenburg, *The Conflict Between El and Ba'al in Canaanite Religion*, Leiden 1969, pp. 164–184. For the use of the name *Baal* in the worship of God, see: Burney, *The Book of Judges*, pp. 201–202.

[73] Burney, *The Book of Judges*, p. 201. Many explanations are given to this root, for a summary of the various interpretations see: Bluedorn, *Yahweh Versus Baalism*, pp. 101–105. Soggin thinks the name ירבעל is a wordplay on the roots רבב which means "to be great" and ריב which means to "put on trial" or to "defend" in a legal context. Soggin, *Joshua*, pp. 124–125.

[74] See: Y. Zakovitch, "The Synonymous Word and the Synonymous Name in Name-Midrashim", *Shnaton: An Annual for Biblical and Ancient Near Eastern Studies* 2 (1977), 105–106 (Hebrew); M. Garsiel, "Homiletic Name-Derivations as a Literary Device in the Gideon Narrative: Judges VI–VIII", *VT* 43 (1993), pp. 305–306. The verbs כרת and נדע are synonymous and appear as variants in biblical parallelism, see e.g.: Isa 22:25. In the instructions to destroy idol worship, the verb כרת is used (Exod 34:13) as well as the verb נדע (Deut 7:5). Garsiel claims that the name Abiezer derives from the root עזר which means *help*, and corresponds to the mission of deliverance assigned to Gideon. M. Garsiel, *Biblical Names: A Literary Study of Midrashic Derivations and Puns* (trans. P. Hackett), Ramat-Gan 1991, p. 107. Schneider

The name "Gideon" reflects the first part of the passage, in which Gideon destroys the Baal's altar, and the name "Jerubbaal" reflects the second part of the passage, in which the men of Ophrah act on behalf of the Baal against Gideon.[75] Both names reflect the two outlooks associated with Gideon in his combat: the name "Gideon" reflects his belief in God and his war against the Baal, and the expectations that he will deliver Israel from Midian. On the other hand, the name "Jerubbaal" reflects the Baalists' hope that Gideon will lose his war against the Midianites as revenge for his attack on the Baal.[76]

Now the reader expects to see how Gideon will succeed in the battle against the Midianites. The next section will deal with this subject.

7. *Deployment for Battle, and Gideon's Hesitancy (6:33–40)*

Initially the account goes on to describe the Midianite deployment: "And all Midian, Amalek, and the Kedemites came together; they crossed over and encamped in the Valley of Jezreel" (v. 33).

In this verse the syntactical order is the reverse of the usual Biblical syntax, the subject in the verse (וכל מדין ועמלק ובני קדם—"And all Midian, Amalek, and the Kedemites") comes before the predicate (נאספו "came together") instead of the regular order ויאספו כל מדין ועמלק ובני קדם. This word order is designed to emphasize the subject in the verse and to set it against what came before. Indeed, the

---

indicated that the name Abiezer means "my father is help"; in her opinion the name refers to Joash's assistance to his son Gideon. Schneider, *Judges*, p. 103.

[75] According to the Gideon account, the name Gideon is the original name, and the name Jerubbaal was given to him after he destroyed the Baal altar. Albright on the other hand considers that Jerubbaal was his name, and the name Gideon was given to him following the destruction of the altar. Albright, *Yahweh and the Gods of Canaan*, p. 199 n. 101. Support for this suggestion is the use of the name Jerubbaal in 1 Sam 12:11. Indeed, the root נדע is related to the fight against idolatry: e.g.: Deut 7:5; 12:3.

[76] For another explanation of the use of the two names see: Boling, *Judges*, p. 144. Some scholars claimed that Gideon and Jerubbaal were different men, and because the stories about them were alike they were merged together and Gideon was identified with Jerubbaal. See e.g.: Noth, *The Deuteronomistic History*, p. 74 n. 3; Martin, *The Book of Judges*, pp. 77–78. This approach was disputed by J. A Emerton, "Gideon and Jerubbaal", *JTS* NS 27 (1976), pp. 289–312; Lindars, "Gideon and Kingship", pp. 324–325.

conjunctive *waw* of the word וכל ('and all') has the meaning of the conversive *waw*.[77] Possibly, the intention of the verse is to show the deployment of the Midianites, who in the meantime received reinforcements for their army through the addition of Amalek and the Kedemites, in contrast to Gideon who was opposed even in his father's house and his city, as seen in the previous passage. In light of the increase in the Midianite army the anticipation of seeing how Gideon will succeed against the Midianites without support is even greater.

The successful Midianite deployment does not deter Gideon, and he also proceeds to organize an army after the spirit of the Lord envelops him, to fight the Midianite oppressor and their allies, vv. 34–35.

> (A) "The spirit of the LORD enveloped Gideon;
> (B) He blew the horn, and the Abiezrites rallied behind him. And he sent messengers throughout Manasseh, and they too rallied behind him. He then sent messengers through Asher, Zebulun, and Naphtali, and they came up to meet the Manassites".

The Israelite leader requires both God's support (A) and the people's support (B); without God's support or Israel's support, the leader will be doomed to failure. Moreover, the appointment of the leader depends on two approbations: God's and the people's. In this way, it is possible to explain the dual crowning of Saul (1 Sam 10:1; ibid. 10:21–27; 11:14–15) and of David (1 Sam 15:13; 2 Sam 2:4, 2 Sam 5:3).

Verse 34 determines that God is with Gideon: "The spirit of the LORD enveloped Gideon". The Othniel and Jephthah accounts contain the phrase: "Then the spirit of the LORD came upon . . ." (3:10; 11:29) and the Samson account the phrase: "The spirit of the LORD rushed on him" (14:6; 15:14).[78] The verb לבשה (lit. = "clothed") has a connotation of warming and protection and in this context the

---

[77] For the syntactic order of the predicate and subject in a biblical sentence see: *Gesenius' Hebrew Grammar* (second English edition by A. E. Cowley), Oxford 1910, § 142 (pp. 455–456).

[78] The verb לבש is not used elsewhere in the Book of Judges in this sense, but it is found in 1 Chr 12:19; 2 Chr 24:20.

verse describes God's presence as "enveloping" Gideon.[79] This verb expresses the totality of God's being with Gideon.[80]

The ingathering of Gideon's soldiers is described in three sentences reflecting three stages in the organization of his army.

(1) He blew the horn,
    and the Abiezrites rallied behind him.

(2) And he sent messengers throughout Manasseh,
    and they too rallied behind him.

(3) He then sent messengers through Asher, Zebulun, and Naphtali,
    and they came up to meet the Manassites.

The first sentence indicates that Gideon blew a horn and then men close to him from the family of Abiezer rallied behind him.[81] In the second sentence, he sent to the more distant circle, to the tribe of Manasseh, and they also rallied behind him; and in the third stage, he sent to an even wider circle, to neighbouring tribes—Asher, Zebulun, Naphtali—and they also rallied behind him.[82] These stages reflect the gradual process of forming of Gideon's camp, first in the circles close to him, and gradually in wider circles. This gradual description shows the ever growing confidence of the people in Gideon. The detailed description of the stages in ingathering of Gideon's army has a further significance. The length of the first part of each of the three sentences gradually increases, the first part of the first sentence being the shortest, and the first part of the third

---

[79] Similar metaphorical use of the verb לבש is widespread in the Bible, for instance: Isa 59: 17 (put on righteousness—וילבש צדקה; he put on the garments of vengeance—וילבש בגדי נקם) Ezek 7:27 ("clothed with desolation"); Ps 104:1 ("you are clothed with honour and majesty"); 109:18 ("He clothed himself with cursing as his coat"); 132:9 ("be clothed with righteousness"); 132:16 ("clothe with salvation"); 132:18 ("I will clothe with disgrace"); Job 29:14 ("I put on righteousness, and it clothed me"). For metaphorical use of לבש in the context of strength see: Ps 93:1; Isa 51:9; 52:1.

[80] Klein, *The Triumph of Irony in the Book of Judges*, p. 55. For a discussion on this expression in its ancient near east setting, see: N. M. Waldman, "The Imagery of Clothing, Covering, and Overpowering", *JANES* 19 (1989), pp. 161–170.

[81] Abiezer is one of the larger clans of the Manasseh tribe, see: Josh 17:2. Gideon belonged to this clan: Judg 6:11, 24; 8:32; 8:2.

[82] Malamat noted that the fact that the Midianites encamped in the valley of Jezreel explains why the tribes that settled in the surrounding area were most affected by the oppression. This is why the tribes that fought against the Midianites were Manasseh, Asher, Zebulun and Naphtali. Issachar did not take part in the battle apparently because they settled in the actual valley and could not revolt. Malamat, "The War of Gideon and Midian", p. 111.

sentence the longest. In this way, Gideon's activity is characterized: he is initially hesitant, and his confidence increases on a parallel to the increased response to his call to join his army. Initially, he does not speak at all, he blows a horn. In the second stage, he already sends a verbal message, but only to the tribe of Manasseh. Only in the third stage does his confidence reach a climax and then he sends a summons to three more distant tribes.

These verses, therefore, show Gideon's successful assumption of the role of deliverer. He receives support from God and the people, and the people's support gradually increases. On a parallel, as more soldiers join, Gideon's actions are clearly less hesitant and more decisive. The impression received in these verses is that at the beginning of the battle Gideon has several factors that are important for success: divine assistance, the people's support, and the confidence of the actual leader.

The emphasis therefore on the description of Gideon's army's deployment is not on the military aspect but on the morale aspect of Gideon and his soldiers.

The stage that should come after gathering of the army and strengthening of Gideon is that of Gideon's war against the Midianites. However, instead, there is a reversal in the situation, with Gideon doubting whether God is with him:[83]

> And Gideon said to God, 'If You really intend to deliver Israel through me as You have said—here I place a fleece of wool on the threshing floor. If dew falls only on the fleece and all the ground remains dry, I shall know that You will deliver Israel through me, as You have said'. (vv. 36–37).

Gideon's expression of doubt recalls the dialogue between the angel and Gideon in the account of his appointment. Gideon here contents

---

[83] Scholars have not dealt with the shaping of Gideon's personality, with the doubts and the swings from one extreme to the other, and they have not entirely grasped the complexity of Gideon's character. Therefore, Moore considers that this passage in which Gideon expresses doubts in God belongs to a separate and parallel source to Gideon's appointment in 6:11–24. Moore, *Judges*, p. 198. Soggin rejects Moore's interpretation, but also completely negates the possibility that these doubts occur after the spirit of the LORD enveloped Gideon, Soggin, *Judges*, pp. 131–132. He considers that the place of these verses is after 6:11–24, and they constitute a continuation of the account of Gideon's commission. Similarly, see: Kaufmann, *Sefer Shoftim*, p. 170. These interpretations completely distort the meaning of the account, as will be seen in greater detail subsequently. The aim of the account is to show Gideon's inconstancy and doubts.

himself with saying "If You really intend to deliver Israel through me" (אם ישך מושיע בידי); at the time of the appointment he said: "is the LORD with us" (ויש ה' עמנו) (6:13). God there promised Gideon: "I will be with you, and you shall defeat Midian to a man" (6:16), and here Gideon contents himself with saying: "If You really intend to deliver Israel through me as You have said". Gideon has already been assured by God that He will be with him, and will deliver Midian into his hands, but once more Gideon is beset by the same doubts. The wording of Gideon's doubts here, which resembles the wording expressing his doubts and God's promise, show Gideon regressing to his starting point, after he has already commenced the campaign against Midian as Israel's commissioned deliverer. The picture appearing is that after having progressed and changed his sceptical attitudes, Gideon now again regresses, despite the signs that he has received in the meantime. The doubt expressed at this point contrasts with the description of Gideon at the beginning of the passage: "The spirit of the LORD enveloped Gideon" (v. 34).

The alienation from God is expressed also by the use of God's two names. In the description of God's nearness to Gideon the Tetragrammaton is used: "The spirit of the LORD enveloped Gideon". Gideon's brusque transition from a state of nearness to God to a state of doubt is expressed in Gideon's appeal to "Elohim": "And Gideon said to God (Elohim)"; this name is used in the entire passage until verse 40. Subsequently, when the bond is again strengthened between Gideon and God, the use of the Tetragrammaton is also resumed (7:3).[84]

Gideon requests two opposite signs, again showing his scepticism. The first sign that he requests is that, in the morning, he will find a fleece of wool with dew on it, but the ground around it will be dry.[85] However, after this request is granted, he requests an opposite sign, that there will be dew on the ground around and only the

---

[84] For a similar explanation see: Boling, *Judges*, pp. 140–141; R. Polzin, *Moses and the Deuteronomist: A Literary Study of the Deuteronomic History*, New York 1980, pp. 169–170.

[85] Burney claims that after the first test, it occurred to Gideon that it was not miraculous because a fleece naturally holds moisture, and this is why he requests a reversed sign, Burney, *The Book of Judges*, p. 204. On the technique of collecting water using a fleece of wool in Ugarit, see B. Margalit, "The Episode of the Fleece (Judges 6:36–40) in Light of the Ugaritic", *SHNATON—An Annual for Biblical and Ancient Near Eastern Studies* V–VI (1981–2), pp. LX–LXII.

fleece of wool will be dry. The need for one sign and then for a similar but opposite sign shows Gideon's uncertainty as to whether God will help him.[86] Gideon's words express the understanding that the second request derives from his own deficiency: "Then Gideon said to God, 'Do not be angry with me'". The duplication of the request and the wording of the second request underscore this: "if I speak just once more, let me make just one more test with the fleece" (v. 39).

The style of the passage reinforces demonstration of Gideon's doubting nature.

	The first sign	The second sign
Request for the sign	Here I place a fleece of wool on the threshing floor. If dew falls only on the fleece and all the ground remains dry	Let the fleece alone be dry, while there is dew all over the ground
Implementation of the sign	And that is what happened. he rose up early the next day, he squeezed the fleece and wrung out the dew from the fleece, a bowlful of water	God did so that night: only the fleece was dry, while there was dew all over the ground

Performance of the first sign is related in the form of a short summary: "And that is what happened" (v. 38). This is immediately followed by an account of how Gideon sees carrying out of the sign: "He rose up early the next day, he squeezed the fleece". In the description of performance of the second sign, there are several differences. Instead of the short summary "And that is what happened" (ויהי כן) as in the description of the first sign, it is said: "God did so that night". In the first sign the sight seen by Gideon in the morning is described; the second sign is narrated from the narrator's

---

[86] In several cases when it is wished to clarify that a sign or miracle is not fortuitous, it occurs twice, as in the Gideon account. This phenomenon was discussed by Zakovitch who called it "control mechanisms in stories of miracles", Y. Zakovitch, *The Concept of Miracle in the Bible* (The Broadcast University Library), Tel Aviv 1987, pp. 35–49 (Hebrew).

point of view: "only the fleece was dry, while there was dew all over
the ground". From what does this difference derive? Why is the first
sign presented from Gideon's point of view and the second from the
narrator's? Through this changed perspective, Gideon's scepticism is
shown, even after carrying out of the first sign as he had requested.
In the first sign it is said "And that is what happened" (ויהי כן) without expressly determining that God generated the sign as is explicit
in the second sign: "God did so that night" (ויעש אלהים כן). In addition to this difference, the first sign is related from Gideon's point
of view and the second from the narrator's. The description from
Gideon's point of view does not relate what he saw but what his
practical reaction was: "he squeezed the fleece and wrung out the
dew from the fleece, a bowlful of water". Thus Gideon is shown as
sceptical even after the first sign. On the other hand, the second
sign is related from the narrator's point of view, and the determination is that it was God who generated the sign, and that it happened exactly as Gideon had expected.[87] After the two signs, Gideon
regains his confidence: "Then Jerubbaal . . . rose early" (7:1). However,
presentation of the second sign from the narrator's point of view
leaves the reader in doubt as to the way in which Gideon ultimately
receives the second sign, whether his doubts have been removed
or not.

In this passage too, the motif of "day" and "night" plays the same
role as previously. The belief in God and the "night" motif are
related, as are the disbelief in God and the "day" motif. The sign
given by God is performed at night: "God did so that night", and
Gideon's doubts are in the daytime: "He rose up early the next
day . . ." (vv. 38–39). Thus we saw also in the preceding units, Gideon
acted in God's name at night, whereas the Baalists pursued Gideon
in the daytime. This motif is designed to show the critical situation
of belief in God. The belief in God "prevails" at night, whereas the
Baal or doubts in God "prevail" in the daytime.[88]

---

[87] Gaster has shown that the idea of rain falling in one place but miraculously
leaving the surrounding area dry or vice versa is common in legends of saints. See:
T. H. Gaster, *Myth, Legend and Custom in the Old Testament: A Comparative Study with
Chapters from Sir James G Frazer's Folklore in the Old Testament*, New York 1969, pp.
419–420.

[88] For another variant explanation of the motif of "day" and "night" see Klein,
The Triumph of Irony in the Book of Judges, pp. 58–59.

8. *Screening of Gideon's Army (7:1–8)*

Then Jerubbaal—that is, Gideon—and all the troops that were with him rose early and encamped above En-harod, while the camp of Midian was north of them, below Gibeath-moreh, in the valley (7:1).

Following the signs, Gideon apparently feels confident; the description of how he rises early in the morning in his army camp opposite the Midianite camp shows him as ready for combat.[89] This verse takes us back to the description of the location of the Midianite camp in verse 33. This repetition of the location highlights the digression from the description of the military confrontation and the detailed description of the signs showing Gideon's doubts. Now too, with the return to the description of the deployment of the armies, the "day" and "night" motif functions as in the preceding passages. After having received the signs from God, Gideon acts in daytime: "Then Jerubbaal . . . rose early".

Gideon is called here by both his names—"Jerubbaal—that is, Gideon". The use of both the names here indicates the internal tension related to Gideon's struggle against the Midianites. When he set out for battle some saw him as Jerubbaal—a man who will be punished by the Baal; others saw him as Gideon—a deliverer sent by God. This increases the tension prior to commencement of the combat: what will the results of the battle be and which expectations will be fulfilled?[90]

The location of the Israelite camp is in En-harod. This location is not noted in principle for purposes of understanding the topography and the strategy.[91] Rather it is in order to create an affinity between the name עין חרד (En-Harod) and Gideon's subsequent

---

[89] For the motif of rising early in the morning (וישכם בבוקר) as an expression of promptitude see Sifra Tractate Tazria Chapter 1:3–5: "Those who are prompt perform mitzvoth early as it is said: 'And Abraham rose early in the morning and saddled his ass'". See also: *Mekilta de-Rabbi Ishmael*, Tractate Beshallah, ch. 2, p. 199; Rashi to Gen 22:3. Also: Assis, *The Literary Structure of the Conquest Narrative in the Book of Joshua (Chs. 1–11) and its Meaning*, pp. 167, 209.

[90] Contrary to the opinion of some scholars that the name Jerubbaal is secondary (see e.g. Richter, *Traditionsgeschichtliche Untersuchungen zum Richterbuch*, p. 186) or that the name Gideon is secondary (see e.g.: Burney, *The Book of Judges*, p. 205).

[91] Malamat ("The War of Gideon and Midian", p. 112), explains that they did not camp there but at the foot of the northeastern slopes of Mount Gilboa, as emerges from the next part of the passage: "*bring them down* to the water" (8:4). This assumption is logical topographically and strategically.

proclamation מִי יָרֵא וְחָרֵד יָשֹׁב וְיִצְפֹּר מֵהַר הַגִּלְעָד ("Let anybody who
is timid and *fearful* turn back, as a bird flies, from Mount Gilead").
Indication of the location of the Israelite camp at En-Harod is a
preliminary intimation of the fear that will overcome the Israelite
camp and which will lead to the departure of over two-thirds of the
soldiers.[92]

The two armies, the Israelite army and the Midianite army, face
each other prior to the battle, but again the battle is postponed.
This time, however, it is God and not Gideon who postpones it:
"The LORD said to Gideon, 'The troops with you are too many for
me to give the Midianites into their hands'" (7:2). God raises the
concern that the people might attribute the victory to itself by virtue
of its large army: "Israel might claim for themselves the glory due
to Me, thinking, 'Our own hand has brought us victory'", and therefore He demands that Gideon reduce the size of his army: "Therefore,
announce to the men, 'Let anybody who is timid and fearful turn
back, as a bird flies, from Mount Gilead'. Thereupon, twenty-two
thousand of the troops turned back and ten thousand remained"
(7:3). The sending away of the fainthearted seems surprising in light
of the attempt to show God's might as a factor in victory. The aim
of this action seems to have been to show that the great majority
of the army who answered Gideon's call were fainthearted and took
the first opportunity to return home; over two-thirds departed. The
verse therefore underscores the great number of those who left and
the number of those who remained. The departure of the fainthearted from the battlefield reveals the great number of those who
do not trust in their might and in Gideon, and it also certainly contributes to demoralization of those who remain.[93]

There is no precedent in the Biblical accounts for concern that
the victory would be attributed to the people rather than to God
even before the start of the battle. There is also no precedent for
reducing the army to an impossible size through God's open intervention, in order to prevent erroneous interpretation by the people
of the reason for the victory. In the other judge accounts, the return

---

[92] Burney, *The Book of Judges*, p. 205; Boling, *Judges*, p. 144.

[93] In Kaufmann's opinion (*Sefer Shoftim*, pp. 170, 171) the original story was that
the people abandoned the campaign because of Gideon's irresolution, and thus only
three hundred soldiers remained. This story took on a fictitious form. According to
Kaufmann, in this account, the reduction in the number of soldiers is intentional.

to God occurs apparently at the stage of the lament to God after the punishment and before the actual battle. Even if the lament to God does not reflect a return to God, the people interpret the judge's victory as a result of divine intervention and therefore they remain loyal to God throughout the judge's life. The fact that in the Gideon account God raises the concern that Gideon's victory will not be interpreted as God's victory as in the other accounts, indicates again the serious spiritual situation in the time of Gideon, and the great effort to be made to restore the people to worship of God.

God does not limit Himself to reducing the number of the soldiers to ten thousand, and He further orders Gideon: "The LORD said to Gideon, 'There are still too many troops, bring them down to the water and I will sift them for you there. Anyone of whom I tell you, This one is to go with you, that one shall go with you; and anyone of whom I tell you, This one is not to go with you, that one shall not go'" (v. 4). God demands that the army be further reduced even though it is clear that the ten thousand remaining soldiers are few for carrying out the mission, as will be concluded by the reader when he learns that the Midianite army was enormous and "as numerous as the sands on the seashore" (7:12). Even when Gideon had thirty-two thousand soldiers, he asked God for signs that he would be victorious in the war. Thus, the reduction of the army at this stage when it numbers only ten thousand is certainly very surprising and even frightening for Gideon and the people. Nonetheless, some degree of confidence can be derived from God's words. God tells Gideon to take them all down to the water, where He will *sift* (יצרף) the people.[94] The verb צרף is figurative here; its meaning is

---

[94] There is a play on words in the description of the sifting of the soldiers in the two stages. In the first stage it is said: "Let anybody who is timid and fearful turn back, *as a bird flies* (ויצפר), from Mount Gilead" (v. 3), in the second stage it is said: "bring them down to the water and *I will sift them* (ואצרפנו) for you there" (v. 4). In the first stage it is the fainthearted who abandon the campaign, in the second stage the impression is given that there is a further refining, and God will sift the good soldiers out of all those remaining. Isaiah di Trani considers that ויצפר (will fly) means ויצרף (will sift) by metathesis of ויצרף, like the metathesis of כבש and כשב (a lamb). However the meaning of the word is perhaps the meaning of בוקר=צפר (morning), in the sense of rising early, or of turning back, see Kimchi. See also Burney, *The Book of Judges*, p. 207. At the same time, there is a clear relation between ויצפר and ויצרפנו. Possibly, the fact that the motif of going down appears in both stages is significant. In the first sifting the fainthearted go down from Mount Tabor, and in the second stage those being sifted go down to the

"to refine", and it is frequently used in the context of refining gold and silver.[95] The use of this verb can give a certain measure of encouragement to Gideon that God will refine his army and will leave only the best. The association of refining gold and silver gives a feeling of an action that will leave the choicest soldiers. This feeling is further reinforced by God's direct intervention in the sifting process: "bring them down to the water *and I will sift them for you* there. *Anyone of whom I tell you,* This one is to go with you, that one shall go with you; and *anyone of whom I tell you,* This one is not to go with you, that one shall not go" (7:4) It is God who carries out the refining action and it is He who decides who will fight. God's decision is dual. He will say who will fight together with Gideon and He will also decide who will not go to war with him. Even though Gideon certainly does not understand exactly what is going to happen, God has taken upon Himself the screening process; Gideon, who already has a small army, can perhaps take comfort from God's intervention.

Gideon carries out God's directive: "So he took the troops down to the water" (v. 5ₐ). At this point, he receives a new directive:

> Then the LORD said to Gideon,
> "All those who lap the water with their tongues, as a dog laps, you shall put to one side;
> and all those who kneel down to drink, (v. 5)
> "Now those who 'lapped' the water by hand into their mouths numbered three hundred;
> and all the rest of the troops got down on their knees to drink water (v. 6).

This difficult sentence has been a source of great perplexity. There are two main problems. The first is that the sentence "and all those who kneel down to drink" (5ₐ) is incomplete. The general tendency is to complete it with the first part of the verse and the words "you

---

water. The root ירד (to go down) appears twice: הורד אותם אל המים . . . ויורד את העם אל המים. The motif of going down here possibly expresses the diminishing of Israel in the process of selecting the soldiers in accordance with God's initial fear that Israel would ascribe the victory to themselves. On the meaning of the word ויצפר, see: S. Aḥituv, "ישב ויצפר מהר הגלעד (Judges 7:3)", *Beer-Sheva* 15 (2002), pp. *20–*23 (Hebrew).

[95] See e.g.: Isa 1:25; 48:10; Mal 3:2–3.

shall put to the other side" are generally added.[96] The second problem is even more difficult and even more significant. God's directive instructs that those who lap as a dog laps should be put to one side. However subsequently the account refers to putting to one side those who lap the water by hand into their mouth, and there is no reference at all to those who lap as a dog laps.

One tendency is to put the words "by hand into their mouths" at the end of verse 5 (Thus the NRSV reads: "all those who kneel down to drink, putting their hands to their mouths, you shall put to the other side"). According to this interpretation, it is not those who lapped the water by hand into their mouth, but those who got down on their knees.[97] According to this interpretation those who lapped prostrated themselves on the ground and drank without using their hands, whereas the position of those who got down on their knees was bending of the knees and raising the water to their mouths using their hands. According to this interpretation, three hundred prostrated themselves on the ground and were chosen, and the rest were sent home. On the other hand, according to the wording of the Masoretic Text the three hundred who lapped drank while kneeling so that their knees were on the ground and their legs were bent (and sitting on their heels), and so they filled their hands with water and drank from their hands. The remaining nine thousand seven hundred prostrated themselves and inclined their heads forward on the ground and drank directly from the water without using their hands (this position is the position of the Moslems who prostrate themselves and their head touches the ground).[98] Since a man does not drink using his tongue like a dog in any position, the distinction of the test is in the position of the body: three hundred drank

---

[96] This is so in the NRSV. For different attempts to reconstruct the original version see e.g. Boling, *Judges*, p. 145; Soggin, *Judges*, p. 137.

[97] See e.g. D. K. Budde, *Die Bucher Richter und Samuel, ihre Quellen und ihr Aufbau*, Giessen 1890, p. 12 n. 3; Budde, *Das Buch der Richter*, p. 58. A similar interpretation is found in the commentaries of Moore and Burney, although they place these words at the end of v. 6. Moore, *Judges*, p. 202; Burney, *The Book of Judges*, p. 210. According to Malamat, both those who kneeled to drink and those who lapped like dogs were rejected, a third group, who lapped the water from their hands without kneeling were chosen. Malamat, "The War of Gideon and Midian", p. 117.

[98] For a similar interpretation see A. Mez, "Nachnal Ri. 7:5, 6", *ZAW* 21 (1901), pp. 198–200; See also Kaufmann, *Sefer Shoftim*, pp. 173–174.

from the water in a kneeling position, and nine thousand seven hundred drank in a position of prostration, and this position is called getting down on the knees.[99] According to the wording of the Masoretic Text, those who lap as a dog laps are those who lap the water by hand into their mouth, and even though the dog does not drink using its paw.[100]

If this explanation is correct, the dog comparison seems irrelevant. How can this comparison in God's directive be explained? Why should a misleading image be used, and particularly since it seems that neither of the groups drank as a dog drinks? Scholars who solved these problems by amending the wording ignored the dramatic element of the test. The dog is a despised animal in the Bible,[101] and therefore by the comparison of the lappers with the dog, the impression received is that those who lapped were those who would not be selected as soldiers to fight with Gideon. The directive that those who lapped are to be put to one side means that they are the ones who should be removed as undesirables. This may be the reason why the second part of this sentence is incomplete as regards those getting down on their knees, in order to reinforce the mistaken feeling that those who get down on their knees are the soldiers who will be chosen to fight together with Gideon.

This feeling increases when it becomes clear that there were three hundred who lapped, whereas the rest got down on their knees in order to drink. Now however, after this test, which certainly took a long time, comes God's command: "Then the LORD said to Gideon, 'With the three hundred that lapped I will deliver you, and give the Midianites into your hand; let all the rest of the troops go to their homes'" (v. 7). The drama reaches its climax when after this long test Gideon hears that God has not reduced his army by three hundred undesirable soldiers, but has winnowed out of his army nine thousand seven hundred, and has left three hundred soldiers only.

---

[99] As opposed to Kaufman (*Sefer Shoftim*, p. 174), who considers that the distinction between the groups is not in the body position but in the manner of drinking, whether they lap (ילוק) or drink (לשתות).

[100] On this issue see Kara.

[101] Today, the dog is considered as man's best friend, in the Bible in almost all occurrences the dog is mentioned in a context of contempt. See e.g.: Exod 22:30; Deut 23:19; 1 Sam 17:43, 24:14; 2 Sam 3:8; 9:8; 17:9; Isa 56:11; Ps 59:7; 68:24, etc. In the Ancient East the dog lived as a scavenger whether in or outside the towns. See: E. Firmage, "Zoology", *ABD*, vol. 6, New York 1992, p. 1143.

Scholars and commentators have endeavoured to understand the reason for this test. How does this method distinguish between those worthy of being included in Gideon's army and those who are not worthy?[102] In the Jewish medieval exegesis, the widespread explanation is that the test distinguishes the idolaters who used to get down on their knees before the Baal (1 Kings 19:18).[103] However, this explanation is difficult. Firstly, those who worshipped God also got down on their knees before God (1 Kings 8:54; Isa 45:23; Ezra 9:5), and it is also difficult to accept that the context of getting down on ones knees to drink water would teach something regarding the cultic habits of thirsty people. Another interpretation is that this test selects the most talented soldiers, those cautious in face of the enemy and guarding themselves from attackers, so that even when drinking, they do so in a way that will allow them to discern approaching danger, as opposed to the majority who carelessly prostrate themselves on the ground.[104] However, selection of the most capable soldiers does not correspond to the initial concern raised by God "Israel might claim for themselves the glory due to Me, thinking, 'Our own hand has brought us victory'" (v. 2). On the contrary, in keeping with God's concern it was not necessary to select the best soldiers but rather those less suitable. Therefore, others argued that this test rather selects gentle people unsuited for war. Those who drank the water by hands into their mouths and did not get down on their knees to drink are the gentle people with soft hands. God

---

[102] For the test of drinking water in parallel cultures see: Gaster, *Myth, Legend and Custom in the Old Testament*, pp. 420–422.

[103] See for instance: Tanhuma (Buber), vol. 1, Toldot 6.19, p. 165, and also Rashi, Kimchi.

[104] Mez, "Nachnal Ri. 7:5, 6", pp. 198–200; Gaster considers that those who drank standing up proved themselves to be alert and ready for any sudden attack, while those who lay down could not be vigilant. Gaster, *Myth, Legend and Custom in The Old Testament*, p. 420. Gersonides claimed that the lapping of the water was a sign of diligence, but those who kneeled were lazy. According to Malamat, the object of the test was to find the best soldiers. The water-drinking test was designed to find the quiet soldiers who did not make the same kind of noises that dogs make when drinking. Malamat, "The War of Gideon and Midian", pp. 116–117. In Lindars' opinion, ("Gideon and Kingship", p. 319) the test winnowed out the brave soldiers who lapped the water like dogs when drinking from a flowing spring. In accordance with the opinion that those who prostrated themselves were selected, they were selected because they showed an ability to fight when crawling on their bellies. See Y. Yadin, *The Art of Warfare in Biblical Lands In Light of Archaeological Discovery* (trans. M. Pearlman), London 1963, p. 257.

chose precisely the weak people who are not suited for war.[105] This
explanation is difficult since it does not fit with God's first command
in which he sent home precisely the fainthearted.[106] The best explanation is that the test is arbitrary and does not determine anything.
The way in which the soldiers drink changes nothing and the
significance of selection of the soldiers by a criterion that is irrelevant to the military field is that when God intervenes on behalf of
Israel it does not matter who goes into battle. The intention is to
transmit the message that God will win the war with any three hundred men who are chosen.[107]

However, if this is the explanation, why was it necessary to perform the test at all? One cannot ignore the complexity of the test,

---

[105] *Josephus: Jewish Antiquities*, vol. 5, H. St. J. Thackery and R. Marcus (ed. and
trans.), London and Cambridge Mass. 1934, p. 99; Boling (*Judges*, pp. 145–146)
considers that those who prostrated themselves were selected and that they are the
weak ones, and thus there is glorification of God. Burney (*The Book of Judges*, pp.
211–212), who agrees with Budde that "by hand to their mouths" describes those
who got down on their knees, considers that most of the soldiers got down on their
knees and thus they were cautious before the enemy. The three hundred who prostrated themselves and drank were not cautious and they were selected so that God's
might might be increased. Also: Soggin, *Judges*, p. 137.

[106] In Amit's opinion (*The Book of Judges*, pp. 241–242), it is possible to decide
between the methods, whether the weak or the strong were selected, only according to the context. She claims that the context shows the aim of the text to be
highlighting of the hand of God and therefore it is proved that the weak were
selected. In light of the contradiction between the first stage, in which the fainthearted were sent away, and the second stage, in her opinion the fainthearted were
selected. She asserts that the three hundred who were selected are even more fainthearted, since they were afraid even to admit their fear (p. 242). However, this
interpretation is extremely problematical. These three hundred were prepared to
go and fight, so how can they be defined as more fainthearted than the twenty-
two thousand who immediately returned home? It is evident that Amit was reduced
to this in order to adapt the story of the test to what she saw as the redactional
theme of this part of the account.

[107] For a variation on this, see: Soggin, *Judges*, p. 137. Gros Louis ("The Book
of Judges", p. 154) claimed that the selection of the three hundred was random.
In the opinion of Wellhausen (*Die Composition des Hexateuchs und der historischen Bücher
des alten Testaments*, Berlin 1889, p. 226), and subsequently Gray (*Joshua, Judges, Ruth*,
p. 304), Gideon had already selected the three hundred soldiers in advance. They
were members of his clan, the Abiezer clan, and the test was conducted so that
the other soldiers would not be offended and would cooperate with him later
in the battle. D. Daube ("Gideon's Few", *JJS* 7 (1956), pp. 155–161) considers that
the lapping of the water like dogs symbolized the custom of licking the enemy's
blood before the battle as a forewarning of what is about to happen. In his opinion, the significance of this custom was already unknown in Gideon's time. In the
opinion of Webb (*The Book of Judges*, p. 57), those with the "bestial" approach were
sent away and those with the "human" approach were chosen. These ideas seem
to have little relation to the passage.

the tactical difficulty of carrying out a test of drinking water by ten thousand men at a small spring such as En-Harod. The test occupies a large place in the account, and its length in the "narrative reality" is also long and tedious; it therefore creates expectations both for Gideon and his soldiers and for the reader vis-à-vis its nature and its results. The contrast between the length and complexity of the test and the fact that retrospectively it emerges that it did not examine anything is the intention of the account. During the test, it seems that God is selecting the good men for Gideon. This emerged explicitly when He commanded that the fainthearted be sent home. It also emerged from the style of God's words: "and I will sift them for you there" (v. 4), and it emerged when God told Gideon that He would indicate to him which man would fight and which man would not. Such an indication seems to show that God, who knows man's innermost thoughts, knows what no mortal knows, and therefore this intervention is welcome. However, ultimately it emerges that God did not intervene for the building of a select army, but to transmit a theological message, and this through dramatization of the screening process in which finally it becomes evident that it is of no assistance to Gideon and his soldiers.

The reduction in the number of soldiers from thirty-two thousand to three hundred only is certainly traumatic for Gideon.[108] An army of three hundred soldiers cannot overcome the vast and strong Midianite army that has already oppressed Israel for seven years. Gideon does not enjoy the full support of the people, he has strong opponents; now this support is further undermined. Gideon is shown in a ridiculous light; he takes a large army but reduces it to an impossibly small size.[109]

---

[108] In Soggin's opinion (*Judges*, pp. 138–139), the original Gideon account described Gideon's war with three hundred soldiers. However, a late, but pre-Deuteronomistic editor wished to describe a war in which several tribes participated under Gideon's leadership. In order not to discard any of the descriptions, the late editor had to invent the screening method initiated by God. There is no basis to this assumption, which is detrimental to the dramatic development of the account.

[109] For a discussion of the question of the reality of the large size of Gideon's army, see: G. E. Mendenhall, "The Census Lists of Numbers 1 and 26", *JBL* 77 (1958), pp. 52–66, and particularly n. 53; S. Tolkowsky, "Gideon's 300: Judges vii and viii", *JPOS* 5 (1925), pp. 69–74; Malamat, "The War of Gideon and Midian", p. 114; Yadin, *The Art of Warfare in Biblical Lands*, p. 257.

How will this situation affect Gideon, who until now has frequently expressed doubts in God? This will be discussed below. Gideon's behaviour here and the fact that he now has only three hundred soldiers undermines the faith of these soldiers: "So they (the lappers) took the provisions and horns that the other men had with them, and he sent the rest of the men of Israel back to their homes, and he retained the three hundred men" (v. 8).[110] Gideon now sends away all the other men who came to fight under him, after the three hundred soldiers remaining with Gideon take from them the provisions and their horns. This information seems superfluous initially, but at a second glance it emphasizes just how problematic the military situation of Gideon's soldiers is. Not only are they a very small group, but the only equipment that those departing give them is food and horns. There is no reference to weapons. Gideon's strange behaviour in the eyes of the people and the departure of the main part of the army are not received gladly by the three hundred selected men. Gideon has to restrain them ("and he retained the three hundred men"), apparently because they do not wish to remain with Gideon after the irrational screening of the army, and the leaving of such a small army.

If Gideon had doubts as to whether God would be with him and he would succeed against the Midianites when he had thirty-two thousand soldiers, it is not difficult to imagine his situation after he remains with only three hundred. This will be seen in the next passage.

Verse 8 again takes us back to the battle arena: "The Midianite camp was below him, in the valley".[111]

After Gideon's destruction of the Baal, the attack against the Midianite camp was twice delayed. The first time the delay was

---

[110] There are many difficulties in the verse: The subject of the phrase ויקחו את צדה העם ("So they took the provisions") is unclear. The expression צדה העם (provisions) is also problematic. There is incompatibility between the verb ויקחו (and they took) in the plural and the verb שלח (he sent) in the singular. Various suggestions were made for corrections. See: Moore, *Judges*, p. 204, Burney, *The Book of Judges*, p. 212.

[111] The almost identical wording in verses 1ᵦ and 8ᵦ does not prove that the verses between them are a late addition as several scholars claim (see for instance: Richter, *Traditionsgeschichtliche Untersuchungen zum Richterbuch*, p. 120; Soggin, *Judges*, p. 135). As we saw, these verses are a further delay in the start of the war, this time by a trial that God set for Gideon, after several delays instigated by Gideon who tested God.

because of Gideon's scepticism, and the second time God delayed the commencement of the battle until reduction of the numbers of the army. Now again the confrontation stage arrives. The anticipation of the battle in the three stages is marked by mention of Midian's deployment in the valley, and thus the following structure is received:

> "*And all Midian*, Amalek, and the Kedemites came together; they crossed over and encamped *in the Valley* of Jezreel" (v. 33).
>
> The signs of the fleece (vv. 36–39)
>
> "*The camp of Midian* was north of them, below Gibeath-moreh, *in the valley*" (7:1)
>
> Screening of Gideon's soldiers (7:2–7)
>
> "*The camp of Midian* was below him, *in the valley*" (v. 8)
> The Midianite's dream (vv. 9–14)

It should be noted that initially, when Gideon gathered the soldiers, God did not ask him to reduce the number of soldiers, and the delay in going out to war was because of Gideon's scepticism. God's delay came only after Gideon's delay. Therefore, it seems that God's command to reduce the number of soldiers was a response to Gideon's request for the signs. Hence, there is a connection between the signs requested by Gideon from God and the reduction of the number of soldiers that God demands of Gideon. Gideon delayed the commencement of the battle when he asked for the signs; God delayed the commencement of the battle subsequently when He reduced the number of soldiers. Gideon asked for corroboration that God would be with him through a sign, God changed the event into something extraordinary and whose exclusive interpretation will be that He is the cause of the victory. Gideon doubted God's power, and in response God turned Gideon's army into an insignificant force so that there would be no doubt that God was responsible for the victory. In Gideon's request for the signs, there are two stages and the transition from one stage to the next shows how great Gideon's doubt was. In screening of the soldiers, there were two stages, and in wake of the second screening there will be no doubt that war is not won by a human force, but by divine assistance only.[112]

---

[112] Compare: Bluedorn, *Yahweh Versus Baalism*, pp. 113–118.

9. Gideon Receives Encouragement through the Midianite's Dream (7:9–15)

> That same night the LORD said to him,
> Arise, *go down to the camp*; for I have given it into your hands.
> But if you fear *to go down*, go down with Purah your servant *to the camp*.
> And listen to what they say, after that your hands shall be strength-
> ened and you should *go down to the camp*",
> *So he went down* with his servant Purah to the outside of the armed
> men that were *in the camp*. (7:9–11).

After receiving of the signs and screening of the soldiers, the battle
stage arrives. This is marked by a description of the Midianite deployment in verse 8: "The camp of Midian was below him, in the valley". After receiving the signs of the fleece, Gideon seems to be
acting in God's name and he acts for the first time in the daytime
(7:1). However, after reducing of his army, Gideon resumes his scepticism, and accordingly the "night" motif again appears in this passage: "That same night" (7:9).

God initiates the beginning of the battle when he commands
Gideon: קום רד במחנה כי נתתיו בידך ("Arise, *go down to the camp*; for
I have given it into your hands") (v. 9). The use of the verb רד ("go
down") is particularly exceptional in the context of war. In God's
words to Gideon the root ירד serves as a keyword, appearing five
times. This verb has two meanings in this passage. The meaning of
the phrase לרדת במחנה with the preposition ב is to fight (see for
instance 1 Sam 26:10; 29:4)[113] and the meaning of the phrase ירד אל,
with the preposition אל, is to descend. The use of ירד in war in
the sense of fighting is very rare and appears in a few isolated
places.[114] It is employed here as a pun. God gives Gideon two possibilities: to go down to fight or to go down to hear. If Gideon is

---

[113] Thus, the JPS translates this whole passage as follows: (9) "That same night
the LORD said to him, 'Get up, *attack* the camp; for I have given it into your hand.
(10) But if you fear *to attack*, go down to the camp with your servant Purah; (11)
and you shall hear what they say, and afterward your hands shall be strengthened
to *attack the camp*'. Then he went down with his servant Purah to the outposts of
the armed men that were in the camp". This translation rightly distinguishes between
the two separate meanings of the verb ירד; however, with this translation the play
on words is destroyed.

[114] Kimchi explains that the concept of going down in war means to descend,
since generally the war was in a valley. Kimchi, *Sefer HaShorashim*, entry ירד (pp.
298–300). On the figurative meaning of the word ירד see: Ibn Ganah, *Sepher
Haschoraschim*, entry ירד (p. 204).

not afraid he will go down to the Midianite camp and fight against them, and if he is afraid, he must go down to the camp where he will hear something that will strengthen him. Gideon is at a crossroads and he has two contrasting possibilities before him. The author intentionally used one verb with two opposite meanings, one meaning being courage and might, and the opposite being in the context of fear, in order to emphasize Gideon's fear when he should have been confident. Gideon decides to descend to the camp (וירד+אל), because he fears to fight against the camp (רד+ב). The expectation is that Gideon will not be afraid, God says to him as He has already said to him several times in the past "I have given it into your hands". However, Gideon again does not trust this promise, and his faith does not withstand the test of reality, Gideon was and remains doubtful of his God who sent him to fight against Midian.

The contrasting possibilities before Gideon also emerge from a comparison between God's opening and closing words:

The opening words:

Arise, *go down to the camp*;   for I have given it into *your hands*

The closing words:

after that *your hands* shall be strengthened and you should *go down to the camp*

In the opening words there is the demand that Gideon go down to fight without delay out of belief that God will deliver the Midianite camp into his hands. Notwithstanding, the closing words are that he will go down only after he has been strengthened by the sign. The contrast between the state of confidence reflected in the opening sentence and the state of fear emerging in the closing sentence is expressed stylistically also in the chiastic reversal between the two sentences.

Gideon takes with him his servant Purah out of fear.[115] The servant here is a marginal figure. Generally, in the Bible the name of

---

[115] I disagree with Soggin (*Judges*, p. 142) who sees here a determination that even the leader appointed by God still depends on Him. Rather this must be seen

marginal figures is not given explicitly. The mention of the servant's name twice (7:10–11) is designed to highlight Gideon's fear in that he relies on the presence of this obscure boy. Gideon does not trust God's promise that He will be with him (v. 9), just as he did not trust that God would be with him in his war against Midian in his conversation with the angel when he was commissioned as deliverer, and he required a sign to prove who was speaking to him. Even after he recruits his army, he still requires signs that will confirm that God will deliver the Midianites into his hand. Here, for a third time Gideon requires a sign that God will deliver Midian into his hands, therefore he goes down to the Midianite camp to hear what they are saying there. Unlike the previous times when there was no justification for Gideon's scepticism, here Gideon's fear can be understood in light of the fact that only three hundred soldiers remain with him to confront the mighty Midianite army, although even now it is expected that Gideon will trust in God.

Again, this third time Gideon receives a sign that God is with him. In the two preceding times it was Gideon who asked for the sign: the first time he asked God for a sign that He was speaking with him (6:17), and the second time he initiated the fleece signs (6:36–40). However, this time Gideon does not ask God for a sign, it is God who speaks to Gideon and proposes the sign of the dream to him. Gideon's attitude changes gradually in relation to the signs. The first time he argues with God and casts accusations before he asks for the sign (6:13–17). The second time he asks for signs out of submission (6:17–19). The third time God suggests to Gideon that He give him a sign because Gideon was silent (7, 10–11). These stages demonstrate the process undergone by Gideon from his first encounter with God in which he behaves antagonistically until he stands submissive and helpless before God. Gideon's failure to react derives from his very difficult spiritual situation and from his lack of confidence in his ability to overcome the Midianite camp with three hundred soldiers. This insecurity leads to paralysis; he is in a situation in which he is not even able to ask for a sign. He has reached the lowest point since the beginning of the account. When we first

---

as a lack of confidence expressed by the fact that instead of going down against the Midianite camp as God commanded, Gideon required another sign. Soggin also errs in emphasizing the fact that the boy here has no function in the aim of the story.

met Gideon, he voiced many complaints, he responded fiercely to the angel's greeting. He was well able to express his doubts in God. Here Gideon appears shocked and unable to express himself. He cannot even ask for a sign. How will Gideon be able to free himself from this situation and lead the people to victory in God's name? This will be discussed presently. However, this low point well serves the account's object. The next sign that Gideon will receive will be the last sign that he will need, and from that point onwards Gideon will have unswerving and unhesitating faith in God. At this point, it is evident that all the signs that Gideon requested were of no avail. The only sign that will indeed strengthen Gideon will be the sign that comes on God's initiative. The fact that the initiative for the last sign comes from God shows Gideon's helplessness, and this is in keeping with God's intention in screening the soldiers (7:2).

> (12) Now Midian, Amalek, and all the Kedemites were spread over the valley, as thick as locusts; and their camels were without number, as numerous as the sands on the seashore.
> (13) Gideon came there just as one man was narrating a dream to another. 'Listen', he was saying, 'I dreamt this dream and in it a loaf of barley bread was whirling through the Midianite camp. It came to a tent and struck it, and it fell; it turned it upside down, and the tent collapsed'.
> (14) And his comrade answered, 'This is no other than the sword of Gideon son of Joash, a man of Israel; into his hand God has given Midian and all the army'.
> (15) When Gideon heard the telling of the dream and its interpretation, he bowed low. Returning to the camp of Israel, he said, 'Arise! The LORD has given the Midianite camp into your hands!' (7:12–15).

Gideon's words to the people, "*Arise! The LORD has given the Midianite camp into your hands!*", (v. 15) are a quotation of God's words to him before He proposed the possibility of going down to hear the dream in the Midianite camp: "*the LORD said* to him *Arise, go down to the camp; for I have given it into your hands*" (v. 9). However, initially Gideon did not accept God's words of encouragement and certainty. After hearing the dream, he can profess faith in God and draw the people after him to fight against Midian. How did the dream change Gideon from a sceptic, doubting in God, to a leader taking his small army into battle against a great, strong and confident enemy?

This reversal in Gideon's situation is emphasized by the opening of the dream episode with the description of the Midianite camp's might and size: "Now Midian, Amalek, and all the Kedemites were

spread over the valley, as thick as locusts; and their camels were
without number, as numerous as the sands on the seashore" (7:12).
As in 6:33, here also the Midianite camp is described with its different
components, and Gideon is thus shown as facing, with his puny
forces, a coalition of cooperating tribes: "And all Midian, Amalek,
and the Kedemites". Two metaphors are used in this verse to describe
the tremendous size of the Midianite army. The metaphor "as thick
as locusts" describes the tremendous size of the Midianite army, and
the description of the number of camels contains the metaphor "as
numerous as the sands on the seashore". The locust metaphor indicates the tremendous size of the Midianite army, but also the helplessness in face of this army, like the helplessness of someone faced
with a locust plague.[116] The camel adds a great military advantage
to the Midianite army in contrast with Gideon's poorly armed army.
Yet the likening of the great number of camels to sand on the
seashore does not indicate the number of camels only. This image
is ironic in light of God's promise to Abraham that his seed will be
as sand on the seashore, and here the situation is the opposite:
Gideon's army is small and the metaphor of the sand on the seashore
applies precisely to the Midianites.[117]

This description of the might of the Midianite army is the most
impressive of the descriptions of this army until now. Its object is
to show the reasons for Gideon's despair on the one hand; but on
the other hand, it intensifies the incisive change in Gideon's personality following the dream. How does the dream influence Gideon?

The dream heard by Gideon is a sign to Gideon that God is with
him. God told him to go down to the Midianite camp and then he
would be strengthened. When he goes down and he is precisely in
the right place at the right time to hear the dream, he sees God's
might and this is another sign that God is indeed with him. The
fleece that Gideon requested previously was linked to the subject of
the war artificially by him. On the other hand, the sign given to
him by God is directly connected to the subject of the war.

Until now, God told Gideon that He would be with him. Gideon
also received support from some of the people alongside opposition
by another part of the people. For the first time Gideon sees the

---

[116] See Joel 1:4 ff.
[117] Gen 32:1; 41:49; Hos 2:1.

Midianite attitude towards him and what he hears constitutes a kind of military intelligence. The Midianites rule over Israel and Israel is greatly inferior to them. Likewise, God's promise and the support of some of the people did not give Gideon tools to evaluate his strength in relation to Midian. Through the dream, Gideon hears that the Midianites not only relate to him very seriously but that they also fear him.

However, beyond this, there is a meaning to the fact that this message is transmitted to Gideon through a dream. The dream in the Bible and in the Ancient East is a medium by which God transmits messages to men. In this way, Gideon can see in the dream a divine message.[118] Transmitting of the message through the Midianite shows Gideon that God has made the Midianite camp fear God and Gideon.[119]

The Bible also relates to psychological aspects of dreams.[120] In this respect, Gideon hears how the Midianite's fears have also invaded his dreams. Psychologically, the interpretation of the dream by the Midianite who hears it is important. The Midianite who interprets does not see in the dream the words of God, but expressions of the dreamer's fear. These fears are also well reflected in the interpreter's words. His interpretation of the dream exposes his own fears, since there is no clear correspondence between the dream and its interpretation, and many other interpretations could have been given.[121]

---

[118] See e.g.: Gen 20:3; 31:11; 40:8; 41:25; Num 12:6; Deut 13:2; 1 Kings 3:5; Jer 23:28; Job 33:14–16; Dan 2:26, etc. On this matter see: Y. Kaufmann, *The Religion of Israel: From Its Beginnings to the Babylonian Exile* (trans. and abridged by M. Greenberg), Chicago 1960, pp. 48–49.

[119] On the "dream" in the Bible see: J. Pedersen, *Israel, Its Life and Culture*, I–II, London and Copenhagen 1926, pp. 133–140. For a comprehensive study of the "dream" in the Ancient East see: A. L. Oppenheim, *The Interpretations of Dreams in the Ancient Near East* (Transactions of the American Philosophical Society, 46,3), Philadelphia 1956. See also J.-M. Husser, *Dreams and Dream Narratives in the Ancient World* (trans. J. M. Munro, The Biblical Seminar, 63), Sheffield 1999.

[120] Thus for instance Joseph's brothers considered Joseph's dreams to be a sign of his arrogance and not the word of God, Gen 37:5, 8. The psychological basis of the dream is what allows Jacob to reprimand Joseph in relation to his dream, *ibid.* 37:10. See also: Isa 29:8: "And it shall be as when a hungry man dreams, and, behold, he eats, but he awakes, and his soul is empty"; Eccl 5:2.

[121] The meaning of the word צְלִיל is apparently "loaf" (see Targum Jonathan); Kimchi interprets it as deriving from the words צְלִי אֵשׁ (fire roast), or in the sense of הַצִּילֶנָּה שְׁתֵּי אָזְנָיו (his two ears will save), and the intention is to the noise of the loaf of barley bread when it whirled through the Midianite camp. Driver explained that the meaning of the word צְלִיל is mildew (עוּבָשׁ) as in Arabic. Driver, "Problems

His sure knowledge that this is the meaning of the dream shows his own fears, and it is the interpreter who makes the connection between Gideon and God: "This is no other than the sword of Gideon . . . into his hand God has given Midian and all the army" (7:14).

The dream and its interpretation influence Gideon to such an extent that his doubts vanish completely. The dream is the turning point of the account. From now on Gideon will trust in God: "When Gideon heard the telling of the dream and its interpretation, he bowed low. Returning to the camp of Israel, he shouted, 'Get up! The LORD has given the Midianite camp into your hands!'" (7:15). Gideon now has sufficiently strong faith to stand before the people and to express his faith, and to declare his understanding that God will deliver the Midianite camp into his hands. We will never again see Gideon express scepticism regarding God's help. In other words, to sum up, the dream fulfils two functions: firstly, it shows the attitude of the Midianites towards Gideon, and secondly, it shows God's attitude towards Gideon.

10. *Gideon's Battle in the Midianite Camp (7:16–22)*

a. *Gideon's instructions to his soldiers before the battle (7:16–18)*

Gideon does not wait for the people's response and that same night he begins to organize his army (v. 16) and gives them orders (vv.

---

in Judges Newly Discussed", p. 13. In a comprehensive study of the root צלל, Tal proved that the meaning of the root is emptiness and dryness. A. Tal (Rosenthal), "צליל לחם שעורים", Y. Bahat, et al. (eds.), *heqer veiyun: Studies in Judaism*, Haifa 1976, pp. 103–106 (Hebrew, Eng. Summary p. XII). This explanation is found in *Midrash Rabbah, Leviticus*, 28:6 (p. 364): "What is the meaning of the expression 'A cake (zelil) of barley bread? Our Rabbis explain: it alludes to the fact that the generation in question was bare (zalul) of righteous men". According to Burney (*The Book of Judges*, p. 214), the loaf of barley bread symbolizes that the Israelites are in a state of poverty. Soggin (*Judges*, p. 142) considers that the loaf symbolizes Israel, whose life is based on agriculture, whereas the tent symbolizes the Midianites and their nomadic way of life. According to Boling, (*Judges*, p. 146), the meaning of לחם שעורים, the loaf of barley bread, in the dream is לוחמי השערים—"the warriors of the gates". The fact that the interpretation of the dream does not clearly derive from the dream is in Zakovitch's opinion intentional so that the dream will be ambiguous, Y. Zakovitch, אחת דבר אלוהים שתים זו שמעתי: "מבעים דו-משמעיים בסיפורת המקראית" לזכרו של פרופי מאיר וייס, Jerusalem 1999, pp. 33–37 (Hebrew). One meaning emerges from the words of the Midianite's comrade, another meaning is seen by the reader trying to bridge between the dream and its interpretation, the third meaning of the dream is given by Gideon who finds in it intimations of how he must act in order to defeat Midian.

17–18). Nor does he postpone the attack on the Midianite camp, commencing it at the end of the first watch of that night (v. 19). Gideon's immediate and energetic activity demonstrates the tremendous change in him.

Gideon is now ready to go into battle, but he has only a very small force of a mere three hundred soldiers. How will he combat the tremendous Midianite army? Since it is God who decreased the number of his soldiers so that victory will be attributed to God and not to a human agency, Gideon could have waited for a miraculous divine intervention. God, however, expects an initiative from Gideon, as emerges from His command to Gideon even before the dream: "Arise, go down to the camp" (7:9) Gideon indeed does not expect divine intervention and he begins to act immediately in a military campaign, despite his small force.

> He divided the three hundred men into three columns and equipped every man with a ram's horn and an empty jar, with a torch in each jar (7:16).

Gideon's first action is to divide his army into three groups that will encircle the Midianite camp. To each of the soldiers he gives a torch in a jar and a horn. There is no mention of equipping the army with weapons, and at this stage the function of the horns and the torches in the jars is not explained either. The main emphasis in these verses is Gideon's order to his soldiers:

> *Watch me, and do the same.*
> When I get to the outposts of the camp,
> *as I do so you should do the same* (7:17)

ויאמר אליהם ממני תראו וכן תעשו
והנה אנכי בא בקצה המחנה
והיה **כאשר אעשה כן תעשון** (ז', י"ז)

The specific instructions are absent in his words. He commences with a sentence that appears truncated: "When I get to the outposts of the camp". Possibly this information is indeed missing, and perhaps the object was to emphasize the previous sentence and the next sentence, in which Gideon's instruction to the soldiers to do as he does is repeated. This illogical sequence underscores Gideon's leadership. The emphasis also emerges from an additional pattern in Gideon's words:

"Watch *me*,	and *do the same*.
When *I* get to the outposts of	
the camp,	
as I do so	*you should do the same*
When I blow the horn, I and all	*then you* also blow the horns
who are with me,	around the whole camp,
and shout, 'For the LORD and	
for Gideon!' (7:17–18)	

Gideon's instructions do not contain specific orders as to what the soldiers are to do, apart from the instruction that when Gideon blows the horn, they should do the same (v. 18). This sentence has two parts: the first part—Gideon's action, and the second part—the soldiers' action in imitation of Gideon's action. It is not incidental that of all the orders that Gideon certainly gave to his soldiers, this action precisely is explicit, since this action indicates Gideon's personal example and his leadership. In the same way, the other sentences in verses 17–18 are divided into two. In the first part is the act of Gideon and in the second his order to the people to do the same, as the above schema illustrates. It is clear, therefore, that the main emphasis in Gideon's words is his leadership, the responsibility that he assumes, and the feeling of confidence that he wishes to inspire in his soldiers.

Gideon ends his words in the sentence: "and shout, 'For the LORD and for Gideon!'" (v. 18). In the battle, the soldiers are to call out in the name of the Lord and in the name of Gideon. This call again shows that the main emphasis is not on Gideon's tactical orders but on the significance of the battle. This sentence summarizes his words to them. Initially Gideon declared to his soldiers that God would deliver the Midianites into their hands: "Get up! The LORD has given the Midianite camp into your hands!" (7:15). Subsequently, he emphasized his leadership (vv. 17–18). In conclusion, Gideon wants his soldiers to go out to battle with God's name and his name on their lips. Thus, Gideon does exactly what is expected of him in light of the people's doubts in God and in light of the opposition to Gideon. Gideon must reinforce his status with the people, and the recognition that God is working through them for Israel. Therefore, there is a difference between Gideon's call prior to the battle and the call of Ehud and Deborah who mention God only. Before the battle, Ehud cries out: "Follow after me; for the LORD has given your enemies the Moabites into your hand" (3:28). A moment before the battle Deborah says to Barak: "Up! For this is the day on which the

LORD has given Sisera into your hand" (4:14). The difference certainly lies in the special circumstances confronted by Gideon. In this account there is doubt both about the presence of God and about Gideon, and the extent of Gideon's success depends on acceptance of his leadership by the people. However, the combination of Gideon alongside God equally—"For the LORD and for Gideon"—is discordant. Does Gideon in this sentence take too much credit which is due to God?[122] The comparison of Gideon's words with those of the interpreter of the dream (7:14) reinforces the feeling that Gideon was excessive in his words. The interpreter of the dream said: "This is no other than the sword of Gideon . . . into his hand God has given Midian and all the army". Gideon in his words relates to the words of the interpreter of the dream, but the interpreter distinguishes between Gideon who wages war and God who places victory in Gideon's hands. Gideon makes no distinction between his act and God's act—"For the LORD and for Gideon" (v. 18). The reader, however, does not have sufficient data at this stage to determine whether Gideon's words are to be interpreted precisely in this way and whether Gideon indeed takes credit that is not due to him; at this point a doubt remains that will be clarified subsequently.

b. *The attack on Midian (7:19–22)*

> Vv. 19–20: Gideon and the hundred men with him arrived at the outposts of the camp, at the beginning of the middle watch, just after the sentries were posted. They sounded the horns and smashed the jars that they had with them. And the three columns blew their horns and broke their jars. Holding the torches in their left hands and the horns for blowing in their right hands, they shouted, 'A sword for the LORD and for Gideon!'

Despite Gideon's military inferiority, he does not rely on divine aid and he uses several clearly tactical means. He takes the Midian camp by surprise, attacking them at the beginning of the middle watch, at the time of the changing of the guards, when the guards are not alert. Gideon cannot overcome the Midianite army, which is larger

---

[122] See also: Marais, *Representation in Old Testament Narrative Texts*, p. 112. For a combination of God and king in the Bible, see Exod 22:27; 2 Sam 15:21; 1 Kings 21:13; Prov 24:21. Williamson relates to this an inscription from Tel Miqne (Ekron). See: H. G. M. Williamson, "Isaiah 8:21 and a New Inscription from Ekron", *Bulletin of Anglo-Israel Archaeological Society* 18 (2000), pp. 51–55.

than his, in a direct attack. Therefore, he uses an additional tactic. Rather than fighting them directly, he creates panic in the Midianite camp and gives them the impression of being attacked by an enormous army. Accordingly, there is no mention of equipping Gideon's soldiers with weapons. Rather, each of the three hundred soldiers receives a horn in one hand and a torch in the other, and the Midianites, surrounded on all sides, think that Gideon's soldiers are an enormous army.[123] The noise of the horns and the smashing of the jars, and the sight of the torch flames in the dark of the night, surrounding them on all sides, panics the Midianite camp: "They remained standing where they were, surrounding the camp; but the entire camp ran about[124] yelling, and took to flight". (v. 21).

The use of the two stratagems explains the duplication of the report of blowing the horn in verses 19 and 20. In verse 19, the blowing of the horn is cited in order to indicate the timing stratagem: "just as the sentries were posted, they sounded the horns". In verse 20, the blowing of the horn is again cited in order to indicate the second stratagem of instilling fear in the Midianites, together with the noise of the breaking jars and the sight of the torches.

The people's call 'for the LORD and for Gideon' precisely as instructed by Gideon shows that the people accept Gideon's leadership. It also shows that they accept Gideon as God's emissary and thereby recognize that Gideon is acting in God's name.

Verse 22 repeats the contents of verses 20–21, as shown in the following table:

Verses 20–21	Verse 22
and the three columns blew their horns and broke their jars. Holding the torches in their left hands and the horns for blowing in their right hands, they shouted, "A sword for the LORD and for Gideon!"	*The three hundred horns were blown,*

---

[123] Compare: Budde, *Das Buch der Richter*, p. 60.

[124] It is improbable that the meaning of the word ויד is to flee, from the root רוץ, since this is the meaning of the verb וינוסו later in the verse. Therefore, Driver ("Problems in Judges Newly Discussed", p. 13) explained that the meaning of the word is התרוצצו, ran about, from the root רצץ, as in Gen 25:22; Joel 2:9. He rejects Moore's proposed a correction (*Judges*, p. 212), replacing ויד by ויקץ (awakened).

They remained standing where they were, surrounding the camp; but the entire camp ran about yelling, *and took to flight.*

The LORD turned every man's sword against his fellow throughout the camp, and the *entire host fled* as far as Beth-shittah and on to Zererah—as far as the outskirts of Abel-meholah near Tabbath.

The first part of verse 22 repeats the blowing of the horn, mentioned in verses 20–21, and the second part indicates the resultant reaction in the Midianite camp, and this report is parallel to the contents of verse 21.[125] The repetition of the same stage in the war is designed to present this decisive stage of the battle from two different points of view. The first description (v. 20) emphasizes the human activity that leads to victory, the timing of the attack and the acts carried out by Gideon's soldiers to instil fear. After these acts, Gideon's soldiers continue to stand in their positions, surrounding the Midianites ("They remained standing where they were, surrounding the camp", v. 21$_a$), and this leads to the Midianite flight: "but the entire camp ran about yelling, and took to flight" (v. 21$_b$). On the other hand, the second description attributes the terror in the Midianite camp to God, who causes the Midianites to kill each other at the time of their flight: "the LORD turned every man's sword against his fellow, throughout the camp, and the entire host fled as far as Beth-shittah and on to Zererah—as far as the outskirts of Abel-meholah near Tabbath" (22$_b$).[126] The magnitude of the Midianite defeat is imprinted in the national memory under the name "day of Midian" (Isa 9:3). Now it is also possible to understand the strange wording of verse 22: ויתקעו שלש מאות השופרות ("The three hundred horns were blown"). Scholars amend the verse in different ways because there is no subject in the verse for the verb

---

[125] As is usual in such cases, some scholars saw this repetition as a combination of different sources, Moore, *Judges*, p. 211; Burney, *The Book of Judges*, pp. 215, 218. Others see the blowing of the horn in this verse as relating to the continued blowing by Gideon's soldiers at the time of the flight of the Midianites: Kaufmann, *Sefer Shoftim*, p. 179.

[126] Therefore, Soggin (*Judges*, p. 145) is mistaken in considering that the entire victory is ascribed to God, that the blowing of the horn has a liturgical significance only and not a realistic meaning, and that therefore the human dimension is not expressed. He is also incorrect is determining that v. 22 corrects v. 21. On the contrary, the two verses describe the event from two points of view; the human aspect appears in this verse on a parallel to the divine aspect.

"blew" (וַיִּתְקְעוּ).[127] However, according to the duplication designed to present the parallel between Gideon's action that leads to deliverance and God's action that leads to deliverance, the act of blowing the horn in verse 22 is not attributed to the soldiers, and the horn itself is the subject of the verb "blew". The people does not play a role, it is as if the horns blew themselves.

The dual description of the defeat of the Midianite camp corresponds to the Biblical concept regarding "dual causality". One description ascribes the victory to God and a separate description ascribes the victory as a human military achievement.[128] Possibly, the use of the dual causality principle here differs from other places in which it appears in the Bible. One of the ways of expressing an idea of "dual causality" in the Bible is by a report of the same event twice, with emphasis on a human activity in one description and ascribing of the deliverance to God in another description. In this case, there may well be an additional significance in the dual description of the war. Possibly, the dual description here is related to Gideon's words to the people previously: "For the LORD and for Gideon" (vv. 18 and 20). In relation to this sentence, we asked whether this cry does not derive from the reinforcing of Gideon's status in his own eyes to the detriment of God. Perhaps the separate description of Gideon's tactics, that are not described negatively here, precedes subsequent stages of the account in which Gideon is presented as being concerned with his status and his name, even at the expense of his fidelity to God.[129] This will be seen subsequently.

---

[127] The Septuagint reads: וַיִּתְקְעוּ בִּשְׁלֹשׁ מְאוֹת הַשּׁוֹפָרוֹת—"And they blew the three hundred horns". Burney (*The Book of Judges*, p. 218) suggests: וַיִּתְקְעוּ בְּשׁוֹפָרוֹת שְׁלֹשׁ הַמֵּאוֹת—"and the three hundred blew horns".

[128] On the idea of "dual causality" in the Bible see: I. L. Seeligmann, "Menschliches Heldentum und Göttliche Hilfe—Die doppelte Kausalität im alttestamentlichen Geschichtsdenken", *TZ* 19 (1963), pp. 385–411. Kaufmann coined the term dual causality for the concept that events occur through divine support and natural causes, see his commentary on the Ai narrative: Y. Kaufmann, *Sefer Yehoshua*, Jerusalem 1976⁵ (1956¹, Hebrew), p. 128. On this issue see also: Y. Amit, "The Dual Causality Principle and Its Effects on Biblical Literature", *VT* 37 (1987), pp. 385–400. The Psalmist expresses the idea of dual causality clearly in ch. 127: 1–2: "Unless the Lord builds the house, those who build it labor in vain. Unless the Lord guards the city, the guard keeps watch in vain. It is in vain that you rise up early and go late to rest, eating the bread of anxious toil; for he gives sleep to his beloved".

[129] On the military tactics adopted by Gideon with his small army, in order to conquer the large Midianite army, which based itself on the use of camels for military campaigns, see: Malamat, "The War of Gideon and Midian", pp. 113–116.

11. *Gideon's Pursuit of the Midianites, his Clashes with the Ephraimites,*
the Men of Succoth and of Penuel, and the Execution of the Kings
(7:23–8:21)

This part is divided into two. The first part of the account describes
Gideon's clash with the Ephraimites and the second part with the
men of Succoth and of Penuel. Before both the first and the second clash, there is a description of the pursuit of the Midianites.
The confrontation at Succoth and at Penuel is divided into two parts.
In the first part, when his request for assistance is denied, Gideon
promises that he will punish them. Subsequently the account returns
to the pursuit of the Midianites, and then comes Gideon's revenge
on the two cities.

> First description of the *pursuit*: 23–25
> The *clash* with the Ephraimites: 8:1–3
> Second description of the *pursuit*: 8:4
> The first *clash* with the men of Penuel and Succoth, 8:5–9
> The continued *pursuit*: 8:10–12
> The *clash* with the men of Succoth and of Penuel, 8:13–17.

It is evident that the main element in the description of Gideon's
pursuit of the Midianites is not the actual pursuit and the surren-
der of the oppressor, but Gideon's clashes with various sectors of his
countrymen. The descriptions of the battle are only a background
for these clashes. This is an exception from the accounts seen until
now. In the Othniel, Ehud and Deborah accounts, the descriptions
of the war were designed to show the greatness of God who helped
the deliverers to win the Israelite wars. What then is the intention
behind the emphasis on Gideon's clashes and transfer of the actual
battle to the background of the account?

a. *The pursuit and the clash between the Ephraimites and Gideon*
(7:23–8:3)

> And the men of Israel were called out from Naphtali and from Asher
> and from all Manasseh, and they pursued after the Midianites.
>   Gideon also sent messengers all through the hill country of Ephraim
> with this order: 'Go down ahead of the Midianites and seize their
> access to the water as far as Beth-barah, and also the Jordan'. So all
> the men of Ephraim were called out and they seized the access to the
> water as far as Beth-barah, and also the Jordan (vv. 23–24).

Here the description passes to the second stage of the war. The first stage was the battle and the second stage is the pursuit.[130] The first stage determined the victor, and in the second stage, in the pursuit, the victorious side wishes to destroy the vanquished side and thereby to determine a clear victory. In a case such as here, where the Israelites had been under Midianite domination, this stage is extremely important, since in it Israel will succeed in considerably weakening the Midianites, and thereby ending their oppression. In the first stage of the war, Gideon was constrained to have a small army because of God's concern that otherwise the Israelites would attribute the victory to themselves and not to divine assistance. Thus, only three hundred soldiers participated in the actual battle, and at this stage the miracle of the victory of the few over the mighty and well equipped Midianite army was clearly seen. Now, already there is no reason for additional soldiers not to come to Gideon's aid for the pursuit stage, in which Israel will endeavour to eliminate the Midianite threat.[131]

This stage (vv. 23–25) does not concentrate on the actual pursuit but mainly on the participation of additional soldiers. The expansion of Gideon's army is described in two stages marked by the verb

---

[130] There are other examples in the Bible where the description of war is divided into these two stages. See for instance the conquest of the South in the Book of Joshua, 10. The first part of the description highlights the hand of God in the victory, and the second part describing the pursuit underscores the human action. See: Assis, *The Literary Structure of the Conquest Narrative in the Book of Joshua (Chs. 1–11) and its Meaning*, pp. 246–270. Similarly, in Boling's opinion (*Judges*, p. 148) Ch. 7 gives a theological perspective to the war described in Ch. 8. On the other hand, scholars who adopt the documentary hypothesis consider that the Gideon account is divided into two sources, one presenting a religious description (6:1–8:3), and the second a natural, realistic version of the events (8:4–21). See: J. Wellhausen, *Prolegomena to the History of Ancient Israel*, Cleveland and New York 1957, pp. 242–245; Moore, *Judges*, pp. 174–177; Burney, *The Book of Judges*, pp. 182–183. In the Deborah account scholars of this school also determined that there were two versions, one realistic in ch. 5 and the other religious in ch. 4, see: Wellhausen, *op. cit.*, pp. 241–242. Kaufmann (*Sefer Shoftim*, pp. 148–151) disagreed with these scholars and showed that the account is one continuous story. As regards the two versions of Deborah's war, Amit rightly asserted (*The Book of Judges*, p. 213, n. 57) that the Song in chapter 5 also underscores the hand of God. Both approaches miss the intention of the passage. Indeed, in the account there are two different points of view: in one God is at the centre and in the other the emphasis in on Gideon's actions.

[131] This theological explanation deriving directly from 7:2 contradicts Soggin (*Judges*, pp. 147–148) who asserted that the initial sending away of the soldiers by Gideon and their return at this stage are absurd.

ויצעק (called out). In a first stage, the men of Naphtali, Asher and Manasseh joined. "And the men of Israel were called out from Naphtali and from Asher and from all Manasseh, and they pursued after the Midianites" (v. 23). In a second stage, the Ephraimites were also called out: "So all the men of Ephraim were called out and they seized their access to the water as far as Beth-barah, and also the Jordan" (v. 24ᵦ). The actual pursuit is pushed to the side while the main emphasis is on the two-stage influx into the army. Naphtali, Asher and Manasseh gathered to pursue Midian without being summoned by Gideon. Only subsequently is it related that Gideon called out the Ephraimites who carried out a mission only after they were summoned.

The fact that the first three tribes joined the pursuit of the Midianites without being asked by Gideon stands out, in light of the fact that the tribe of Ephraim came only after being called out. This fact was emphasized in that it continues the question of Gideon's status in the eyes of the people, which is connected directly with the subject of belief in God among the Israelites. Following the smashing of the Baal, Gideon stood at the centre of a confrontation between those who believed in God and the Baalists who awaited Gideon's failure. The participation of the three tribes without being called shows that the idea represented by Gideon in his appeal to the people was accepted. Gideon was recognized as succeeding in his mission with God's assistance. In the deployment stage, a large number of soldiers feared from the battle and went home at the first opportunity (7:3). Now the people returned on their own initiative to the battlefield, apparently after their doubts were removed and they were sure of Gideon's leadership and success.

Acceptance of Gideon's leadership is shown also by the fact that the Ephraimites responded to Gideon's call without hesitation and carried out his order exactly. This idea is expressed in the passage by a quotation of the wording of the implementation in detail, in the same words of the order, despite the tedium and superfluity of this repetition:[132]

---

[132] Concerning the word-for-word repetition between the command and the implementation to show that those carrying out the action did so precisely as ordered, see: Sternberg, *The Poetics of Biblical Narrative*, p. 121; F. Polak, *Biblical Narrative: Aspects of Art and Design* (The Biblical Encyclopaedia Library, XI), Jerusalem 1994,

The order:

> Go down ahead of the Midianites
> *and seize their access to the water as far as Beth-barah, and also the Jordan.*
> (v. 24ₐ)

The implementation:

> So all the men of Ephraim were called out
> *and they seized their access to the water as far as Beth-barah, and also the Jordan*
> (v. 24_b_).

At the same time the Ephraimites, unlike the men of Naphtali, Asher and Manasseh, do not come on their own initiative but only after Gideon's request. We have already explained that the object of this distinction was to highlight the spontaneous mass arrival of the three tribes to Gideon. The description of the participation of the Ephraimites only after being called out by Gideon is designed to present Gideon in a positive light in his subsequent clash with the Ephraimites, as will be discussed below.

> V. 25: They captured the two captains of Midian, Oreb and Zeeb; they killed Oreb at the rock of Oreb, and Zeeb they killed at the wine press of Zeeb; they pursued the Midianites. They brought the heads of Oreb and Zeeb to Gideon beyond the Jordan.

The Ephraimites, acting on Gideon's order, are successful beyond all expectations. Gideon told them to seize the bridges of the Jordan in order to catch the Midianites as they fled to Jordan: "and seize their access to the water as far as Beth-barah" (7:24). However, the Ephraimites succeed far beyond this, capturing the two Midianite captains, Oreb and Zeeb. The verse emphasizes their execution by the Ephraimites. The importance of this action is shown by the fact that the localities in which they were executed were called after them: "they killed Oreb at the rock of Oreb, and Zeeb they killed at the wine press of Zeeb".[133] The action is credited to the Ephraimites

---

pp. 68–72 (Hebrew); Assis, *The Literary Structure of the Conquest Narrative in the Book of Joshua (Chs. 1–11) and its Meaning*, pp. 230–231.

[133] In Böhl's opinion, these names were used in order to diminish the princes' honour and to present them as evil beasts of prey. F. M. T. Böhl, 'Wortspiele im Alten Testament', *JPOS* 6 (1926), p. 203. Martin (*Judges*, p. 100) asserts that it is not reasonable that the Midianite captains were called Oreb and Zeeb, and therefore in his opinion the object of the story is to explain the source of the names of a specific rock and a specific wine press.

who carried it out and to Gideon who gave them a detailed order in the matter.

Immediately afterwards it is written: "they pursued the Midianites" (7:25). Gideon did not order them to do so. Thus, the Ephraimites are presented positively as contributing to the war effort beyond the orders that they received. On the other hand, however, this statement is short and not detailed, and it seems that the continuation of the pursuit was cut off in order to bring the heads of Oreb and Zeeb to Gideon: "They brought the heads of Oreb and Zeeb to Gideon beyond the Jordan" (v. 25$_2$). This is not an act that contributes to the war effort against Midian, and it derives from the wish to gain repute on account of their deeds. Since the pursuit was not yet concluded, as clearly shown subsequently in the account, interruption of the pursuit by the Ephraimites, who came to Gideon in the midst of the battle for a matter that could have been postponed, is designed to present them even before their explicit complaint against Gideon, as the negative side in the clash, as will be made clear immediately.

Not only do the Ephraimites suspend the pursuit in order to bring the heads of the Midianite captains to Gideon, but they disturb Gideon at the height of battle with a complaint based on a desire for glory rather than a wish to complete the military campaign: "And the men of Ephraim said to him, 'What have you done to us, not to call us when you went to fight against the Midianites?'" (8:1). They bring the heads of the Midianite captains to Gideon in order to seek praise, and to complain that they had not been given a more significant part in the battle. Not only do they interrupt their pursuit, and cause Gideon to temporarily interrupt the pursuit, for the sake of glory, but their complaint is serious and the potential of a crisis emerges from its seriousness: "And they rebuked him severely".[134]

Gideon faces a significant test: Will he succeed in preventing an internal clash within his people, and this at a time when the national mission against Midian is still at its height? In his response to the Ephraimites Gideon appears in all his greatness. He does not relate to his own prestige; he is concerned with the continued pursuit of

---

[134] On the root ריב with the meaning of a legal complaint, see: J. Limburg, "The Root *rib* and the Prophetic Lawsuit Speeches", *JBL* 88 (1969), pp. 289–304, in particular pp. 293–294.

Midian, which will be resumed immediately after the clash with
Ephraim (v. 4). He waives the Ephraimite insult to his honour, and
even attributes the main victory to them, deeming their execution
of the Midianite captains to be of greater importance than his own
actions: "He said to them, 'What have I done now in comparison
with you? Is not the gleaning of the grapes of Ephraim better than
the vintage of Abiezer?'" (8:2). The Ephraimites are motivated by
a desire for glory; Gideon gives them this glory thereby satisfying
their desire and averting an internal conflict. Gideon reveals here
that his motives are for the good of the people in opposition to the
Ephraimites who are motivated by glory. The Ephraimites indeed
answered Gideon's call for assistance, but even though they continued the pursuit, they interrupted it immediately afterwards for the
sake of their honour. Gideon on the other hand solves the internal
problem quickly in order to return to the pursuit and to complete the
people's victory over the Midianites. In contrast to Jephthah who
faced a similar situation and waged a bloody war against the Ephraimites, Gideon wisely settles the matter peaceably.[135] Gideon is aware
of the Ephraimites' feeling of injustice, since they consider themselves a leading tribe to whom the glory of victory is due. He therefore gives them a feeling of glory and pride, ascribing excessive
importance to their part in the event—the execution of the Midianite
captains, and he thereby averts a confrontation with them.[136]

---

[135] Some scholars consider that the account of Jephthah's confrontation with the
Ephraimites is a late addition based on Gideon's confrontation with Ephraim, others are of the opposite opinion, see: Moore, *Judges*, p. 216. Moore considers that
these are two independent accounts that have a similar beginning, but which develop
in completely different ways. He rightly argues that it was natural that the tribe of
Ephraim, an important tribe with lofty aspirations, expressed bitterness on more
than one occasion when leaders did not include them in important events. Similarly,
see: Burney, *The Book of Judges*, p. 226; Gray, *Joshua, Judges, Ruth*, p. 339.

[136] In contrast to my assertion that Gideon is presented here as a skilled diplo-
mat averting a destructive confrontation, Jobling maintains that the reader identifies
with the Ephraimites because they are right, and Gideon did not summon them.
In his opinion, Gideon's conciliating and pleading note is a result of the fact that
they were justified in their claim. D. Jobling, "Structuralist Criticism: The Text's
World of Meaning", G. A. Yee (ed.), *Judges and Method: New Approaches in Biblical
Studies*, Minneapolis 1995, pp. 91–118. Webb (*The Book of the Judges*, pp. 70–71) considers that the difference between the confrontations with the Ephraimites does not
lie in differences of approach between these leaders, but in the different approach
of the Ephraimites in the two cases. The Ephraimites' claims against Jephthah were
far more serious than their confrontation with Gideon, since they threatened Jephthah:
"We will burn your house down on you" (12:1). Moreover, they approached Gideon

Now the reason for which Gideon was appointed leader appears justified. In the account of the commissioning, it was clarified that the main attribute for which Gideon was appointed was the deep-seated concern that he expressed for the fate of the people. Gideon felt the people's pain and therefore he was chosen to deliver the people. Here his national motive is put to the test and he passes with flying colours. Gideon was unable to face the men of Ophrah after he destroyed the altar of the Baal, and there Gideon's failure to respond to the harsh claims of the men of Ophrah and his father's intervention on his behalf stand out.[137] When Gideon needs to protect the people's interests he does so very successfully.[138]

The importance of this clash for elucidation of Gideon's character emerges also from its presentation in a chiastic structure:

A מֶה הַדָּבָר הַזֶּה עָשִׂיתָ לָּנוּ לְבִלְתִּי קְרֹאות לָנוּ כִּי הָלַכְתָּ לְהִלָּחֵם בְּמִדְיָן
    B וַיְרִיבוּן אִתּוֹ **בְּחָזְקָה**
        C וַיֹּאמֶר אֲלֵיהֶם מֶה **עָשִׂיתִי** עַתָּה **כָּכֶם**
            D הֲלֹא טוֹב עֹלְלוֹת אֶפְרַיִם מִבְצִיר אֲבִיעֶזֶר
            בְּיֶדְכֶם נָתַן אֱלֹהִים אֶת שָׂרֵי מִדְיָן אֶת עֹרֵב וְאֶת זְאֵב
        'C וּמַה יָכֹלְתִּי **עֲשׂוֹת כָּכֶם**
    'B אָז רָפְתָה רוּחָם מֵעָלָיו
'A בְּדַבְּרוֹ הַדָּבָר הַזֶּה

This structure contains two different structures within it. Gideon's words are in a chiastic structure and contain the elements CDC' (C: וַיֹּאמֶר אֲלֵיהֶם מֶה **עָשִׂיתִי** עַתָּה **כָּכֶם**—"What have I done now in comparison with you?"; C': וּמַה יָכֹלְתִּי **עֲשׂוֹת כָּכֶם**—"what have I been able to do in comparison with you?"). Gideon's words are within an additional chiastic framework of the narrator's words that contain the elements AA'BB'. The chiasmus in the narrator's words expresses reversal. Before the vehement words of the tribe of Ephraim (A "What have you done to us, ... severely"—מֶה הַדָּבָר הַזֶּה ... בְּחָזְקָה)

---

before the end of the battle with the Midianites, and therefore Gideon had no choice but to avoid a confrontation. However, they clashed with Jephthah two months after the victory over the Ammonites. Abravanel's interpretation also goes in this sense. On the reverse analogy between the accounts, and its meaning, see Y. Zakovitch, *Through the Looking Glass: Reflection Stories in the Bible* (Hillal ben Haim Library), Tel Aviv 1995 pp. 39–40 (Hebrew).

[137] Exum, "The Center Cannot Hold", p. 418. She points out the linguistic similarity between the question of the men of Ophrah: "Who did this thing", 6:29, and the question of the Ephraimites: "What have you done to us", 8:2.

[138] Exum, "The Center Cannot Hold", pp. 410–431, in particular p. 418.

Gideon succeeds in calming them and as a result of his words (Λ' בְּדַבְּרוֹ הַדָּבָר הַזֶּה—"when he said this") then "Their anger against him abated" (אָז רָפְתָה רוּחָם מֵעָלָיו).[139]

In the chiastic structure of Gideon's words there is no reversal, and there is no focusing on the centre either; the chiasmus serves another purpose. Gideon's words show his ability to deal with the Ephraimites diplomatically. He does not enter into a confrontation with them and gives them the credit of the victory; for this, he uses sophisticated rhetoric. Gideon, apparently, applies a known aphorism to the present situation: "Is not the gleaning of the grapes of Ephraim better than the vintage of Abiezer".[140] Through the use of the adage Gideon gives his words complete and universal validity.[141] The style of Gideon's speech in a chiastic structure is a further rhetorical tool, giving an impression of measured, well thought out words that should be accepted.[142]

b. *The continued pursuit and Gideon's clash with the men of Succoth and of Penuel (8:4–17)*

After the confrontation with the Ephraimites Gideon is able to continue pursuit of the Midianites, v. 4: "Gideon came to the Jordan and crossed it, he and the three hundred who were with him were famished, but still in pursuit".

---

[139] The word רפה is opposite in meaning to the word חזק, see for instance: E. Assis, "'How Long are You Slack to Go to Possess the Land' (Jos. xviii 3): Ideal and Reality in the Distribution Descriptions in Joshua xiii–xix", *VT* 53 (2003), pp. 17–18.

[140] Boling, *Judges*, p. 151. In Kaufman's opinion (*Sefer Shoftim*, p. 183), this is a fragment of the Wisdom Literature. As regards the use of the Wisdom Literature in order to express an absolute idea, see: E. Assis, *From Despair to Prayer: Literary Study of the Third Lament in the Book of Lamentations*, Thesis, Bar Ilan University 1995, pp. 101–103.

[141] The tendency in the research is to see the sentence uttered by Gideon, "Is not the gleaning of the grapes of Ephraim better than the vintage of Abiezer?" as a well-known aphorism. See for instance: Gray, *Joshua, Judges, Ruth*, p. 308. The rhetorical use of an adage is based on the timeless nature of adages. On aphorism, see: J. A Cuddon, *Dictionary of Literary Terms and Literary Theory*[3], London 1991, p. 52. The use of an aphorism as part of a rhetoric of persuasion is found in David's speech to Saul, 1 Sam 24: 13: "As the proverb of the ancients says: Out of the wicked comes forth wickedness".

[142] On the use of the chiastic structure to create an impression of well-considered and planned things, see: E. Assis, "Chiasmus in Biblical Narrative: Rhetoric of Characterization", *Prooftexts* 22 (2003), pp. 273–304. It is interesting to note that the adage also cited in the preceding note appears in a chiastic framework in verses 12 and 15.

What is strange in this verse is that again Gideon is with the three hundred soldiers with whom he commenced the battle, and it is unclear why there is no reference to the large army that joined him in the meantime (7:23–24). Above we saw that the battle was divided into two stages. In the attack stage, God instructed that there would be three hundred soldiers only so that Israel would not ascribe the victory to themselves. After Israel's victory with the three hundred soldiers, other soldiers joined for the actual pursuit. How can the disappearance of these other soldiers be explained? This matter will be clarified after discussion of Gideon's clash with the men of Succoth and of Penuel.

The description of the actual battle is again interrupted, this time by a description of a clash with the men of Succoth and of Penuel in verses 5–9. The account then resumes the description of the battle, vv. 10–13. This is followed by the description of Gideon's revenge on the men of Succoth and of Penuel (vv. 14–17), and finally the execution of the Midianite Kings, Zebah and Zalmunna (vv. 18–21). Thus, a structure is obtained that describes alternately Gideon's clash with the men of Succoth and of Penuel and Gideon's confrontation with the Midianites:

1. 4—Gideon's pursuit of the *Midianites*
2. 5–9—Gideon's request for support from the men of *Succoth and of Penuel*
1. 10–13—the continued pursuit of *Midian* and the capture of the *Midianite* kings.
2. 14–17—Gideon's revenge on the men of *Succoth and of Penuel*
1. 18–21—Execution of the *Midianite* kings by Gideon.

Why is the affair of Succoth and of Penuel integrated in this way in the story of Gideon's pursuit of and victory over the Midianite army? The answer to this question lies in the analysis of the story of Gideon's clash with the men of Succoth and of Penuel.

c. *Gideon's clashes with the men of Succoth and of Penuel (8:5–9, 13–17)*

> (5) He said to the people of Succoth, 'Please give some loaves of bread to the men who are following me, for they are famished, and I am pursuing Zebah and Zalmunna, the kings of Midian'.
> (6) But the officials of Succoth said 'Are the hands of Zebah and Zalmunna already in your hands, that we should give bread to your troops?'

(7) Gideon replied, 'therefore when the LORD delivers Zebah and
Zalmunna into my hands, I'll thresh your bodies upon desert thorns
and briers!'
(8) From there he went up to Penuel and spoke to them likewise; but
the people of Penuel gave him the same reply as the people of Succoth.
(9) So he said to the people of Penuel as well: 'When I come back
safe, I'll tear down this tower!' (vv. 5–9)

In his request for bread from the men of Succoth, Gideon stresses
his status: "and *I am pursuing* Zebah and Zalmunna, the kings of
Midian" (v. 5).[143] In addressing the men of Succoth he makes no
attempt to associate them and praise them on their part in the war,
but presents his personal achievements, which he sees as justification
for his request for their support. Nor does he indicate the acts of
heroism of his soldiers; rather he emphasizes their need for bread.
He attributes the fatigue to the people, while referring to the pursuit in the singular and attributing it to himself. In the response of
the princes of Succoth, it is clear that their opposition derives from
their scepticism over Gideon's achievements: "*Are the hands of*[144] *Zebah
and Zalmunna already in your hands*, that we should give bread to your
troops?*" (v. 6). Gideon in his response seems to some extent to correct the emphasis on his achievements, attributing the victory to
God: "*therefore when the LORD delivers Zebah and Zalmunna into my hands*"
(v. 7). Gideon then promises to punish them for their refusal to
proffer assistance: "I'll thresh your bodies upon desert thorns and
briers!" (v. 7).[145] Here it seems that Gideon wishes to punish them

---

[143] Burney (*The Book of Judges*, pp. 228–229) claims that these are not original
names. In his opinion, the meaning of the names is related to the fate of the kings.
Böhl, "Wortspiele im Alten Testament", pp. 203–204, is of the same opinion. Burney
also notes that the name צלם (Zalam), is the name of a god of Têma in Northern
Arabia.

[144] Yadin (*The Art of Warfare in Biblical Lands*, p. 260) explained this expression in
relation to a usage in the ancient East of cutting off the hands of the enemies. See
also: J. B. Pritchard, *The Ancient Near East in Pictures Relating to the Old Testament*, New
Jersey 1954, pp. 104, 118; also: U. Cassuto, The Goddess *Anat: Canaanite Epics of
the Patriarchal Age* (trans. I. Abrahams), Jerusalem 1971, pp. 86–89. On the other hand,
this seems rather to be a metaphorical concept as in: ויתנם ה' ביד מדין שבע שנים
("and the LORD delivered them into the hand of Midian seven years"), 6:1.

[145] The intention of the act is unclear. Some interpret the verse to mean that
he will strike them with thorns, see: Kimchi; Amit, *Judges*, p. 150. Martin (*The Book
of Judges*, p. 104) considers that the intention is that he will trample them under-
foot without concern for their fate, as he would have done to thorns and briers.
See also: Soggin, *Judges*, pp. 149–150.

because they prejudiced God's victory.[146] However, when he asked for help he did not ascribe the victory to God and therefore it seems rather that when he includes God in justification of the punishment he does so in order to conceal that the main motive for their punishment is the offence to him and not the offence to God. This is further reinforced by his answer to the men of Penuel who also refused, like the men of Succoth, to help him: "So he said to the people of Penuel as well: 'When I come back safe, I'll tear down this tower!'" (v. 9). Again, Gideon attributes the victory to himself as if he were acting alone in the campaign. He does not refer to the action of his soldiers, even though it is for them that he is requesting the loaves. In contrast to his answer to the men of Succoth, he does not promise a punishment to the men of Penuel but that he will tear down the tower when he comes back safely.

The passage describing the request for assistance from the men of Succoth and of Penuel commences and ends with Gideon's words that emphasize how focused he is on himself and his success. Inclusion of the accounts of Gideon's request to the men of Succoth underlines the change that has occurred in Gideon's personality.

This subject is further underscored when Gideon returns from the war victorious. His first action is not to complete the victory over Midian. Instead of executing the Midianite kings because of the evil that they did to his people, he first goes to take vengeance on the men of Succoth and of Penuel, vv. 13–17.

> (13) Gideon son of Joash returned from the battle at the Ascent of Heres,
> (14) He captured a boy from among the people of Succoth and questioned him; and he listed for him the officials and elders of Succoth, seventy-seven in number.[147]

---

[146] See Gersonides (in his commentary on vv. 7–8). Dishon ("Gideon and the Beginnings of Monarchy in Israel", p. 259), in accordance with her positive approach towards Gideon's outlook and actions, considers that the account of the punishment of Succoth and of Penuel emphasizes that Gideon acted lawfully and justly. Soggin (*Judges*, pp. 155–156) considers that the Bible justifies Gideon's acts as legitimate reprisals.

[147] C. Feigenbaum (*The Story of Gideon*, M.A. diss., Bar Ilan University 1989, p. 86) notes that the number seventy-seven recalls Lamech's arrogant words: "If Cain shall be avenged sevenfold, truly Lamech seventy and sevenfold" (Gen 4:24). This connection was designed to link Gideon's killing of the men of Succoth to the murder committed by Lamech.

(15) Then he came to the people of Succoth and said, 'Here are Zebah and Zalmunna, about whom you mocked me, saying, Are Zebah and Zalmunna already in your hands, that we should give your famished men bread?'
(16) And he took the men of the city and, bringing desert thorns and briers, he punished the people of Succoth with them.
(17) As for Penuel, he tore down its tower and killed the men of the city.

This part commences with the statement: "Gideon son of Joash returned from the battle at the Ascent of Heres". (8:13). This sentence describes Gideon's return from the battle campaigns after the description of his impressive achievements of destroying the Midianite camp and capturing the Midianite kings. What will Gideon do when he returns from war? Initially he does not complete the mission of executing Israel's oppressors of the last seven years. This he leaves until after the second stage. First, he proceeds to punish the inhabitants of Succoth and of Penuel. Gideon captures a boy who gives him inside information on the heads of the city of Succoth. This act recalls a like stratagem of the house of Joseph receiving inside information from the men of Beth-El that allows them to conquer the city (1:22–26). Yet Gideon applies this stratagem against an Israelite city. He uses war stratagems against his own people for whom he fought in order to deliver them from the Midianite oppression. However, the narrator does not go on to describe immediately the punishment of the men of Succoth. Firstly, he indicates Gideon's words to the men of Succoth, in which he notes that his entire intention in punishing them is only because they dishonoured him: "Then he came to the people of Succoth and said, 'Here are Zebah and Zalmunna, *about whom you mocked me*, saying, Are Zebah and Zalmunna already in your hands, that we should give your famished men bread?'" (8:15). Gideon does not content himself with the punishment, but he explains to them that the reason for the punishment is that they mocked him. He does not initially proceed to the execution of the Midianite kings because he wishes to show that he indeed succeeded in capturing Zebah and Zalmunna despite the doubts expressed by the men of Succoth and of Penuel. Moreover, the fact that he first deals with the men of Succoth and of Penuel indicates Gideon's aims. Firstly, he deals with his honour and his status, first he must punish those who dishonoured him and only then will he punish the Midianite Kings who harmed his people.

Gideon's interests appear also in the description of carrying out of the punishment: "And he took the men of the city and, bringing desert thorns and briers, he punished the people of Succoth with them" (v. 16). The punishment described here is nothing other than Gideon's maltreatment of the men of Succoth, with the aim of showing them his might and his honour. Perhaps the use of the verb ידע here with the meaning of punished[148] was chosen in order to give a connotation of a message that Gideon wishes to transmit to the men of Succoth. It is not known whether this maltreatment led to the death of the men of Succoth, but what emerges is that Gideon's actions here are guided by personal motives. Moreover, the report in verse 7: "I'll thresh your bodies upon desert thorns and briers!" raises in association the first scene in which Gideon appeared to the reader: "His son Gideon was then beating out wheat inside a winepress" (6:11). The similarity between the agricultural activities indicates the reversal that has occurred in Gideon's personality. In the context of the same scene at the beginning of the Gideon account, he appears as a man deeply concerned by his people's plight. Tearing of the flesh of the men with the briers and thorns of the wilderness is an injury to the people for the benefit of his honour.

Gideon's behaviour towards the men of Penuel highlights this even more. When they refused to give bread to his soldiers, he said to them: "When I come back safe, I'll tear down this tower!" (v. 9). However, in fact, the punishment that he metes out is even more rigorous: "As for Penuel, he tore down its tower and killed the men of the city" (8:17).[149] From the time that they dishonour him until

---

[148] See: *DCH*, 4, p. 111. See also for instance: Ezek 19:7; Isa 53:3; perhaps also Hos 9:7; Gen 18:21. On the root ידע like the root יסר meaning "to educate", "to teach" and also "to punish", see: *DCH*, 4, pp. 238–240. The Septuagint determined here וידש ("tore") instead of וידע (as in 8:7), as does Burney, *The Book of Judges*, p. 233. Reider proposes reading וירע instead of וידע in several places, including in the verse under discussion, where the root is not easily explained. The root of the verb is רעע and the intention of the verse is the breaking of the men of Succoth with the briers. J. Reider, "Etymological Studies: ידע or ירע and רעע", *JBL* 66 (1947), pp. 315–317. For an extensive study of the meaning of the root ידע, see: J. A Emerton, "A Consideration of Some Alleged Meanings of ידע in Hebrew", *JSS* 15, 2 (1970), pp. 145–180.

[149] Kimchi notes in this respect: "Perhaps they fought against him when he came to tear down the tower". Similarly: L. Wood, *Distressing Days of the Judges*, Grand Rapids 1975, p. 224. However, the Bible does not suggest this situation, and therefore it seems that the intention is to show that Gideon's actions went far beyond his words.

he comes to punish them, Gideon's anger does not abate, and he
carries out his plan with the greatest rigour and cruelty. He does
not only tear down the tower, but he also slays the men of the city.
Moreover, the act of tearing down the tower of Penuel brings to
mind the destruction of the Baal and the sacred post at the beginning of the account, and in both the same verb root is used ("tore
down", נתץ): "since it is his altar that has been *torn down*" (6:31),
"As for Penuel, he *tore down* its tower" (8:17). The similarity between
the two actions is designed to emphasize the tremendous difference
that occurred in Gideon's approach between the former stage and
this stage. Then Gideon destroyed the altar on God's command in
order to combat the Baal and to proclaim that the deliverance is in
God's name. Here Gideon tears down the tower in order to make
a name for himself. In the story of the destruction of the Baal,
Gideon was unable to face his opponents and to justify the war
against the Baal and the worship of God that he founded there. Now,
however, Gideon fights energetically because of the offence to him.

Now the meaning of the structure of the description of the war
against Midian and the clash with the men of Succoth and of Penuel
becomes quite clear. We saw above how the clash with Succoth and
with Penuel is integrated into the war account, and twice the account
alternates between description of the war and the clash with Succoth
and with Penuel. The incorporation of the description of Gideon's
cruel treatment of the men of Succoth and of Penuel within the war
account shows his absorption with his personal interest and not the
people's interest. The aim is to show Gideon's self-centred motives
in his war against Midian at this stage. Presentation of these two
themes alongside each other shows that Gideon used his war against
the Midianites in order to make a name for himself.[150] Therefore,
Gideon comes with his captives—the Midianite kings—to the men
of Succoth and of Penuel.

The two accounts, Gideon's clash with the Ephraimites and the
clash with the men of Succoth and of Penuel, which are interpo-

---

[150] Scholars noted that in this part of the account Gideon becomes someone who
enjoys using force, even to take savage vengeance, as opposed to the first part of
the account in which he lacked confidence (see for instance: Marais, *Representation
in Old Testament Narrative Texts*, p. 113). However, in general they did not discuss
the internal contradictions in Gideon's actions and the role of these contradictions
in shaping his personality and in the meaning of the account. This will be discussed below in detail.

lated in the description of the pursuit of the Midianites, are in marked contrast to each other. The Ephraimites complain to Gideon that he dishonoured them, Gideon appeals to the men of Succoth and of Penuel so that they will give him the honour due to him. When the Ephraimites came to Gideon seeking honour, Gideon acceded, thereby averting a disaster. When Gideon demands honour from the men of Succoth and of Penuel they refuse, and Gideon this time does not avert a disaster.[151] Rather he takes vengeance on them for not honouring him. The Ephraimites are motivated by injury to their honour, and in the account of Penuel and Succoth Gideon is motivated by injury to his honour. The Ephraimites complain that they did not take a more significant part in the battle, Gideon requests assistance in order to continue the battle. In the first description the theme is the execution of the Midianite princes, in the second the execution of the Midianite kings.[152]

d. *Gideon pursues and defeats the Midianites (8:4, 10–12)*

After the clash with the Ephraimites, the account resumes the description of the pursuit. Reference was made above to the surprising fact that Gideon was again with the three hundred soldiers who had been with him in the initial stage of the war (v. 4). The narrative reality behind this fact is unclear for the reader. However, given that we clarified above the personal motivations in Gideon's clash with the men of Succoth, we might assume that the reduction of his army

---

[151] All this, assuming that the cities of Succoth and Penuel are Israelite cities. See also: Kaufmann, *Sefer Shoftim*, p. 149. Reviv, on the other hand endeavours to establish that these cities are gentile enclaves. H. Reviv, "Two Notes to Judges VIII, 4–17", *Tarbiz* 38 (1969), pp. 309–317 (Hebrew, Eng. Summary p. I). Malamat also thinks that the cities were non-Israelite. In his opinion Gideon expected support from these cities because of vassal-treaty that existed between Gideon and cities of north Transjordan. See: A. Malamat, "The Punishment of Succoth and Pennuel by Gideon in Light of Ancient Near Eastern Treaties", C. Cohen, A. Hurvitz and S. M. Paul (eds.), *Sefer Moshe: The Moshe Weinfeld Jubilee Volume: Studies in the Bible and the Ancient Near East, Qumran and Post-Biblical Judaism*, Winona Lake 2004, pp. 69–71. See also: Moore, *Judges*, 219; Y. Aharoni, *The Land of the Bible: A Historical Geography*[2] (trans. A. F. Reiney), London 1979, p. 211. The fact that Gideon expects to receive assistance from these cities, and also the name of the city "Penuel" make it more likely that they are Israelite cities.

[152] In light of these connections, Boling (*Judges*, p. 152) is incorrect in asserting that the verses describing the confrontation between the Ephraimites and Gideon do not fit into the same context.

is related to the matter of his personal status. Gideon requests bread for his soldiers from the men of Succoth, on account of his personal actions. Presentation of the request in this manner is in keeping with the fact that the three hundred soldiers are his personal regiment. It is also difficult to ignore the fact that in the previous passage he shares his achievements with the Ephraimites, and here there is a regression: he does not share his victory with others, and the others do not exist at all: "Gideon came to the Jordan and crossed it, he and the three hundred who were with him were famished, but still in pursuit" (8:4).

> (10) "Now Zebah and Zalmunna were at Karkor with their army of about fifteen thousand men; these were all who remained of the entire host of the Kedemites for one hundred twenty thousand men bearing arms had fallen.
> (11) Gideon marched up the road of the tent dwellers, up to east of Nobah and Jogbehah, and smote the camp, which was off guard.
> (12) Zebah and Zalmunna took to flight, and he pursued them, and captured Zebah and Zalmunna, the two kings of Midian, and threw the whole army into panic. (vv. 10–12).

The description of the Midianite camp commences with mention of the Midianite kings, Zebah and Zalmunna, who occupy an important place from this stage of the account. It is therefore surprising that they were not mentioned previously. In the Ehud account, in which the killing of the king is also the focus of the story, the king is mentioned already from the outset (3:12). In the Deborah account, the execution of Siserah has an important role and is mentioned already at the outset (4:2). In the Gideon account, in comparison, there is detailed reference to the execution of the kings, but the reader had no previous knowledge of the kings. The account concerning the Midianite kings is all the more surprising, in that the reader had already heard about the execution of the Midianite captains by the Ephraimites, and believed them to be the Midianite leaders. This was certainly Gideon's intention when he said to the Ephraimites: "Is not the gleaning of the grapes of Ephraim better than the vintage of Abiezer" (8:2).

The Midianite kings are mentioned for the first time in verses 5–6 when Gideon requests support from the men of Succoth for his soldiers since he is in pursuit of the Midianite kings. We saw that this request was made in the context of Gideon's desire to make a name for himself. It seems therefore that the introduction of the new motif

of the Midianite kings at this stage of the account is designed to
serve the personal element in Gideon's motives. Here too an expla
nation of the dual motif of the Midianite leaders is necessary. The
Ephraimites, in relation to their honour, indicated their deeds in
capturing the Midianite captains (two). Introduction of the motif of
the Midianite kings (also two) serves the same actual idea of the victor's honour, but this time it is Gideon's honour that is in question.
The duality here is designed to serve the duality in Gideon's personality, and to serve as preparation for the subject of the kingship
that will arise subsequently in the Gideon account and in the Abimelech
account. In the Oreb and Zeeb account, Gideon appeared as someone concerned with the good of the people, and in the Zebah and
Zalmunna account as someone concerned with his own good. In
order to contrast these two facets of his personality, the author intentionally duplicated the subject of execution of the Midianite leaders,
so that each description stresses one facet.[153]

The emphasis on the Midianite kings in verse 10 also serves this
object. This verse distinguishes between the Midianite kings and the
Midianite camp. This distinction was not made previously (see for
instance: 6:33; 7:1, 12, 22 etc.), and it is designed here to precede
the theme of Gideon's capture of the Midianite kings.

For the first time in this story, the size of the Midianite camp is
given: the remaining army has fifteen thousand soldiers, and one
hundred and twenty thousand soldiers fell in the Midianite camp
(8:10). This information was given precisely now because here it
comes to serve the emphasis on Gideon's great achievements and
the change that occurred in his worldview. Initially the situation of
the people was his main concern, but the more attainments that he
has to his credit the more he focuses on his personal status. At the
beginning of the account, Gideon with his small army of three hundred soldiers faced an enormous Midianite army, the exact size of

---

[153] Therefore, even though there is a kind of duality between the report of the
killing of Oreb and Zeeb by the Ephraimites and the killing of Zebah and Zalmunna
by Gideon, this is not to be seen as the result of different sources, one religious
and the other realistic, as claimed by Wellhausen (*Prolegomena to the History of Ancient
Israel*, pp. 242–243; Burney, *The Book of Judges*, p. 182). This approach was opposed
also by: Martin (*The Book of Judges*, p. 103) and Soggin (*Judges*, p. 152). Boling
(*Judges*, p. 152) is also incorrect in maintaining that in the present context Gideon
was placed in an embarrassing situation after it emerged that the Ephraimites had
brought him the wrong heads.

which was not given, rather it was described metaphorically: "as thick as locusts; and their camels were without number, as numerous as the sands on the seashore" (7:12). Gideon defeated this enormous army with divine intervention. The number of fifteen thousand is a real number not a metaphorical one and it comes in the second part of the account, in the pursuit part. At this point, the account passes to a description of war without explicit divine assistance, and then Gideon's army is swelled with the arrival of soldiers from the tribes of Naphtali, Asher, Manasseh and Ephraim. In these two stages, together one hundred and twenty thousand Midianite soldiers were killed. Now Gideon faces fifteen thousand soldiers but with him again he has only three hundred exhausted soldiers. This introduction therefore is designed to emphasize the courage and might of Gideon, who with such a small army faces an army fifty times larger. Moreover, the tremendous number of those who died in the battle in the Midianite camp, coming at this point precisely and without mention of divine intervention (as was indicated, for instance, in Joshua 10:11), again illustrates here highlighting of the changes in Gideon's attitude towards his war against the Midianites.[154]

Verse 11 also specifically stresses Gideon, this time at the expense of his three hundred soldiers fighting with him. The attack on the Midianite camp in this verse is attributed to Gideon alone: "Gideon marched up . . . and smote the camp". This kind of description is exceptional in the Gideon account. For instance, in 7.19 the action is ascribed both to Gideon and to his soldiers: "Gideon and the hundred men with him arrived"; and in 8:4: "Gideon came to the Jordan and crossed it, he and the three hundred who were with him". In 7:21, the action is ascribed to the soldiers and Gideon is not distinguished: "They remained standing where they were, surrounding the camp". The description here is exceptional, relating to Gideon alone. This corresponds to the object in these verses of presenting the context in which Gideon concentrates on his status.

In the description of the capture of the kings in verse 12, the same emphasis also emerges.

---

[154] Contrary to the opinion that the indication of the three hundred men attests here to a source other than that described in ch. 7, see: Wellhausen, *Prolegomena to the History of Ancient Israel*, p. 242; Moore, *Judges*, pp. 174–175.

Zebah and Zalmunna took to flight,
and he pursued them,
and captured Zebah and Zalmunna, the two kings of Midian,
and threw the whole army into panic (8:12)

After the attack on the Midianite camp the passage describes the
flight of the kings ("Zebah and Zalmunna took to flight") only in
order to again hear of Gideon's further success in the pursuit ("and
he pursued them") and capture ("and captured Zebah and Zalmunna").
Twice in this verse the name of the kings is mentioned and their
title is also cited again "Zebah and Zalmunna took to flight, . . . and
captured Zebah and Zalmunna, the two kings of Midian". The preference given to the more complex and longer wording over a short
and good wording ("Zebah and Zalmunna took to flight and he pursued them and captured") is designed to emphasise Gideon's personal achievement in capturing the kings. Again, in this verse all the
actions relate to Gideon, and the role of the soldiers in the success
of the campaign is clearly ignored.

In verse 13, the account reverts to the theme of Gideon's punishment of the men of Succoth and of Penuel. Above we already
analyzed these verses and we saw that this action precedes the execution of the kings, and Gideon's priorities are reflected in them.
He is more concerned with his status than with completing the mission for which he assumed the role—delivering Israel from the
Midianites. We will now study the description of the execution of
the kings and we will see also in this passage how Gideon's priorities are expressed.

e. *Gideon executes the Midianite kings (8:18–21)*

> (18) Then he said to Zebah and Zalmunna, 'Where are the men whom
> you killed at Tabor?' They answered, 'As you are, so were they, every
> one of them; they resembled the sons of a king'.
> (19) He said: 'They were my brothers, the sons of my mother. As the
> LORD lives, if you had spared them, I would not kill you'.
> (20) So he said to Jether his firstborn, 'Go kill them!' But the boy did
> not draw his sword, for he was timid, because he was still a boy.
> (21) Then Zebah and Zalmunna said, 'Come, you slay us; for as the
> man is, so is his strength'. So Gideon went over and killed Zebah and
> Zalmunna, and he took the crescents that were on the necks of their
> camels. (8:18–21)

We saw that the object of Gideon's dialogue with the men of Succoth
and of Penuel is to show them Gideon's intention in punishing them.

The dialogue between Gideon and Zebah and Zalmunna also serves the same object. On a parallel to this account, Joshua executes the five kings of the south (Josh 10:22–27). In both cases, Gideon and Joshua wish to humiliate the vanquished kings. Joshua humiliates the kings by asking the officers who went with him to place their feet on their necks. Gideon also wishes to humiliate Zebah and Zalmunna. In the Joshua account, there is no dialogue with the kings. Gideon, however, conducts such a dialogue, and in it his wish to make a name for himself is again reflected.[155]

Gideon asks the kings: איפה האנשים אשר הרגתם בתבור. The meaning of the word איפה is where.[156] This question therefore seems meaningless and there is no real information that he wishes to receive from them. His main intention is to hold a discussion with them. The reply of the Midianite kings, "As you are, so were they, every one of them; they resembled the sons of a king" is also unclear, and does not answer Gideon's question. The vagueness both in Gideon's question and in the kings' reply is designed to emphasize the new element in the kings' words. They describe Gideon as a king.[157]

Gideon replies to the kings: "They were my brothers, the sons of my mother. As the LORD lives, if you had spared them, I would not kill you" (v. 19). The term אחי (my brothers) has a broad meaning that includes an extended family, tribe or national relationship. This being so, the Bible uses the term "my brothers the sons of my mother" to indicate a family relationship of blood brothers.[158] From Gideon's words it now becomes clear that his family was directly injured by the Midianite oppression and his relatives died in these events. Until now, we had heard nothing of this event and of personal injury to Gideon in the Midianite oppression. The next part

---

[155] On the other hand, Amit (*Judges*, p. 148) considers that the dialogue between Zebah and Zalmunna, in which they related to Gideon as a king, is in juxtaposition to the attitude of the Ephraimites and the men of Succoth and of Penuel towards Gideon.

[156] See: *DCH*, vol. 1, p. 221. According to Kaufmann (*Sefer Shoftim*, p. 187), the text should read נהגתם rather than הרגתם. The meaning of the question would then be "where are the men whom you took captive at Tabor?" Driver ("Problems in Judges Newly Discussed", p. 15) explains that the intention of the question is what happened with the men whom you killed. Many farfetched interpretations have been given to the intention of this question, but the best explanation would seem to be that Gideon does not expect any answer.

[157] See: Dishon, "Gideon and the Beginnings of Monarchy in Israel", p. 260.

[158] See for instance Deut 13:7; and on the other hand, Deut 17:15.

of the sentence is the main point and it is for this that the matter is mentioned. Gideon tells the Midianite kings that he would have pardoned them had they not harmed his brothers. These words are surprising, and not in keeping with Gideon's character as it appeared at the beginning of the account. The Midianite kings are responsible for the harsh oppression of Israel, and for this they deserve Gideon's reaction. However, Gideon determines that had they not killed members of his family, he would have spared them. These words of Gideon are all the more forceful in that they are expressed in the form of an oath using God's name: "As the LORD lives" (v. 19).[159] Gideon's statement shows that the meaning given to the execution of the kings is personal vengeance because of the injury to him and to his family.[160]

Gideon executes the kings only after two further dialogues. Firstly, he tells his firstborn Jether[161] to execute the kings: "So he said to Jether his firstborn, 'Go kill them!' But the boy did not draw his sword, for he was timid, because he was still a boy" (8:20). Since his son fails to do so, this request seems superfluous.[162] The object of indicating Gideon's request is again to present Gideon's personal aim in executing the kings. Execution of the kings by someone not of the rank of the person executed is ignominious.[163] Thus, Abimelech considers it ignominious to die at a woman's hands and asks his

---

[159] For the meaning of the expression "As the LORD lives", see: M. Greenberg, "The Hebrew Oath Particle *hay/hē*", *JBL* 76 (1957), pp. 34–39.

[160] Similarly, see: Webb, *The Book of Judges*, p. 151. Boling (*Judges*, p. 157) justifiably considers that the statement that the Midianite kings had killed Gideon's mother's sons at Tabor is surprising since there had been no mention of this until now.

[161] The name "Jether" is apparently a contraction of the name "Jethro". This name appears in Israel in the Bible only in the Book of Exodus (4:18) in relation to Jethro, Moses' Midianite father-in-law. The fact that Gideon's son is called by the Midianite name "Jether" may possibly indicate an influence of the Midianite oppression in his period. Klein saw this as a further connection between Gideon's and Moses' personalities, see: Klein, *The Triumph of Irony in the Book of Judges*, p. 62.

[162] Webb (*The Book of Judges*, p. 151) explained that the dialogue was designed to show the contrast between Gideon now and his previous conduct, reflected here in his firstborn son's irresolution. Similarly, Exum ("The Center Cannot Hold", p. 418) insists that Jether inherited his father's timidity as expressed in Gideon's lack of response to the claims of the men of Ophrah (6:25–31) and the fact that Gideon was rescued by his father.

[163] Pedersen, *Israel, Its Life and Culture*, p. 379; in Abravanel's opinion, Gideon asked his son to kill the Midianite kings in order to honour his son and to show that he saw him as his successor; likewise Dishon, "Gideon and the Beginnings of Monarchy in Israel", p. 261.

servant to kill him after being wounded by a woman (9:53–54). Saul
also asked his arms bearer to kill him in order not to die at the
hands of the Philistines (1 Sam 31:4). Since the kings had harmed
his family Gideon wishes to humiliate them and have them executed
by a member of his family. His firstborn son is the person closest
to him, and because he is a boy, this is a humiliation. At the same
time to have them executed by Jether expresses the personal injury
done to Gideon. Zebah and Zalmunna wish to die honourably and
entreat Gideon to execute them personally, so that their death will
be more honourable, similarly to the requests of Abimelech and Saul
cited above. From the viewpoint of the Midianite kings, it is preferable to die honourably at the hands of the actual leader. As far as
Gideon is concerned, he himself reaps the praise for his defeat of
the Midianite kings, and thus his status is enhanced.[164]

If the main topic of the passage was the execution of the Midianite
kings, with this report the passage should have ended. However, as
we saw, the execution of the kings derives from Gideon's personal
motives and this is the main emphasis in the description. Therefore,
the passage ends with a detail that seems on the face of it unim-
portant: "and he took the crescents that were on the necks of their
camels" (v. 21$_b$). It is not clear what exactly the crescents were, but
it seems that they were royal ornaments that adorned the royal
camels that bore the kings.[165] The report that closes the story of the
execution of the kings does not deal with the elimination of the kings
but the royal booty taken by Gideon. In this, Gideon is again presented as a royal leader who vanquished the Midianite kings and in
the way of the kings took the royal booty. Again Gideon's personal
side is emphasized in this act instead of the national interest.

At the end of this passage the reader is exposed to several motifs
that underline royal aspects in Gideon's behaviour: the humiliation
of the kings by his firstborn son; execution of the kings by Gideon
after the kings ask to die by the most senior personage and who
corresponds to the Midianite kings; and also Gideon's taking of the

---

[164] On "honour" and "vendetta" as the main subject of the dialogue between
Gideon and the kings, see: Pedersen, *Israel, Its Life and Culture*, p. 379.

[165] The "crescents" are mentioned only on one other occasion in the Bible in
relation to women's jewellery, Isa 3:18. The root of the word סהר indicates that
the ornament was made apparently in the form of a crescent. See: Pritchard, *The
Ancient Near East in Pictures Relating to the Old Testament*, p. 22.

royal crescents. All these motifs assembled together in the topic of execution of the Midianite kings surprise the reader, who expects to see highlighting of Israel's national victory at the end of the account. The focus on the royal motifs here precedes the people's request to Gideon to reign over them. Thus the reader receives the impression that Israel's request does not appear out of nowhere. It seems that Gideon himself contributed to a great extent to the offer of kingship made to him.

12. *Gideon's Refusal of Kingship and the Setting Up of the Ephod in Ophrah (8:22–28)*

After Gideon adopted regal characteristics it is not surprising that the people asked him to found a monarchic dynasty:[166] "Then the men of Israel said to Gideon, 'Rule over us—you, your son, and your grandson as well; for you have saved us from the Midianites'" (8:22). The concept of king does not appear in the people's request,[167] but it is clear that this is their intention since they indicate the transfer of the rule from father to son: "you, your son, and your grandson as well". Even though the attempt to institute a monarchy is related to the regal characteristics adopted by Gideon, possibly the initiative to make him king comes here in the book after several accounts of judges who were successful, but whose deaths were followed by instability. Here, after Gideon's success, there is an attempt to solve the problem of instability inherent in the judge leadership model.

Gideon adamantly rejects the people's proposal: "Gideon said to them, 'I will not rule over you myself, nor shall my son rule over you; the LORD shall rule over you'" (8:23). This refusal contrasts with the regal conduct that he adopted in execution of the Midianite kings, and the royal status that the Midianite kings attributed to him.[168] In his refusal, Gideon again does not express his personal

---

[166] See also: Webb, *The Book of Judges*, p. 152.

[167] In Soggin's opinion (*Judges*, p. 158) the people do not use the word מלך— since this title refers only to the rule of God in ancient sources. From many sources it is clear that the word משל ("rule") is close, if not equal, in meaning to the word מלך. See for instance: Gen 37:8; Isa 49:7; Jer 34:1, Mic 4:5; Ps 22:29; 37:8; 103:19; 105:10; 145:13; Dan 11:3, 4, 5; Neh 9:37; etc.

[168] Scholars disagree as to the period of the anti-monarchic approach reflected

interest but the right course of action to take. Gideon here expresses
a theocratic outlook that sets God at the centre of the people's existence. God, according to this outlook, is the king of Israel, and any
human monarch conflicts with this outlook.

However, immediately after this refusal, Gideon goes on to ask
the people: "And Gideon said to them, 'I have a request to make
of you: Each of you give me the earring he received as booty', for
they had golden earrings, because they were Ishmaelites"[169] (8:24).
This request is a continuation of the dialogue between the people
and Gideon. Gideon refuses to rule but immediately demands that
they give him their booty. Given the consecutive sequence in the
dialogue between Gideon and the people, it is necessary to examine the nature of the relation between what appear initially to be
two unrelated issues.

The people willingly comply with Gideon's request:

> 'We will willingly give them', they answered. So they spread a gar-
> ment, and everyone threw onto it the earring he had taken as booty.
> The weight of the golden earrings that he had requested was one thou-
> sand seven hundred shekels of gold; beside the crescents and the pen-
> dants and the purple robes worn by the kings of Midian and beside
> the collars on the necks of their camels. Gideon made an ephod of it
> and set it up in his own town, in Ophrah, and all Israel prostituted
> themselves to it there, and it became a snare to Gideon and his house-
> hold (8:25–27).

The said request and the people's willing compliance recall Aaron's
request for the people to give him their golden rings, from which
he prepared a molten calf:

> Aaron said to them, 'Take off the gold rings that are on the ears of
> your wives, your sons, and your daughters, and bring them to me'.

---

in Gideon's statement. There is a detailed discussion of this subject in the conclusion
of this monograph. For the conception God as King in the Bible see: K. Seybold,
"melek", *Theological Dictionary of the Old Testament*, VIII, trans. D. W. Stott, Grand
Rapids and Cambridge 1997, p. 366, and the bibliography there.

[169] The confusion between "Ishmaelites" and "Midianites" can also be seen in
the story of Joseph, Gen 37:25–28, on this see: Burney, *The Book of Judges*, pp.
184–185. Since the names Midian and Ishmael serve together in this account, and
given that the prevalent opinion today is that the E and J sources are not to be
found in the Gideon account, it is necessary to reconsider the assumption of the
scholars in relation to the Joseph account that the E source uses the name "Midianites"
and the J source the name "Ishmaelites". See: J. Skinner, *Genesis* (ICC), Edinburgh
1910, p. 443; S. R. Driver, *An Introduction to the Literature of the Old Testament*, Edinburgh
1913, pp. 17–18.

> So all the people took off the gold rings from their ears, and brought them to Aaron. He took the gold from them, formed it in a mold, and cast an image of a calf; and they said, 'These are your gods, O Israel, who brought you up out of the land of Egypt!' (Exod 32:2–4).

In both cases the leader asks the people to give golden jewellery including earrings.[170] The people comply willingly in both cases. From the jewellery Aaron makes a molten calf, and Gideon an ephod.[171] In the Aaron account the people transgress in worship of the calf, and in the Gideon account the people transgress in worship of the ephod.[172]

In the calf account, the people's distress was due to Moses' disappearance:

> When the people saw that Moses delayed to come down from the mountain, the people gathered around Aaron, and said to him, 'Come, make gods for us, who shall go before us; as for this Moses, the man who brought us up out of the land of Egypt, we do not know what has become of him' (Exod 32:1).

The calf transgression is the result of a leadership crisis: Moses' disappearance and the people's need for a leader. The same is true in the Gideon account. Gideon's request for the people's jewellery derives also from a leadership crisis. Sick and tired of the instability deriving from the absence of permanent centralized leadership, the people therefore ask Gideon to rule over them and to be the first in a dynasty of leaders.

The main problem in the Gideon account is Gideon's self-contradiction. He refuses to accede to the office of king since he sees

---

[170] On the דים see Burney, *The Book of Judges*, 235.

[171] Various opinions have been put forward as regards the nature of the "ephod". Some see in it a garment like the Priest's ephod (Burney, *The Book of Judges*, pp. 236–243; M. Haran, "The Ephod According to Biblical Sources", *Tarbiz* 24 (1955), p. 388 (Hebrew, Eng. Summary: pp. II–III); others consider that the ephod is a statue of God (Moore, *Judges*, pp. 230–231). Some see the ephod as a cultic instrument for consulting God (T. C. Foote, "The Ephod", *JBL* 21 (1902), pp. 1–47). On the "ephod" and the meaning of the word according to Assyrian and Ugaritic sources, see: Albright, *Yahweh and the Gods of Canaan*, pp. 200–203. See also: Burney, *The Book of Judges*, ibid.

[172] According to Klein (*The Triumph of Irony in the Book of Judges*, p. 65) the ephod is a garment, and therefore she links this to the expression at the beginning of the battle: "The spirit of the LORD enveloped Gideon". In her opinion the meaning of this connection is that initially the spirit of the LORD "enveloped" him whereas now another spirit "envelops" him. However probably there is no connection between the two.

this as prejudicial to God's sovereignty. However, he immediately initiates the building of an ephod that is also prejudicial to the worship of God. How can this direct contradiction in Gideon's actions be explained?

The explanation lies in the elements making up the ephod. Gideon asks the people "Each of you give me the earring he received as booty" (8:24) and they immediately comply: "and everyone threw onto it the earring he had taken as booty" (8:25). A summary is then given of all that was collected: "The weight of the golden earrings that he had requested was one thousand seven hundred shekels of gold" (8:26$_a$). However, the summary does not end here, and the verse continues with a further description: "beside the crescents and the pendants and the purple robes worn by the kings of Midian and beside the collars on the necks of their camels" (8:26$_b$). The people were not asked to bring these objects, and indeed, they brought only earrings. The nature of the crescents, the pendants, the purple raiment and the chains as an addition to what was collected appears also syntactically: ". . . beside the . . . and beside the . . .". The listing of these objects separately was designed to emphasize them.[173] These were given not by the people who brought the earrings as requested, but by Gideon himself. Above we saw that Gideon took the royal crescents that were on the necks of the royal camels as booty of the victorious king from the vanquished kings. Here "the crescents and the pendants and the purple robes worn by the kings of Midian" and "the collars on the necks of their camels" were added, emphasizing the royal nature of this booty. This serves to show the nature and object of the ephod. The elements making up the ephod were the royal booty given by Gideon. This booty, taken by Gideon from the Midianite kings, is part of the motif used to show Gideon as a king who triumphed over the Midianite kings. Therefore, the fact that the stressed elements of the ephod are the royal booty that Gideon took from the Midianite kings would seem to show that the significance and purpose of the ephod must be sought in this context. Probably, the ephod was built as a monument to commemorate Gideon's victory over the Midianite kings. In ancient times kings used to exhibit the royal booty that they took in their wars, and

---

[173] In Moore's opinion (*Judges*, p. 232), the second half of verse 26 is a late addition. Burney, *The Book of Judges*, p. 236, disagreed.

particularly booty that could glorify their name in relation to the kings that they had vanquished. Gideon acts in the way of kings to glorify his name.

Thus we will understand the emphasis on the location where this victory monument is set up: "Gideon made an ephod of it and set it up in his own town, in Ophrah" (8:27). The fact that the monument was set up in Ophrah, Gideon's town, shows that its aim was to glorify Gideon. Victorious kings frequently built monuments in their capital city, in order to focus greater attention around them and to earn the admiration of their subjects. By placing this monument in Ophrah Gideon certainly makes Ophrah a centre for pilgrimage and perpetuation of his name, and this is the situation reflected in the sentence: "and all Israel prostituted themselves after it there" (v. 27).

What is the nature of the cult formed around the ephod and represented by the verb זנה ("prostituted")? Possibly this is an idolatrous cult,[174] but there may be an additional dimension here. It may well be a personality cult of Gideon.[175] ויזנו כל ישראל אחריו שם "and all Israel prostituted themselves after it there" (v. 27). To what does the word אחריו (literally, "after it" or "after him") refer? Syntactically it is possible that they prostituted themselves after the ephod, but it can also be understood that they prostituted themselves after Gideon. In my opinion, the ambiguity is intentional. Even if there was a real

---

[174] McMillion (*Judges 6–8*, pp. 252–253) considers that the ephod account is a continuation of Gideon's refusal to rule. In his opinion, Gideon built the ephod so that it would serve as a means for the rule of God. In Kaufman's opinion (*Sefer Shoftim*, p. 190), Gideon intended to make an ephod for God's sake. Kaufmann maintains that Gideon built the ephod as a symbol of his rule, through it he stood at the head of the people as a spiritual leader, and used the ephod to carry out the priestly role of consulting God (see p. 193). Amit (*The Book of Judges*, pp. 261–262) considers that there is a uniform redactional line between Gideon's refusal to rule and his initiative to build the ephod. Since she considers that Gideon meant what he said, when he refused to rule because of his wish to underscore God's place, she also interprets the act of building the ephod as the continuation of his refusal to rule: his intention in building the ephod was to create a cultic symbol of God's deliverance (see also, *ibid.*, pp. 91–92). However, the method of determining the meaning according to the context does not take into account the possibility of inconsistency in Gideon's actions. Moreover, in order to establish her claim, Amit determines that the ephod is cited principally in positive contexts. This claim, however, is groundless. The ephod was a priestly garment, but, as here, it is cited in several places in negative contexts, e.g.: Judg 17:5; Hos 3:4.

[175] This is the opinion of Kimchi in his commentary. However, his interpretation that only after Gideon's death Israel worshipped the ephod is farfetched.

cult here, it derived from the people's adoration of Gideon and not
religious or ritual aspirations. The cult of the ephod as representing
Gideon materializes the people's adoration of Gideon following his
victories which led them to wish to make him king. In this context
precisely, we must understand Gideon's request from the people to
contribute their earrings. Building of the ephod by Gideon is a direct
continuation of his refusal to rule over them. They requested a king,
he refused, but he immediately acts for construction of an ephod.
He diverted the people's adoration for him from their wish to make
him king to the cult of the ephod.

The result of construction of the ephod also shows Gideon's aim:
"and it became a snare to Gideon and his household" (v. 27$_b$).[176]
There is a new motif here, "his household". What is the nature of
the household? The household here implies the establishment created around Gideon's personality. Even though he refused to be
king, we hear here about his household, which is not his private
household but a governmental institution created around him, and
reminiscent of a royal house.

Gideon's explicit refusal to be king (8:23), which derives from
understanding of God's status on one hand and an attitude of humility and altruism on the other, sharply contrasts with his request to
construct the ephod, which derived from his wish to consolidate his
status in the eyes of the people, and corresponds to his regal conduct. His monarchic attitude will receive additional aspects later in
the account. This contradiction led several scholars to the conclusion that Gideon in fact did not mean what he said when he refused
to be king.[177] However, it seems that this contradiction is an essen-

---

[176] Since this verse does not correspond to the general intention of the account,
Kaufmann (*Sefer Shoftim*, p. 190) and Amit (*Judges*, p. 155) delete it. However, we
have already seen throughout the account that Gideon's inconsistent behaviour is
a main motif in his personality, and deleting of the verse prejudices the shaping of
the character of Gideon, who on one hand expresses concern for God's monarchy,
but on the other hand causes prejudice to it.

[177] The contradiction between Gideon's opposition to the monarchy and his adopting of monarchic manners gave rise to three exegetic orientations. One possibility
is that of attributing the different motifs to different sources (see: Moore, *Judges*, pp.
229–230; Burney, *The Book of Judges*, pp. 183–184, 235) A second possibility is that
although it seems that Gideon refuses to rule he in fact did rule (or held another
similar office). A third possibility is to detract from the importance of the items that
indicate that he is king. Davies considers that Gideon in fact accepted the monarchy and his opposition is only a polite refusal and indeed he accepted the offer,
see: G. H. Davies, "Judges VIII 22–23", *VT* 13 (1963), pp. 151–157. In Davies'

tial part of the account and of Gideon's personality, as already seen above. Gideon oscillates between a positive and a negative approach to his leadership. He refuses to rule, expressing a clear theological outlook that places God in the centre, despite his very human wish for rule. Gideon knows the correct path to adopt and he intends to act accordingly. However, the urge to rule prevails in that he nonetheless seeks to make an ephod and to thereby perpetuate his deeds.[178]

---

opinion, the context proves that Gideon indeed reigned, as shown by his personal wealth, his children, wives and concubines, his temple, and the quarrel between his sons as to who would succeed him (pp. 155–156). Davies also emphasized that in Jotham's fable there is not one word against the monarchy, but only that the wrong man received the monarchy. The ephod that Gideon made, like Saul and David, is a royal characteristic. Soggin, *Judges*, p. 160 and Gerbrandt disagreed with him (See: G. E. Gerbrandt, *Kingship According to the Deuteronomistic History* (SBL Dissertation Series, 87), Atlanta 1986, p. 126). Kaufmann appears undecided. On one hand (*Sefer Shoftim*, pp. 191–193), he considers that Gideon refused to rule, but the continued negotiations between him and the people in which he accepted the offer was omitted, in order to leave the nice impression of Gideon's words expressing his loyalty to God. On the other hand, Kaufmann emphasizes (*ibid.*, p. 191) that the large number of wives and sons, and the fact that he called his son Abimelech are not monarchic characteristics. Unconvincingly, Kaufmann also argues (*ibid.*) that Gideon does not express the view that the monarchy is a transgression but that there is no advantage in it. For other variations, see also: Malamat, *History of Biblical Israel*, pp. 122–125. Dishon ("Gideon and the Beginnings of Monarchy in Israel", p. 266) asserts that Gideon did not refuse to rule, nor did he express agreement. Rather he declared that changing of the regime and establishment of a monarchy is possible in the framework of the rule of God. In her opinion, Gideon refused to rule as a despot, but did agree to rule in a democratic manner. This theory seems very remote from the literal meaning of the verses, in which it is expressly stressed that Gideon rejected the request for him to rule. For criticism of this approach, and in particular of Dishon's article, see: S. E. Loewenstamm, "The Lord Shall Rule Over You (Judges VIII 23)", *Tarbiz* 41 (1971–2), pp. 444–445 (Hebrew, Eng. Summary p. V). In Halpern's opinion, Gideon refused to accept the monarchy, but he adopts the role of the priest whose function is to mediate between God and Israel. B. Halpern, "The Rise of Abimelek Ben-Jerubbaal", *Hebrew Annual Review* 2 (1978), pp. 84–85. According to Gerbrandt (*ibid.* pp. 127–129), Gideon does not express an anti-monarchic outlook. He maintains that when the people said to Gideon "Rule over us . . . for you have saved us" they thus did not acknowledge God's deliverance and attributed the deliverance to Gideon, just as God had feared: "Israel might claim for themselves the glory due to Me, thinking, 'Our own hand has brought us victory'". Gideon opposed such a monarchy that was contradictory to God's kingship. What characterizes all these solutions is that they all assume that there must be uniformity in Gideon's conduct, and that his actions must correspond to his words. However, all these interpretations miss the point of the account. The simple meaning of the reading shows that Gideon indeed refused to rule, but on the other hand he conducted himself like a king.

[178] McMillion (*Judges 6–8*, pp. 274–282) discussed the paradoxes in Gideon's personality, but did not reach the conclusions that emerge in the analysis in this work.

Gideon's action in building the ephod was not directed at founding an alternative cult to worship of God and his intention was not to cause prejudice to God. His aim was to glorify himself and this also caused prejudice to God. There is a contradiction between Gideon's intention and his acts, but this contradiction was the intention of the account. This contradiction is shown in order to demonstrate the destructive results of the action of a leader who is driven by personal interests. This idea is highlighted by means of the clear irony between the beginning and the end of the account. At the beginning of the account, Gideon opposes his father's house and the men of his city and he destroys the Baal worship in the city of Ophrah. Now at the end of the account, after having vanquished the Midianites and proved the supremacy of God who commissioned him as opposed to the Baal against whom he fought, he establishes in exactly the same place, in his city of Ophrah an alternative cult: "Gideon made an ephod of it and set it up in his own town, in Ophrah, and all Israel prostituted themselves to it there, and it became a snare to Gideon and his household" (8:27). It is extremely ironical that Gideon, who destroyed the Baal in the city of Ophrah at the beginning of the account, returns and establishes worship of the ephod precisely in the same place at the end of the account.[179] Although this cult is not as serious as the Baal worship, the irony is clear; its object is to present a critical evaluation of the results of Gideon's personal motivations.

The account departs from this negative description of Gideon's acts in order to present a positive summary of his period and his deeds: "Thus Midian submitted to the Israelites and did not raise its head again; and the land had rest for forty years in Gideon's time" (8:28). This verse returns us to the detailed description of the Midianite oppression at the beginning of the account, which showed the harshness of the Midianite rule over Israel. Gideon solves this problem. Not only did the confrontation between Israel and Midian

---

[179] See: Webb, *The Book of Judges*, p. 153; Exum, "The Center Cannot Hold", p. 419. Gooding sees a chiastic structure in the Gideon account: A—Gideon challenges the idolatry by destroying the altar of the Baal (6:1–32), B—Gideon fights Israel's enemies (6:33–7:25). B'—Gideon fights his own people (8:1–21), A'—Gideon himself tends to idolatry (8:22–32). D. W. Gooding, "The Composition of the Book of Judges", *Eretz Israel* 16 (1982), p. 74. However, the opposite is true. We saw already that the structure of the account in general is different and more complex.

end with the defeat of Midian, but also with a further statement: "and did not raise its head again". The fall of Midian is absolute. They cannot recover from it. It is interesting that indeed no Midianite agency is subsequently involved in any injury to Israel in the Bible.

The Gideon account seemingly ends here with the report of the defeat of the Midianites by Gideon and the summary of the number of years in which he judged Israel. The Ehud account ends in the same way: "And the land had rest eighty years" (3:30). The Deborah account also ends in this way (5:31$_b$).[180] However, the account here does not end with this positive appreciation of Gideon. The text then resumes the description of the harm caused by Gideon.

13. *Gideon's Death (8:29–32)*

(29) And Jerubbaal the son of Joash went and dwelt in his house.
(30) Now Gideon had seventy sons, his own offspring, for he had many wives
(31) His concubine who was in Shechem also bore him a son, and he named him Abimelech.
(32) Gideon son of Joash died at a good old age, and was buried in the tomb of his father Joash at Ophrah of the Abiezrites (vv. 29–32).

The description in these verses of the end of Gideon's life after deliverance of the people is exceptional in the judge accounts. The Ehud and Deborah accounts conclude with the end of the war against the enemy, as does the Samson account.[181] What is the significance of this description in the Gideon account?

These verses describe regal characteristics in Gideon's leadership. Gideon's many wives and his many sons, seventy in number,[182] are

---

[180] The place of 5:31$_b$ should be at the end of Ch. 4, see: B. Lindars, "Deborah's Song: Women in the Old Testament", *Bulletin of the John Rylands University Library of Manchester* 65, 2 (1983), p. 158.

[181] The Jephthah account likewise does not end at the victory stage, and there the continuation after the victory is even more remarkable than in the Gideon account. This will be studied below.

[182] Ahab also had seventy sons. Possibly the number seventy is designed to present a monarchic institution; there are also seventy elders in Exodus 24. According to Fensham, the number seventy is symbolic, expressing the princes in the royal family who are called "seventy". F. C. Fensham, "The Numeral Seventy in the Old Testament and the Family of Jerubbaal, Ahab, Panammuwa and Athirat", *PEQ* 109 (1977), pp. 113–115. On this matter see also: C. W. Wolf, "Traces of Primitive

clear characteristics of a monarch, as described in the Bible.[183] This
is also true of the mention of Gideon's concubine, concubines being
a royal usage.[184] In light of this, we will also understand the verse
that appears initially unclear: "And Jerubbaal the son of Joash went
and dwelt in his house" (8:29). Clearly, this sentence does not mean
that Gideon merely went on one occasion to his house. Another possibility is that after Gideon was asked to rule and refused, he then
retired from office in order to lead his private life: according to this
interpretation, "in his house" symbolizes his private life as against
his public office.[185] This possibility is improbable since apparently
Gideon continues to be a public figure, as emerges from the regal
conduct that he adopts. Therefore, the meaning of the word ביתו
(his house) would seem to be בית המלכות (the royal palace). The
house symbolizes Gideon's governmental establishment. The meaning of the word ישב is to enter into office, and the meaning of the
passage therefore is that Gideon went and sat on his throne of leadership, and the passage seeks to intimate that this resembled a royal
dynasty.

This explanation fits well with the report that Gideon named his
son by his concubine in Shechem "Abimelech" (= אבי—Abi] my
father [מלך—Melech] is king). Clearly, the aim of this report is to
introduce the next chapter in the book, and the end of the Gideon
account is combined with the beginning of the Abimelech account.[186]
However, first and foremost, this report belongs to the Gideon

---

Democracy in Ancient Israel", *JNES* 6 (1947), p 99. Martin, on the other hand
(*The Book of Judges*, p. 110), considers that this information is compatible with the
report of the many sons of the minor judges.

[183] Deut 17:17; 1 Kings 11:1–3; See: Webb, *The Book of Judges*, p. 154; Dishon,
"Gideon and the Beginnings of Monarchy in Israel", p. 260.

[184] Saul had a concubine: 2 Sam 3:7; as did David: 2 Sam 5:13; 17:21; and
Solomon: 1 Kings 11:3. See: Soggin, *Judges*, p. 159. On these motifs as intimating
the monarchy founded by Gideon, see also: Malamat, *History of Biblical Israel*, pp.
123–124; Dishon, "Gideon and the Beginnings of Monarchy in Israel", p. 260;
Webb, *The Book of Judges*, p. 154.

[185] This is the opinion for instance of Burney (*The Book of Judges*, p. 264), and
therefore he considers that the place of this verse is after Gideon's refusal to rule
in verse 23; Moore, *Judges*, p. 233, is also of this opinion. They consider that this
verse was placed after the story of the ephod since first it was necessary to relate
that on the same occasion that he refused to rule he asked the Israelites to give
him the booty.

[186] In Moore's opinion (*Judges*, p. 234), vv. 30–32 are an introduction to the
Abimelech account.

account. The fact that he calls his son "Abimelech" (= my father is king) shows that Gideon sees him as the son of a king and one way or the other he sees himself as king.[187] The irony is clear.[188] Gideon coined the sentence: "I will not rule over you myself, nor shall my son rule over you; the LORD shall rule over you" (v. 23). Not only will his son rule as will be seen below in the next account, but when he calls his son Abimelech he gives himself the status of king.[189] The regal conduct adopted by Gideon was prejudicial to worship of God. It was Gideon who indicated the contradiction between a mortal king and the reign of God, and therefore, when actually he conducts himself as king, this is followed immediately by prejudice to worship of God: "and all Israel prostituted themselves to it there" (8:27).

Now we also understand the reason that Gideon is called Jerubbaal in verse 29. The use of the name Jerubbaal is not fortuitous; and there is a change in this use at this point. Until now we explained that the use of both names expressed the dissent in the people, around belief in God or in the Baal. The use of the name Jerubbaal is designed to indicate here the fall of Gideon who ultimately became "Jerubbaal" instead of continuing to be "Gideon". As noted, the name "Gideon" expressed Gideon's battle against the Baal on behalf

---

[187] D. Jobling, *The Sense of Biblical Narrative: Structural Analyses in the Hebrew Bible*, II (JSOTsup, 39), Sheffield 1986, p. 69, Dishon, "Gideon and the Beginnings of Monarchy in Israel", p. 260. Compare: S. Abramsky, "Abimelech's Leadership—King, Chief and Ruler", A Even-Shoshan et al. (eds.), *The Book of Siwan: A Collection of Studies and Essays in Memory of the Late Jerusalem Publisher Shalom Siwan*, Jerusalem 1979, p. 170 (Hebrew). Abramsky explains that the use of the exceptional phrase וישם את שמו אבימלך shows that "naming is designed for the aim of fulfilment of a specific thought regarding the person bearing the name". In his opinion, Gideon planned a priori that his son Abimelech would rule in Shechem. Therefore, in other places where the exceptional form וישם שמו appears the intention is to an objective, see for instance: 1 Kings 17:34; Neh 9:7; Dan 1:7. However, contrary to Abramsky's thesis, this verse is not designed to justify Abimelech's monarchy, but on the contrary, to present Gideon in a negative light in that despite his refusal to rule he nonetheless tended towards the monarchy. On the meaning of the name "Abimelech" and its origin, see: Boling, *Judges*, pp. 162–163; Soggin, *Judges*, pp. 166–167. While Moore (*Judges*, p. 235) may be right in arguing that the meaning of the names "Abimelech" and "Ahimelech" may be that God is the king, one cannot deny the irony in the fact that Gideon who refused to rule called his son Abimelech, nor can one negate that in the present context there is a special meaning to giving of this name.

[188] Boling, *Judges*, p. 164; Webb, *The Book of Judges*, p. 154.

[189] Prof. Y. Zakovitch drew my attention to a further irony: Abimelech is perhaps the son of the king, but he was not the father of a king as his name means.

of God, and "Jerubbaal" expressed the attitude of Gideon's opponents who hoped and believed that the Baal would take vengeance
on Gideon. When Gideon is called "Jerubbaal" here, it seems that
ultimately the Baal fought Gideon and triumphed; therefore he is
called "Jerubbaal" at this point. This meaning appears clearly from
the fact that Jerubbaal is the only name appearing in the Abimelech
account, in which the name Gideon does not appear even once. The
fact that Gideon is called Jerubbaal here indicates that ultimately
Gideon failed in his attempt to restore the people's belief in God.[190]

   Just as we found throughout the account a combination of positive and negative descriptions of Gideon, the closing verse here is
both positive and negative: "Gideon son of Joash died at a good old
age, and was buried in the tomb of his father Joash at Ophrah of
the Abiezrites" (8:32).[191] In the closing verse again the name "Gideon"
is used, three verses after he was called "Jerubbaal". The verse also
indicates that Gideon died "at a good old age". This indication
occurs in the Bible in relation to only two people other than Gideon:
Abraham and David (Gen 15:15; 25:8; 1 Chr 29:28). The indication of Gideon's good old age placed him in this distinguished group.
On the other hand, Gideon is called here "Gideon son of Joash".
This name seemingly is not intended as a compliment since Joash
is mentioned in the account as a Baal worshipper. It also seems that
the object of the passage is indeed to present him as Joash's successor, and therefore it is indicated that he was buried in his father's
tomb. This indication "and was buried in the tomb of his father
Joash at Ophrah of the Abiezrites" is an indication usually used in
the Bible to refer to kings. Its object in this verse is to show Gideon
as a link in a dynasty of leaders, or kings, contrary to his refusal to
rule over Israel.[192] The fact that Gideon is presented as the son of

---

[190] For a similar explanation see: Polzin, *Moses and the Deuteronomist*, p. 169.

[191] However, there is no paradox here as noted by Marais (*Representation in Old
Testament Narrative Texts*, p. 114), but an internal contradiction in Gideon's personality and conduct—a well-known human manifestation.

[192] Apart from Gideon and Samson, it is not said of any judge that he was buried
in the tomb of his father or with his fathers. In the pre-monarchic period, "burial
with one's father" was unknown. This is characteristic of most of the kings, of whom
it is said that they were buried with their fathers. See for instance, in relation to
Saul and Jonathan, 2 Sam 21:14; David, 1 Kings 2:10; Solomon, 1 Kings 11:43;
Rehoboam, 1 Kings 14:31; Abijam, 1 Kings 15:8; Asa, 15:24, etc. For another
explanation of this indication, see: Boling, *Judges*, p. 164.

Joash and the father of Abimelech who founded a corrupt monarchy, shows the negative side of Gideon's leadership and personality.

14. *After Gideon's Death (8:33–35)*

(33) As soon as Gideon died, the Israelites relapsed and prostituted
themselves with the Baals, making Baal-berith their god.
(34) The Israelites did not remember the LORD their God, who had
rescued them from the hand of all their enemies on every side.
(35) And they did not show loyalty to the house of Jerubbaal, that is,
Gideon, in return for all the good that he had done to Israel (8:33–35).

These verses are part of the Gideon account,[193] and they contain a
negative and unequivocal criticism of Israel's conduct. However, as
in the previous verses, the evaluation of Gideon is ambivalent. The
Bible clearly determines that Israel went astray after the Baal only
after Gideon's death: "As soon as Gideon died, the Israelites relapsed
and prostituted themselves with the Baals, making Baal-berith their
god" (v. 33). The gravity of the transgression appears from the rare
expression: "making Baal-berith their god". Generally, the expression: "worship other Gods" appears in the Bible.[194] In our account,
there is a decision to adopt idol worship and to institute the Baal
cult. The verse explicitly accuses the people, of being ungrateful to

---

[193] See for instance: Soggin, *Judges*, p. 161. Several scholars consider these verses
to be the beginning of the Abimelech account. See for instance: Jobling, *The Sense
of Biblical Narrative*, pp. 67–68; Amit, *The Book of Judges*, pp. 100–102. According to
this opinion, the verses are composed according to the model in the Book of Judges
at the beginning of an account, 3:7; 12; 4:2. However, unlike other accounts in the
Book, here the description of the transgression includes details of Gideon's acts and
the negative attitude of the people towards him. According to Budde (*Das Buch der
Richter*, p. 68), Moore (*Judges*, p. 234) and Burney (*The Book of Judges*, p. 266), these
verses are a description of Israel's apostasy and the ingratitude towards Gideon's
house (8:33$_b$, 35$_a$), which are reported in detail in the Abimelech account, ch. 9,
and they are placed here instead of in ch. 9 in the form of a conclusion. This
opinion derives from the fact that the Abimelech account is not in keeping with
the Deuteronomistic model in the Book of Judges: transgression, punishment and
deliverance. Therefore, the account was omitted by the Deuteronomist and instead
he introduced a summary of the account in vv. 33–35. At a later stage, the Abimelech
account was reintroduced in the book. However, as the verses are now composed,
it must be said that the intention of the account is to show that the problems
appearing in the Abimelech account lie already before this in the end of the Gideon
account.
[194] See for instance: Deut 4:28; 7:4; 8:19; 11:16; Judg 2:19.

God who delivered them from their enemies: "The Israelites did not
remember the LORD their God, who had rescued them from the
hand of all their enemies on every side" (8:34). However, the accusation is not only ingratitude towards God, but also towards Gideon:
"and they did not show loyalty to the house of Jerubbaal, that is,
Gideon, in return for all the good that he had done to Israel" (8:35).
Hence, the verses seem to exempt Gideon from blame. This is not
however the case.

Firstly, the name "Jerubbaal" again appears here. If the attitude
in these verses were only positive, probably only the name "Gideon"
would appear. The artificial combination of both names of Gideon that do not appear in a habitual syntactic sequence—עם ביח
ירבעל גדעון ("to the house of Jerubbaal, that is, Gideon")—shows
that these verses seek to assess him both as Gideon[195] (as we have
already seen), and as Jerubbaal (as we will now discuss).

After Gideon's death it is said: "the *Israelites* relapsed and *prostituted themselves* with the Baals" (וישובו בני ישראל ויזנו אחרי הבעלים)
(8:33). In Gideon's lifetime the people went astray after the ephod:
"and *all Israel prostituted themselves* to it there" (ויזנו כל ישראל אחריו שם)
(8:27). The worship of the ephod is not as serious as the Baal worship. The worship of the ephod was worship of God, but with a
forbidden cult. The Baal worship is idolatry. However, the use of
the word זנה (prostituted) in both places is significant even though
it does not refer to the same transgression or the same seriousness
of transgression. The use of the same verb in two completely different
transgressions creates a relationship and continuity between them.
The intention is to determine that the roots of the Baal transgression are latent precisely in the worship of the ephod established by
Gideon. Before the deliverance from Midian, and before Gideon
came into the picture only some of the people worshiped the Baal-
berith. Why precisely after Gideon's deliverance did all the people
worship the Baal? The answer to this question is related to what
happened in the meantime—Gideon's actions. Gideon delivered the

---

[195] On the other hand Burney (*The Book of Judges*, p. 266) argues that the name
Gideon is used here so that we will know that he is known by both names (see
also: Moore, *Judges*, p. 236), but it is not clear why the narrator would bother to
explain this precisely now at the end of the account.

people and united them around him. However, rather than bringing the people to worship God, he united them around his personality and the cult of the ephod. These verses leave the impression
that when Gideon disappeared, that unity obtained by Gideon in
his life continued after his death, and the orientation that commenced
with worship of the ephod continued to worship of the Baal. In this
way, the Bible blames Gideon who was the one who turned the people away from God and brought them to worship the ephod, and
when he died the people turned to Baal worship.

Another hint of the blame laid on Gideon by these verses can be
found in the juxtaposition of two sentences that are syntactically
exceptional. The giving of the name Abimelech by Gideon is worded:

וישם את שמו אבימלך ("and he named him Abimelech") (8:31)

The straying after the Baal is worded:

וישימו להם בעל ברית לאלהים ("making Baal-berith their god") (8:33).

In our separate discussion of these two verses we saw that the use
of the verb שים in both cases is exceptional, and this use shows the
intention behind the act. The giving of the name "Abimelech" by
Gideon indicates an intention existing in the meaning of the name,
and the going astray after the Baal is presented as a conscious decision to worship another god. The relation between the two sentences
reinforces Gideon's responsibility for the people's transgression. He
led the people astray through his wish to elevate his status, and after
his death they took a further step in the same direction.

As indicated above, in the other judge accounts, it is not said that
the people again went astray. In the other accounts, this is indicated
subsequently, in the following judge account. The Ehud account ends
with eighty years of peace after Ehud's victory. It is in the exposition of the Deborah account that it is reported that Israel again did
evil (4:1): "The Israelites again did what was evil in the sight of the
LORD". The Deborah account ends with the destruction of the
Canaanites: ". . . until they destroyed King Jabin of Canaan" (4:24),
and with forty years of peace after the victory: "And the land had
rest forty years" (5:31). Again it is only at the beginning of the
Gideon account that the reader learns that this situation changed
after the forty years of peace: "The Israelites did what was evil in
the sight of the LORD" (6:1). The Gideon account does not end with

forty years of peace, but with Israel's transgression after Gideon's death.[196] This would therefore seem to mean that the serious transgression that commenced after Gideon's death is a result of Gideon's failure. The aim of the verses is to establish that Gideon's personal motives, which are at the basis of building of the ephod, and which appear also in other actions in the second part of the Gideon account, are what ultimately led the people to again do evil in God's eyes. On the other hand, the impression received in the judge accounts until now, and from the theological introduction of the book, is that the fact that the people again did evil in God's eyes after the deaths of Ehud and of Deborah is due to the disappearance of the leaders and the forgetting of God's deliverance after the death of the judges. Even though this is the explicit explanation of Israel's transgression after Gideon's death, the verses also indicate that Gideon himself was at fault.

15. *The Structure and the Meaning of the Gideon Account*

The Gideon account is clearly divided into two almost equal parts, according to the structure of the plot and the nature of Gideon's character. In the first half of the account, Gideon is shown as a sceptic, insecure in his belief in God (until 7:14). Gideon does not trust in God and he also harshly criticizes God initially; subsequently he doubts as to whether God will help Israel or not. There is no parallel to Gideon's personality in the Book or Judges or in the Bible in its entirety. There is no other example of a person chosen by God and expressing such fierce doubt towards God. The turning

---

[196] Therefore, Burney (*The Book of Judges*, p. 266) is mistaken in considering the information given here to be a normal manifestation in the Book of Judges, i.e. that after the death of every judge the people transgressed again. What is unique in the Gideon account is that this fact is related in the framework of the actual account. This of course is in light of our assumption, which is controversial, regarding the question of whether these verses are part of the Gideon account or part of the Abimelech account. It is also possible that vv. 33–35 serve both as the conclusion of the Gideon account and the introduction of the Abimelech account, a phenomenon that Zakovich calls a suspended conclusion. Y. Zakovitch, *The Life of Samson (Judges 13–16): A Critical-Literary Analysis*, Jerusalem 1982 (Hebrew), p. 72, and note 160a there. Such a phenomenon is found in Judges 13:25, which constitutes a conclusion of the account of Samson's birth but also anticipates the future, the story of Samson's heroic acts. For a further example see *ibid.*, p. 120.

point in Gideon's personality is the Midianite's dream, after which Gideon's doubts completely disappear, and for good (from 7:15). However, even in the second part of the account Gideon's personality is unstable, but in a completely different area. In the second part of the account, Gideon's behaviour is inconsistent. He sometimes seems to have the good of the people and the will of God at heart, even at the expense of his personal benefit; at the same time, however, he also behaves in the opposite way. Sometimes he acts out of personal motives to the detriment of the people and even of God.[197]

Let us outline the expressions of the pendulum motif in Gideon's personality in both parts of the account. When God's angel appears to Gideon to commission him as leader, Gideon appears very estranged from God. In his reply to the angel's greeting "The LORD is with you" (6:12) he makes harsh accusations against God, verging on apostasy: "is the LORD with us" (6:13). Gideon's doubts continue and he demands proof that it is God who is speaking with him: "give me a sign that it is You who are speaking to me" (6:17). The extremely detailed description of the angel's appearance to Gideon is designed to show the very great extent of the estrangement from God. At the end of this encounter Gideon arrives at clear recognition that it is God who is speaking with him, and like the patriarchs he builds an altar to God as an expression of the relationship created: "So Gideon built there an altar to the LORD and called it Adonai-shalom" (6:24).

Gideon's relation to God is now expressed practically when he prepares to carry out God's command to destroy the altar of the Baal: "So Gideon took ten of his servants and did as the LORD had told him" (6:27$_a$). However, immediately there is a regression. Gideon is gripped by fear and does not carry out the mission in daytime: "but as he was afraid to do it by day, on account of his father's household and the townspeople, he did it by night" (6:27$_b$).

---

[197] Crüsemann shows the contrast between the figures of Gideon and Abimelech, and presents Gideon as a positive character in contrast to the negative character of Abimelech. Gideon saves Israel and Abimelech wreaks destruction on Israel. F. Crüsemann, *Der Widerstand gegen das Königtum* (Wissenschaftliche Monographien zum Alten und Neuen Testament, 49, Neukrichen Vluyn: Neukrichenre Verlag, 1978), p. 42. Although Crüsemann effectively shows the contrasts between the figures, Gideon's character is complex and the account's message likewise is not in the positive presentation of Gideon's character.

After the destruction of the Baal, Gideon organizes an army, in order to combat the Midianites. He goes into battle in God's name and the verse attests to a special relationship between Gideon and God: "The spirit of the LORD enveloped Gideon" (6:34). With this divine inspiration he is able to mobilize many soldiers to fight with him (6:34–35). However, this attitude is again replaced by Gideon's doubt as to whether God will indeed assist him against the Midianites, and he asks God for signs in this respect. Gideon's doubt is not resolved after God carries out the first sign of the fleece for him and he asks for a second sign of the fleece (vv. 36–40).

Gideon's oscillation from one extreme to the other does not end at this stage. God now initiates the next delay and commands Gideon to reduce the number of his soldiers, and in a long process, Gideon's army is reduced from thirty-two thousand soldiers to a small army of three hundred soldiers only (7:1–8). Gideon's doubting reaction is almost immediate. Gripped by fear, he does not respond positively to God's words to go and fight against Midian (7:9–11), even though God has told him that He will be with him (v. 9). There is no other judge to whom God directly promises divine assistance as He does to Gideon, and there is no one other than Gideon who expresses so many doubts in God.[198]

Because of his fear and his doubts as regards God's promise to be with him, Gideon chooses to go down into the Midianite camp as God has suggested, and there he expects to hear something that will strengthen him. When he goes down and hears the Midianite's dream and its interpretation that Gideon will vanquish the Midianites with God's assistance, he is strengthened and returns to hearten his army: "Get up! The LORD has given the Midianite camp into your hands!" (7:15). From this point onwards Gideon will not doubt God again or the assistance that God has promised him. There is no further mention of doubts in the rest of the account, and the oscillation between belief and doubt ends here.

Gideon prepares for combat, and although he no longer expresses any doubt, he is still characterized by oscillation. Henceforth he swings between noble behaviour in which he makes concessions in

---

[198] Klein, *The Triumph of Irony in the Book of Judges*, p. 68; Exum, "The Center Cannot Hold", p. 416.

favour of national and divine interests, and self-interested and ego-centric behaviour.[199]

The noble behaviour is expressed clearly in the confrontation with the Ephraimites (8:1). In his response to the Ephraimite claim, Gideon exalts their contribution to the victory over the Midianites while playing down his own deeds. He averts a confrontation within Israel at the price of making light of his own actions, and does so out of concern for the national interest (8:2–3). It is because of this concern that Gideon was appointed leader despite his doubts in God, as shown in his response at a national level to the words of the angel of God (6:13).

His behaviour is in complete contrast in his confrontation with the men of Succoth and of Penuel. Here he takes vengeance because of their refusal to assist him and to accord him the honour that he sees as his due (8:15–17). The verses expand on this point and stress that his behaviour in this case derives from the priority given to personal interests over the national interest. Gideon's concern for his honour and his status appears in the description of the execution of the Midianite kings (8:18–21).

Gideon's self-interested behaviour is manifest in the many details that underscore his concern for his status as leader and the numerous regal characteristics mentioned in the descriptions of Gideon's confrontation with the men of Succoth and of Penuel on one hand, and the Midianite kings on the other. However, this is not the last change in Gideon's personality in the account. After Gideon's adoption of several regal characteristics, the reader is not very surprised to hear that the people ask Gideon to institute a monarchy that will continue subsequently through his descendants (8:22). However, Gideon vehemently refuses, and instead of thinking of himself, he expresses in one short sentence one of the most impressive theological axioms in the Bible: "I will not rule over you myself, nor shall my son rule over you; the LORD shall rule over you" (8: 23). Even though the way was paved for Gideon to establish his leadership, he does not "take up the gauntlet" due to considerations based on God's status among the people and not on Gideon's status. Again Gideon nobly sets aside his own wishes, in order to take the correct

---

[199] On the contrasts between Gideon's actions in this part of the account, see: Klein, *The Triumph of Irony in the Book of Judges*, p. 63.

and proper action for the good of the people and in God's eyes, and not because he does not want to be king.

The Gideon account does not end with this noble response and again, like a pendulum, Gideon swings back, expressing his own personal wishes. While refusing to accept the monarchy, he initiates building of an ephod, which is none other than a monument to perpetuate his status within the people. He sets this monument up in his hometown (8:24–26). This act leads the people to turn aside from God. Gideon's victories do not lead the people to recognize God's sovereignty, as Gideon himself asserted they should; rather the people go astray after the ephod that represents Gideon: "Gideon made an ephod of it and set it up in his own town, in Ophrah, and all Israel prostituted themselves to it there, and it became a snare to Gideon and his household" (8:27). Although Gideon refused to be king for altruistic reasons, in fact he behaved like a king for egocentric reasons. Ultimately, because of this behaviour, the people who strayed after Gideon and the ephod while Gideon was alive then strayed after the Baal after Gideon's death (8:33–35).

Throughout the account, Gideon is characterized by oscillating behaviour; in all the stages of the account, his actions are contradictory and he constantly passes from one extreme to the other. In the first part of the account, Gideon goes from doubt to trust in God, whereas in the second part, the account goes from deeds based on national and altruistic considerations to acts based on egocentric interests prejudicial to the people.[200]

---

[200] As indicated above, scholars of the documentary school divided the Gideon account into two different sources: the first part ch. 6:1–8:3 and the second part 8:4–21. The two parts differ on many points but in general the first description according to this hypothesis is a fictitious description and the second a realistic description. On this see: Wellhausen, *Prolegomena to the History of Ancient Israel*, pp. 237–243, *Die Composition des Hexateuchs und der historischen Bücher des alten Testaments*, pp. 223–227; Moore, *Judges*, pp. 174–177; Burney, *The Book of Judges*, pp. 182–183. On the other hand, several scholars noticed changes in presentation of Gideon's character in both parts of the account, but the division of the account into two parts differs from one scholar to another, and there is no consensus on the definitions of the character in the two parts. In my opinion, the explanations cited below are inexact since they do not take into account all the details in the account. According to Webb (*The Book of Judges*, p. 151) the first part is characterized by the fact that Gideon does not participate in the campaign willingly, he does not rely on himself but on God only. The war that he wages is a holy war in which the victory is not his personal achievement but a gift from God. On the other hand, in the second part of the account, there is no indication of God's involvement, and the motifs of

How can this oscillating behaviour be explained? His swings of faith from doubt to trust in the first part of the account are intellectual and emotional. They are certainly related to Israel's inferior status in relation to Midian. Gideon's origin also certainly contributed greatly. His home is not a home where God is worshipped, and nor is his town. In Gideon's home his father occupied a central role in Baal worship, and the residents of his town were devout Baalists. After the angel appeared to Gideon and commissioned him as leader to deliver Israel, Gideon underwent a transition. It is not difficult to understand that this change in his world-view did not occur instantly. He underwent a long religious and intellectual process before being convinced of the new direction adopted.

Gideon's transitions in the second part of the account between altruistic and egocentric actions are more at the psychological level. Basically, Gideon has an altruistic approach, and he was appointed because of his great concern for the people's situation. After he assumed the office of deliverer, and began to fight against the Midianites, he began to attach more and more importance to his own status. We found a similar problem in the case of King Saul. Saul initially was humble and shy; after being anointed, he returned home as if he had not received such an elevated and important office (1 Sam 10:22, 26). However, after he assumed office, this humility was replaced by egocentric attachment to the office, manifestly to the prejudice of the people. This change in Saul's attitude to his office was expressed in his refusal to accept Samuel's decree

---

holy war are completely absent. The victories in this part are due to Gideon's strong character and his tactical ability. Amit (*The Book of Judges*, pp. 232–246) also considers that the Gideon account is divided into two parts; the first part highlights God's involvement in the events through supernatural signs, whereas the second part deals with leadership problems. The aim of the first part is to lead to the conclusion that Israel's deliverance depends on God's will, and Gideon is only his emissary. The second part ends with the presentation of two opinions concerning leadership. The people wish for an orderly monarchic rule and not the judge-deliverer leadership system, whereas Gideon expresses the view that human leadership is temporary and God's rule is permanent. In opposition to Amit's approach, it should be noted that the supernatural signs and phenomena are merely a response to the spiritual situation of the people, and essentially the aim in this part is to highlight Gideon's doubts and his inconstancy. For some reason Amit did not consider this matter also in her comprehensive discussion of Gideon's character in the first part of the account (pp. 238–239). Since Amit did not correctly define the focus of each part, she also did not discern the unique pendulum structure in each of the parts (pp. 228–229).

that God had rejected him (1 Sam 15); in his cruel slaughter of the men of Nov, the city of the priests, because he suspected them of assisting David (1 Sam 22:9–23), and in his ceaseless pursuit of David in order to kill him. A like process occurred in the case of Gideon. Although he was modest and humble when he assumed office, we witness an accelerated process of egocentric conduct. However, unlike Saul whose personality becomes egocentric, in Gideon the two conflicting lines of conduct exist simultaneously. He became egocentric but at the same time his concern for the good of the people did not disappear. These two characteristics serve together in Gideon's personality; each trait is expressed alternately. Gideon still cares about the people and he has not forgotten his role as leader, but the office of leadership has an impact on him and already he cannot separate his impulses from his actions.

Gideon's personality is certainly one of the most fascinating and colourful in the Book of Judges. What is the object of such a description of his character? The above analysis shows that the main parts of the account, which contain far more details than other judge accounts, focus on the nature of Gideon's personality as oscillating between belief and doubt in the first part; and in the second part, once his personality stabilizes in his belief in God and the ability to be His loyal emissary, a second oscillation commences between expression of his altruistic tendencies and his egocentric tendencies. The answer to the question posed is also the answer to the question of the aim of the Gideon account.

The main aim of the Gideon account is to show the two parameters by which an Israelite leader is examined.[201] The first parameter is the extent of his loyalty to God, and it is expressed in the

---

[201] Many scholars hold that the main meaning of the account is to describe Israel's disloyalty during the time of Gideon, which is described in very great detail in this account. See for instance: Webb, *The Book of Judges*, pp. 156–157. In Polzin's opinion (*Moses and the Deuteronomist*, p. 171) the object of the account is to show how Israel, even when they have been delivered by God, swing between loyalty to God and worship of other gods. The irony in the account in his opinion is that the result of the deliverance by God through Gideon is the passage from partial to total worship of the Baal-berith. Bluedorn (*Yahweh Versus Baalism*, in many places, e.g. p. 51) believes that the main aim of the Gideon and Abimelech accounts is to present God's supremacy as opposed to the Baal. However, even though this subject occupies a central place in the Gideon account it does not make all the other parts of the account disappear. Marais (*Representation in Old Testament Narrative Texts*, pp. 113–118) oversimplifies in claiming that the aim of the Gideon and Abimelech accounts is to present a criticism of the monarchy. The complex picture of Gideon's

first part of the Gideon account. In the first part of the account, Gideon undergoes a process of building a relationship with and belief in God. Until he absolutely recognizes that it is in God's hands to bring him victory in the war he cannot commence the campaign. In this process Gideon had to deal with and combat the belief in the Baal before he could assume his office; in this way it will become clear that his future achievements are a result of divine assistance.

The leader's personality is the second parameter by which the measure of his suitability and success in office is examined. Gideon is chosen as deliverer because of his concern for the plight of the people, as already seen above in Gideon's reply to the angel's greeting (6:13).

The second part of the Gideon account deals with the personality aspects of Gideon's suitability for the office that he occupies. This part of the account shows how Gideon's character, which oscillates between altruistic and egocentric tendencies, led the people astray, and resulted in a negative evaluation of Gideon as leader. Gideon's suitability for the office of leader in the field of his relations with God, and even his initial suitability for the office because of his personality, does not guarantee his success; ultimately, his main consideration was his own personal benefit.

*

The analysis of the Gideon account and of Gideon's personality has implications as regards the theory of Biblical criticism. In classical Bible study inconsistencies and tensions constitute an indication of the complex composition of the Biblical text from different and conflicting sources. In new literary studies, that interpret the work on its own merits ignoring the process of the growth of the composition, very frequently inconsistencies and tensions in the account are ignored, on the assumption that these features are part of a

---

personality stands in opposition to both Kariv's presentation of Gideon as a perfect and exemplary figure, and to the assertion made by van Midden that Gideon is not a hero, and that he leads Israel into evil. See: A. Kariv, *The Seven Pillars of the Bible: Essays of Biblical People and Biblical Ideas*, Tel Aviv 1971, pp. 61–66 (Hebrew); P. J. van Midden, "Gideon", J. W. Dyk, et al. (eds.), *The Rediscovery of the Hebrew Bible* Amsterdamse Cahiers voor Exegese van de Bijbel en zijn Tradities, Supplement Series 1), Maastricht 1999, pp. 51–67.

discipline that is separate from the literary questions under investigation. Between these two orientations I wish to present a third possibility. In a study of the account of the crossing of the Jordan (Josh 3–4), I examined the application of diachronic and synchronic approaches in analysis of the account. It emerged that the attempts to uncover the sources of the account did not properly solve the inconsistencies discussed by scholars. On the other hand, harmonistic solutions of inconsistencies and tensions in the text by scholars, adopting a synchronic approach, seem forced. In the aforesaid work I argued that the inconsistencies and repetitions have a purpose in shaping the meaning of the account. Sometimes the authors of the Bible wished to express a multidimensional idea presented from different points of view, and to these ends different stages of the account are presented alongside each other, expressing each time a different angle. Hence, precisely the observation of inconsistencies and repetitions can lead the reader to a multidimensional view and accurate comprehension of the account.[202]

In analysis of the Gideon account, it emerged that another type of tension in the text led scholars to deal with the sources of the text. However, I showed that in these cases too these are intentional tensions constituting an integral part of shaping of the meaning of the account. The inconsistency in Gideon's acts, behaviour, world-view and thoughts led scholars to find different sources in the account. Thus, for instance, there is a contradiction between Gideon's basic opposition to the monarchy for theological reasons and his desire not to prejudice God's sovereignty, and the fact that he builds an ephod and leads the people astray after the cult of the ephod. Scholars both with a diachronic or with a synchronic orientation, all according to the tools at their disposal in the discipline that they adopted, tried to solve this contradiction so that there would be no inconsistency in Gideon's actions. Some attributed the different actions to different sources, or omitted one verse or another and thus created a smooth account without inconsistencies. Others unified Gideon's actions, either by explaining that Gideon did not really object to the monarchy, or in fact did not lead the people astray. While the methods of the two schools are completely different, they are based on

---

[202] See: Assis, *The Literary Structure of the Conquest Narrative in the Book of Joshua (Chs. 1–11) and its Meaning*, pp. 139 ff.

a shared assumption: there can be no inconsistencies in the text and the exegesist must remove them in the course of his exegesis. A third possibility is to leave the account as it is with its inconsistencies and tensions. In the above analysis, I explained that Gideon contradicts himself and behaves inconsistently. If this possibility is correct, any attempt to achieve harmony in Gideon's personality and actions, either by removing "inconvenient" verses from the text or by "sophisticated" interpretations, misses the point of the account. It is the exegesist's duty primarily to examine how inconsistencies, repetitions and tensions in the text shape its meaning. It is the understanding of the contradiction in Gideon's personality that revealed to us the ideology and the aim of the account.

16. *The Structure of the Book of Judges and Its Meaning*

The structure and meaning of the Gideon account shed light on the meaning of the Book of Judges as a whole.[203] The Book of Judges contains seven accounts describing the actions of seven leaders: Othniel (3:7–11), Ehud (3:12–30), Deborah (chap. 4), Gideon (chaps. 6–8), Abimelech (chap. 9), Jephthah (chaps. 10–12:7) and Samson (chaps. 13–16). The first three judges—Othniel, Ehud and Deborah—are positive untarnished characters, both as regards their conduct and their personality. In contrast, the last three figures, Abimelech, Jephthah and Samson, are problematic. What they have in common is that they are focused on their personal benefit, each to a different extent and in each account the gravity of the results differs. Abimelech kills his brothers in order to be king, and he wages a bloody war in order to retain sovereignty. In agreeing to be commander of the army in the war against Ammon, Jephthah is motivated by a wish to be head over all the inhabitants of Gilead, and he institutes a savage civil war against the tribe of Ephraim since they did not offer

---

[203] Malamat attempted to explain the order of the judge accounts according to a geographical principle, from south to north. A. Malamat, "השופט המושיע כמנהיג בתקופה השופטים" *Types of Leadership in the Biblical Period*, Jerusalem, 1973, p. 13 (Hebrew). Zakovitch considers that the Book of Judges is ordered by associative links between every two adjacent episodes. Y. Zakovitch, "The Associative Arrangement of the Book of Judges and Its Use for the Recognition of Stages in Formation of the Book", A. Rofé and Y. Zakovitch and (eds.), *Isac Leo Seeligmann Volume: Essays on the Bible and Ancient World*, I, Jerusalem 1983 (Hebrew), pp. 164–183.

him the honour he considered his due. Samson's actions against the
Philistines are revenge for the offence to him; he does not act to
deliver the people, and in fact does not deliver the people at all.
On the contrary, the people suffer more from the Philistine oppression because of his acts, and when the tribe of Judah complains he
explains his personal motives: "He replied, "As they did to me, so
I have done to them" (15:11).

Personal considerations do not play any role in the actions of the
first three judges. They deliver the people from Israel's enemies and
make no personal demands. Othniel delivers the people from the
Aramites, even though the Aramite oppression did not affect him or
his tribe since he dwelt in Judah in the south of the country. Ehud
acts alone, placing himself at great personal risk. Both these men
neither seek nor receive office or any other personal benefit after
they deliver the people. This is also true of Deborah, whose account
anticipates the Gideon account. Deborah is a prophetess and she
appoints Barak to deliver Israel; he agrees to take part in the campaign only if Deborah is present alongside him. Likewise, the angel
of the Lord commissions Gideon and he expresses doubts. Despite
the relation between Barak and Gideon, in the Gideon account the
angel who appoints Gideon is a marginal figure, while in Judges 4–5
Deborah is the central figure, the figure of the judge (5:7). It is her
character as a leader that must be compared with Gideon's character. Deborah is presented as an untarnished figure. In the Song
of Deborah the main subject is the willingness of the different tribes
to volunteer for the good of the people. These are positive personalities also in their relation to God. Deborah is a prophetess and all
her actions are in the name of God; Ehud acts out of belief that
God delivers his enemies into his hands and it is with this statement
that he appeals to the people (3:28). The problem presented in this
part of the book is the disloyalty to God after the death of these
leaders. Therefore, the three accounts that present positive leadership both in relation to God and to the people are relatively short
accounts, and on the other hand, the last three accounts that present problematic figures are long, and show the nature of the problems in detail. The Gideon account, which centralizes both religious
problems and leadership problems, is the longest account.[204]

---

[204] For another explanation of the place of the Gideon account at the centre of
the book and the length of this account, see: Amit, *The Book of Judges*, pp. 262–266.

Thus the figures in the Book of Judges are presented in a symmetrical structure: the first three judges whose attitude towards God was positive, and the last three judges whose main consideration was furthering of their own interests. At the centre is the Gideon account that is divided into two parts. The first part corresponds to the theme of the first three judges, and the second to the theme of the three personalities in the second part of the book. The first part of the Gideon account focuses on the question of Gideon's belief in God, and this in parallel to the first protagonists of the book; the second part of the Gideon account deals with Gideon's inconstancy, sometimes concerned for the people and sometimes for himself, and this part precedes the description of the actions of the three protagonists who follow him.[205]

The introduction and the conclusion of the Book of Judges also correspond to this structure. The introduction deals with religious problems: the failure to expel the Canaanites (1:1–2:5) and the failure to eradicate an idolatrous cult (2:6–3:6), and it constitutes a clear introduction to the entire book. However, this subject is further highlighted precisely in the accounts of the first three judges. On the other hand, the conclusion of the Book of Judges (chaps. 17–21) deals with leadership problems and constitutes a continuation and closing of the description of the leadership problems as described in the accounts of the three protagonists described in the second part of the book (chapter 17 that deals with the construction of idolatry by Micah is in the framework of the criticism of lack of leadership: "In those days there was no king in Israel; all the people did what was right in their own eyes", 17,6). Thus a structure is received that can be described through the following schema:

---

[205] Several scholars have noted that the book has a symmetrical structure, see for instance: Gooding, "The Composition of the Book of Judges", pp. 70–79. This structure was espoused by J. P. Tanner, "The Gideon Narrative as the Focal Point of Judges", *Bibliothea Sacra* 149 (1992), pp. 149–150. However, Tanner suggests another structure for the Gideon account. On the structure of the Book of Judges, see also: Amit, *The Book of Judges*, pp. 118–119. Dewitt's opinion that the Book of Judges is made up of a chiastic structure with the Gideon account at the centre is farfetched. D. S. Dewitt, *The Jephthah Traditions: A Rhetorical and Literary Study in the Deuteronomistic History*, Diss., Andrews University 1987, pp. 261–313. Williams' opinion on the structure of the book is also improbable. J. G. Williams, "The Structure of Judges 2:6–16:31", *JSOT* 49 (1991), pp. 77–86.

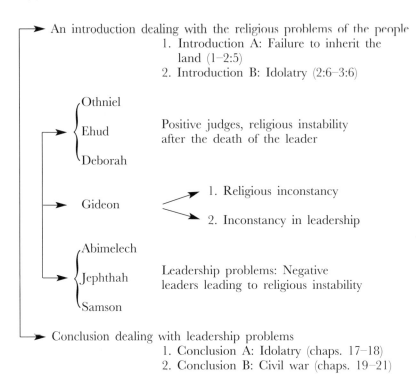

An introduction dealing with the religious problems of the people
>   1. Introduction A: Failure to inherit the
     land (1–2:5)
>   2. Introduction B: Idolatry (2:6–3:6)

Othniel

Ehud   Positive judges, religious instability
              after the death of the leader

Deborah

Gideon   1. Religious inconstancy

              2. Inconstancy in leadership

Abimelech

Jephthah   Leadership problems: Negative
              leaders leading to religious instability

Samson

Conclusion dealing with leadership problems
>   1. Conclusion A: Idolatry (chaps. 17–18)
>   2. Conclusion B: Civil war (chaps. 19–21)

CHAPTER TWO

THE ABIMELECH ACCOUNT (9)

The Abimelech account is preceded by a passage that deals with transgression (8:33–35), and contains details related to the Abimelech account. In the structure of the Book of Judges, the description of transgression is generally followed by the deliverance by the judge. Hence, the author wished to create the expectation that Abimelech would deliver Israel. The Abimelech account, however, is not a deliverance account. It differs from all the deliverer accounts in the Book of Judges, and does not correspond to their cyclical pattern, as outlined at the beginning of the Book (2:11–23). The Abimelech account is preceded by the information that the people again abandoned God and worshiped another god (8:33), but there is no account of punishment by God in the form of an oppressor who fights against Israel. Unlike the other protagonists in the book, Abimelech does not deliver the people.[1] What then is the function of the account in

---

[1] Because of the fact that the Abimelech account is not in the historiosophic framework of the Book of Judges, as presented at the beginning of the book (2:11–23), several scholars concluded that it was inserted by a late redactor. See: Budde, *Das Buch der Richter*, p. 50; Moore, *Judges*, p. 238; Burney, *The Book of Judges*, p. 268; Cooke, *The Book of Judges*, p. 98. Soggin (*Judges*, pp. 163–164) considers that, unlike the other judge accounts, this account is not in the Deuteronomistic framework and does not deal with theological aspects. He therefore concluded that it is based on historical material such as chronicles and annals and its main importance is in the historical aspects. For historical conclusions from the account, see *ibid.*, pp. 169–170. On the other hand, Abramsky ("Abimelech's Leadership—King, Chief and Ruler", pp. 163–176) sees Abimelech as Israel's deliverer from the oppression of Canaanites living in Shechem (see p. 165). In his opinion, the author did not call him deliverer because of the circumstances of his accession to the kingship and because of the murder of his brothers. However, in the account there is no mention of the people's plight and of a confrontation with Shechem. Likewise, nowhere in the account is it indicated that the war was between groups of different peoples. Even if the Bible did not wish to emphasize that Abimelech was a deliverer there is no satisfactory explanation as to why it also concealed the nature of the war described in the account. In Abramsky's opinion, the information that "after Abimelech there arose to save Israel Tola the son of Puah" (10:1) is evidence of the deliverance by Abimelech. Similarly, see also Kimchi on 10:1. However, the meaning of the verse is not necessarily that Abimelech delivered Israel, but that Tola delivered Israel and that he succeeded Abimelech. Amit (*The Book of Judges*, pp. 40–42) sees the Abimelech account as an element of the punishment after the idolatry described prior to the

the Book of Judges and how does it fit into the framework of the
other deliverance accounts in the book?[2]

The Abimelech account is the continuation of the Gideon account.[3]
It commences with reference to information about Abimelech given
at the end of the Gideon account (8:31). Abimelech's desire to be king
derives from the fact that he considers that Gideon was king; the question now is which of his sons will succeed him. The monarchy issue
was raised explicitly when the people asked Gideon to rule (8:22), and
Gideon adopted royal manners prior to and above all after this request.
Abimelech, in his character and actions, to a very great extent recalls
his father, whether by similarity or by contrast. The connections

---

Gideon account. She sees the Tola son of Puah account as the deliverance account.
This explanation seems very unrealistic. Amit seems prepared to ascribe improbable meanings to passages as long as this explains the redactional layer. Heller considers that the account corresponds to the emphasis of the Book of Judges. R. L.
Heller, "The Disappearing Deity and the Wages of Sin: The Theology of Divine
Retribution in the Books of Judges," *Berkeley at Yale* 1 (1999), pp. 10–13. The account
describes Israel's oppression by Abimelech, but this account is presented from the
oppressor's viewpoint. The killing of Abimelech by the woman at Thebez was the
deliverance, and the information that Abimelech ruled over Israel for three years
is not parallel to the years of peace after the Judge but the years of oppression at
the beginning of the judge accounts (3:8, 14; 4:3; 6:1).

[2] Malamat (*History of Biblical Israel*, pp. 168–170) considers that the Abimelech
account was included in the Book of Judges in order to present an anti-judge model,
which is the antithesis of the charismatic judge. In Marais' opinion (*Representation in
Old Testament Narrative Texts*, pp. 113–118) the aim of the account is to present an
anti-monarchic view. Similarly, see: M. Weinfeld, "Zion and Jerusalem as Religious
and Political Capital: Ideology and Utopia", R. E. Friedman (ed.), *The Poet and the
Historian: Essays in Literary and Historical Biblical Criticism* (Harvard Semitic Studies),
Chicago 1983, p. 86. In Klein's opinion (*The Triumph of Irony in the Book of Judges*,
p. 78) the meaning of the account is to warn Israel not to enter into relations with
non-Israelites. Abimelech the son of a concubine from Shechem does not deliver
the Israelites, but kills them. In Boogaart's opinion, the object of the account is to
present the idea of retribution. T. A. Boogaart, "Stone for Stone: Retribution in
the Story of Abimelech and Shechem", *JSOT* 32 (1985), pp. 43–56. O'Brien considers that the Abimelech account is the culmination of the Book of Judges. This
account relates an attempt to change the leadership system in Israel and its failure
because the change was not instituted by God. M. A. O'Brien, *The Deuteronomistic
History Hypothesis: A Reassessment* (Orbis Biblicus et Orientalis), Göttingen 1989, p. 31.
Although this insight is correct, we will see below that the account discusses the
attributes of the leader who is suited to rule over Israel. In Gray's opinion (*Joshua,
Judges, Ruth*, p. 316), the purpose of the Abimelech account is to criticize the monarchic institution. For a summary of the research into the Abimelech account and its
meaning, see: Bluedorn, *Yahweh Versus Baalism*, pp. 15–50. On humour, ambiguity
and wordplay in the Abimelech account, see: A. D. Crown, "A Reinterpretation of
Judges IX in the Light of its Humour", *Abr-Nahrain* 3 (1961–62), pp. 90–98.

[3] See also: Kaufmann, *Sefer Shoftim*, p. 195.

between the two accounts show that the Abimelech account does
not stand alone, but is part of the Gideon account, and it is for this
reason that it does not correspond to the judge-deliverer account
model. The two accounts are closely related, both thematically and in
style and literary structure, and it is in this context that the significance
of the account must be sought.

1. *The Structure of the Abimelech Account*

The Abimelech account is clearly divided into three parts:

1. Abimelech's accession to kingship (9:1–6) = transgression
2. The Jotham fable (9:7–21) = rebuke
3. The disagreement between Abimelech and the citizens of Shechem,
   and Abimelech's defeat (vv. 22–57) = punishment

This structure denotes the object of the account. The first part is the
shortest; it describes Abimelech's accession to the throne. After murdering his brothers, Abimelech planned and worked to become king in
cooperation with the citizens of Shechem. In the second part, Abimelech's brother Jotham opposes Abimelech as king, forecasting a dispute
between the citizens of Shechem and Abimelech. The third part is
the longest part of the account. It describes the fulfilment of Jotham's
prediction, with Abimelech's defeat following a dispute with the citizens of Shechem.[4] The object of the account is to present Abimelech's
rule in a negative light. It does not deal at all with a description of
the three years of his reign, but with a description of its rise and
fall. In our study of the account, we must examine the nature of this
negative perspective. Does it represent opposition to the monarchic
institution in general or opposition to Abimelech's reign?

---

[4] Therefore, I disagree with Fritz's assertion that Jotham's words are unneces-
sary for an understanding of the plot development. V. Fritz, "Abimelech und Sichem
in Jdc. IX", *VT* 32 (1982), p. 132. According to Fritz, the Jotham account is a late
addition that sought to present the account as a criticism of the monarchy. For a
structural analysis of the Abimelech account, see: J. P. Fokkelman, "Structural
Remarks on Judges 9 and 19", M. Fishbane and E. Tov (eds.), *"Sha'rei Talmon":
Studies in the Bible, Qumran and the Ancient Near East Presented to Shmaryahu Talmon*,
Winona Lake 1992, pp. 33–40.

2. Abimelech's Accession to Kingship (9·1–6)

The object in the account of Abimelech's kingship is to show his actions negatively, through the contrast between his acts and those of his father Gideon.[5]

> (1) Abimelech son of Jerubbaal went to Shechem to his mother's brothers, and spoke to them and to the whole clan of his mother's family. He said, (2) 'Speak, I pray you, in the ears of all the men of Shechem: Which is better for you, to be ruled by seventy men—by all the sons of Jerubbaal—or to be ruled by one man? And remember, I am your own flesh and blood' (9:1–2).

Abimelech's appeal to the men of Shechem could have begun immediately with a dialogue, as did the appeal of the men of Israel to Gideon: "the men of Israel said to Gideon, 'rule over us'" (8:22). However, here the appeal begins: "Abimelech son of Jerubbaal went to Shechem to his mother's brothers, and spoke to them". In this way, from the outset the account seeks to show Abimelech's efforts to become king.[6] The people asked Gideon to rule. Abimelech, on the other hand, was not asked and acted to seize power for himself. Abimelech does not appeal to his brethren or the men of Ophrah, his father's town, since presumably he knows that he will not obtain his object in this way. He appeals to his mother's family in Shechem. Gideon has seventy sons, and there is no reason why Abimelech should be favoured over his other brothers in Ophrah, even more so in that he is the son of a concubine. Therefore, he goes to his mother's family in Shechem, where he is more likely to receive support. The relationship between Abimelech and the men of Shechem is the only basis for preferring of Abimelech. This is why the family

---

[5] See: Crüsemann, *Der Widerstand gegen das Königtum*, p. 42; U. Simon, "The parable of Jotham (Judges IX, 8–15): The Parable, Its Application and Their Narrative Framework", *Tarbiz* 34 (1964), pp. 30–32 (Hebrew); Amit, *The Book of Judges*, pp. 103–104.

[6] This brusque beginning of the account is intentional. Boling (*Judges*, p. 170) and others (see above n. Error! Bookmark not defined.) wrongly consider this verse to be a direct continuation of 8:31, omitting the redaction's addition in vv. 32–35. Scholars who consider that vv. 33–35 are part of the Abimelech account distort the intention both as regards Gideon and as regards Abimelech. Verses 33–35 describe a transgression and also point an accusing finger at Gideon. The sudden opening of the Abimelech account with וילך presents him immediately at the start of the account as someone only concerned with bringing his wish to rule to fruition.

relationship is emphasised twice in the verse: "Abimelech . . . went . . . *to his mother's brothers . . . and to the whole clan of his mother's family*".

Abimelech asks his relatives in Shechem to persuade the men of Shechem (בעלי שכם), the town leaders,[7] to make him king, and he hints that in exchange for their support he will grant them benefits: "And remember, I am your own flesh and blood". In his persuasive appeal, Abimelech uses sophisticated rhetoric in order to obtain his wish. He presents two possibilities to the men of Shechem, one of which is unreasonable. One possibility is that all seventy of Gideon's sons will rule over them, and the other is that one man will rule over them. Through this presentation of the two possibilities, the men of Shechem are accorded the honoured status of people having the power to decide on the leadership arrangements. However, the decision between the two possibilities is simple; the first possibility is completely unreasonable in contrast with the second. Given that this presentation of the possibilities points to the possibility of making one man king, he immediately reminds them of the family relationship between them. Abimelech's cunning lies in the fact that he omitted a third possibility, that none of Gideon's sons will rule over them.[8] This is exactly the possibility adopted by Gideon: "I will not rule over you myself, nor shall my son rule over you" (8:22).

The object of the first two verses of the account is to show Abimelech's personal interests in ruling. Firstly, the verses show that he intrigues and takes actions to become king. Secondly, he appeals to the men of Shechem who are related to him and not to his other brothers, and he clearly intimates that they will receive benefits in

---

[7] For a discussion of the meaning of the expression בעלי העיר and the distinction between this institution and the institution of the elders, see: A. Altman, "בעלי העיר in the Bible", S. Ettinger et al. (eds.), *Milet: Everyman's University Studies in Jewish History and Culture*, II, Tel-Aviv 1985, pp. 5–33 (Hebrew, English summary, p. V). In his opinion, the בעלי העיר is a group of wealthy men who rule over the town replacing the traditional leadership of the elders.

[8] Abramsky ("Abimelech's Leadership—King, Chief and Ruler", p. 167) and Soggin (*Judges*, p. 160) conclude from Abimelech's words, "Which is better for you, that all the sons of Jerubbaal, who are seventy persons, rule over you", that after Gideon's death his sons seized power by right of inheritance. However, as noted, it is possible that Abimelech's words are merely rhetoric that he uses in order to manipulate the men of Shechem so that they will establish him as king (similarly, see: Amit, *The Book of Judges*, p. 100 n. 75). Moore (*Judges*, p. 241) is also correct in indicating that Abimelech's words do not constitute an in-depth analysis of the advantages of the monarchy vis-à-vis the disadvantages of the patriarchal leadership (as interpreted by Wellhausen).

exchange for their support. Thirdly, in his appeal to the men of
Shechem he also uses rhetorical sophistication so that they will decide
that they want to adopt the possibility of making one man king.

Abimelech's strategy is successful:

> His mother's brothers said all this in his behalf to all the citizens of
> Shechem, and they were won over to Abimelech; for they thought,
> 'He is our kinsman' (9:3).

His mother's brothers from Shechem bring Abimelech's request to
the citizens of Shechem, who agree. Their decision also derives from
self-interest, given the possibilities latent in their relationship with
Abimelech: "for they thought, he is our kinsman". This sentence is
an echo of Abimelech's words: "And remember, I am your own
flesh and blood" (v. 2).[9]

The citizens of Shechem support Abimelech financially:

> (4) They gave him seventy shekels from the temple of Baal-berith; and
> with this Abimelech hired some worthless and reckless fellows, and
> they followed him.
> (5) Then he went to his father's house in Ophrah and killed his
> brothers, the sons of Jerubbaal, seventy men on one stone, only Jotham,
> the youngest son of Jerubbaal, survived, because he went into hiding
> (9:4–5).

The support offered to Abimelech by the citizens of Shechem is surprising. The impression received was that Abimelech was asking the
citizens of Shechem to make him king. Now it emerges that they
cannot do so at this stage and that Abimelech's request was for
financial backing in order to form an army of mercenaries and to
take the kingdom by force.[10]

The money given to him comes from the Baal-berith. Not only
does Abimelech not deliver the people. In contrast to his father he
does not combat the Baal, but rather uses the Baal to further his aims.

---

[9] Boogaart, ("Stone for Stone", p. 55, n. 8) pointed out the irony in the fact
that while they are shown as brothers by blood relationship at the beginning of the
account, they are seen to be also brothers by nature—all are treacherous and mur-
derers. This expression also appears in: Gen 3:23; 29:14; 2 Sam 5:1; 19:12–13. On
the expression עצמכם ובשרכם in the Bible, see: W. Brueggemann, "Of the Same
Flesh and Bone (Gen 2:23a)", *CBQ* 32 (1970), pp. 532–542.

[10] The financial support of seventy shekels is very little. This sum coincides with
the number of Abimelech's brothers whom he murdered, perhaps to show the low
price that he paid for each of his brothers. See: Moore, *Judges*, p. 242.

Abimelech does not express any belief in God, and does not object to receiving assistance from the Baal.

Abimelech savagely murders his seventy brothers. His wickedness is expressed in the verse by the indication that he killed all seventy of his brothers with one stone: "and killed his brothers, the sons of Jerubbaal, seventy men on one stone".[11] This cruel act is carried out with the aid of "worthless and reckless" fellows who are paid to assist him in the crime.[12] His relation with his mother's house is based on interests; his cruelty towards his father's house stems from his ambition to be king.

After killing all his brothers, Abimelech returns to Shechem and there he is crowned by the men of the city: "All the citizens of Shechem and all Beth-millo convened, and they went and made Abimelech king at the terebinth of the pillar at Shechem" (9:6). Now it emerges that the citizens of Shechem could make Abimelech king, and since the next part of the account shows that the borders of Abimelech's kingdom did not go beyond the area of Shechem, it becomes clear that killing of his brothers was merely so that nobody would contest him as king, and there would be no heir to the throne to endanger his status. The citizens of Shechem could have made Abimelech ruler of the city without the death of all his brothers.[13]

The indication of the place where Abimelech was made king is significant: "at the terebinth of the pillar at Shechem" (9:6). The appointment of Abimelech at the terebinth (אלון) recalls Gideon's meeting with the angel who came to commission him as deliverer "under the terebinth" (אלה) (6:11). In that episode, we saw that indication of the terebinth intimates an idolatrous connection, we observed Gideon's alienation from God at the beginning of the encounter,

---

[11] In the same way, Jehu kills Ahab's seventy sons, 2 Kings 10:1–10, 12–14. In both cases a dynasty is destroyed. The cruelty of the killing on one stone emerges from the comparison with the slaughter of the cattle on a stone by Saul. See 1 Sam 14:33 ff.

[12] Abramsky ("Abimelech's Leadership—King, Chief and Ruler", p. 167), in keeping with his approach, which presents Abimelech's monarchy in a positive light, interpreted that the expression אנשים רקים does not mean worthless men, but men who had no property, like Jephthah's men. However, the sources cited by Abramsky in support of his thesis (2 Sam 6:20; 2 Chr 13:7; Neh 5:13) point to a negative meaning of the word. In any case, the word פוחז certainly indicates a negative characteristic.

[13] On the sociological context at the basis of the confrontation between Abimelech and his brothers, see: N. Steinberg, "Social Scientific Criticism", G. A. Yee (ed.), *Judges and Method: New Approaches in Biblical Studies*, Minneapolis 1995, pp. 45–64.

and how he gradually drew near, until he built an altar to God in place of the terebinth. The commissioning of Abimelech at the terebinth is parallel to the motif of the terebinth in the Gideon account. This parallel is designed to show the difference between the two appointments. While Gideon builds an altar to God instead of the terebinth when he is commissioned to deliver Israel, Abimelech receives his office at the terebinth with its idolatrous connotations.[14]

Abimelech's aspirations and desires are the only considerations motivating him. His aspiration to be king is what brings him to intrigue and to act forcefully to these ends. He manipulates the citizens of Shechem through his family and bribes the men of the city. He influences them with cunning and, above all, he is prepared to perpetrate the cruel mass murder of his brothers. Abimelech is quite willing to use money from the Baal to carry out his plans. The citizens of Shechem also support Abimelech out of self-interest only, out of a wish to be related to royalty. They are therefore prepared to collaborate and to support these crimes financially The account does not deal with the people's plight or needs at all, and even the place of God is completely absent. The citizens of Shechem and Abimelech use the Baal-berith since this serves the aim. The account does not describe their espousal of the Baal, like the men of Ophrah in the Gideon account, or opposition to it; the only consideration is that of the personal interests of Abimelech and his allies in Shechem.[15]

Abimelech's actions contrast with the actions of Gideon, his father, throughout the account. Yet, Abimelech sees himself as continuing in his father's footsteps and resembles him in a number of ways.[16] Abimelech intrigues and acts forcefully to become king. In contrast, when the angel of the LORD wishes to commission Gideon to deliver Israel, Gideon, because of his humility, has reservations. Gideon's humility shows that he is worthy of the task. Likewise, when the people seek to make Gideon king, he refuses. Abimelech's eagerness to be king shows just how unworthy he is of this position.

---

[14] For another explanation, see: Boling, *Judges*, p. 172.

[15] The account clearly presents Abimelech's unsuitability for kingship through his egocentric and cruel personality and not, as claimed by Jobling (*The Sense of Biblical Narrative*, p. 77), through the fact that he is the son of a concubine (9:18).

[16] Klein (*The Triumph of Irony in the Book of Judges*, p. 70) emphasizes Gideon's part in the shaping of Abimelech's character by the use of the verb שׂם in relation to the naming of Abimelech by Gideon: "and he called his name Abimelech" (8:31). His ambition to be king is a result of the name that Gideon gave to him (*ibid.*, p. 71).

Gideon's attitude towards God is a prominent element in the account. This attitude is not one-dimensional. Gideon defies God, doubts whether He will help him to deliver Israel, until finally he professes faith and declares to the people that victory depends on God. Gideon is most outstanding in this field in his war against the Baal and in setting up an altar to God in its stead. Abimelech, however, does not relate to God at all either in work or action, neither positively or negatively. He does not refer to God at all and the object of all his actions is to have himself made king.[17] Moreover, Abimelech uses the money of the Baal-berith for this endeavour. However, he does not accept the support of the Baal-berith because he believes in it, but only out of self-interest. In both accounts, there is a tree motif that highlights the contrast between father and son. Gideon opposes his family and at God's command cuts down the sacred post belonging to the Baal worship (6:27); the terebinth in Shechem is indicated as the place where Abimelech was made king.

The people answered Gideon's call en masse. Abimelech has to hire men to fight his war. Gideon screens his soldiers, whereas Abimelech takes "worthless and reckless" fellows.

Despite the sharp contrast between Abimelech and his father, Abimelech sees himself as continuing his father's monarchy. When he appeals to his mother's family, his assertion is that one of Gideon's sons will inherit and reign over Israel, the question is who among his sons will reign. Gideon indeed said: "I will not rule over you myself, nor shall my son rule over you; the LORD alone shall rule over you" (8:23), but Abimelech already assumes that one of his sons will rule, and he uses the same root משל that Israel and Gideon used in the previous account: "Which is better for you, to be ruled by seventy men—by all the sons of Jerubbaal—or to be ruled by one man?" (9:2). Abimelech not only sees himself and presents himself as continuing after his father, he also acts accordingly. Abimelech "learnt" the 'ambush' tactic from his father. Gideon divided his army into three and outflanked the Midianite camp (7:16 ff.); in Abimelech's war against Shechem he divided his army into four (9:34) and then in his attack on the people in the field, he divided his soldiers into

---

[17] Klein, *The Triumph of Irony in the Book of Judges*, p. 70. She also stresses that in the Abimelech account only the name אלהים appears whereas the ineffable name does not appear at all.

three columns (9·43). Gideon presents himself as a role model: "Watch me, and do the same" (7:17), and similarly Abimelech asks his soldiers to do as he does: "What you saw me do—quick, do the same" (9:48). A distinction should immediately be made, in that Gideon employs the military tactics against his enemies, and Abimelech uses them against his subjects. Abimelech's vicious treatment of his seventy brothers recalls Gideon's cruel treatment of the men of Succoth and of Penuel. The men of Succoth and of Penuel refused to support Gideon in his battle against Midian. Abimelech, however, murdered his brothers without any threat on their part. In both cases, nonetheless, Gideon and Abimelech act out of self-interest. Gideon attacked the men of Succoth and of Penuel because they dishonoured him, and questioned his ability to strike the Midianite kings. Abimelech, in his efforts to become king, follows this example, but is more extreme.[18]

The analogies between Abimelech and his father Gideon serve to show that Abimelech is the antithesis of his father. Gideon is shown as worthy to lead the people. Abimelech's self-centred avidity, on the other hand, shows his unsuitability for the office that he craves. The Gideon account, however, does reveal an egocentric side to Gideon's personality. It is this aspect of his father's personality that Abimelech adopts fanatically and totally. In shaping of his character in the account there are absolutely no other facets beyond this. This is why Abimelech throughout the account is called the "son of Jerubbaal" and not the "son of Gideon". The name Gideon expresses his action against the Baal, whereas the name Jerubbaal is used in the context of the Baal worshippers' outlook or in the context of Gideon's negative actions. The use of both names in the Gideon account reflects both kinds of behaviours adopted by Gideon. Abimelech is called the son of Jerubbaal throughout the account, and this means that he followed in the path of Jerubbaal and not of Gideon.[19]

---

[18] See: Simon, "The Parable of Jotham", pp. 30–32. However, in Simon's opinion, the aim of the similarity and the difference between the personalities is to show the difference between a judge-deliverer who receives God's blessing and a king who was not anointed by God, and despite all his capabilities brought about a disaster. In my opinion the difference is not between a king and a judge; the object of the two accounts is to illustrate the basic attribute that must be in the personality of the leader.

[19] Polzin, *Moses and the Deuteronomist*, p. 173. On the other hand, in Abramsky's opinion ("Abimelech's Leadership—King, Chief and Ruler", p. 167), the name "Abimelech son of Jerubbaal" is more authentic and implies Jerubbaal's right to rule, even though Abimelech acted immorally.

3. The Jotham Fable (9:7–21)

At the end of the previous part of the account, Abimelech killed all seventy of his brothers except for the youngest, Jotham: "only Jotham, the youngest son of Jerubbaal, survived, because he went into hiding" (9:5). This serves as a prelude to the next section of the account, in which Jotham will express his opposition to the appointment of Abimelech as king. At the same time, this information shows how ruthless Abimelech is, and it confirms that the report of the murder of the brothers is no exaggeration, and of all Gideon's sons only Jotham remains.

Jotham escaped from Abimelech.[20] This may have been because he was the youngest of the sons, and therefore was not considered a real threat to Abimelech's scheme to become king.[21] However, it is precisely from this unexpected direction that the first opposition to Abimelech as king will come.[22]

The destruction of Gideon's family by Abimelech seems effective, and Jotham's opposition is expressed only in a speech that he makes to the citizens of Shechem from the top of Mount Gerizim: "Jotham was informed, and he went and stood on top of Mount Gerizim and cried aloud and said to them" (9:7). This oration is the only thing that Jotham can do. Abimelech has been accepted as king by the citizens of Shechem, and Jotham must flee and hide from Abimelech (9:21). Jotham's opposition is very important at the declarative level. He uses sophisticated rhetoric designed to influence through an interesting fable that gains the listener's sympathy. The citizens of Shechem, however, remain indifferent to his words. The trees asked three different fruit trees to reign over them, but the three

---

[20] The root of the name Jotham (יותם) is תמם. The narrator thus wished to present Jotham as perfect, while the meaning of the name Abimelech shows his negative character. Boling (Judges, p. 171) suggested that the name יותם (Jotham) is connected to the word יתום (orphan). While Abimelech through his name declares that his father Gideon was king, Jotham declares that his father is the God of Israel. However, there is no relation between these two words.

[21] Maly claims that the fact that Jotham is the youngest son is designed to present the irony of his awareness of the dangers involved in kingship, while the citizens of Shechem show no such awareness. E. Maly, "The Jotham Fable—Anti-monarchical?", CBQ 22 (1960), p. 300.

[22] Similarly, Joash the son of Ahaziah was saved from Athaliah who killed all the king's sons, and ultimately he reigned instead of Athaliah, who was executed, 2 Kings 11:1–16.

fruit trees refused. In the fourth attempt, they asked the thornbush, which accepted.[23] What function does Jotham's oration serve in the account, and what does Jotham seek to achieve thereby?

The fable:

> (7) Listen to me, you lords of Shechem, so that God may listen to you.
> (8) The trees once went out to anoint a king over themselves.
>   So they said to the olive tree,
>   'Reign over us'.
> (9)   The olive tree answered them,
>   'Shall I stop producing my rich oil
>   by which gods and mortals are honored,
>   and go to hold sway over the trees?'
> (10) Then the trees said to the fig tree,
>   'You come and reign over us'.
> (11)   But the fig tree answered them,
>   'Shall I stop producing my sweetness
>   and my delicious fruit,
>   and go to hold sway over the trees?'
> (12) Then the trees said to the vine,
>   'You come and reign over us'.
> (13)   But the vine said to them,
>   'Shall I stop producing my wine
>   that cheers gods and mortals,
>   and go to hold sway over the trees?'
> (14) So all the trees said to the thornbush,
>   'You come and reign over us'.
> (15)   And the thornbush said to the trees,
>   'If in good faith you are anointing me king over you,
>   then come and take shelter in my shade;
>   but if not, let fire come out of the thornbush
>   and devour the cedars of Lebanon.' (9:7–15)

The moral:

> (16) Now then, if you acted truly and uprightly in making Abimelech king, and if you have done right by Jerubbaal and his house and have requited him according to his deserts—(17) considering that my father fought for you and saved you from the Midianites at the risk of his life, (18) but you have risen up against my father's house this day, and killed his sons, seventy men on one stone, and set up Abimelech, the

---

[23] This fable is constructed in the form of the three-four model. On this see: Y. Zakovitch, *The Pattern of Numerical Sequence Three-Four in the Bible*, Ph.D. Diss., The Hebrew University, 1977, pp. 244–249 (Hebrew).

son of his handmaid, as king over the citizens of Shechem just because
he is your kinsman—
(19) If, I say, you have this day acted truly and uprightly toward
Jerubbaal and his house, have joy in Abimelech and may he likewise
have joy in you.
(20) But if not, let fire come out from Abimelech, and devour the lords
of Shechem, and Beth-millo; and let fire come out from the lords of
Shechem, and from Beth-millo, and devour Abimelech! (9:16–20)

Many scholars have discussed the important differences between the
fable and the reality to which it refers, and between the fable and the
moral.[24] In the fable, the trees asked the three fruit trees, the olive,
the fig and the vine, to reign over them, and they refused. On the
other hand, in the account, it is Abimelech who uses bribery in
order to be made king.[25] In the fable, the thornbush agrees to rule
over the trees, but threatens and intimidates them.[26] In the account,
Abimelech seeks to influence and win over the citizens of Shechem.

There is also a difference between the fable and the moral. While
the main part of the fable deals with the commissioning of a king, the
moral deals principally with the ingratitude of the citizens of Shechem
towards Gideon. The connection between the fable and the moral
seems at first sight artificial and relies on the linguistic connection
between the thornbush's words and Jotham's words in the moral:
"If in good faith . . . but if not" (אם באמת . . . ואם אין) (vv. 15, 16,
19–20), and on the motif of fire both in the thornbush's words and

---

[24] Moore, *Judges*, p. 245; Burney, *The Book of Judges*, p. 275; Maly, "The Jotham
Fable—Anti-monarchical?", pp. 301–302; Simon, "The Parable of Jotham", pp.
1–3; Richter, *Traditionsgeschichtliche Untersuchungen zum Richterbuch*, p. 349; B. Lindars,
"Jotham's Fable—A New Form-Critical Analysis", *JTS* 24 (1973), 355–360.

[25] In Budde's opinion (*Das Buch der Richter*, p. 72), the fruit trees in the fable are
Gideon's slain sons. However, this explanation does not bring the fable closer to
the reality, since there is no mention of Gideon's brothers having opposed the
monarchy. In Jobling's opinion (*The Sense of Biblical Narrative*, p. 76), the trees' refusal
to reign was in comparison with Gideon's refusal to reign. Jobling himself admits,
however, that Gideon's reason for refusal of the kingship is not the same as that
of the trees.

[26] I disagree with the opinion that the thornbush's answer is ironical, that its
words do not show any intention of accepting the kingship, and are rather a kind
of jest since the thornbush does not give shade. (Lindars, "Jotham's Fable—A New
Form-Critical Analysis", pp. 356–357; Fritz, "Abimelech und Sichem in Jdc. IX",
p. 140; Jobling, *The Sense of Biblical Narrative*, p. 76). It is difficult to see irony or a
jest in the thornbush's threat, "and if not let fire come out of the thornbush", unless
of course we delete 15ₐ. See for instance: Crüsemann, *Der Widerstand gegen das Königtum*,
p. 19; Lindars ("Jotham's Fable—A New Form-Critical Analysis", p. 359) also considers that this verse is a separate axiom, not related to the present context.

in Jotham's words in the moral: "but if not, let fire come out of the
thornbush / but if not, let fire come out from Abimelech" (9:16–20).[27]

These differences have led scholars to different conclusions. Some
consider that Jotham did not compose a fable suited to the event to
which he refers, but took a readymade fable, which did not coincide with reality in all the details. Others stress that it is not unusual
for the fable not to coincide fully with reality and with the moral.[28]

Since the fable does not correspond either to the reality or to the
moral, it is first necessary to examine the meaning of the fable separately from the moral or the reality, and to bear in mind the possibility that there is significance in the differences between the fable
and the reality and the moral.[29]

A widely held opinion is that the fable expresses an anti-monarchic
outlook.[30] The fruit trees' rejection of the monarchy parallels Gideon's

---

[27] On further differences, that I consider insignificant, between the fable and the
moral, see: Jobling, *ibid.*, pp. 73–74.

[28] Moore, *Judges*, p. 245, Maly, "The Jotham Fable—Anti-monarchical?", p. 301;
Lindars, "Jotham's Fable—A New Form-Critical Analysis", pp. 355–359; Soggin,
Judges, p. 175. Moore (*Judges*, pp. 245, 250–251) and Burney (*The Book of Judges*,
p. 275) do not consider it exceptional that the fable and the moral do not coincide in all the details, but are alike in the main matter. However, in order to
decrease the difference between the fable and the moral they assert that v. 19$_b$ is
the continuation of 16$_a$ and 16$_b$–19$_a$ is a late addition (Moore, *ibid.*, p. 151; Burney,
ibid., p. 275). In this way, the argument in v. 16—"if you acted truly and uprightly"—
relates to the loyalty to Abimelech as in the fable in v. 15. Kaufmann (*Sefer Shoftim*,
p. 199) emphasizes that the fact that the fable and the moral do not fully coincide
in all the details is characteristic of fables. Simon ("The Parable of Jotham", pp.
14–15) considers that the trees are not real characters. The trees were designed to
serve as a contrast to the pursuit of power by the thornbush, which was easily
identified as Abimelech, since it was worthless and reckless (Judg 9:4). In Simon's
opinion, the fable differs from the reality factually, in that it ascribes to the trees
the initiative of crowning a king. However, as regards the meaning, it faithfully
reflects the fact that Abimelech became king because of the lack of interest of the
citizens of Shechem. Similarly, Amit (*The Book of Judges*, pp. 106–107, 110–111)
considers that if the reader understands the fable in its context, he can find the
similarities between the fable and the reality, notwithstanding the differences. She
also explains that Jotham's failure to convince the citizens of Shechem derives from
the difference between the fable and the reality (p. 100). On the interest of Israel
in fables, see: O. Eissfeldt, *The Old Testament, An Introduction* (trans. P. R. Ackroyd),
Oxford 1974, pp. 37–38.

[29] Sternberg (*The Poetics of Biblical Narrative*, p. 143) notes that the fact that the
fable deviates from the reality allows presentation of the problem from a new angle.

[30] On Jotham's fable Buber states (*Kingship of God*, p. 75): "The Jotham fable, the
strongest anti-monarchical poem of world literature, is the counterpart of the Gideon
passage . . . This kingship, so teaches the poem . . ., is not a productive calling. It is
vain, but also bewildering and seditious, that men rule over me. Every one is to
pursue his own proper business, and the manifold fruitfulnesses will constitute a

refusal, whereas the anointment of the useless thornbush reflects ideological opposition to the institution of monarchy. In this opinion, Jotham's fable is one of the strongest sources against the institution of monarchy. Some scholars have gone even further, claiming that this source reflects the theocratic post-exilic outlook.[31]

There is indeed an anti-monarchic outlook in several sources in the Bible, for instance in Gideon's words: "I will not rule over you myself, nor shall my son rule over you; the LORD alone shall rule over you" (8:23); or in God's words: "and the LORD said to Samuel, 'Listen to the voice of the people in all that they say to you; for they have not rejected you, but they have rejected me from being king over them'" (1 Sam 8:7). Nonetheless, the fruit trees do not express fundamental opposition to the institution of monarchy. They do not wish to reign because they do not wish to abandon production of their fruit. In the words of the three trees the expression "Shall I stop producing my . . . and go to hold sway over the trees?" is repeated. The fruit trees do not use the wording of the trees' proposal in their reply: "You come and reign over us". This shows that they do not basically object to the idea of being king, but are not inclined to perform the function that requires going "to hold sway over the trees". The office of royalty requires an action of holding sway, which would prevent continued production of their fruits. The trees turn to the thornbush as a direct result of having internalized the fruit trees' message. Now they address their request to a barren tree that is not occupied with fruit production and that will have time to hold sway over the trees. On the other hand, Gideon's refusal to be king is

---

community over which, in order that it endure, no one needs to rule—no one except God alone". See also: Richter, *Traditionsgeschichtliche Untersuchungen zum Richterbuch*, p. 285; Soggin, *Judges*, p. 177; Jobling, *The Sense of Biblical Narrative*, pp. 72–73. See also: Crüsemann, *Der Widerstand gegen das Königtum*, pp. 19–32. Daube conjectured that the law in the book of Deuteronomy 17:15, "one from among your brethren shall you set king over you; you shall not put a foreigner over you, who is not your brother" relates to Abimelech who was the son of a Shechemite woman. He indicates that this law seems strange, since it is not reasonable that Israel would wish to set a foreign king over them, and indeed there was no such initiative in the history of Israel, apart from the Abimelech account. In Daube's opinion, the law was written in opposition to Abimelech's kingship, and the opposition to Abimelech's kingship relates to this law. D. Daube, "One From Among Your Brethren Shall You Set King Over You", *JBL* 90 (1971), pp. 480–481. While I accept the opinion that Shechem was a Canaanite city, it is not clear that the concubine from Shechem was a Canaanite, see: Kaufmann, *Sefer Shoftim*, p. 194.

[31] See in my discussion in the epilogue of this monograph.

not practical, but fundamental: the reign of a human king is opposed
to God's reign.

There is no objection to the institution of monarchy in the moral
of Jotham's fable either. Jotham tells the citizens of Shechem that
they have requited good with evil by making Abimelech king. Jotham
speaks of personal injury to Gideon and not basic opposition to the
actual appointing of a king. He notes the way in which they ill
requited Gideon, killing his seventy sons. He does not object to the
fact that they appointed a king, but that the king appointed is unworthy—the son of Gideon's concubine, and that they killed the seventy
sons who were worthy. Jotham says expressly that if they have done
right by Jerubbaal: "have joy in Abimelech and may he likewise have
joy in you" (v. 19). The problem is that they did not act honorably
and loyally towards Jerubbaal and therefore "let fire come out from
Abimelech" (v. 20). Jotham's words imply that he agrees that one
of Gideon's sons should have reigned, but that the wrong man has
been appointed. It is therefore apparent that theologically there is no
anti-monarchic argument in the fable or in the moral, as in Gideon's
words or in God's words in 1 Sam 8.

In Kaufmann's opinion the fable is a pro-monarchic document
which criticizes the fruit trees that were worthy of reigning but were
not prepared to sacrifice themselves for this objective, and their avoid-
ance of duty led to the appointment of someone unworthy.[32] The
fable, in his opinion, criticizes the conduct of the people, who did not
recognize the value of the monarchy and were prepared to deliver it
into the hands of a thornbush. Kaufmann insists that the fable corresponds to the reality: the trees acted correctly when they asked the
fruit trees to reign over them, and in reality the people acted wisely
when they wished to make Gideon king. On this point, Kaufmann
is correct since, as indicated above, Jotham does not object to his
father being king, or to one of Gideon's sons being king. Jotham's

---

[32] Kaufmann, *Sefer Shoftim*, pp. 201–202; Maly, "The Jotham Fable—Anti-monarchical?", pp. 303–305. In Maly's opinion the redactor who inserted the fable in the
account took a fable that dealt with the subject of the monarchy and adapted it
to the specific situation. Since the main point here is to show the disaster that will
be caused because of Abimelech, he adapted the thornbush to the figure of Abimelech
through adding of the motif of fire that will devour the cedars of Lebanon. This
opinion is shared by Lindars, "Jotham's Fable—A New Form-Critical Analysis", pp.
365–366; Fritz, "Abimelech und Sichem in Jdc. IX", p. 140; Boling, *Judges*, p. 174.

argument is that the citizens of Shechem acted badly towards Gideon in murdering Gideon's sons and appointing Abimelech who is not worthy of the office. However, I disagree with Kaufmann's interpretation that the fable criticizes the fruit trees for refusing to reign. This is not the simple meaning of the fable. According to the fable, the negative thornbush was contrasted with the fruit trees that are presented positively.[33] Nor does the fable criticize the other trees, since they first approached the right trees, and only in face of their refusal did they approach the thornbush. When the trees asked the thornbush, and the thornbush agreed, the fable also shows their powerlessness against the thornbush's threats to burn the cedars of Lebanon.[34]

The meaning of the fable must be based on its simple understanding, without relation to the reality against which the fable is recounted or the moral.[35] The fable contrasts the refusal of the three trees to be king with the thornbush's acceptance of the offer. The reader expects an answer other than that uttered by the thornbush, since this is a three and four structure common in the Bible, and the request to the thornbush is the fourth. Moreover, the request made to the three fruit trees is addressed in the feminine form, and only the thornbush is masculine. However, the main reason is that the thornbush differs from the other fruit trees cited. After the fruit-bearing trees refused three times, the request is made to the thornbush, which is not a fruit-bearing tree, and therefore it has time "hold sway over the trees". The thornbush indeed agrees to the proposal. However, its response contains a surprising transition; its place at the end of the fable shows that this is its sting. The thornbush does not respond

---

[33] Therefore, Maly ("The Jotham Fable—Anti-monarchical?", p. 303), who also asserted that the fable is designed to criticize the trees' refusal to rule, claims that the thornbush's words concerning the fire that will come out from it and devour the cedars of Lebanon are an addition of the redactor who inserted the fable in its present context.

[34] Gerbrandt (*Kingship According to the Deuteronomistic History*, pp. 130–132) does not agree that the fable is pro-monarchic. While he does consider that the fable originally was an anti-monarchic document, in its context in the account, there is no criticism of the crowning of Abimelech but there is criticism of the killing of Gideon's sons and, like the entire account, the fable also criticizes Abimelech and the citizens of Shechem.

[35] In contrast to Amit's methodological approach (*The Book of Judges*, pp. 105–106), which she applies also to several other problematic episodes, whereby the fable must be interpreted according to its context.

affirmatively to the proposal but replies with a threat: "If truly you
are anointing me king over you, then come and take shelter in my
shade;[36] but if not, let fire come out of the thornbush and devour the
cedars of Lebanon". Not only does the thornbush accept the proposal, but it threatens them that henceforth they will not be able to
retract it, and if they do not accept its rule, it will harm them. This
answer reveals the thornbush's innermost secrets. The thornbush is
so avid to reign that it will not be prepared to be deposed, and if
the trees do not accept it, it will harm them. Hence, it does not
seek the good of the trees in its willingness to reign over them, but
fulfilment of its personal desires. The thornbush offers its patronage
if they accept it, but threatens to destroy them by fire if not. The
thornbush's avidity to reign contrasts with the fruit trees' reservations
about assuming office.

Scholars of literature determine that the meaning of a fable is
clear in itself, even when the moral is not given.[37] We will therefore
now seek to understand the moral without direct connection to the
fable. After establishing the meaning of the fable and the moral separately, I will discuss the nature of the relation between them.

Jotham words are divided into two parts, and both open with the
words "if you acted truly and uprightly" (vv. 16, 19). This repetition
is due to the length of the sentence that commences in verse 16.

> (1) Now then, if you acted truly and uprightly in making Abimelech
> king, and if you have done right by Jerubbaal and his house and
> have requited him according to his deserts—
> (17) considering that my father fought for you,
> risked his life,
> and saved you from the Midianites
> (18) but you have risen up against my father's house this day,
> and killed his sons, seventy men on one stone,

---

[36] The king's shadow (צל = "shade" and "shadow") is a prevalent motif in the
conception of the monarchy of Egypt and Mesopotamia, see: A. L. Oppenheim,
"The Shadow of the King", *BASOR* 107 (1947), pp. 7–11. This motif also appears
in the Bible, see: Lam 3:20; Ps 91:1.

[37] J. T. Shipley, *Dictionary of World Literature*, Totowa 1966, p. 297. Shipley makes
a distinction between a fable, which usually has human characters and a closely
related moral, and a fable in which the characters are animals or plants or even
inanimate objects, and the moral is self-evident. In a fable, the moral must be
related because it deals with human beings; without an explicit moral the fable
night not be understood as such. However, because the characters of the fable are
not human, the moralistic nature is self-evident.

and set up Abimelech, the son of his handmaid, as king over the
citizens of Shechem
just because he is your kinsman—
(2) (19) and if you acted truly and uprightly toward Jerubbaal and his
house,
have joy in Abimelech
and may he likewise have joy in you.
(20) But if not, let fire come out from Abimelech, and devour the
lords of Shechem, and Beth-millo;
and let fire come out from the lords of Shechem, and from Beth-
millo, and devour Abimelech!

This repetition shows a kind of inner contradiction in Jotham's words.
The phraseology "and if you acted truly and uprightly" presents
them objectively. Even though this opening is neutral, the next part
of the sentence is not. The objective phraseology is that of the second
sentence, which states that there are two possibilities contained in
the acts of the citizens of Shechem who made Abimelech king. If they
acted truly and uprightly in making him king, the result will be
mutual joy of Abimelech and the citizens of Shechem: "have joy in
Abimelech and may he likewise have joy in you" (v. 19). However,
if they did not act truly and uprightly, ultimately the result will be
mutual hatred between Abimelech and the citizens of Shechem that
will be expressed in reciprocal aggression.

Yet, Jotham does not really present a neutral position and two
possibilities. Even though the first and the second sentence commence
in a similar way, in the next part of the first sentence Jotham clearly
and unequivocally argues that the citizens of Shechem have betrayed
Gideon. This argument is developed through three statements describing Gideon's sacrifice on their behalf: (1) "my father fought for you",
(2) "risked his life", (3) "and saved you from the Midianites". Against
these three phrases Jotham utters three phrases describing the way
in which the citizens of Shechem betrayed Gideon: (1) "you have
risen up against my father's house this day", (2) "and killed his sons,
seventy men on one stone", (3) and set up Abimelech, the son of his
handmaid, as king over the citizens of Shechem". Jotham says expressly
that their betrayal of Gideon derives from personal interests—from
their wish to be close to the king: "just because he is your kinsman".

Jotham clothes his address to the citizens of Shechem and presentation of their intentions in objectivity. However, the address is
very lengthy because he also evaluates the matter. The rhetorical use
of the fable and presentation of the two possibilities shows that

Jotham's intention is to persuade the citizens of Shechem to change
their mind about making Abimelech king. Jotham's attempt at persuasion is very similar to the sophisticated words of persuasion used
by Abimelech with the citizens of Shechem. Abimelech also addressed
a seemingly neutral question to them: "Which is better for you, to
be ruled by seventy men—by all the sons of Jerubbaal—or to be
ruled by one man?" (v. 2). This neutral presentation was cut short
immediately by Abimelech's next words in which he intimated that
it would be of benefit to them to make him king: "And remember,
I am your own flesh and blood" (v. 2). As in Abimelech's question
to the citizens of Shechem, that reflects rhetorical sophistication and
an explicit statement of how they should act, Jotham's highly ingenious
rhetorical presentation also poses a question with the answer alongside it. However, Abimelech and Jotham differ on a significant point
in transmitting of the messages. Abimelech asks his immediate family
in Shechem to persuade the citizens of Shechem, whereas Jotham
stands at the top of Mount Gerizim and delivers a public oration.
Abimelech acts secretly, in the way of criminals, whereas Jotham,
who seeks justice, speaks publicly on Mount Gerizim in the manner
of the prophets delivering a rebuke at the gate. Jotham also stood
at the top of Mount Gerizim, undoubtedly, because he had to keep
his distance from the citizens of Shechem so that he would be able
to flee.[38] At the same time, the location is certainly related to the fact
that this was the site of the ceremony of blessing and cursing the
people. This further reinforces the two possibilities that Jotham presents to the people, one positive (benediction) and one negative (curse).

The parallel between Jotham's and Abimelech's words again underscores the negative decision of the citizens of Shechem in favour of
Abimelech rather than listening to Jotham. Whereas they took immediate action to make Abimelech king, Jotham's words fall on deaf
ears and the citizens of Shechem fail to respond, preferring their
own interests to acting "truly and uprightly".

There is a further analogy between Abimelech's actions and Jotham's
words. The table below presents a comparison of Abimelech's and
Jotham's opening and closing words:

---

[38] Maly, "The Jotham Fable—Anti-monarchical?", p. 300.

	Abimelech and the citizens of Shechem (vv. 1–6)	Jotham and the citizens of Shechem (vv. 7–21)
Opening words	Abimelech son of Jerubbaal *went* to Shechem to his mother's brothers, and spoke to them and to the whole clan of his mother's family.	Jotham was informed, *and he went* and stood on top of Mount Gerizim and cried aloud and said to them, "Listen to me, you lords of Shechem, so that God may listen to you.
Closing words	All the citizens of Shechem and all Beth-millo convened, *and went* and made Abimelech king at the terebinth of the pillar at Shechem.	And Jotham ran away, and fled, *and went* to Beer, and dwelt there, for fear of Abimelech his brother

This analogy underscores the condemnation of the citizens of Shechem who preferred Abimelech for the benefits that he promised, rather than accepting Jotham's words and acting faithfully towards Gideon. They make Abimelech king, whereas Jotham is obliged to flee.

Let us now go back to the relation between the fable and the moral. The scholars are correct in arguing that the fable and the moral do not coincide. The question is whether they should be expected to coincide. Moreover, a difference between the fable and the moral is obligatory if we want the fable to be profound, and to make us think about it and discuss it; a fable that is a transparent reflection of the moral is superfluous to the person hearing it. An analysis of the fable and the moral shows that they do not coincide and any attempt to unify them is doomed to complete failure.

The main argument of the fable is against the thornbush's eagerness to be king.[39] There is no argument either against the other fruit trees or against the trees. On the other hand, in the moral, even though Abimelech's crime is clear, the main argument is against the citizens of Shechem. Therefore, it seems that the object of the moral is not to interpret the fable, since the fable is clear and does not require interpretation. The moral raises other arguments that complete

---

[39] There are scholars who insisted that the fable criticizes Abimelech's conduct, but they failed to explore the relation between the fable and the lesson: See: Webb, *The Book of Judges*, p. 155 and p. 254, n. 95. He considers that the main meaning is not in the actual fable but in application of the fable to the present situation, in that they did not act truly towards Jerubbaal.

the fable. In the fable, the main argument is against Abimelech's eagerness to be king, and the danger that it therefore represents for the people. After censuring Abimelech through the fable, Jotham goes on to preach in narrative style and to censure the acts and motives of the citizens of Shechem. Here the main argument is that in making Abimelech king, they betrayed Gideon. In this way, Jotham's words contain a complete and comprehensive set of arguments, in the fable against Abimelech and in the subsequent narrative against the citizens of Shechem. That the main argument in the fable is against Abimelech can be seen in that the fire comes from the thornbush only (*"If truly* you are anointing me king over you, then come and take shelter in my shade; *but if not, let fire come out of the thornbush and devour the cedars of Lebanon"*, v. 15). However, the subsequent narrative explanation refers to mutual fire that will come out both from Abimelech and from the citizens of Shechem (*"and if you acted truly and uprightly* toward Jerubbaal and his house . . . *but if not, let fire come out from Abimelech, and devour the lords of Shechem, and Beth-millo*; and let fire come out from the lords of Shechem, and from Beth-millo, and devour Abimelech!"*, vv. 19–20).

The advantage of this interpretation is that it corresponds to the convention that there is not an explicit moral alongside a fable. Another advantage is that unlike other interpretations, which ignored the fact that the fable did not coincide with Jotham's subsequent words, or that tried by force to settle the contradiction, in this interpretation the differences between the fable and Jotham's subsequent words, written in prose, are intended to present a set of different and complementary arguments.

Abimelech is censured for his avidity to rule, which reflects his self-interest and therefore his unsuitability for the office. The citizens of Shechem are also censured in like manner, for having appointed a man unworthy of being king, preferring their interest over their obligation to Gideon. Jotham presents Gideon as a model of fitting kingship. Gideon endangered himself for the sake of the people, and preferred the good of the people over other considerations. Jotham predicts that fire will come out from Abimelech against the citizens of Shechem and from the citizens of Shechem against Abimelech. At the end of the account, it is clear that Jotham is cursing them because of their wickedness (9:57).[40] However, at the same time Jotham's

---

[40] Simon ("The Parable of Jotham", pp. 3–9) defines the genre of Jotham's words as a curse.

words are not recognizably a curse. They can also be seen as a logical evaluation of the future implications of appointment of a king for reasons of self-interest. Jotham censures the self-interest of the parties, predicting that fire will come out from them and that they will fight Abimelech when the reasons for which they appointed him are no longer relevant. Jotham indicates the risk inherent in appointing a king whose motives are personal and not national.

Despite the differences, the fable and Jotham's subsequent words are complementary. They are, however, identical in the perception that appointment of a king out of self-interest is liable to lead ultimately to a conflict of interests that will result in disaster. Jotham's fable is not a pro or anti-monarchic declaration. It is a censure of Abimelech's egocentric personality, his unsuitability for the office of king, and the egotistical motives of the citizens of Shechem in making him king.

4. The Dispute between Abimelech and the Citizens of Shechem (vv. 22–57)

a. *Theological introduction (vv. 22–24)*

> Abimelech ruled over Israel for three years.
> God sent an evil spirit between Abimelech and the citizens of Shechem, and the citizens of Shechem broke faith with Abimelech—to the end that the crime committed against the seventy sons of Jerubbaal might be avenged, and their blood recoil upon their brother Abimelech, who had slain them, and upon the citizens of Shechem, who had abetted him in the slaying of his brothers (vv. 22–24)

After Jotham's opposition to Abimelech failed to influence the citizens of Shechem, the first thing that we learn is the fact that Abimelech ruled over Israel for three years. Even though there is no description of Abimelech's reign, an allusion should perhaps be seen to the negative evaluation of his reign by use of the rare verb וישר ("ruled"). The use of this verb, other than in our account, does not describe a monarchic rule.[41] Its use here is generally explained by the fact that the verse seeks to describe Abimelech's reign as one of domination

---

[41] See for instance: Num 16:13; Isa 32:1; Hos 8:4; Prov 8:16; Esth 1:22; I Chr 15:22. In these sources it is used generally in relation to the governmental action of the prince (Isa 32:1; Prov 8:16; 1 Chr 15:22), or a government that is not of a king (Num 16:13; Esth 1:22) and therefore the appropriate verb is used. An exception, it seems, is the source in Hosea, where this verb is used to bring diversity of the poetic Biblical parallelism.

and oppression.[42] However, generally it does not seem that this verb describes a despotic kingdom (other than in Numbers 16:13). The use of this verb seems to be related to the meaning of the Acadian words *šarrum* and *malāku*. The word *šarrum* means king, and the word *māliku* means counsellor, advisor the opposite of the Hebrew. שר means chieftain, ruler, official, captain, prince. In Hebrew also there is an indication that the root מלך (to reign) is related to a viceroy in the sense of taking counsel, seeking advice. Possibly the use of the word וישר in the Abimelech account in the sense מלך as in Acadian is designed to describe Abimelech's monarchy as working along the lines of monarchy in the Near Ancient East, which is regarded with disfavour in several biblical accounts.[43]

This may well be the explanation behind the foreign background of the Abimelech account. The residents of Shechem seem to be Canaanites who have some partnership with Israel, as can be deduced from the expression: "They entered the temple of their god" (v. 27). This background is designed to show that this monarchy is an adoption of a foreign model and the Biblical narrator wished to present it as foreign to the Biblical concept.[44]

---

[42] Rashi, Kimchi, Kaufmann, *Sefer Shoftim*, p. 206; Malamat, *History of Biblical Israel*, pp. 128–129; Amit, *Judges*, p. 174. In Brawer's opinion, the author did not wish to give Abimelech the title of king, even though he was crowned by the citizens of Shechem and did not in fact "judge", in order to create a distinction between Abimelech and the judge-deliverers par excellence. Therefore, he chose the verb שרר, which indicates government through seizing power by force. A. J. Brawer, " 'וישר אבימלך על ישראל' [= And Abimelech ruled over Israel]' ", *Beit Mikra*, 16 (1963), pp. 120–121 (Hebrew). Abramsky ("Abimelech's Leadership—King, Chief and Ruler", pp. 168–169) disagreed and tried to show that there is no negative connotation in the verb וישר. However, he fails to explain why the Biblical narrator chose to use this rare verb here. Boling (*Judges*, p. 175) considers that the word שר indicates long-term leadership, and he emphasizes that in no place in the account is it written that Abimelech was king. However, this contradicts the explicit statement in verse 6: "and they made Abimelech king" (9:6). It should be noted that the expression מלך appears three times consecutively in this verse.

[43] Similarly see also: Abramsky, "Abimelech's Leadership—King, Chief and Ruler", p. 169. However, he does not see in this criticism of Abimelech's kingship. On the Canaanite nature of Abimelech's kingship, see: Kaufmann, *Sefer Shoftim*, pp. 196–197.

[44] The prevalent opinion is that the residents of the city of Shechem were gentiles. See, for instance: Moore, *Judges*, p. 236; Burney, *The Book of Judges*, pp. 266–267; M. Haran, "Shechem Studies", *Zion* 38 (1973), pp. 18–21 (Hebrew, English Summary: p. I); Abramsky, "Abimelech's Leadership—King, Chief and Ruler", p. 170; Segal also considers that the residents of Shechem are Canaanites, and in this context indicates the antiquity of the account. M. Z. Segal, "Studies in the Book of Judges", *Tarbiz* 2 (1930), pp. 1–4 (Hebrew). (On the antiquity of the account, see also: Moore, *Judges*, p. 238). In light of the foreignness of the city of Shechem, Burney

The fact that the length of Abimelech's reign is indicated at the beginning of the account is exceptional in relation to the other accounts. Normally, the number of years in which the judge ruled is indicated at the end. Moreover, the duration of Abimelech's reign is indicated even though no information is provided about the reign. Instead, the account goes on to summarize the subsequent contents of the account: the betrayal of Abimelech by the citizens of Shechem. This betrayal is explained as God's retribution against Abimelech for the crime of killing his brothers, and against the citizens of Shechem for the crime of assisting him.[45] The evil spirit sent by God between the citizens of Shechem and Abimelech is the opposite of the spirit of God that clothes Gideon and which gives him the strength to fight the Midianites.[46] Thus, the Abimelech account opens with a summary of Abimelech's confrontation with the citizens of Shechem that is described later in the account (9:25–57). The description of the confrontation also ends with a similar theological conclusion, determining that God requited Abimelech and the citizens of Shechem for their wickedness (9:56–57). From this, we may conclude that the description of the confrontation between Abimelech and the citizens of Shechem is delimited by an enclosing structure of theological expressions explaining the reason for the confrontation.

The theological summary at the beginning of the account prevents any build-up of tension, and the reader's curiosity about the

---

determines that the indication that Abimelech ruled over "all Israel" derives from a late perspective that considered that the tribes of Israel in that period were already an integrated unit (*ibid.*, p. 267). On the other hand, in Haran's opinion, this indication (as also in v. 55), attests to the fact that Abimelech's rule extended far beyond the city of Shechem and this was the reason for his inclusion in the list of Israelite leaders (*ibid.*, p. 20). Possibly the relations between Shechem and Israel are reflected in the relations between Shechem and the Habiru. On this, see for instance: Abramsky, "Abimelech's Leadership—King, Chief and Ruler", pp. 170–171. However, there is no basis to Wellhausen's assertion (*Die Composition des Hexateuchs und der historischen Bücher des alten Testaments*, pp. 227–228) that the account is in fact a description of the war between the Canaanites and Israel. Nielson considers that the city before Abimelech was Canaanite, and it was Abimelech that made it into an Israelite city. E. Nielsen, *Shechem, A Triditio-Historical Investigation²*, Copenhagen 1959, pp. 169–170. In contrast, Kaufmann (*Sefer Shoftim*, pp. 196–197) deems that in Abimelech's time the city was Israelite. See also: N. Na'aman, "Migdal-Shechem and the 'House of El-berith'", *Zion* 51 (1986), pp. 270–271 (Hebrew). Martin (*The Book of Judges*, pp. 113–114) showed how Abimelech's monarchy is built on the model of city-states as reflected in the Tel Amarna letters.

[45] On this see Webb, *The Book of Judges*, pp. 154–155.

[46] Klein, *The Triumph of Irony in the Book of Judges*, p. 73.

subsequent plot evaporates even before the story commences. There
is a similar structure at the beginning of the account of Joshua's first
war against Ai and his failure following Achan's transgression (Josh
7:1). In both cases the theological significance of the events is explained
even before the description of the event. The account of the confrontation between the citizens of Shechem and Abimelech is long
and complex. To ensure that the meaning of the account is not
obscured, the express theological explanation is given at the outset
as part of a summary of the future events. The author wished to
transmit an unequivocal theological message at the beginning of the
story, even at the expense of impairing the poetics of the account, so
that there would be no doubts or alternative readings of the events.

The account now goes on to describe in detail the confrontation
between Abimelech and the citizens of Shechem. This is a complex
story with many scenes and it is filled with many details; it is sometimes difficult to follow the plot development. The account opens
with the betrayal of Abimelech by the citizens of Shechem and the
transfer of their loyalty to Gaal son of Ebed who declares a revolt
against Abimelech (9:25–29). Zebul, the governor of the city, knows
of the preparations; he informs Abimelech and advises him how to
fight the rebels. Abimelech accepts his advice and lies in wait on
Shechem with four columns (9:30–34). Gaal, who is in the city,
observes the events, but Zebul, who is with him in the city, deceives
him, and thus allows Abimelech to surprise him (9:35–38). In the
war, Abimelech scores a clear victory over Gaal (9:39–41). In the
second stage of the battle, Abimelech fights against the people in
the field (9:42–44). He then goes on to the third stage, in which he
fights against the city of Shechem and again scores a clear victory.
This is followed by the burning of the tower of the city of Shechem
with all the people in it (9:45–49). In the fourth stage, Abimelech
goes to fight against the city of Thebez. He also captures this city,
but when he goes to burn the tower, as he did in Shechem, a woman
throws an upper millstone on his head and injures him. In order to
minimize the shame, Abimelech asks his attendant to kill him. Upon
Abimelech's death, his supporters disperse (9:50–55). The account
closes with a theological conclusion parallel to the opening, in which
the meaning of the account is established: God requited the wickedness of Abimelech and the citizens of Shechem (9:56–57).

The account is characterized by lack of clarity in many substantial
details. This is expressed in surprising transitions from one stage to

another, with ambiguity as regards the winning sides: who fights against whom, and why they are fighting against each other.[47] A study of the verses describing the confrontation shows that their main object is to leave the reader in uncertainly, even though he receives a great deal of detailed information.

b. *The betrayal of Abimelech by the citizens of Shechem and their preference of Gaal son of Ebed (vv. 25–29)*

> (25) The citizens of Shechem planted ambuscades against him on the hilltops; and they robbed whoever passed by them on the road, and it was reported to Abimelech.
> (26) Then Gaal son of Ebed and his kinsfolk came passing through Shechem, and the citizens of Shechem put their confidence in him.
> (27) They went out into the fields, gathered the grapes from their vineyards, trod them, and celebrated. They entered the temple of their god, and they ate and drank and they cursed Abimelech.
> (28) And Gaal the son of Ebed said, 'Who is Abimelech, and who is Shechem, that we should serve him? Is not he the son of Jerubbaal? and Zebul his officer? Serve the men of Hamor the father of Shechem: for why should we serve him?
> (29) Oh, if only this people were under my command, I would rid myself of Abimelech! He said to Abimelech, Increase your army, and come out'! (vv. 25–29).

This description commences suddenly without any prior explanation to the context of the betrayal of Abimelech by the citizens of Shechem. The impression is that the citizens of Shechem cease to support Abimelech only out of a wish to increase their wealth: "The citizens of Shechem planted ambuscades against him on the hilltops; and

---

[47] The transitions in the account were explained by the scholars as the result of a combination of different sources. See for instance: Moore, *Judges*, pp. 237–238, Burney, *The Book of Judges*, pp. 266–268. Boling (*Judges*, p. 176) disagreed with this approach. In contrast to the scholars who found a combination of E and J sources in the account, Fritz ("Abimelech und Sichem in Jdc. IX", pp. 129–144) considered that the different sources are local accounts. In his opinion, the account is made up of three separate stories that were adapted at different stages by several redactors. On the other hand, other scholars read the account as a complete and continuous whole. See: Kaufmann, *Sefer Shoftim*, pp. 195–196; Segal, "Studies in the Book of Judges", pp. 1–4. Boogaart, "Stone for Stone", pp. 45–56. In Abramsky's opinion ("Abimelech's Leadership—King, Chief and Ruler", pp. 163–175), the Jotham fable is not part of the Abimelech account; after leaving out the late additions, he finds a uniform story that criticizes the citizens of Shechem and supports Abimelech. Conversely, on the narrator's disapproval of Abimelech, see: Boling, *Judges*, p. 170.

they robbed whoever passed by them on the road" (v. 25). They joined Abimelech when they believed that it would be worth their while to do so. Now they abandon him when they see that they can rob him on the roads and make a greater profit. It was greed that led them to support Abimelech and greed that led them to withdraw their support. Abimelech hears of this: "and it was reported to Abimelech", but does not respond. His lack of response contrasts with his energetic activity to become king. Since Abimelech achieved his position with the self-interested support of the citizens of Shechem, and not because they were in his favour, without their support he is powerless.[48]

In the next stage it is related that Gaal the son of Ebed came into the city and the citizens of Shechem put their confidence in him: "Then Gaal son of Ebed and his kinsfolk came passing through Shechem, and the citizens of Shechem put their confidence in him" (v. 26).[49] We do not know who Gaal son of Ebed is, and why the citizens of Shechem put their confidence in him.[50] This uncertainty is inten-

---

[40] Contrary to Soggin's opinion (*Judges*, p. 188), that Abimelech's silence is a literary technique to show that Abimelech does not speak but only acts. Moore (*Judges*, p. 245) was aware of the problematic nature of this passage, but instead of seeing here Abimelech's helplessness, he used textual criticism to show Abimelech's war against Shechem (v. 42 ff.) as the direct continuation of v. 25.

[49] On the meaning of the name "Gaal" see: Burney, *The Book of Judges*, p. 278. The designation "son of Ebed" is also designed to present him negatively. However, the original meaning of the name is certainly עובד ה׳ (servant of God), see. Burney, *op. cit.*, p. 278. There is a play of words between נעל בן עבד, (Gaal son of Ebed), and his appeal, 9:28:

ומי שכם כי נעבדנו ... עבדו את אנשי המור אבי שכם ומדוע נעבדנו אנחנו

On this point see Klein, *The Triumph of Irony in the Book of Judges*, p. 74. On the meaning of the name, see Boling, *Judges*, p. 176. In Nielson's opinion (*Shechem, A Triditio-Historical Investigation*[2], p. 158), Gaal was not an Israelite.

[50] Moore (*Judges*, pp. 237–238) and Burney (*The Book of Judges*, pp. 267–268) consider that the Gaal story is out of place in the account of the confrontation between Abimelech and the citizens of Shechem. Verses 22–25 speak of an evil spirit sent by God between the citizens of Shechem and Abimelech, which led to the confrontation between them. On the other hand, verses 26 onwards indicate that the situation was caused because of Gaal's intervention. Following the passage dealing with the confrontation with Gaal, in verse 42 the account resumes the description of the confrontation between Abimelech and the citizens of Shechem. Burney, therefore, concludes that the continuation of the account of verses 22–25 is in verses 42 onwards, whereas the Gaal story in verses 26–41 is from a separate source. The main story belongs to the E source and the Gaal story belongs to the J source. Burney based this division on the fact that after the plundering of Abimelech's property we expect a reaction that fails to come in the account. On the other hand, after Abimelech defeats Gaal in verses 26–41, Abimelech's reaction against the citizens of Shechem appears in verses 42 onwards. However, a synchronic solution better suits the intention of the passage. As noted above, the abrupt transitions

tional and is designed to show the ease with which the citizens of Shechem commission a man as king and then reject him and take another in his stead. Gaal was not a native of the city but was passing through (v. 26). Nonetheless, the citizens of Shechem put their confidence in him and commissioned him to represent them against Abimelech.[51] The intention is to present them as always acting out of a narrow and temporary interest. The fact that he is called "Gaal *son of Ebed*" (עבד = servant, slave) recalls the fact that Abimelech is the son of a concubine[52] (9:18; and see also 8:33). The object is to show that the citizens of Shechem always support people who are unworthy.

The next scene describes the holding of the festival of thanksgiving for the grape picking, at which time they cursed Abimelech: "They went out into the fields, gathered the grapes from their vineyards, trod them, and celebrated. They entered the temple of their god, and they ate and drank and they cursed Abimelech" (v. 27).[53] Again the context of the verse and its place in the account is not at all clear. It is not clear who went out to the field. After gathering the grapes from their vineyards, they celebrate and then enter the temple of their god. It is not clear which temple of god they entered, or even who the god in question is. However, it is clear that the

---

between the stages of the story are designed to convey the feeling of an event that evolves irrationally, with the aim of presenting the self-interested motives of each of the sides. Abimelech did not react to the action of the citizens of Shechem in verse 25 because he had lost the main basis of his status and was helpless. This situation will change subsequently when he finds another support. In this matter, see also below.

[51] Reviv ("The Government of Shechem in the El-Amarna Period and in the Days of Abimelech", pp. 252–257) discussed the similarities between the Abimelech account and the description of the actions of the rulers of the city of Shechem in the El-Amarna period. In particular, he noted the fact that Abimelech and Gaal are not residents of the city, like those who came to rule Shechem in the El-Amarna period. He therefore concludes that it was usual in Shechem to accept rulers from outside the city.

[52] Jotham presents Abimelech as the son of a handmaid. In chapter 8, v. 31, it is said that he is the son of a concubine. It seems that the status of the handmaid was lower than that of the concubine; the former was intended for slavery, whereas the latter had marital relations with the master, but apparently without inheritance rights. There is no contradiction between the sources. Apparently, Jotham is trying to demean Abimelech's status, and, therefore, Burney (*The Book of Judges*, p. 276) is incorrect in his assertion that this difference proves that this is a late source

[53] On the grape festival see: Moore, *Judges*, p. 255, Burney, *The Book of Judges*, pp. 278–279.

narrator wished to show the estrangement of the celebrants: "They entered the temple of *their god*". They worship their god and curse Abimelech who is not included in this group. The description of the celebration is not just a background to the description of the betrayal. It helps to create an impression of randomness and fortuity in the act of betrayal; the cursing of Abimelech is only in the context of drunkenness and debauchery.[54]

Only in the next verse is the explanation of their betrayal of Abimelech presented: "And Gaal the son of Ebed said, 'Who is Abimelech, and who is Shechem, that we should serve him? Is not he the son of Jerubbaal? and Zebul his officer? Serve the men of Hamor the father of Shechem: for why should we serve him'?" (v. 28).[55] Gaal's words show that the citizens of Shechem consider themselves the original inhabitants of Shechem—the descendants of Hamor the son of Shechem. Gaal presents the wish of the citizens of Shechem to be ruled again by Hamor's family rather than by Abimelech who is of Israelite origin.

However, this is clearly not the intention behind the reasoning of the citizens of Shechem. Firstly, these wishes did not prevent them from making Abimelech king in the first place. Secondly, at least on his mother's side, Abimelech is connected to Shechem, and thirdly, the betrayal of Abimelech comes before this explanation. The friction commenced when the citizens of Shechem robbed Abimelech, only afterwards was a justification presented. Transfer of the support to Gaal resembles the commissioning of Abimelech. On both occasions the motives were of self-interest disguised as reasoning.[56] Fourthly, this claim is expressed by Gaal, the son of Ebed, whose identity is

---

[54] Soggin, *Judges*, p. 185.

[55] For a discussion of the meaning of the verse and of its syntax, see: Burney, *The Book of Judges*, pp. 279–280; R. G. Boling, "'And Who Is *Š-K-M*?' (Judges IX 28)", *VT* 13 (1963), pp. 479–482.

[56] Boogaart, "Stone for Stone", shows that the Gaal account does not contradict the Abimelech account and does not prejudice the continuity of the account, as claimed by many scholars, but demonstrates how the conspiracy between Abimelech and the citizens of Shechem returns as retribution against them. The citizens of Shechem joined Abimelech as opposed to the legitimate rule of the dynasty of Jerubbaal; in the same way, they joined Gaal against the rule of Abimelech. Just as Abimelech emphasized his kinship with the citizens of Shechem, so did Gaal. Janzen also developed this theme. J. G. Janzen, "A Certain Woman in the Rhetoric of Judges 9", *JSOT* 38 (1987), pp. 34–37. Gerbrandt (*Kingship According to the Deuteronomistic History*, pp. 132–133) also maintained that retribution is the main subject of this account.

unknown. However, we do know that he is not a native. Therefore the fact that this sentence comes precisely from him, and that the citizens of Shechem accept Gaal's authority, proves that they did not desire the distinction of being ruled by a "Shechemite". Gaal's request for the people's support in combating and driving out Abimelech even though Gaal is not from Shechem is ironical, and it serves to present the narrow self-interest of the citizens of Shechem.

Gaal seeks the people's support in order to remove Abimelech and he incites them to war: "Oh, if only this people were under my command, I would rid myself of Abimelech! He said to Abimelech, Increase your army, and come out!" (v. 29). The situation created is ironic. Gaal who is not from Shechem, aided by the citizens of Shechem, fights Abimelech, who is "half Shechemite", and who was supported in the past by the citizens of Shechem, for the control of the city of Shechem in which both are foreigners.

c. *Zebul's support of Abimelech and the deployment against Gaal (vv. 30–34)*

(30) When Zebul, the governor of the city, heard the words of Gaal son of Ebed, he was furious.

(31) He sent messages to Abimelech at Tormah to say, 'Gaal son of Ebed and his kinsfolk have come to Shechem and they are stirring up the city against you.

(32) Therefore, set out at night you and forces you have with you and conceal yourself in the fields. (33) Then early in the morning, as soon as the sun rises, get up and rush on the city; and when he and the troops that are with him come out against you, and you will do to him whatever you find possible'.

(34) So Abimelech and all the troops with him got up by night and lay in wait against Shechem in four companies (vv. 30–34).

Until this stage the reader saw how Gaal promoted the confrontation, while Abimelech appeared powerless. Abimelech's reinforcement comes from an unexpected quarter—Zebul the governor of the city of Shechem. Zebul was mentioned by Gaal as loyal to Abimelech, but there his identity was unknown. Now, in verse 30, Zebul appears as the governor of the city.[57] When Zebul hears of Gaal's intentions,

---

[57] On the "governor of the city" see: N. Avigad "'The Governor of the City' Bulla", H. Geva (ed.), *Ancient Jerusalem Revealed*, Jerusalem 1994, pp. 138–140; G. Barkay, "A Second 'Governor of the City' Bulla", H. Geva (ed.), *Ancient Jerusalem Revealed*, Jerusalem 1994, pp. 141–144; N. Avigad, "On 'A Second Bulla' of a Sar Ha-'ir", *Qadmoniot* 11 (1978), p. 34 (Hebrew).

he sends a message of support to Abimelech and advises him how
to act against Gaal. Until now we thought that it was the citizens
of Shechem who betrayed Abimelech, and when Gaal chanced to
come to the city they supported him, and he conducted the campaign against Abimelech on behalf of the citizens of Shechem. Now
it emerges that there is not unanimity among them, some betrayed
Abimelech and transferred their loyalty to Gaal, but Zebul, the governor of the city, supports Abimelech. This, then, is a war between
Gaal and Abimelech for the rule of the city of Shechem and each has
support within the city; Gaal is supported by the citizens of Shechem
and Abimelech by Zebul. Anyone wishing to understand the nature
of the dispute in Shechem will not find the answer in the account.

There appears to be symmetry between the previous cooperation
between Abimelech and the citizens of Shechem and the cooperation between Zebul and Abimelech. The citizens of Shechem helped
Abimelech to kill his brothers, and Zebul helped Abimelech to kill
Gaal.

Following Zebul's advice to Abimelech, the reader concludes that
he does not properly understand even what seemed clear to him until
now. According to verse 31, Abimelech is in Tormah,[58] and Zebul
who is in Shechem, sends him a message there, whereas Gaal is
with the citizens of Shechem in the field of the city of Shechem. From
the beginning of Zebul's words, it seems that Gaal intends to besiege
Shechem in order to besiege Abimelech within the city of Shechem
(v. 31). Therefore, Zebul suggests to Abimelech that he lie in wait
in the field on Gaal's army when he draws near to the city (v. 32).
However, from his next words it seems that Gaal is in the city and
Zebul suggests that Abimelech set upon the city and capture Gaal
(v. 33). From this, we do not know whom the inhabitants of Shechem
support, Abimelech or Gaal. Will Abimelech fight against the city
or will Gaal fight against the city? An attempt to resolve the ambiguity here misses the intention of the narrator, who wished to give
an impression in the account of everyone against everyone, without

---

[58] According to Kimchi's interpretation, the intention is to Arumah mentioned
in v. 41. Also: Burney, *The Book of Judges*, p. 281; Boling, *Judges*, p. 178. According
to another interpretation, he sent to him בתרמה, deceitfully, Kimchi, and Soggin,
Judges, p. 187. Moore (*Judges*, p. 259) asserted that if this was the intention the
verse would have used the word בסתר (in secret).

any clarity as to who is fighting whom. This situation was designed to highlight the intrigues and interests at the basis of the struggle

Abimelech did not react to the rebellion of the citizens of Shechem, since his kingdom was based only on his and their interests. Now that the governor of the city of Shechem has declared his support for him, he can act, and he indeed does exactly as advised; he gathers his army and lies in wait on the city of Shechem from four directions.

Abimelech's helplessness until approached by Zebul recalls Gideon's reservations before he was ready to start fighting Midian. Gideon's attitude changed when he heard the Midianite's dream, and received inside information on the state of morale in the Midianite camp. Likewise, Abimelech's confidence was restored after he received inside information on the organization of the citizens of Shechem from Zebul, the governor of Shechem. In both cases, immediately after they are strengthened, they deploy for combat. Gideon divides his army into three companies for the attack on Midian, and Abimelech divides his army into four companies in his attack on Shechem. However, there is a highly significant difference between the two accounts. Gideon's attitude changed when he realized that God was indeed with him, whereas Abimelech's attitude changed when he realized that he had a new ally on whom he could rely in order to maintain his rule. Gideon's confidence derived from God, Abimelech's confidence from Zebul.

d. *Zebul deceives Gaal (vv. 35–38)*

> (35) When Gaal son of Ebed came out and stood at the entrance to the city gate, Abimelech and the army with him emerged from concealment.
>
> (36) Gaal saw the army and said to Zebul, 'That's an army marching down from the hilltops!' Zebul said to him, 'The shadows of the hills look to you like men'.
>
> (37) Gaal spoke up again, 'Look, an army is marching down from Tabbur-erez, and another column is coming from the direction of Elon-meonenim'.
>
> (38) Then Zebul said to him, 'where is your boast, Who is Abimelech that we should serve him? There is the army you sneered at; now go out and fight it'! (vv. 35–38).

Again the reader is surprised in this passage by additional details that do not correspond to what has gone before. According to the previous passage, Gaal seemed to be coming from outside Shechem in order to attack Shechem where Abimelech was (v. 31). Now it becomes

apparent that Gaal is in Shechem (v. 35) and he is waiting for
Abimelech's attack (vv. 36–37). Further, according to the previous
passage he apparently does not know of Abimelech's intentions.

There is a further surprise in the account. Gaal had already made
known his assumption that Zebul was Abimelech's ally (v. 28). However, in this passage Zebul is alongside him in the preparations for the
battle against Abimelech. Moreover, this passage makes manifestly
clear that Gaal relies on and trusts Zebul. When Gaal sees people
coming down from the tops of the mountains, Zebul misleads him,
saying that this is the shadow of the hills, and Gaal trusts Zebul
even though previously he saw him as Abimelech's ally. Moreover,
when Gaal sees even more men coming down and approaching, and
he can even identify the direction in which one of the companies is
moving ("Look, an army is marching down from Tabbur-erez, and
another column is coming from the direction of Elon-meonenim",
v. 37), he continues to trust Zebul and does not suspect that he might
have deceived him. It is Zebul who discloses that he is collaborating with Abimelech, when he sarcastically and cynically refers to Gaal's
pretension to fight Abimelech: "Then Zebul said to him, 'where is
your boast, Who is Abimelech that we should serve him'? There is
the army you sneered at; now go out and fight it!" (v. 38). Gaal's
blind trust in Zebul is surprising when a priori he knows of the relations between Zebul and Abimelech. It is difficult to know what happened exactly in the meantime. However, probably some tie was
formed between Zebul and Gaal. Yet the Biblical narrator withholds
this information from the reader, who cannot therefore reconstruct
the dual and changing loyalties of the characters, so that this impression will remain etched in the reader's awareness.

e. *The war between Gaal and Abimelech, Abimelech's victory (vv. 39–41)*

> (39) So Gaal went out at the head of the citizens of Shechem and
> gave battle to Abimelech.
> (40) Abimelech pursued him and he had to flee before him, and
> many fell slain, all the way to the entrance of the gate.
> (41) Abimelech stayed in Arumah, and Zebul expelled Gaal and his
> kinsfolk and kept them out of Shechem (vv. 39–41).

It is again recalled that Gaal did not act alone but in collaboration
with the citizens of Shechem: "So Gaal went out at the head of the
citizens of Shechem". Thus Gaal's downfall is also their downfall, and
Abimelech's victory is also Zebul's victory against the rest of the cit-

izens of Shechem, and Zebul drives Gaal's brethren from the city.
The reader is ignorant, however, as to Zebul's motives in siding with
Abimelech and against the citizens of Shechem.

The difficulty in following the events and the logic behind them
continues also in this passage. In the verse it did not seem that Gaal
came from outside Shechem in order to conquer Shechem from
Abimelech who was in the city. In verse 35 Gaal was in the city
waiting for Abimelech's attack. Now that Abimelech has defeated
Gaal it is not clear why Abimelech, who fought against Gaal in
Shechem, goes to dwell in Arumah. Why does Abimelech, who fought
against Gaal, not take his place in Shechem? Why does Zebul take
this action? Is it possible that Zebul, who was the source of Abimelech's
support in Shechem, prevented Abimelech from entering Shechem?
Here too there does not appear to be a solution, thus allowing the
reader to imagine a variety of possible intrigues.

f. *Abimelech's war against Shechem (vv. 42–49)*

(42) The next day, the people went out into the fields, Abimelech was
informed.

(43) He took the army, and divided it into three columns and lay
in ambush in the fields; and when he saw the people coming out of
the city, he pounced upon them and struck them down.

(44) While Abimelech and the column that followed him dashed ahead
and took up a position at the entrance of the city gate, the other two
columns rushed upon all that were in the open and struck them down.

(45) Abimelech fought against the city all that day. He captured the
city and massacred the people in it; he razed the town and sowed it
with salt.

(46) The citizens of the Tower of Shechem heard, and they went
into the tower of the temple of El-berith.[59]

(47) Abimelech was informed that all the citizens of the Tower of
Shechem had gathered, (48) So Abimelech went up to Mount Zalmon,

---

[59] There is disagreement on whether the "temple of el-Berith" here is identical
to the "temple of Baal-berith" in verse 4. On this see: Cross, *Canaanite Myth and
Hebrew Epic: Essays in the History of the Religion of Israel*, p. 39; Na'aman, "Migdal-
Shechem and the 'House of El-berith'", pp. 264–265, 270–271; J. A. Soggin, "The
Migdal Temple, Migdal šᵉkem Judg 9 and the Artifact on Ebal", M. Augustin and
K. D. Schunk (eds.), *Wünschet Jerusalem Frieden: Collected Communications of the XIIth
Congress of the International Organization for the Study of the Old Testament, Jerusalem 1986*,
Frankfurt am Maine 1988, pp. 115–119; on the identity of El/Baal-Berith, see in
detail: R. E. Clements, "Baal-Berith of Shechem", *JSS* 13 (1968), pp. 21–32; T. J.
Lewis, "The Identity and Function of El/Baal Berith", *JBL* 115 (1996) 401–423.

he and all the troops that were with him Abimelech took an ax in his hand, Abimelech lopped off a tree bough and lifted it onto his shoulder. Then he said to the troops with him, "What you saw me do—quick, do the same!

(49) So each of the troops also lopped off a bough; then they marched behind Abimelech and laid them against the tower, and set fire to the tower over their heads. Thus all the people of the Tower of Shechem also perished, about a thousand men and women (vv. 42–49).

After Abimelech scored his victory over Gaal's army, and Gaal's brethren were driven out of the city, the confrontation seemed to be at an end. Surprisingly, however, the battle continues with the conquest of Shechem. This corresponds to the general intention of the account, which is to show that when people act out of self-interest, the killing and dissension spread in unexpected directions.[60]

Abimelech's war against Shechem is divided into three stages: In the first stage, Abimelech fights against the people in the field (vv. 42–44). In a second stage he goes on to conquer Shechem (v. 45), and in the third stage he burns the tower of Shechem where all the citizens of Shechem had gathered (vv. 46–49).

In this part too the nature of the events is unclear to the reader. Abimelech hears that the people are going out to the field, and he divides his army into three columns, lies in wait and strikes them. Again, in this stage of the war he divides his army into three columns, in order to ambush the people who are going out into the field. However, it is not clear against whom he is fighting at this point. The people going out to the field would seem to be to the residents of the city of Shechem. However, Abimelech has already fought against Gaal's army and Zebul has already driven Gaal's brethren out of the city. Moreover, the Bible presents the men attacked by Abimelech as

---

[60] This explanation is according to the synchronic analysis of the account proposed here. It is an explanation that corresponds more closely to the purpose of the passage, which is to maintain the uncertainty as to Abimelech's aims in continuing the war against Shechem. Amit (*The Book of Judges*, pp. 40–43, 111–112) adopted a similar stance. In her opinion, there is no convincing reason in the account of the destruction of Shechem and of Thebez, in order to present the Abimelech events as a punishment of the transgression of idolatry described at the end of chapter 8. According to Moore (*Judges*, pp. 262–263), it is impossible to understand why Abimelech wages war on Shechem after defeating Gaal. Therefore, he considers that these verses are not a continuation of what went before, but a continuation of verse 25. On this see above, n. 50. Segal ("The Composition of the Abimelech Affair, Judges 9", p. 138) who considers the account to be uniform, admits that something was omitted before verse 42.

simple men going about their agricultural labours, and who are not threatening Abimelech and are not prepared for his attack. Why does Abimelech fight them? There is no answer to this question in the account.[61]

In the second stage Abimelech goes on to fight against the actual city of Shechem:

> Abimelech fought against the city all that day.
> He captured the city
> and massacred the people in it;
> he razed the town
> and sowed it with salt (v. 45).

The lengthy description of Abimelech's conquest of the city is designed to emphasize the destruction that he sowed there. It could have been thought that it would have sufficed for Abimelech to conquer Shechem and impose his rule. However, he killed all the inhabitants and destroyed the city. The duality of the expressions "he razed the town" and "sowed it with salt",[62] gives a feeling of total destruction of the city.

In the third stage of the conquest, Abimelech focuses on the tower of Shechem where all the people of the city had gathered.[63] This tower is fortified and unassailable by normal combat. Without delay, Abimelech cuts down trees and orders his soldiers to do the same. Using these trees they set fire to the tower with the many people who are inside. Abimelech is shown in this passage as a shrewd leader in organization of his soldiers, using military ingenuity according to the special circumstances.

---

[61] See Boling, *Judges*, p. 179.

[62] This is the meaning of the expression also in Deut 29:22, Jer 17:6; Ps 107:33–34; perhaps also Gen 19:26. On the sowing of salt in a place destroyed, in the ancient East, see: Gaster, *Myth, Legend and Custom in the Old Testament*, pp. 428–430; and also: Burney, *The Book of Judges*, p. 285. Some interpret the meaning of the sowing of salt to be a preliminary stage for imposing a taboo on the city, see S. Geviratz, "Jericho and Shechem: A Religio-Literary Aspect of City Destruction", *VT* 13 (1963), pp. 52–62. Boling rightly disagreed with this, asserting that there is no trace of a ḥerem motif in the account of the destruction of the city. For other explanations, see: Boling, *Judges*, p. 180; F. C. Fensham, "Salt as Curse in the Old Testament and the Ancient Near East", *BA* XXV (1962), pp. 48–50.

[63] On the "tower of Shechem" as a separate city, close to Shechem and not encompassed by a wall, see: Moore, *Judges*, p. 264. On this matter, see also: Na'aman, "Migdal-Shechem and the 'House of El-berith'", pp. 260–265. Wright considers that the "tower of Shechem" is the temple of a god. G. E. Wright, *Shechem: The Biography of a Biblical City*, New-York and Toronto 1965, pp. 126–127. See also: Soggin, "The Migdal Temple, Migdal šᵉkem Judg 9 and the Artifact on Ebal", pp. 115–119.

Abimelech's war against the citizens of Shechem is understood in light of their betrayal. However, the Bible emphasizes that Abimelech killed "about a thousand men and women" in the tower of Shechem. The degree of cruelty employed against Shechem is not surprising, given Abimelech's cold-blooded murder of his seventy brothers. In this action Abimelech again appears as unworthy of leadership. Abimelech kills the very men over whom he wished to rule. His wish to be king did not derive from a wish to benefit the people. Abimelech murdered his brothers with the assistance of the citizens of Shechem in order to be king. Now he murders the citizens of Shechem who refuted his crown.

As in the previous stages of the confrontation, in this stage too there is a lack of clarity as regards the object of Abimelech's action against the city of Shechem: the killing of the citizens of Shechem in the field in the first stage, the destruction of the city and killing of its inhabitants in the second stage, and the burning of the thousand men and women in the tower of Shechem in the third stage. Gaal's threat had already been removed and Abimelech was victorious in this confrontation, so it is unclear what he wished to achieve with the destruction of Shechem. Moreover, again it is not clear against whom Abimelech was fighting. Zebul, the governor of the city, who had supported him, dwelt in the city, and it seems that he had already taken control (v. 41).[64] The ambiguity in this part reaches a further climax. Abimelech's struggle seemed to derive from a wish to restore his rule over Shechem, following the betrayal of the citizens of Shechem and the new leadership of Gaal the son of Ebed. However, Abimelech himself destroys his regime. His motives in this act are unclear.

g. *Abimelech's conquest of Thebez, his defeat by a woman, and the disintegration of his kingdom (vv. 50–55)*

(50) Then Abimelech went to Thebez; he encamped at Thebez and occupied it.

(51) Within the town was a fortified tower; and all the men and women and all the citizens of the town, took refuge there. They shut themselves in, and went up on the roof of the tower.

---

[64] In the opinion of several scholars verses 46 onwards are another tradition of the same war that is described in verses 43–45, and the redactor placed them after each other. See for instance: Wright, *Shechem*, p. 126; Boling, *Judges*, p. 181. In Martin's opinion (*The Book of Judges*, p. 127), the war over the tower of Shechem was waged prior to the destruction of Shechem.

(52) Abimelech came to the tower, and attacked it. He approached the door of the tower to set it on fire.

(53) But a woman dropped an upper millstone on Abimelech's head and cracked his skull.

(54) He immediately cried out to his attendant, his arms-bearer, 'Draw your dagger and kill me, that they may not say of me, A woman killed him!' So his attendant stabbed him, and he died.

(55) The men of Israel saw that Abimelech was dead, and every-one went home (vv. 50–55).

The ambiguity regarding Abimelech's goals and the identity of his opponents reaches a climax in this part of the account. Now it is related that Abimelech goes to conquer Thebez. He tries to take control of the tower where the town's residents have gathered, thereby repeating his achievement in Shechem. Here too men and women are gathered in the tower that Abimelech seeks to burn. Why does Abimelech fight against Thebez? Again there is no explanation of Abimelech's act in the account. The reader is also extremely surprised, since this is the first mention of the town of Thebez.

Abimelech's downfall comes from an unexpected direction. When Abimelech approaches the town's tower in order to subdue it, a woman throws an upper millstone on his head, seriously injuring him.[65] Out of concern for his honour after his death, Abimelech does not want it to be said that he was killed by a woman, and asks

---

[65] In Tanhuma [(Buber) Wayyera, 4.28, p. 114], the millstone dropped on the head of Abimelech is retribution for his slaughter of his brothers on one stone (9:5). "The Holy one said to Abimelech Son of Gideon (of Jud 9): O wicked one, see the honour that Abimelech paid to Abraham! Now you have arisen and killed your brothers, (according to v. 5) 'seventy men on one stone'. Woe to that man, for thus Solomon has spoken (in Eccl. 10:8): 'The one who digs a pit will fall into it'. Accordingly, he also was not killed other than by means of a stone, as stated (in v. 53): 'Then a certain woman cast a millstone . . .'. The Holy One said to him: I have written in my Torah (in Prov. 10:27) 'The fear of the LORD increases one's days, but the years of the wicked will be shortened'. Now you have killed your brothers. By your life, I am shortening the life of that man (i.e., Abimelech). He therefore reigned three years, as stated (in Judg. 9:22): 'Now Abimelech ruled over Israel three years'". On this matter see also: Boogaart, "Stone for Stone", p. 51. This Midrash explains Abimelech's kingship as retribution for Gideon's positive reaction in his refusal to rule over the people, *ibid.*, p. 52. When they said to him, "Rule over us—you, your son, and your grandson as well" (8:22), he said to them: I will not rule over you myself, [nor shall my son rule over you; the LORD shall rule over you] (Judg 8:23). They said three things to him, and he said three things to them. God said to him, Upon your life, I am setting up from you a son who will reign three years against the three things that you said, humility should come before honour. Therefore, Abimelech reigned [over Israel for three years] (*ibid.*, 9, 22)".

his attendant to kill him. Abimelech scored an impressive victory in his struggle against the citizens of Shechem. It is therefore ironic that when the war is almost over he is defeated by a woman unskilled in the martial arts.[66]

The irony of Abimelech's death is even greater. Abimelech's aim in having himself made king was completely selfish. His endeavours to achieve a high status were totally egocentric, as expressed in the murder of his brothers and the merciless killing of the citizens of Shechem. In his death, however, he was humiliated and degraded.

Abimelech's death is also the end of his kingdom: "The men of Israel saw that Abimelech was dead, and everyone went home" (v. 55). The end of the account with the disintegration of Abimelech's kingdom contrasts with the commencement of the account: "Abimelech son of Jerubbaal went to Shechem" (9:1).[67] The fact that the people abandoned Abimelech's kingdom and did not try to continue it in any way is significant. Abimelech was made king as Gideon's heir, and it could have been expected that upon Abimelech's death there would be some attempt to crown an heir. The dispersal of the people immediately after Abimelech's death expresses their disappointment and dissatisfaction with his rule. The body of "men of Israel" that disperses, with the clear intention of putting an end to Abimelech's kingdom, is the same body that initially wished to make Gideon king (8:22). This shows the people's disillusionment with the first attempt to found a monarchy in Israel. However, in contrast to the opinion of the scholars who consider that the Abimelech account is fundamentally anti-monarchic, here it seems clearly that the people's regret derives from Abimelech's leadership, as shown in the account.

h. *Theological conclusion (vv. 56–57)*

> (56) Thus God repaid Abimelech for the evil he had done to his father by slaying his seventy brothers; (57) and God also made all the wickedness of the people of Shechem fall back on their heads, and on them came the curse of Jotham son of Jerubbaal (vv. 56–57).

This theological conclusion parallels the theological introduction describing the confrontation between Abimelech and the citizens of Shechem at the beginning of the war account (vv. 23–24). Throughout

---

[66] It is a further irony that in the historical memory it will be perceived that it was a woman who killed Abimelech, 2 Sam 11:21.

[67] Abramsky, "Abimelech's Leadership—King, Chief and Ruler", p. 164.

the account uncertainty passed as a leitmotif through the entire description of the confrontation between Abimelech and the citizens of Shechem. The natural explanation of this is that Abimelech and the citizens of Shechem were motivated by personal interests, and had no concern for the good of the people, or any other ethical constancy. Therefore the loyalties are not unequivocal and do not last. Abimelech betrayed his brothers, the citizens of Shechem betrayed Gideon. The citizens of Shechem then betrayed Abimelech, and Zebul betrayed the citizens of Shechem and supported Abimelech. Now, on conclusion of the account, the reader can explain the confusion over the nature of the aims and actions of the characters by God's direct intervention to punish Abimelech and the citizens of Shechem for the murder of Abimelech's brothers. This prevented any possibility of human reasoning.

5. *The Meaning of the Abimelech Account*

The Abimelech account does not correspond to the pattern of the other judge accounts in the Book. Abimelech does not deliver the people and the account does not deal with the oppression of Israel by an enemy. This account tells of Abimelech's reign, and is a direct continuation of the Gideon account. Gideon refused the office of king, for theological reasons. Abimelech, his son, ignores these considerations and employs immoral means to become king. The object of the account is to show the result of a monarchy that is brought about by negative motives.

The Abimelech account has three parts that are interconnected in a clear thematic continuity. The account opens with Abimelech's successful endeavours to become king of Shechem (vv. 1–6). The second part describes in detail Jotham's oration opposing the appointment of Abimelech as king, and his curse, predicting that a dispute between Abimelech and the citizens of Shechem will lead to their downfall (vv. 7–21). The third part is constituted by the fulfilment of Jotham's words, and a detailed description of the violent confrontation between Abimelech and the citizens of Shechem (vv. 22–57). The close connection between the parts of the account manifests the unity of the idea emerging from all the parts of the account.

The account of Abimelech's accession to kingship shows his actions in a negative light, through the contrast between his acts and those of his father Gideon. Abimelech craves to be king, and stops at nothing

to obtain his object. He puts all his energy into becoming king. He
bribes his family in Shechem to intervene with the citizens of Shechem,
and in exchange for their support he promises them benefits. They
make him king because of the benefits that they expect to receive.
His egotistical desire to be king led him to the cold-blooded, savage
murder of his seventy brothers. Abimelech is the example of a negative leader.[68] His wish to be king regardless of the good of the people sharply contrasts with Gideon's identification with his people,
and his objections to accepting the role of deliverer at the beginning of the account and the role of king at its end. Notwithstanding,
the cruelty demonstrated by Abimelech towards his brothers for egotistical reasons, recalls Gideon's acts against the men of Succoth and
of Penuel for like reasons. There are contradictions in Gideon's personality and acts. In some cases, he acted out of national motives
and self-sacrifice. In others, he acted for personal reasons of status
and honour. Abimelech's personality is one-dimensional. His desire
for honour and power are extreme, whereas he shows no regard for
national considerations or God's will. From this point of view, certainly, Abimelech is an anti-judge figure. He is shown as having a
personality unworthy of office. The account is not anti-monarchic,
as many scholars purport. Rather it presents a model of an egocentric leader, who is only concerned with his own good, and who
is unworthy of leadership.[69] The negative attitude towards Abimelech
is expressed by the fact that throughout the account the word אלהים
only is used to designate God.[70]

Jotham's fable continues the censure of Abimelech's personality
showing him as unfit to be king. The force of his rebuke is that
Abimelech's personal ambition to be king will one day conflict with

---

[68] Klein (*The Triumph of Irony in the Book of Judges*, p. 70) calls Abimelech an anti-
judge. On Abimelech's negative personality throughout the story, see Boling, *Judges*,
p. 170; Marais, *Representation in Old Testament Narrative Texts*, p. 115.

[69] See above n. 2.

[70] Polzin, *Moses and the Deuteronomist*, p. 173. On the relationship between the
figure of Gideon and the figure of Abimelech, see also: Simon, "The Parable of
Jotham", pp. 30–32; M. Garsiel, "Models of Analogy and Sets of Comparison in
the Bible: With Specific Reference to Judges and Samuel", S. Ettinger et al. (eds.),
Milet: Everyman's University Studies in Jewish History and Culture, II, Tel-Aviv 1985, pp.
38–43 (Hebrew). Crüsemann (*Der Widerstand gegen das Königtum*, p. 42) notes that
Gideon is appointed by God, delivers Israel and refuses to rule. Abimelech, on the
other hand, seizes the monarchy though violence and does not seek God's assistance. Gideon dies at a good old age and Abimelech is killed.

the good of the people, who will ultimately pay the price for Abimelech's egotism. Jotham's rebuke is also against the citizens of Shechem who ill requited Gideon, collaborating with Abimelech to kill Gideon's sons and make Abimelech king.

The third part of the account describes the fulfilment of Jotham's words. This part describes the dispute between Abimelech and the citizens of Shechem, which derived from incompatibility between the selfish motives of each of the sides. The account opens with the betrayal of Abimelech by the citizens of Shechem, but without any explicit explanation of the context. The impression is that they betrayed him out of greed and a wish to increase their wealth at his expense. This is the main motif in the account. They made Abimelech king because of personal interests, and rebelled against him for the same reason. The transfer of loyalties from one side to the other derives from the constant wish to advance their personal interests. What characterizes the account is that it is not clear who supports whom and who opposes whom. The citizens of Shechem use Gaal, who is an obscure personality and not a citizen of Shechem. It is not clear what his motives are and it is also not clear why the citizens of Shechem placed their confidence in him. The loyalties among the citizens of Shechem are also unclear. Abimelech is powerless in face of the betrayal of the citizens of Shechem, but his hope comes from an unexpected quarter. Zebul the governor of the city does not support the citizens of Shechem, but supports and assists Abimelech. His motives, however, are obscure. It is also unclear what happened in the meantime that led Gaal to trust Zebul, when attacked by Abimelech's force. After Abimelech overcomes Gaal and Zebul drives Gaal's brethren from the city, surprisingly the incident is not over. Now again, Abimelech fights against Shechem after Zebul his ally has taken control of the city, and it is impossible to understand the circumstances. The ambiguity continues when Abimelech goes to conquer the town of Thebez which was not mentioned previously. Once more, it is not clear why the war develops in this direction.

The ambiguity in the description of the war is a tool to show that one cannot predict developments when a leader seizes power out of self-interested motives and is supported by allies who are self-interested; allies will become enemies, and there will be no clear distinction between friend and foe.

CHAPTER THREE

THE JEPHTHAH ACCOUNT (10:6–12:7)

1. *Transgression, Punishment and Lament (10:6–18)*

The Israelites again did what was offensive to the LORD.
They served
the Baalim
and the Ashtaroth,
and the gods of Aram,
the gods of Sidon,
the gods of Moab,
the gods of the Ammonites,
and the gods of the Philistines;
they forsook the LORD and did not serve Him. (10:6).

This description of Israel's transgression is the longest and most serious in the Book of Judges. In the other accounts, there is one short sentence to summarize the transgression: "The Israelites (again) did what was offensive to the LORD" (3:12; 4:1; 6:1).[1]

The description of the transgression commences with a general allegation that "The Israelites again did what was offensive to the LORD" as do the parallel descriptions in the other accounts. However, here the account departs from the usual wording and goes into extensive details of the other gods that Israel worshipped. The passage specifies seven idolatrous cults adopted by Israel. The number seven is probably typological, and expresses totality.[2] It shows Israel as adopting foreign cults of all types, and the forsaking of God is more serious than in any other account in the Book. At the same time, this list has another meaning. It is arranged in the chronological

---

[1] The description of the first transgression in the Othniel account is slightly longer than the other accounts, except for the Jephthah account: "And they did what was offensive to the LORD, and forgot the LORD their God, and served the Baalim and the Asheroth" (3:7).

[2] For a bibliography on the subject, see: Zakovitch, *The Pattern of Numerical Sequence Three-Four in the Bible*, p. 22, n. 132.

order of the accounts in the Book of Judges.[3] Before the appearance
of Othniel, it is recounted that Israel: "served the Baalim and the
Asherahs" (3:7), and accordingly the Baal and the Ashtaroth appear
first in the list in the introduction to the Jephthah account. Then the
"gods of Sidon" are cited, which do not appear elsewhere in the
Book. The next in the list of the foreign cults partially corresponds
to the order of the oppressors in the Book of Judges: the gods of
Aram (Cushan-rishathaim in the Othniel account), the gods of Moab
(Eglon king of Moab in the Ehud account), the gods of Ammon (in
the Jephthah account) and the gods of the Philistines (in the Samson
account).[4] Mention of the foreign cults in this order is designed to
show that not only did the Israelites not learn the lesson from all
the different oppressions that they suffered in the period of the judges,
but on the contrary, they learnt the negative lesson and adopted the
oppressor's gods.

The description of the Israelites' idolatrous transgressions ends with
another general and serious allegation that expresses both the
affirmative and the negative actions present in the transgression:
"they forsook the LORD and did not serve Him" (10:6). However,
beyond its rhetorical meaning, the expression contains an ideological

---

[3] W. Richter, *Die Bearbeitungen des "Retterbuches" in der deuteronomischen Epoche* (Bonner
Biblische Beiträge, 21), Bonn 1964, p. 16.

[4] In this order, there is no mention of the "Canaanite gods", which should have
come after the Ehud account, as representative of the Deborah account. The reason is perhaps that this included the worship of the Baal, which had already been
mentioned or that, as indicated by Moran, Sidon, which is cited in the verse, is
identical to Canaan. W. L. Moran, "A Study of the Deuteronomic History", *Biblica*
46 (1965), p. 227. However, the Sidonians are also cited in v. 12, even though
there is no mention in the Bible of Israel's oppression by the Sidonians. Moore
(*Judges*, p. 280) disagreed on the correlation between Sidon and the northern
Canaanite peoples. In his opinion, the mention of Sidon in v. 12 is merely to correspond to their mention in v. 6. However, this explanation is improbable since
the two lists fail to correspond in most of the details. Presumably, the worship of
the Midianite gods is not mentioned because this cult perhaps was not institutionalized, as a result of the nomadic nature of the Midianites. Indeed, we have information on the cults of the peoples cited in the list, but not on the Midianite cult.
In this context, Moran (*ibid.*, p. 228) suggests reading "Midian" in verse 12, instead
of "Maon", and this is also the Septuagint version. Rabbi Avraham ben Shlomo
(*Piruš 'al nevi'im rišonim: Yehoshua, Shoftim* (Rabbi Joseph Kapach edition) Kiryat Ono
1999, p. 229, a 15th century Jewish interpreter from Yemen), considers that "Maon"
means "Midian". Accordingly, "Midian" does not appear in the list of gods, but it
does appear in the list of the peoples from whom God delivered Israel. Notwithstanding,
Amit (*Judges*, p. 191) rightly asserts that it is difficult to accept the substitution of
a rare name for a well-known name.

assessment and a theological definition of the transgression. It is not just a question of doing evil and transgressing, but of forsaking God. What emerges here is that, unlike other cases in the Bible, the people do not merely adopt a foreign cult without forsaking God, but they forsake God in favour of other gods.

The response to these serious transgressions is the usual retribution visited by God in the Book of Judges:

> (7) And the LORD, incensed with Israel, surrendered them to the Philistines and to the Ammonites. (8) That year⁵ they battered and shattered the Israelites—for eighteen years—all the Israelites beyond the Jordan, in what had been the land of the Amorites in Gilead. (9) The Ammonites also crossed the Jordan to make war on Judah, Benjamin, and the House of Ephraim. Israel was in great distress (10:7–9).

This time God sent the Philistines and the Ammonites against Israel.⁶ However, Jephthah will deliver Israel in fact only from the Ammonites and there is no mention of deliverance from the Philistines. Moreover, in details of the punishment in these verses, only the actions of the Ammonites are described, firstly beyond the eastern Jordan, and then their expansion to the west side. If so, what is the place of the Philistines in this introduction? This question will be left open for now, and discussed later.

The description of the Ammonite oppression is divided into two stages. In the first stage, they take control on the east side of the Jordan: "all the Israelites beyond the Jordan, in what had been the land of the Amorites in Gilead" (v. 8), and in the second stage they pass over the Jordan and take control of extensive areas on the west side of the Jordan: "The Ammonites also crossed the Jordan to make war on Judah, Benjamin, and the House of Ephraim" (v. 9). The

---

⁵ Moore (*Judges*, p. 277) considers that the words "eighteen years" are an addition, and the verbs at the beginning of the verse better correspond to a short oppression; he opines, therefore, that the version "in that year" is preferable. See also: *Ibid.* p. 278. The interpretation of the words "in that year" as meaning from the year onwards is unlikely. See for instance: Kimchi and Kara. The understanding of the Septuagint, "in that year—in that period" is more probable, like the word יום that is interpreted in the sense of "period". "In that year" can perhaps be interpreted as "in the eighteenth year of the oppression". This is also the case in Jer 32:1: "in the tenth year of Zedekiah . . . which was the eighteenth year of Nebuchadrezzar".

⁶ Boling (*Judges*, p. 191) indicates that the mention of the Philistines and the Ammonites, in the reverse order of their mention in verse 6, is a stylistic tool designed to connect the two verses through chiasmus.

description of the Midianite oppression in the Gideon account is long, and the principle hardship there was the serious damage to the lives of the Israelites and their possibilities of livelihood (6:2–6). The description here does not specify the acts of the Ammonites but principally the tremendous areas that they occupied, and the many tribes that were subject to their rule. This is not the first time that a people dwelling on the east side passes over the Jordan. This is the case in the Ehud account. There, Moab possessed the city of the palm trees, and in Ehud's war against Moab he takes the fords of the Jordan in order to trap the ten thousand Moabite soldiers who crossed the Jordan (3:28–29). However, there the stages of Moab's expansion and the scope of their occupation are not mentioned.[7] This is not so in the Jephthah account. Here, there are two stages of the Ammonite occupation: first, the suffering of the Israelites on the east side of the Jordan is mentioned, and then in the second stage, the crossing to the west side of the Jordan. The second stage describes the Ammonites' war in extremely extensive areas of the west side that affected three tribes: Judah, Benjamin and Ephraim. The fact that Ammon attacked Judah is unique. This is the first time in the Book of Judges that the tribe of Judah was affected by the oppression of a foreign enemy.

What lies behind this unique description of the Ammonite oppression? Possibly the object of this description is to show Israel's helplessness and their inability to provide a deliverer even though many tribes were subject to the Ammonite occupation, both on the east and the west sides of the Jordan.[8] The fact that there was no local leader to take the initiative and fight against the Ammonite oppression, as there had been until now in the book, is all the more marked in light of the fact that the Ammonite conquest was carried out in several stages.

As in the other judge accounts, the next stage is the people's lament to God: "Then the Israelites cried out to the LORD" (10:10$_a$). This sentence is identical to the formula in the other judge accounts (3:9; 3:15; 4:3; 6:6). However, in the other accounts the short state-

---

[7] In Webb's opinion (*The Book of the Judges*, p. 56), the Ammonite conquest of the area of Moab is the result of Israel's victory over Moab in Chapter 3. In this context, he also indicates the mention of Ammon in the Ehud account, 3:13.

[8] In general, the judge was a local deliverer who rose up in the area of distress. On the local nature of the action of the Judges, see: Eissfeldt, *The Old Testament, An Introduction*, p. 259; Malamat, *History of Biblical Israel*, p. 98.

ment of the lament is followed immediately by a comprehensive account of the deliverance of Israel from their plight. Notwithstanding, in this introduction there is a long dialogue between God and Israel that includes the contents of the lament to God: "we have sinned before You, for we have forsaken our God and served the Baalim" (10:10_b). Certain scholars rightly stress that the contents of the lament to God in the judge accounts do not include repentance,[9] and therefore the lament to God following the Ammonite oppression is exceptional: this is repentance *par excellence*; it includes an acknowledgement that they transgressed "we have sinned before You", and precise details of the transgression: "for we have forsaken our God and served the Baalim". This avowal is greatly reinforced in that it parallels the description of Israel's transgression related by the narrator in the introduction:

v. 10_b
"for we have forsaken our God and served the Baalim"

v. 6_b
"they forsook the LORD and did not serve Him"

This repentance seems sincere and therefore a further departure of the account from the usual model in the Book of Judges is particularly conspicuous:

(11) But the LORD said to the Israelites,
"I have rescued you from the Egyptians, from the Amorites, from the Ammonites, and from the Philistines. (12) The Sidonians, Amalek, and Maon also oppressed you; and when you cried out to Me, I saved you from them.
(13) Yet you have forsaken Me and have served other gods, therefore, I will not deliver you again.
(14) Go cry to the gods you have chosen; they will deliver you in your time of distress! (vv. 11–14)

God presents to the Israelites a brief historic review commencing with the exodus from Egypt, recalling the conquest of Canaan and other events that are not cited in the Bible.[10] God indicates that in

---

[9] There are scholars who consider that this stage expresses the people's repentance. See, for instance: Wellhausen, *Prolegomena to the History of Ancient Israel*, p. 231, Kaufmann, *Sefer Shoftim*, pp. 156; H. W. Wolff, "Kerygma of the Deuteronomic Historical Work", W. Brueggemann and H. W. Wolff (eds.), *The Vitality of the Old Testament Traditions*, Atlanta 1975, p. 98. Brueggemann disagrees with this hypothesis. Brueggemann, "Social Criticism and Social Vision in the Deuteronomic Formula of the Judges", pp. 108–109.
[10] Kaufmann, *Sefer Shoftim*, p. 219. It is evident that this list does not correspond

all these events the pattern is repeated: Israel cries out to God because of their oppressors, God delivers them, but each time Israel forsakes God and returns to idolatry. This description resembles the historio-sophical introduction to the Book of Judges (2:11–3:6), but here God decides that He is now putting an end to this repetitive cycle: "there-fore, I will not deliver you again". God now ironically tells Israel to cry out this time to the gods that they worshipped for deliverance: "Go cry to the gods you have chosen; they will deliver you in your time of distress" (v. 14).

How is this scathing response by God to be understood? Does He really mean that He will not deliver them in the future? How can one understand the appearance of this resolute decision precisely after the most complete repentance of Israel, a repentance unparal-leled in the Book of Judges? Are God's words merely rhetoric designed to shock the Israelites and to spur them to better repentance? Such a possibility is negated by the people's response to God's harsh words.

They are not indifferent, but manifest even more impressive repen-tance, vv. 15–16:

> The Israelites said to the LORD:
> 'we have sinned,
> You do to us as You see fit;
> only save us this day!'
> They removed the alien gods from among them and served the LORD.

There are four elements in Israel's repentance. The first and the last elements relate to Israel, and the two middle elements relate to actions that they request from God. The first element is the con-fession and it is the shortest: חָטָאנוּ ("we have sinned"). On the other hand, the last element is the remedying of the transgression and it is the longest. The avowal "we have sinned" is short, firstly because they had already confessed in the first stage when they appealed to God, and there it appeared in length ("we have sinned before You, for we have forsaken our God and served the Baalim", v. 10). The innovation in this stage is not acknowledgment of the transgression but the practical action performed by Israel in order to extirpate the

---

to the accounts in the book. The "Amorite" perhaps refers to Jabin, King of Canaan, in chapters 4–5. However, conflicts with Sidon and Maon, or the Ammonites, were not mentioned in the book up to this stage. In contrast, Midian is not cited in the list, while Amalek, which was a junior partner of Midian, does appear. Aram and Moab are also not mentioned in the list.

transgression. This stage is the longest, in order to impress the reader not only with the sincerity of their repentance but with the fact that they also worked seriously to solve the problem. The comparison between the first and the last element is also impressive in that it presents Israel as speaking little (חטאנו ["we have sinned"]—one word) and doing much (ויסירו את אלהי הנכר מקרבם ויעבדו את ה, "They removed the alien gods from among them and served the LORD").

The comparison of the structure of the confession and the repentance in Israel's response to God's statement—"I will not deliver you again", and between the expression of regret immediately after the description of the punishment, also shows that it is an improved and better repentance. Initially the lament came at the beginning of the words ("Then the Israelites cried out to the LORD", v. 10) and then the acknowledgement of the transgression ("we have sinned before You", v. 10). Now first there is acknowledgement of the transgression ("we have sinned", v. 15) and the appeal for deliverance comes subsequently ("only save us this day", v. 15), and this only after willingness to receive another punishment from God on account of their transgression.

The act of extirpating the transgression parallels like actions formulated in similar language by Jacob, Joshua and Samuel (Gen 35:2, 4; Josh 24:23; 1 Sam 7:3–4). Placing removal of the foreign gods here on a par with this distinguished group gives authentic validity to Israel's repentance.

The repentance is formulated as the opposite of the transgression: they practiced idolatry and ceased worshipping God, and in contrast they also eliminated the idolatry and resumed worship of God:

(1) "They served the Baalim and the Ashtaroth
    (2) they forsook the LORD and did not serve Him". (10:6)
(1) "They removed the alien gods from among them
    (2) and they served the LORD". (10:16)

The acknowledgement of the transgression is complete in that they do not refuse to receive punishment, they are aware of their responsibility and partially prepared to bear the results: "*You* do to us as *You* see fit" (10:15). However they ask God to remove the Ammonite oppression: "only save us this day", and they wish to receive the punishment directly from God and not from the Ammonites ("*You* do to us as").[11] An important point emerging here is that Israel are

---

[11] A similar situation is found in King David's decision not to be punished by war, but by pestilence, 2 Sam 24, 11–16.

aware that the Ammonite servitude is punishment for their idolatry.

The people's positive response to God's rebuke appears clearly from a comparison between this case and two other analogical rebukes in the Book of Judges, one at the beginning of the book (2:1–5), and the other at the start of the Gideon account (6:7–8).

10:11–14	6:7–9	2:2–5
The LORD *said to the Israelites,*	the LORD sent a prophet to the Israelites who said to them,	Now *the angel of the* LORD went up from Gilgal to Bochim, and said,
"*I have rescued you from the Egyptians,* from the Amorites, from the Ammonites, and from the Philistines. The Sidonians, Amalek, and Maon *also oppressed you;* and when you cried out to Me, I saved you from them.	"Thus said the LORD, the God of Israel: *I brought you up out of Egypt* and freed you from the house of slavery. I rescued you from the *hand of the Egyptians and from the hand of all your oppressors*; I drove them out before you, *and gave you their land.*	"*I brought you up from Egypt, and brought you into the land* that I had promised to your ancestors. I said, 'I will never break my covenant with you.
Yet you have forsaken Me *and have served other gods,*	And I said to you, 'I am the LORD your God. *You must not worship the gods* of the Amorites in whose land you dwell.' But you did not obey Me".	For your part, *do not make a covenant with the inhabitants of this land; tear down their altars.' But you have not obeyed my command.* See what you have done!
Therefore, I will not deliver you again. Go cry to the gods you have chosen; they will deliver you in your time of distress!"		So now I say, I will not drive them out before you; but they shall become adversaries to you, and their gods shall be a snare to you." When the angel of the LORD spoke these words to all the Israelites, the people lifted up their voices and wept.

In these three passages there are three to four shared elements arranged in the same order and containing a similar vocabulary. The three passages commence with God or His representative addressing the Israelites (2:1; 6:8; 10:11). The second element in all the cases is the description of God's acts for Israel, and including in each of the cases mention of the deliverance from the Egyptians and from other peoples (2:1; 6:8–9; 10:11–12). The next stage is a description of the transgression of the Israelites who worshipped other gods despite all that God had done for them (2:2; 6:10; 10:13). Following the transgression in the Jephthah account, God says to Israel that He will not deliver them again, and in the Bochim account, because of the transgression, the angel promises Israel that they will be punished (2:3; 10:13).

In the context of the similarities between the three rebukes, the differences between the situations reflected in them are very conspicuous. I have already discussed the difference between the response to the angel's rebuke at Bochim and the prophet's rebuke at the beginning of the Gideon account. In the first case, the people responded to the angel's rebuke with weeping and accepted the rebuke. However, in the Gideon account, the people remained indifferent to the prophet's rebuke. Moreover, Gideon argues with the prophet, and complains that God has failed to deliver the people. In this case precisely, God delivers the people despite the harsh responses of the people and Gideon. In contrast, in the Jephthah account, the people express remorse for their transgression and return to worship of God. However, precisely in this account, it is God who rejects Israel's repentance and does not send them a deliverer.

God's response to Israel's words and acts is surprising: ותקצר נפשו בעמל ישראל ("and his soul was grieved for the misery of Israel") (v. 16b). This expression is not sufficiently clear. It seems to mean that God no longer wished to see Israel's suffering.[12] This strange response

---

[12] Kimchi; Moore, *Judges*, p. 281; Kaufmann, *Sefer Shoftim*, p. 216. Polzin (*Moses and the Deuteronomist*, p. 177) explained that God's patience had run out following Israel's attempts to repent and to change God's mind. However, it is difficult to accept that the meaning of עמל is Israel's repentance. Therefore, it seems rather that עמל refers to Israel's oppression by the Ammonites. Abravanel explained that Israel's soul was grieved, namely the harsh oppression led Israel to lose patience. Gersonides interpreted עמל as meaning deceit (see Ps 10:7). Namely, God lost patience because of Israel's recurrent lying. However, this interpretation is difficult, since Israel's repentance in this case seems absolutely authentic.

differs from all the accounts in the Book of Judges. At this stage in all the other accounts God sends a deliverer to save Israel from their enemies, but here only God's 'feelings' are related! Moreover, the expression ותקצר נפשו ("and his soul was grieved") always relates to a man who is powerless and requires God's help. This is so in relation to Israel: ותקצר נפש העם בדרך ("and the soul of the people was much discouraged because of the way") (Num 21:4), and also in relation to Samson whose great thirst leads him to think that he is going to die, until God gives him water: ותקצר נפשו למות ("his soul was vexed unto death") (16:16).[13] In this case, indeed, God does not respond with a concrete action and He does not send a deliverer to Israel. God's lack of response recalls the other cases in which it was said about someone ותקצר נפשו and he was helpless. Where the reader expects God to respond concretely, delivering Israel, he hears about God's innermost thoughts. This will be followed immediately by the attempt of the princes of Gilead to find a deliverer and, as will be seen below, this only emphasizes God's lack of response to Israel's request. It is again made clear that God's intention not to appoint a deliverer is serious, but why does God refuse to deliver Israel? This refusal comes precisely when the people repent in a way unparalleled elsewhere in the Book of Judges. Also, in a broader Biblical context, Israel's response is appropriate; it would be hard to find a better response.[14] We will return to this question shortly.

---

[13] See also: Zach 11:8; and Job 21:4–5.

[14] Many solutions have been proposed for the fact that God does not respond to the repentance of the people, and for this deviation from the model presented at the beginning of the book. One point of view is that this account did correspond originally to the model. In Moore's opinion (*Judges*, p. 281), in the original account at this stage, immediately the appearance of the deliverer is recounted, and verses 17–18 are a late addition. According to this interpretation, God answered the people's request to send a deliverer, but these verses for some reason were omitted. Zakovitch considers that the stage of commissioning the deliverer is missing in this account in the redaction framework, since the way in which the judge rises is described in another detailed way subsequently in Jephthah's negotiations with the princes of Gilead. Y. Zakovitch, *The Life of Samson (Judges 13–16): A Critical-Literary Analysis*, Jerusalem 1982, p. 21 (Hebrew). In Martin's opinion (*The Book of Judges*, pp. 135–136), the question of the princes of Gilead: "Let the man who will *begin* to fight" is in fact a question to God (like the question in Judges 1:2), but the answer was omitted from the account. Several scholars maintain that in a first stage the people do not receive a reply because the repentance was not complete; subsequently, in verse 16 they eliminate the idolatry, and then God changes His mind. See for instance: Richter, *Die Bearbeitungen des "Retterbuches" in der deuteronomischen Epoche*, p. 23; Boling, *Judges*, p. 193; Dewitt, *The Jephthah Traditions*, p. 80. However, this explanation is not plausible since Israel's repentance is the most impressive in

In the next verse (v. 17), the deployment of the Israelites and the Ammonites against each other is presented in a balanced structure:[15]

The Ammonites <u>mustered</u> and they <u>encamped</u> <u>in Gilead</u>;
and *the Israelites* <u>massed</u> and they <u>encamped</u> <u>at Mizpah</u>.

וַיִּצָּעֲקוּ **בְּנֵי עַמּוֹן** <u>וַיַּחֲנוּ</u> <u>בַּגִּלְעָד</u>
<u>וַיֵּאָסְפוּ</u> **בְּנֵי יִשְׂרָאֵל** <u>וַיַּחֲנוּ</u> <u>בַּמִּצְפָּה</u>

The use of the verb וַיִּצָּעֲקוּ in relation to the Ammonites and the verb וַיֵּאָסְפוּ in relation to Israel is not incidental, or for the sake of diversification. The root וַיִּצָּעֲקוּ indicates gathering together in a more enthusiastic and confident way, as opposed to the verb וַיֵּאָסְפוּ, and its aim is to show Israel's irresolution and the Ammonites' confidence.[16] This situation contrasts with the description of the deployment of Midian and Israel in the Gideon account 6:33–35:

And all Midian, Amalek, . . . <u>massed</u>; they crossed over and <u>encamped</u> <u>in</u> <u>the Valley of Jezreel</u>.
The spirit of the LORD enveloped Gideon; he blew the horn,
and the *Abiezrites* <u>rallied</u> (וַיִּזָּעֵק) behind him.
And he sent messengers throughout *Manasseh*, and they too <u>rallied</u> behind him.

וכל מדין ועמלק וכל בני קדם <u>נֶאֱסְפוּ</u> יחדו ויעברו <u>וַיַּחֲנוּ</u> בעמק יזרעאל
ורוח ה' לבשה את גדעון ויתקע בשופר <u>וַיִּזָּעֵק</u> **אֲבִיעֶזֶר** אחריו. ומלאכים שלח **בכל**
מנשה <u>וַיִּזָּעֵק</u> גם הוא אחריו.

The description of the gathering together of Midian and Israel is formulated in the same way as that of Ammon and Israel in chapter 10, but in inverted form. The verb אסף, which relates to Israel's

---

relation to all the accounts, even in the first stage. Moreover, God does not answer even after they eliminate the idolatry, and He does not send a deliverer. In contrast to this interpretation, see also Webb, *The Book of the Judges*, pp. 45–46. In contrast to these explanations, Polzin (*Moses and the Deuteronomist*, p. 177) considers that God did not answer the people's request positively. On this matter and a structural analysis of the entire book, see *ibid.*, pp. 176–181. Soggin (*Judges*, pp. 205–206) sees in God's failure to respond to Israel an account that does not meet the criterion of the Deuteronomist, and he also sees the statement that the spirit of the LORD came upon him (11:29) as a late addition. Because God did not answer Israel in this account, and because of other deviations of the Jephthah account from the judge account model, he deems, like Richter (*Traditionsgeschichtliche Untersuchungen zum Richterbuch*, p. 328), that the Jephthah account originally did not belong to the book of the deliverers.

[15] In Webb's opinion (*The Book of the Judges*, p. 49), the stylistic parallel shows the conflict between the two sides.

[16] Compare Webb, *The Book of the Judges*, p. 222 n. 13.

army in the Jephthah account, relates to the Midianite army in the Gideon account, and the verb זעק relates to the Ammonite army in the Jephthah account and to Israel in the Gideon account. What distinguishes between the two sources is that in the Gideon account "The spirit of the LORD enveloped Gideon", and he leads the people into the confrontation with Midian; the response of the tribes to the leader's call is enthusiastic. Therefore, the verb זעק is used as against אסף in relation to Midian. In the account of the war against the Ammonites, there is a marked absence of a leader, and therefore the Ammonites muster enthusiastically, whereas the Israelites are gripped by inertia. In Chapter 10, there is no leader acting in God's name, as opposed to Gideon in his combat against the Midianites. Again God's lack of response to Israel's repentance and to their plea to deliver them from Ammon is highlighted here.

Israel's inferiority is expressed also in indication of the place where they gather. The Ammonites muster in "Gilead", and immediately in the next verse there is reference to the Israelite princes of Gilead. This is designed to stress the fact that the Ammonites gather at a site that is the residence of Israel. Possibly the name of the place where the Israelites camp—מצפה ("Mizpah") is designed to express Israel's anticipation of leadership which will change the balance of power between them and the Ammonites. This wish is expressed in their endeavour to persuade one of their number to assume the leadership of the people in the war.

God's decision not to deliver the people is particularly stressed in the next stage of the account: "The troops—the officers of Gilead— said to one another, 'Let the man who will *begin* to fight the Ammonites be chieftain over all the inhabitants of Gilead' " (v. 18). This account departs very markedly from the judge account model until now, and as it appears at the beginning of the book (2:11–23). As God refused the people's plea to send a deliverer to save them from the Ammonites, the princes of Gilead endeavour to deal with the situation themselves. They try to persuade one of the princes of Gilead to take responsibility and to lead the people into war against Ammon. The leadership plight is expressed in two points. Firstly, the leadership problem is so complex that they cannot cope with it. Therefore, they are prepared to waive their authority and to grant their powers to anyone prepared to take responsibility and to wage war on Ammon, and to appoint such a person chieftain over all the inhabitants of Gilead. Secondly, their distress is so great, that they do not expect that resourceful person to solve the problem, but only to "*begin* to fight against the Ammonites".[17] In their distress, they are willing to content themselves with someone who will begin to lead the people. They apparently hope that then there will perhaps be a momentum that will lead the people to rid themselves of the Ammonite yoke. This exceptional suggestion comprises a significant change in the governmental structure of the people; it reveals very obviously what should have happened in the next stage: commissioning of a deliverer by God. The impression given is that since God refused to appoint a deliverer, and since the princes of Gilead were the leaders of the people, they had to solve the problem themselves without divine assistance.

Now we must once more ask ourselves: How can we understand why, precisely now, God refuses to send a deliverer to Israel? Further, the more difficult question is what is the intention in God's statement: "I will not deliver you again"?

It is impossible to interpret God's words as an intention to never deliver Israel again. On the other hand, this cannot be seen as a kind of incentive to Israel to repent even more, since even after they repent completely God still does not deliver the people.

The only way to understand God's statement is that He will not deliver Israel again with this model of judge-deliverer leadership. Indeed God complains that He has already delivered Israel from various enemies, but each time they do evil again. God's words here are not only an opening to the Jephthah account, but show that He despairs of the judge system as a whole. The claim that this introduction is the conclusion of the Book of Judges until now and an introduction to the next part of the book is proved by two points. Firstly, the list of the gods worshiped by Israel reviews the accounts from the beginning of the Book. Secondly, in description of the punishment, both the Ammonite oppression and the Philistine oppression are mentioned. Therefore, this introduction must also be seen as the beginning of the Philistine oppression, which will accompany the people in the entire process of the transition from the judges until the instituting of the monarchy.[18]

---

[17] Similarly, see: Klein, *The Triumph of Irony in the Book of Judges*, p. 86.

[18] See: Richter, *Die Bearbeitungen des "Retterbuches" in der deuteronomischen Epoche*, pp. 13–23. Boling (*Judges*, p. 193) considers that this introduction is a theological introduction of the second half of the Book of Judges, as against the theological introduction of the first part of the book in chapter 2. In his opinion, God's speech in

It is pointless to send another deliverer if it is clear that the people will not remain true to God and will again commit idolatry. God despairs of such a system after the people are delivered several times and each time return to the path of evil. This cyclical process is expressed in the Othniel, Ehud, Deborah and Gideon accounts. After the downfall of Abimelech's monarchy, the rejection of the old system appears here.

There is no indication in the verses of an alternative system, but it seems that, as in other parts of the Book of Judges, these verses anticipate the next period in the life of the people, the monarchic period.[19] Already, from the introduction to the Book, it is clear that it describes an intermediary period in the life of the people (2:11–3:6). Most exceptionally in the Bible, the book initially contains a historiosophic introduction that summarizes all the judge accounts through a model common to them all, and which has four stages: transgression, punishment, lament and deliverance. The explanation for the existence of this introduction, summarizing the entire period, lies perhaps in the author's wish to inform the reader, already at the beginning of the book, that the governmental model of the judges will fail, and already in the introduction the question of a possible alternative is posed. After the reader has perceived the religious instability following the Othniel, Ehud and Deborah accounts, he then deals intensively with the Gideon account. In this account he will be introduced for the first time to an additional leadership system: the monarchy. However, this model will be criticized both ideologically, in

---

verses 11–16 is part of the same redaction that is responsible for the prophet's words in 6:7–10, and the angel's words in 2:1–5. See also: Soggin, *Judges*, p. 203. Moore (*Judges*, p. 277) and Burney (*The Book of Judges*, p. 293) also consider that in their present form, verses 6–16 constitute an introduction both to the Jephthah account and to the Samson account. Moore, however (*Judges*, p. 276), admits that he has no clear answer as to why this long introduction appears in the middle of the book. My conclusion also contradicts Burney (*The Book of Judges*, pp. 293–294), who considers that there is no reason to include this introduction after the introduction at the beginning of the book, instead of bringing an introduction to the specific Jephthah account. In his opinion, the differences between this introduction and the introductions of the other judge accounts are a result of a late redaction, which is identical to the late layer of E. For a similar orientation, see: Budde, *Das Buch der Richter*, pp. 79–80.

[19] In this context, attention should be paid to the opinion of Weisman, who considers that the charismatic leaders should not be seen as representing the only regime of the period of the judges "but as precursors of a new political regime: the monarchic regime" Z. Weisman, "Charismatic Leaders in the Era of the Judges", *ZAW* 89 (1977), pp. 399–411.

Gideon's words, and practically, in Abimelech's failed attempt to rule
and in the catastrophe that he brought upon Israel.[20] Does this mean
that it is now preferable to return to the Judge system? In the introduction to the Jephthah account the answer to this question is negative. God does not intend to restore the people to this model. The
meaning of God's refusal to send the people a deliverer, even when
the people has repented and deserves to be delivered, is to stress that
the problem is with the leadership method of the judges. The meaning of the introduction is to show that even though the first attempt
to institute a monarchy in Israel was a complete failure, it is impossible to go back to the judge system.

In this introduction, it is likewise stressed that it is also impossible
to go back to the patriarchal method that was the institutionalized
leadership in and before the period of the judges.[21] The helplessness
of the elders of Gilead in face of the Ammonite oppression is designed
to show that this model is not a governmental alternative.

The Jephthah account does not propose an alternative method to
the judges, but at the same time the reader is made aware of the
monarchy issue in the introduction to the account. The princes of
Gilead propose appointment of someone to be chieftain over all the
inhabitants of Gilead. What powers he will have, and what the roles
of the other princes will be subsequently is unclear. However, like
the rule of the king, the object here is to set one man over everyone.
This association certainly arises after the monarchic issue appeared
explicitly in the Gideon and the Abimelech accounts. Again in this
account, after the Gideon and the Abimelech accounts, we have a
situation of human initiative for appointment of a sole leader.[22] This
introduction must be seen as one stage in a gradual process from
the despair with the period of the judges to the institution of the
monarchy.

Indeed, it is evident that both the Jephthah and the Samson accounts
do not correspond to the judge account model. As already seen,

---

[20] On the subject of the monarchy in the Book of Judges, see: Amit, *The Book
of Judges*, pp. 87–90.

[21] On this see: H. Reviv, "Types of Leadership in the Period of the Judges",
Beer-Sheva: Annual Studies in Bible, Ancient Israel and Ancient near East 1 (1973), pp.
204–221 (Hebrew, English summary, pp. 233–234).

[22] Buber's opinion (*Kingship of God*, pp. 67–73) that the issue of the opposition to
the monarchy appears already in chapters 1–5 is implausible. Israel's victory over
Jabin, King of Canaan, and the mention of Eglon, King of Moab, as איש בריא מאד,
"a very fat man", do not constitute mockery of the monarchic institution.

after God sent Ammon to oppress Israel, He does not send them a deliverer, and it is the princes of Gilead who appoint Jephthah to deliver Israel. This is a fundamental departure from the judge account model. Likewise, after the Jephthah account, it is not written that the people again did evil in the eyes of the LORD, and the reason for this is presumably that Jephthah did not bring the people to worship of God in his days. This is compounded by the fact that Jephthah judged Israel for six years only, as opposed to the forty years of leadership or peace in the other judge accounts before him (apart from Ehud who judged for eighty years). The Samson account also departs from the model of the other judge accounts. The most salient point is that Samson does not deliver the people from the Philistines but, on the contrary, causes harm to the people (15:11). Likewise, at the beginning of the Samson account, the people do not cry out to God, and God does not send Samson as a response to their lament. At the end of the Samson account there is no mention of years of peace either.[23]

In the Othniel, Ehud, Deborah and Gideon accounts there are also important diversities in the descriptions of the judges and their actions, but there is uniformity in the structure of the account, corresponding to the historiosophic introduction of the book. In these three accounts, the people cry out to the LORD, who therefore sends them a deliverer who saves the people. After a period of forty years (or twice that period) the people again do evil. This structure does not exist in the Jephthah and Samson accounts.

If the assumption raised here is correct, the question must be asked of why God appoints Samson as deliverer. Likewise, why was the spirit of the LORD upon Jephthah? It will be possible to answer the second question from an analysis of the Jephthah account. As regards the Samson account, in this framework we will only be able to suggest the following orientation, which will be developed more fully elsewhere. The Samson account does not contradict God's decision not to send a deliverer according to the judge-deliverer model, since indeed it does not correspond to this model. The Samson account is one link in the transition between the judge model and the institution of the monarchy. As intimated above, this transition is

---

[23] On these issues see my forthcoming article: Assis, "The Meaning of Samson's Birth Account (Judg 13)".

characterized by the people's struggle against the Philistines, who will be fought not only by Samson, but by Eli, Samuel and then King Saul and King David. These accounts are linked. The Samson and Samuel accounts are firmly linked, and Samuel, who inherited Eli's status, will anoint both Saul and David. Politically, Samson will commence the process of fighting the Philistines: "and he *will begin* to deliver Israel from the hand of the Philistines".[24]

Why did the spirit of the LORD rest on Jephthah even though God decided that He would not again deliver Israel? This will be discussed below.

2. *Jephthah's Background (11:1–3)*

(1) And Jephthah the Gileadite was a mighty man of valour, who was the son of a harlot. Jephthah's father was Gilead;

(2) Gilead's wife also bore him sons, and when the wife's sons grew up, they drove Jephthah out. They said to him, You shall not inherit anything in our father's house; for you are the son of another woman

(3) So Jephthah fled from his brothers and settled in the Tob country. Vain men gathered about Jephthah and went out raiding with him (11:1–3).

The Jephthah account does not commence with the deliverance from the Ammonites, but many years before, when Jephthah was driven out of his father's house by his brothers.[25] The beginning of this account is related to the introduction through the use of the conjunctive *waw* וַיִּפְתָּח (and Jephthah). The object of the *waw* in this sentence is to set Jephthah the Gileadite against "all the inhabitants of Gilead" at the end of the previous verse. The princes of Gilead

---

[24] Scholars also discussed the question of the differentiation between the Book of Judges and the Book of Samuel from a literary perspective, since the judge-deliverer model elements appear in the narratives concerning Eli, Samuel and even Saul. In Noth's opinion (*The Deuteronomistic History*[2], p. 69), Samuel is considered a judge-deliverer. Weisman, ("Charismatic Leaders in the Era of the Judges", pp. 7–9) deems that Eli, Samuel and Saul are considered judges, and only David represents the new monarchic period.

[25] On the question of the legality of Jephthah's expulsion, principally in accordance with Mesopotamian legal records, see: I. Mendelsohn, "The Disinheritance of Jephthah in the Light of Paragraph 27 of the Lipit-Ishtar Code", *IEJ* 4 (1954), pp. 116–119; D. Marcus, "The Legal Dispute Between Jephthah and the Elders", *Hebrew Annual Review* 12 (1990) 105–114; J. Fleishman, "Legality of the expulsion of Jephthah (Judges 11:1–11)", *Diné Israel: An Annual of Jewish Law, Past and Present* 18 (1995–6), pp. 61–80.

proposed that one of their number should volunteer to lead the peo
ple, but no one accepted. At this point, the focus passes to Jephthah
who is also a Gileadite, and a mighty man of valour.[26] The close
connection between Jephthah and Gilead is expressed in the fact that
the name of Jephthah's father is "Gilead".[27] This gives the impression
that Jephthah is the son of an important person in the locality.
Jephthah's importance is also suggested through his father's connection to him: "Jephthah's father was Gilead" (v. 1). However, he
is the son of a harlot.[28] Jephthah is in a contradictory situation: on
one hand, he is a Gileadite and the son of Gilead, and he is also a
mighty man of valour; on the other hand, he is the son of a harlot.
What, then, will his status be? In the next verse another woman enters
the picture, Gilead's main wife who bore other sons to Gilead. These
sons drove Jephthah out of his father's house despite the affinity
between him and his father, because he was the son of a harlot.[29]
Why was Jephthah driven out? It seems from the verse that his
brothers saw him as of inferior status; he was obliged to flee from
his brothers because they were many and he was alone.

Jephthah was driven out of his home and was obliged to go into
exile. Exiled, he found his place on the margins of society, and "vain

---

[26] On the phrase "mighty man of valour" see chapter 1 in the section 'Gideon's
appointment as deliverer (6:11–24)'.

[27] However, the intention is not that Jephthah is the son of Gilead son of Machir
son of Manasseh, but presumably one of his descendants. See R. Isaiah di Trani.
As is known, names recur within dynasties. In contrast to the opinion of Moore
(*Judges*, pp. 284–285), who sees the words "Jephthah's father was Gilead" as a mis-
interpretation inserted by mistake.

[28] It seems that the meaning of the word זונה is harlot (see for instance: R. Isaiah
di Trani; Kaufmann, *Sefer Shoftim*, p. 218). Kimchi considers that the intention is
that she was a concubine. In Zakovitch's opinion, the meaning of the word זונה is
a divorced woman. Y. Zakovitch, "The Woman's Rights in the Biblical Law of
Divorce", *The Jewish Law Annual* 4 (1981), pp. 39–40. He also agrees with Rashi
as regards the concubine of Gibeah of whom it is said: ותזנה עליו פילגשו ("and his
concubine played the harlot against him", 19:2), meaning that she left her husband
to go to her father's house. Another opinion is that she was a woman from another
tribe or a gentile (see Gersonides, who sets forth the first possibility; Burney, *The
Book of Judges*, p. 308, raises both possibilities).

[29] See also: P. Trible, "The Daughter of Jephthah: An Inhuman Sacrifice", *Text
of Terror: Literary-Feminist Readings of Biblical Narratives*, Philadelphia 1984, p. 94; J. C.
Exum, *Tragedy and Biblical Narrative: Arrows of the Almighty*, Cambridge 1992, pp. 47–48.
The tension between the two parts of the verse is intentional. There is no reason
to see in this a contradiction originating in a combination of two sources, as maintained by Simpson, *The Composition of the Book of Judges*, p. 45.

men" gathered about him.[30] This reality strengthened him and made him into a man of valour. What Jephthah and his battalion did is not exactly specified, but it is clear that they had some military activity: "and went out raiding with him" (v. 3). From this we will understand why the princes of Gilead turn to him, and with what military infrastructure he will fight against the Ammonites.

The object of this introduction, relating Jephthah's personal history, was to describe the circumstances in which Jephthah's military power was created, and to explain why the princes of Gilead turned to him. To these ends, the account goes back in time, prior even to the Ammonite menace. However, this explanation is insufficient. The Book of Judges until now did not describe at length the special skills of the judges. The Bible defined Gideon as a "mighty man of valour"; it also noted that Ehud was left-handed. However, it did not describe their military capacities in greater detail, and the Bible does not even mention the nature of Barak's attributes. Why does the passage specify the military capacities and the circumstances that make Jephthah suited for conducting of a military campaign?

It is important for Jephthah's might to be explained since Jephthah is the only deliverer chosen by his fellow men, and the princes of Gilead had these considerations in mind when they turned to Jephthah. The other judges, however, were chosen by God, and the rational explanations of their selection are irrelevant. Thus, these explanatory facts are compatible with the introduction, emphasizing the human side of the selection of Jephthah, as against the divine selection of the other judges.

This introduction reveals an interesting side of Jephthah's personality. Jephthah was forced out of his father's home against his will. Below it will be seen that the elders of Gilead seek to bring him back to Gilead, so that he will agree to conduct the war against Ammon.[31] In

---

[30] It is uncertain whether the word רקים indicates men who have practically no morals or men who have no property. On this matter, see: Burney, *The Book of Judges*, p. 309.

[31] Chapter 10, v. 18 refers to the princes of Gilead, whereas chapter 11, v. 6 refers to the elders of Gilead. In McKenzie's opinion, the two terms are not identical. J. L. McKenzie, "The Elders in the Old Testament", *Biblica* 40 (1959), p. 528. He indicates that the princes were those charged mainly with military matters, whereas the elders constituted a larger group from which the princes were appointed. He does acknowledge, however, that the two concepts do have some common characteristics.

this situation, one is led to wonder what Jephthah will do when asked
to return to Gilead and to save the people who drove him out in the
past. How will Jephthah's personal past be expressed with his return
to the place from which he was expelled? When Jephthah enters
into combat against the Ammonites he will prepare the way for his
return to the society to which he considered himself to belong.[32]

The background of Jephthah's personal story shows the reader his
military capacities, as opposed to the inability of the other princes
of Gilead. At the same time, it explains his personal motivation for
delivering Israel, so that he will be allowed to regain his status in a
place from which he had been expelled.

3. Jephthah's Appointment (11:4–11)

(4) Some time later, the Ammonites went to war against Israel.

(5) And when the Ammonites attacked Israel, the elders of Gilead
went to bring Jephthah back from the Tob country.

(6) They said to Jephthah,   'Come be our chief, so that we can
                                fight the Ammonites'.

(7) Jephthah said to the elders of Gilead,
                                'Did you not hate me, and expel me
                                out of my father's house, so why do
                                you come to me now when you are
                                in trouble?'

(8) The elders of Gilead said to Jephthah,
                                'Nevertheless, we have now turned back
                                to you, so that you may go with us
                                and fight with the Ammonites, and
                                become head over us, over all the
                                inhabitants of Gilead'.

(9) Jephthah said to the elders of Gilead,
                                'If you bring me home again to fight
                                with the Ammonites, and the LORD
                                gives them over to me, I will be
                                your head'.

---

[32] There is no basis to Trible's claim ("The Daughter of Jephthah: An Inhuman
Sacrifice", p. 100) that Jephthah suffered because of his parents' sins, and his daughter will die because of her father.

(10) And the elders of Gilead answered Jephthah,

> 'The LORD Himself shall be witness
> between us: we will do just as you
> have said'.

(11) Jephthah went with the elders of Gilead, and the people made him their head and chief, and Jephthah spoke all his words before the LORD at Mizpah. (11:4–11)

After the flashback, describing Jephthah's banishment from his father's home, the account returns to the events of the war between Israel and the Ammonites: "Some time later, the Ammonites went to war against Israel" (v. 4).[33] The resumption of the account of the current events is presented as a continuation of the account of Jephthah's banishment: "Some time later" (ויהי מימים). This means that Jephthah's banishment in the past is not just informative background, but plays an important role in Jephthah's appointment, as will be expressed in his words: "Did you not hate me, and expel me out of my father's house, so why do you come to me now when you are in trouble?" (v. 7).

God did not respond to Israel's appeal, and the princes of Gilead also failed to appoint one of their number as leader. In their plight, and having no other choice, the elders now sought to appoint Jephthah to deliver Israel. At the point at which we would have expected God to send a deliverer, the elders of Gilead try to find a deliverer from among themselves:[34] "And when the Ammonites attacked Israel, the elders of Gilead went to bring Jephthah back from the Tob country" (v. 5). This verse again expressly emphasizes that the background to Jephthah's return to Gilead is the plight of Gilead vis-à-vis the Ammonites.

After negotiations, the parties reach an agreement, and Jephthah accepts the office, returning with the elders to Gilead: "Jephthah went with the elders of Gilead, and the people made him their head and chief" (v. 11a). The elders' appeal to Jephthah and the dialogue with him is described at length (vv. 5–11). What is the role of the dialogue in the account of Israel's deliverance from the Ammonites?

The elders ask Jephthah: "Come be our chief, so that we can fight the Ammonites" (v. 6). This proposal does not resemble the proposal that they had made previously. Previously, they proposed making

---

[33] Therefore, this verse must not be seen as superfluous. On this matter, see: Moore, *Judges*, p. 286.

[34] Exum ("The Center Cannot Hold", p. 422) sees censure of God in this.

the person who would lead the people into war against the Ammonites head over all the inhabitants of Gilead (10:18), but to Jephthah they propose a military role only—chief, and not head.[35] The difference lies primarily in the fact that the first appeal was made to the princes of Gilead. The governmental structure of the princes was patriarchal, the leadership of the tribe was in the hands of the family heads, and each of them had an equal status. In their distress they were prepared to give to one of them the broadest governmental powers, and to appoint him as head of the tribe. This proposal was not made to Jephthah since he did not belong to the group of princes.

Jephthah does not accept the proposal made to him immediately. He refuses, and blames them for having driven him out:[36] "Did you not hate me, and expel me out of my father's house, so why do you come to me now when you are in trouble?" (v. 7) Jephthah does not wish only to express his distress, but negotiates with them to improve on their offer. The elders understood that Jephthah's prevarication is in fact the opening of negotiations in which they must make a better offer so that he will agree to lead Israel to deliverance. They therefore make the following offer: "Nevertheless, we have now turned back to you, so that you may go with us and fight with the Ammonites,

---

[35] קצין indicates here a military function as in Josh 10:24, and not with the meaning of general leadership as in Isa 1:10. See also: Martin, *The Book of Judges*, p. 138; H. N. Rösel, "Jephtah und das Problem der Richter", *Biblica* 61 (1980), pp. 251–255. Moore (*Judges*, pp. 287 and 289), on the other hand, opines that קצין and ראש have the same meaning. This opinion was also held by Marcus, who therefore considered that the dialogue between Jephthah and the elders of Gilead did not focus on the question of Jephthah's powers, but on Jephthah's inheritance rights. D. Marcus, "The Bargaining between Jephthah and the Elders (Judges 11:1–11)", *JANES* 19 (1989), pp. 95–100. There is no basis for this in the meaning of the verses. Burney (*The Book of Judges*, p. 310) considers that Jephthah does not accept the proposal initially because he does not wish to content himself with an indefinite promise, but wants an oath to be given at the sacred place of Mizpah. For a summary of different meanings that were given in the research to the functions of "chief" (קצין) and "head" (ראש), see: W. M. Timothy, "The Nature of Jephthah's Authority", *CBQ* 59 (1996), pp. 34–35. On the nature of Jephthah's leadership, see: *Ibid.* pp. 33–44. On the powers and functions of the "head", see: J. R. Bartlett, "The Use of the Word ראש as a Title in the Old Testament", *VT* 19 (1969), pp. 1–10.

[36] Some scholars see a contradiction between verse 2, which says that the sons of Gilead drove Jephthah out, and verse 7, that states that the expulsion was an official act of the elders of Gilead (see: Simpson, *The Composition of the Book of Judges*, pp. 45–46, Moore, *Judges*, p. 284; Soggin, *Judges*, pp. 204, 207). However, in truth, there is no contradiction. In verse 2, the story is told from the narrator's perspective, whereas Jephthah presents his viewpoint and harshly condemns the elders for the fact that he had to flee. Similarly: Webb, *The Book of the Judges*, p. 224, n. 24.

and become head over us, over all the inhabitants of Gilead" (v. 8). The elders understand and acknowledge their ironic situation: "Nevertheless, we have now turned back to you". They do not deny that previously they drove him out and now they need him. They do not try to justify the expulsion but acknowledge Jephthah's claim. However, they try to compensate him, through the offer that he will lead the people into war against the Ammonites, and then they will appoint him to be head over all the inhabitants of Gilead.[37] Jephthah agrees: "If you bring me home again to fight with the Ammonites, and the LORD gives them over to me, I will be your head" (v. 9). Jephthah agrees to assume the role of deliverer if he is appointed as head of the tribe. The dialogue ends with the proclaimed acceptance of this by the elders: "The LORD Himself shall be witness between us: we will do just as you have said" (v. 10).

The refusal to accept office is widespread in the Bible, as in the case of Moses, Gideon, Jeremiah. However, the refusal here is completely different. Moses and Gideon refused because they considered themselves unworthy. Such a refusal, expressing humility, is an important element in appointment of the leader, since it shows that the candidate is worthy of the designated office. Jephthah also initially refuses, but for the opposite reason, not because he sees himself as unworthy, but he blames the elders for having driven him out of his father's house in the past, and now that they need him they ask for his aid. Jephthah accepts the office solely because the office includes not only his return to his father's home, but also leadership of the tribe. Jephthah is driven by clear personal motives. There is no indication that he takes into consideration the national concern of delivering Israel from the Ammonite oppression. The Ammonite story, as far as Jephthah is concerned, is merely a means in the context of his personal story, which is his focus of interest. The Ammonite oppression is a means by which Jephthah can return and receive recognition after he was driven out of his father's house. Jephthah, who was cast out of his father's house, is prepared to help his people only if he returns to the tribe, not however as a member of the rank and file but as leader. They drove him out of his home, he forces himself on them as leader.[38]

[37] Boling, *Judges*, p. 198.

[38] Klein (*The Triumph of Irony in the Book of Judges*, p. 90) considers that Jephthah has many merits that qualify him to be a judge; his shortcoming is only that he

The fact that Jephthah agrees to deliver Israel because of personal rather than national motivation recalls Abimelech's negative motives, and the second part of the Gideon account in which Gideon furthers personal interests. On the other hand, there is a further aspect in Jephthah's world that is strongly emphasized. While stressing his personal interest, Jephthah expresses his unequivocal viewpoint that his future victory depends on God being with him: "If you bring me home again to fight with the Ammonites, *and the* LORD *gives them over to me*" (v. 9). The dialogue between the elders and Jephthah ends with an unclear sentence: "and Jephthah spoke all his words before the LORD at Mizpah" (v. 11$_b$). It is not clear to what these words before God refer, but the object of the verse is to present Jephthah's feeling of dependence on God and his belief that he will be successful only with God's assistance.[39]

The introduction and the story of the appointment are parallel in the Gideon and Jephthah's accounts, yet in complete contrast. Both the Midianite and the Ammonite oppressions are harsh. The Midianites are nomadic tribes with no fixed residence, and the Ammonites are a people well defined in their land on the east side of the Jordan. Gideon comes from a well-established family, Jephthah is an outcast from his father's home. Gideon clashes with his father's home and his fellow citizens before he begins to deliver the people, Jephthah finds his way back to a senior status in his tribe before he begins to deliver the people. Both accounts contain a rebuke against the people because of their idolatry after all the good that God did for Israel from the time of the exodus from Egypt onwards. In the Gideon account, this rebuke does not bring the people to change their ways, but God nonetheless appoints Gideon to deliver the people. In the Jephthah account, the rebuke brings the people to change their ways, to desist from the transgression and to return to God, but God refuses to appoint a deliverer, and therefore the elders are obliged to appoint Jephthah as deliverer. Gideon and Jephthah are called "mighty man of valour", and both do not accept the commission immediately.

---

has no father to transmit to him the tradition that is passed down from father to son, and by virtue of which he will be able to renew the alliance with God. There is no basis for this theory in the account (see also: *ibid.*, pp. 98–99).

[39] In Klein's opinion (*The Triumph of Irony in the Book of Judges*, pp. 87–88), Jephthah suggests that God will decide whether he will receive the position of head. If Jephthah wins the war, he will prove that God was with him, and therefore he will be able to continue to hold his office. However, if he fails, he will not hold the position of head.

Gideon refuses because of his humility, and Jephthah refuses because he does not receive the honour that he seeks. Gideon is chosen as leader because of his altruistic attributes and his concern for the fate of the people, Jephthah is prepared to fight for selfish reasons. On the other hand, Gideon defies God, and he doubts whether God will assist him; Jephthah, however, expresses unreserved faith in God, and he knows that his success depends on God alone.

Such close parallels call for a comparison of the accounts, and study of the attributes and actions of the judges. In the Abimelech account, we saw how personal motives of a leader can be disastrous for the people. One wonders, therefore, how the story will develop after commissioning by the people of someone who acts out of personal motives. However, knowing that Jephthah believes his success to be dependent on God, we wait to see how this conviction, that Gideon did not have, will favourably influence Jephthah's success. We must also wonder how Jephthah will succeed since he was appointed by his fellow men and not by God, despite his belief that deliverance lies with God.

4. Jephthah's Negotiations with the Ammonite King (11:12–28)

Once Jephthah has been appointed head and chief, it is to be expected that he will commence the campaign against the Ammonites. He was chosen because of his military attributes and he is supposed to act in this field. Instead, we pass in the next verses to a long dialogue with the Ammonite king, initiated by Jephthah, in an attempt to settle the dispute by negotiations. The report of the negotiations is somewhat surprising, since this is the only time in the Book of Judges that such a method is employed. Moreover, the description of this dialogue is very long, extending over seventeen verses (11:12–28), about a third of the entire Jephthah account. In comparison, the description of the actual war is extremely short, made up of only two verses (11:32–33).[40]

---

[40] In Moore's opinion (*Judges*, p. 283), the object of this passage is to claim Israel's ownership of the entire area between the Arnon and the Jabbok. In Webb's opinion (*The Book of the Judges*, p. 58), through the negotiations Jephthah improved his prestige in the eyes of the people and raised his and their morale. Klein (*The Triumph of Irony in the Book of Judges*, p. 89) considers that the object of noting

The excessive emphasis given to the negotiations is harder to understand in light of the fact that they were fruitless. Jephthah was unsuccessful in his endeavour to solve the problems peaceably; the war was not averted. If so, why are the negotiations described at such great length when they had no concrete results, whereas the description of the war that brought peace to Israel is extremely succinct?[41] In other words, what is the function of the negotiations in the account?

As already noted, the answer to this question is not related to the results of the confrontation between Israel and Ammon. A study of the verse before the dialogue and the verse after it clearly explains the matter:

> And Jephthah spoke all his words before the LORD at Mizpah (v. 11₂).
> [...]
> Then the spirit of the LORD came upon Jephthah, and he passed through Gilead and Manasseh. He passed on to Mizpah of Gilead, and from Mizpah of Gilead he passed on to the Ammonites (v. 29).

The fundamental change between the situation before and after the dialogue is that the spirit of the LORD came on Jephthah (v. 29ₐ). The expression "the spirit of the LORD came upon" recurs in the other accounts of the judges who were appointed and sent by God to deliver

---

Jephthah's diplomacy in the account is to justify the Israelite conquest as a non-aggressive conquest, and to show the place of God who decides the result of the military conflict. The object of the diplomacy is also to present Jephthah as trying to prevent a military conflict. Exum (*Tragedy and Biblical Narrative*, pp. 55–56) compares Jephthah's success in negotiations with the elders of Gilead with his failure in his negotiations with the Ammonite king. She links this failure with his failure in the vow (11:30–40). However, we will see that Jephthah's long oration against the Ammonite King does not present him as someone who failed, but on the contrary, someone concerned for the good of his people, and someone who believes that God will deliver his people. In Gilad's opinion, Jephthah needed time to deploy and he therefore commenced negotiations. Furthermore, the negotiations led to relaxing of the tension in the Ammonite camp. H. Gilad, "Diplomacy and Strategy in Two Wars with Ammon", *Beit Mikra*, 58 (1974), pp. 416–418 (Hebrew, English summary p. 454).

[41] The exceptional fact that Jephthah endeavoured to prevent war through negotiations appears as proof that the negotiations are a late addition to the account. See: Soggin, *Judges*, p. 211. Webb, however (*The Book of the Judges*, 54, and p. 225 n. 30), considers that these negotiations are not exceptional, and Jephthah first tries to negotiate according to an ancient precedent, that he himself recalls in his speech, of sending messengers for negotiations (vv. 17–21). Yet, if we compare this account to the other war accounts in the Bible, we will see that Jephthah's initiative is exceptional. Such a dialogue does not occur either in the conquest of Israel accounts in the Book of Joshua or in the other judge accounts. Wood (*Distressing Days of the Judges*, pp. 282, 286) considers that Jephthah endeavoured to prevent bloodshed. He also praises Jephthah, who was prepared to waive his glory in war against Ammon in order to prevent war.

Israel (3:10; 6:34; 14:6, 19; 15:14). Why did the spirit of the LORD come upon Jephthah when God had declared that He would not send a deliverer to Israel again (10:13)? It will be recalled that God did not change His mind after the people repented. God changed His mind immediately after Jephthah's speech to the Ammonite king. The obvious conclusion is that it was the speech that led God to change His mind, and to retract the decision not to deliver Israel, as announced at the beginning of the account. This would seem to be the explanation for the inclusion in the account of the long speech. Since it brought about a turning point in the account and God's acceptance of Jephthah's leadership, the speech was reported in considerable detail.

Before the speech, Jephthah was at Mizpah, where he spoke his words before the LORD. It is not clear what these "words" were, but it is evident that this sentence is designed to present Jephthah's devoutness and his reliance on God. However, God does not answer Jephthah's words, and does not show any sign that He is with Jephthah. The fact that Jephthah is in Mizpah, in the same place where Israel camped opposite the Ammonites when they were helpless (10:17), shows how problematic Jephthah's situation is. He was chosen by the elders to be the head and to deliver Israel from the Ammonites, and he knows that the deliverance depends only on God, but he is still at Mizpah, waiting for a response from God, and God does not answer him. All this changes immediately after the speech. Then, "the spirit of the LORD came upon Jephthah" (v. 29).

The advantage of this explanation is that it solves two major problems in the account simultaneously. It explains why the dialogue is described in great detail even though it does not contribute to understanding of the confrontation between Israel and the Ammonites, and it also focuses the reader on the turning point from God's previous decision not to send a deliverer.

What is there in the speech that led God to change His position? This will be revealed by a study of the contents and structure of the speech.

The dialogue contains two stages.[42] In the first stage, Jephthah's claim concerning the Ammonite king's aggression towards Israel is

---

[42] For an analysis of the structure of the negotiations between Jephthah and the Ammonite king by the form criticism method, see: C. Westermann, *Basic Forms of Prophetic Speech* (trans. H. C. White), Cambridge and Louisville 1991, pp. 112–115.

moderate: "What is there between you and me, that you have come to me to fight against my land?" (v. 12).[43] The Ammonite king, in reply, makes a counterclaim, alleging that Israel is the aggressor, since they conquered Ammon when they came out of Egypt and now Ammon demands that Israel restore these cities to them (v. 13). The second stage contains Jephthah's answers to the king of Ammon in the form of a long speech containing most of the dialogue (vv. 14–27), and making a further accusation against Ammon. In relation to this accusation, the narrator concludes that Ammon did not accept Jephthah's arguments (v. 28).

Jephthah's speech contains four arguments:

A historic argument:	"Israel did not seize the land of Moab or the land of the Ammonites . . ." (vv. 15–22).
A theological argument:	"Now, then, the LORD, the God of Israel, dispossessed the Amorites before His people Israel; and should you possess their land? Should you not possess what your god Chemosh gives you to possess? And should we not be the ones to possess everything that the LORD our God has conquered for our benefit?" (vv. 23–24)
Threat and intimidation:	"Now, are you any better than Balak son of Zippor, king of Moab? Did he start a quarrel with Israel or go to war with them?" (v. 25)
An ethical argument:	Ammon's arguments are not genuine and it is a fact that for three hundred years[44] they took no action (v. 26); Israel, for its part, did not do any harm to Ammon: "I

---

[43] There is also a claim that opens in this style in 2 Sam 16:10; 19:23; 1 Kings 17:28; 2 Kings 3:13; 2 Chr 35:21.

[44] Moore (*Judges*, pp. 296–297) raised the possibility that the number three hundred years is the sum of all the years of oppression and peace mentioned in the Book of Judges, which totals three hundred and one years (not including the eighteen years of the Ammonite oppression, and the years in which Samson judged). However, this similarity is apparently merely a coincidence. See also: Kaufmann, *Sefer Shoftim*, p. 225; Malamat, *History of Biblical Israel*, p. 138. There is a chronological calculation of the three hundred years in *Midrash Seder 'Olam Rabba* (Dov Ber Ratner ed.), Wilna 1894–1897, chapter 12 (p. 55); Kimchi. For a slightly different calculation, see Rashi.

have not sinned against you; yet you are doing me harm and making war on me" (26–27).

In answering the king of Ammon, Jephthah accuses and threatens him. This answer is in the form of an elaborate rhetorical structure.

Jephthah's four arguments are a reply to the two arguments put forward by the Ammonite king in v. 13:

> (1) When Israel came from Egypt, they seized the land which is mine, from the Arnon to the Jabbok as far as the Jordan.
> (2) Now, then, restore it peaceably.

Jephthah's first and last arguments are an answer to the Ammonite king's first argument, and Jephthah's second and third arguments are answers to the king's second argument. To the Ammonite king's claim: "When Israel came from Egypt, they seized the land which is mine", Jephthah replies firmly: "Israel did not seize the land of Moab or the land of the Ammonites" (v. 15). Here, a historical argument appears and, accordingly, the main part of Jephthah's speech is a historical review that proves his argument. According to this review, Israel did not fight Ammon and Moab, and conquered the area in question from the Amorites who attacked Israel.[45] The difference between the claims of the two sides is expressed in the description of the borders. Ammon defines its land: "from the Arnon to the Jabbok as far as the Jordan" (v. 13). Arnon is the southern border, Jabbok the northern border and the Jordan the western border of the land of Ammon, according to the Ammonite king. On the other hand, Jephthah defines the same area as the area of the Amorites: "all the territory of the Amorites from the Arnon to the Jabbok and from the wilderness to the Jordan" (v. 22). The Ammonite King did not define the eastern border of the area, but Jephthah, who uses the same borders, also adds the eastern border: "from the wilderness to the Jordan". He thereby gives greater credibility to his words in relation

---

[45] On the relation between the account of the wars in the Book of Numbers and the account here, see: J. Van Seters, "The Conquest of Sihon's Kingdom: A Literary Examination", *JBL* 91 (1972), pp. 182–197; J. R. Bartlett, "The Conquest of Sihon's Kingdom: A Literary Re-Examination", *JBL* 97 (1978), pp. 347–351; J. Van Seters, "Once Again—The Conquest of Sihon's Kingdom", *JBL* 99 (1980), pp. 117–119; D. M. Gunn, "The 'Battle Report': Oral or Scribal Convention?", *JBL* 93 (1974), pp. 513–518.

to the vague border indicated by Ammon, but he also indicates the area of Ammon as beyond the wilderness.[46]

Jephthah's fourth argument complements his first argument. After clearing Israel of any blame, he now transfers the blame to Ammon's unjustified aggression. He makes a moral accusation, asserting that they are striking Israel without any justified reason (vv. 26–27).

This structure shows that the historical argument and the moral conclusion are in fact the answer to the Ammonite king's claims. These arguments occupy most of the speech. Hence, the evident conclusion is that if the historical basis of Ammon is false, then the Ammonite king's demand that Israel restore the cities to him peaceably is also void. However, Jephthah does not content himself with the historical argument and adds a theological argument. To the Ammonite king's claim "Now, then, restore it peaceably", Jephthah replies: "Now, then, the LORD, the God of Israel, dispossessed the Amorites before His people Israel; and should you possess their land?" (v. 23). Jephthah asserts that he cannot respond to the request to restore the cities peaceably for theological reasons. The point of view that Jephthah expresses is that Israel's achievements are in fact God's victory and therefore they have no authority to give to another what God gave to them.[47]

This argument put forward by Jephthah is strange both in its logical and in its literary aspect. From a literary viewpoint, the object of the main part of the speech would seem to be to consolidate the historical argument that Israel did not fight against the Ammonites when they came out of Egypt and, therefore, the Ammonites have no justified claim against Israel. This historical argument is on the same plane as the Ammonite argument. Therefore, the conclusion of the historical review is the fourth argument in which Jephthah asserts that Ammon has no claim against Israel and, on the contrary, the Ammonites have done an injustice to Israel. The theological conclusion that immediately follows the historical review is surprising.

---

[46] Compare: Webb, *The Book of the Judges*, p. 55.

[47] Burney (*The Book of Judges*, pp. 314–315) considers that Jephthah's words reflect a polytheistic viewpoint. However, it should not be forgotten that this text is a dialogue between Jephthah and the Ammonite king, and therefore Jephthah's words do not necessarily reflect precisely his beliefs. He may be voicing the Ammonite king's opinion. Similarly, see: Kaufmann, *Sefer Shoftim*, p. 224; Y. Kaufmann, *The Religion of Israel*, p. 131; M. Weiss, "Einiges über die Bauformen des Erzählens in der Bibel", *VT* 13 (1963), p. 471; Wood, *Distressing Days of the Judges*, p. 287.

The theological argument is far stranger logically. Jephthah's logic is that every victory is an achievement of God. He applies this logic universally and in relation to the Ammonite god explicitly: "Should you not possess what your god Chemosh gives you to possess? And should we not be the ones to possess everything that the LORD our God has conquered for our benefit?" (v. 24). Since Jephthah's argument is that what God gives cannot be changed, he thereby includes also what Chemosh gives to Ammon and he thus removes the basis of his claim against the Ammonites.[48] The Ammonites rule over Israel

---

[48] Jephthah refers to Chemosh as god of Ammon, but Chemosh was the god of Moab, and Molech was the god of Ammon. See: Num 21:29; 1 Kings 11:5, 7, 33; 2 Kings 23:13; Jer 48:7, 13, 46. One way of solving the problem is through a diachronic approach. Some scholars are of the opinion that material that related originally to Israel's negotiations with Moab was inserted in this text, and that this passage is a late addition. For different variations of this hypothesis, see: Moore, *Judges*, p. 283, Burney, *The Book of Judges*, pp. 299–300, 315. In Noth's opinion (*The Deuteronomistic History*², p. 76, n. 2) this late addition is post-Deuteronomistic, from the period in which the entire area bordering on Judah in the east was called Ammon, and the ancient history of the area was unclear; Soggin, *Judges*, p. 211. For a further bibliography on the matter of Chemosh and Molech, see Webb, *The Book of the Judges*, p. 225, n. 34. In the opinion of several scholars, "Ammon" should be replaced by "Moab". In all the verses of the negotiations, the *BHS* thus replaces Ammon by Moab (vv. 13, 14, 27, 28, 30, 31). It is unclear why the editor preferred to amend the wording in so many places rather than making one correction: "Molech" instead of "Chemosh" in one place in verse 24. Indeed, Noth (*ibid.*) disagreed with this hypothesis. For a review of the earlier research, see: Moore, *Judges*, p. 295. Boling (*Judges*, p. 201) considers that there is no combination of different sources in this passage. In his opinion (*Ibid.*, p. 203), Ammon defeated Moab and its territorial claims against Israel were on behalf of Moab. This is the reason that Jephthah refers precisely to the god of Moab, Chemosh. For variations on this point of view, see: Kaufmann, *Sefer Shoftim*, pp. 220–222; Y. Elitzur, *Sefer Shoftim* (Daat Mikra), Jerusalem 1976, p. 125; Wood, *Distressing Days of the Judges*, p. 287. A different variation can be found in Webb (*The Book of the Judges*, p. 56), who claims that Jephthah did not make a mistake, but intentionally ascribed to the Ammonite king rule over both Ammon and Moab; Jephthah's argument is that he did not take the land of either Ammon or Moab. However, this argument is not simple, since if this is the case it is not clear why only the Moabite god is mentioned and not the Ammonite god. On this matter, see in detail: W. Richter, "Die Überlieferungen um Jephtah: Ri. 10:17–12:6", *Biblica* 47 (1966), pp. 485–556. On the different redaction stages of this passage, see M. Wüst, "Die Einschaltung in die Jiftachgeschichte Ri. 11:13–26", *Biblica* 56 (1975), pp. 464–479. Another solution to the problem is that Jephthah was mistaken in his words. Klein (*The Triumph of Irony in the Book of Judges*, p. 89), for instance, considers that Jephthah has his facts confused, mixing up people and historical events concerning the Moabites, the Ammonites and the Amorites, and mixing up the national gods. This confusion shows how little he knows of his people, and that his belief in God is practical and not idealistic. Perhaps the confusion in Jephthah's words is designed to show him as someone who does not distinguish between the gods of Israel's neighbours to the east, since he does not attribute any importance or strength to them.

and they conquered the many areas of Israel on both sides of the
Jordan. According to the theological argument presented by Jephthah,
Ammon does not have to restore to Israel what they conquered from
them with the aid of their god. Diplomatically, the theological argument does not seem to help Jephthah; on the contrary, it places him
in a position of inferiority. Therefore, Jephthah goes on to complete
the theological argument with a third argument, which is principally
a threat. Jephthah emphasizes that Ammon's achievement is temporary, and the real war is between the gods, and therefore the
question is which god is stronger. He brings a historic proof of this
in that Balak the king of Moab recognized the greatness of Israel's
God and did not fight Israel.

Not only does the theological argument not help Jephthah; on the
contrary, since according to Jephthah's theological argument he cannot transfer the area given to them by God because Israel's victory
is in God's hands, what point is there to clarification of the historical truth? Now all the negotiations appear superfluous. What, in
fact, can Jephthah obtain from the Ammonites? The Ammonites rule
over the Israelites, who are in a position of inferiority. The best
result that he could request is that the Ammonites would agree to
lighten the yoke in exchange for meeting of their demands. However,
Jephthah does not accept this proposal because of his theological
viewpoint. Possibly, Jephthah could have achieved something for
Israel by diplomatic means if he had been prepared to compromise
his theological arguments, but he does not do so, preferring to wage
war on the Ammonites.

Jephthah cannot remove the Ammonite threat by historical arguments, and certainly not by theological arguments. Nonetheless, the
theological argument and the related threat are at the centre of his
oration. The theological argument is very weak when made against
Ammon, because of Israel's position of inferiority. However, it is
very significant as regards God's attitude towards Israel. Therefore,
the speech is not a factor for any change in the relations between
Ammon and Israel, and it was included in the account in order to
present Jephthah's theological arguments, which constitute a turning
point in the relations between God and Israel. Jephthah, here, expresses an unequivocal viewpoint that Israel's victories in war are
the acts of the LORD, God of Israel. This viewpoint expressed by
Jephthah is so clear and simple that he feels that he cannot decide
to transfer cities conquered by Israel to the Ammonites, even in
exchange for improved living conditions. Jephthah appears here as

someone impregnated with a historical memory; the events determining his viewpoint in the present occurred in the very distant past.
Possibly, it is this very strong faith of Jephthah that led God to
change His plan not to send a deliverer to save Israel. With the
revealing of Jephthah's viewpoint, there was a prospect that this time,
when God delivered Israel from the Ammonites, Jephthah would
instil his faith in his people, and perhaps the faith would be absorbed
by the people. Therefore, immediately after Jephthah's speech, which
does not make any contribution to the war account, it is said "the
spirit of the LORD came upon Jephthah" (v. 29), Jephthah received
a divine commission after being chosen by the elders of the people
because of the potential inherent in his faith, even though God's
plans were not to deliver the people.

The extensive details of the historical argument as it emerges from
Jephthah's speech are to be understood in this context. Israel's main
problem in the period of the Judges is the people's short historical
memory. After the death of the judge, they again do evil in God's
eyes, because they forget the events even from the period of the last
judge. This is precisely God's argument in His refusal to send a
deliverer (10:11–13). Israel's short historical memory prevents them
from achieving stability in their belief in God. The problem of the
historical memory also emerges at the beginning of the Gideon
account in the words of the prophet of Israel, who reminds the people that God brought them out of Egypt and delivered Israel's enemies up to them in the period of the conquest of the land (6:7–10).
Selective historical memory also appeared when Gideon accused God
of not delivering the people as He had done in the past, but ignored
Israel's responsibility, and the prophet's historical reconstruction. With
Jephthah the opposite appears. Jephthah, in his speech to the Ammonite
king, expresses historical awareness of God's responsibility for Israel's
victories three hundred years previously. This information is not theoretical. Jephthah makes immediate political use of it, refusing to
transfer the cities of Israel to the Ammonite King peaceably because
of the same historical awareness that attributes to God the victories
over Israel's enemies even in the distant past. Given Jephthah's solid
outlook, there is a prospect that he will be able to impart to the
people the same historical awareness that will stand firm in time,
just as it influences Jephthah's viewpoint after such a long period.

Jephthah's selection by the elders was supported by God because
of Jephthah's belief in God, as it appeared in his speech to the
Ammonite king, and before this in his words at the time of

commissioning by the elders. The speech was included in the account because it explains why God accepted Jephthah's leadership despite His assertion that He would not send a judge to deliver Israel.[49] On the other hand, at the beginning of the account, Jephthah appeared as someone prepared to deliver Israel for reasons of self-interest rather than for national reasons. This explanation places Jephthah's character in complete contrast to the presentation of Gideon's character in chapter 6. Gideon was chosen because of his sensitivity to the fate of the people, and was shown as sceptical in his belief in God. The creation of the character of these judges as two contrasting figures leads the reader to a comparison between them and between the leadership models emerging in the two accounts.

We already saw that the leader's self-interest led to a certain failure both in Gideon's leadership and particularly in the national disaster of Abimelech's monarchy. This makes the reader wonder about the implications of the self-interest appearing in Jephthah's considerations, and whether Jephthah's faith in God will be expressed in success in leading the people.

5. Jephthah's War against Ammon and his Vow (11:29–40)

After Jephthah demonstrated his belief that his victory depended on God's assistance he received divine inspiration: "Then the spirit of the LORD came upon Jephthah, and he passed through Gilead and Manasseh", now Jephthah can deploy for war against Ammon: "He passed on to Mizpah of Gilead, and from Mizpah of Gilead he passed on to the Ammonites" (v. 29).

After the lengthiness of the account until now, one expects the description of the deployment for battle to be followed immediately by the battle. However, the account passes instead to the vow made by Jephthah before going into battle (vv. 30–31).[50] Several times in the

---

[49] Scholars generally fail to explain why the spirit of the LORD did not come upon Jephthah until this time, and why a change occurred precisely at this point of the account and the spirit of the LORD suddenly rests on him. See, for instance, Klein's comprehensive analysis, *The Triumph of Irony in the Book of Judges*, p. 90; or Webb's analysis, *The Book of the Judges*, pp. 51–60.

[50] Nonetheless, this should not lead us to conclude that the account of Jephthah's vow does not fit in with the verses preceding and following it, as claimed by T. C. Römer, "Why Would the Deuteronomists Tell about the Sacrifice of Jephthah's Daughter?" *JSOT* 77 (1998), p. 28. In Römer's opinion, the connection between

Bible prior to a difficult struggle, a vow is made in order to guarantee success. Jacob for instance vows that if God watches over him on his way to Haran, clothes him and brings him back to his father's home in peace, he will make the stone that he set up as a pillar to be God's house and will give a tenth of all that God gives him to God (Gen 28:20–22). Similarly, Jephthah vows that if God delivers the Ammonites into his hands, he will sacrifice whoever comes forth from his house when he returns in peace from the war (11:30–31). This vow reflects Jephthah's view that his victory depends on God.[51] Immediately afterwards the battle is described very briefly, in only two verses (vv. 32–33). After the short report of Jephthah's victory, the Bible goes back to Jephthah's vow (vv. 34–40). When Jephthah returns, to his bitter chagrin it is his daughter who comes out to meet him. Immediately Jephthah tells her that he cannot retract his vow, to which his daughter also agrees. After she laments her maidenhood for two months, Jephthah carries out his vow. Jephthah's vow leads to a disaster, but the vow is made immediately after it is said that God's spirit came upon Jephthah. What is the cause of this change between God being with Jephthah and Jephthah's disastrous vow? This will be studied below.

In contrast to the short description of the war, the carrying out of the vow is described in great detail. From early exegesis to contemporary research, the account of Jephthah's vow has been studied extensively, mainly in relation to the tragedy of Jephthah and his daughter, and the moral aspects of the event.[52] However, the personal

---

32_a and the end of v. 29 proves that verses 30–31 are a late addition. Many scholars also consider the Jephthah's daughter account to be an independent account inserted at a late date. For a bibliography, see Römer, *ibid.*, p. 29, n. 12. However, as will be discussed below, the fact that Jephthah makes a vow after receiving divine inspiration contributes to the shaping of Jephthah's problematic personality. See also: Webb, *The Book of the Judges*, pp. 62 63. In contrast, Trible ("The Daughter of Jephthah", pp. 96–97) considers the interruption of the war account and the appearance of the vow in the middle to be ironic, in that even though the spirit of the LORD came upon Jephthah, he nonetheless made a vow. This fact shows Jephthah's lack of faith; even though he does not believe in God, he tries to take control of Him and manipulate him through the vow. In my opinion, the problem is not Jephthah's lack of faith, but his egocentricity. Amit (*Judges*, p. 204) considers that the author dwelt at length on the episode of Jephthah's daughter and gave a brief description of the war in order to present Jephthah in a negative light.

[51] Martin, *The Book of Judges*, p. 145.

[52] In recent years, several studies with a feministic orientation have been published. See, for instance: Trible, "The Daughter of Jephthah", pp. 93–116; M. Bal, *Death and Dissymmetry: The Politics of Coherence in the Book of Judges*, Chicago and London

tragedy of Jephthah and his daughter is not the main subject of the account. The main subject is the national tragedy of Israel's oppression under Midian and the strengthening of Israel under Jephthah's leadership. The national account of the liberation from the Ammonite yoke is placed in the shadow of the account of the personal tragedy of Jephthah and his daughter.[53] What were the narrator's considerations in recounting Jephthah's vow in detail and placing the account of the victory over Ammon in the background?

The explanation of the extreme brevity of the description of Jephthah's war against the Ammonites must be related to the purpose of the story of Jephthah's vow, since these two accounts are interpolated, as shown in the following schema:

Deployment for *war* (v. 29)
  Jephthah's *vow* (vv. 30–31)
Jephthah's *war* against the Ammonites (vv. 32–33)
  Carrying out of Jephthah's *vow* (vv. 34–40)
Jephthah's *war* against the Ephraimites (12:1–7)

What then is the significance of the account of Jephthah's vow? Firstly, we will study the actual vow.

> And Jephthah made a vow to the LORD:
> "If you will give the Ammonites into my hand.
> Then whoever comes out of the door of my house to meet me when I return victorious from the Ammonites shall be the LORD's and shall be offered by me as a burnt offering" (vv. 30–31).

1988, pp. 42–68; Exum, *Tragedy and Biblical Narrative*, pp. 65–69; J. C. Exum, "Feminist Criticism: Whose Interests Are Being Served?", G. A. Yee (ed.), *Judges and Method: New Approaches in Biblical Studies*, Minneapolis 1995, pp. 65–90; J. C. Exum, "Murder They Wrote: Ideology and the Manipulation of Female Presence in Biblical Narrative", *USQR* 43 (1989), pp. 19–39. For a further bibliography, see: Exum, "Feminist Criticism", pp. 88–90 and Römer, "Why Would the Deuteronomists Tell about the Sacrifice of Jephthah's Daughter?", p. 27, n. 4.

[53] The brevity of the war account led Wellhausen (*Die Composition des Hexateuchs und der historischen Bücher des alten Testaments*, pp. 228–229) to the conclusion that there are no historical elements at all in the Jephthah account. Moore (*Judges*, p. 284) noted that the fact that the circumstances of the war were not well remembered and were not cited fully in the account does not prove that such a story did not occur. In a like perspective, see also: Burney, *The Book of Judges*, pp. 304–305. It should be noted that claims like those of Wellhausen do not take into account that a Biblical narrative has ideological and educational objectives that are shaped as a literary work, and therefore the fact that a Biblical account is not to a historian's taste does not have to negate the authenticity of the account altogether.

The wording of Jephthah's vow is unclear. It is unlikely that his intention was an animal,[54] since his words "whoever comes out of the door of my house to meet me when I return" show that the one who will come out to great him is a sentient being.[55] However, the possibility that he intended to sacrifice a human being is also unlikely in light of his severe reaction when he saw his daughter coming out to meet him.[56] From Jephthah's reaction it is clear that he did not

---

[54] See *Midrash Genesis Rabba* 60, 3 (vol. II, p. 527); BT Ta'anit, p. 4a. This viewpoint was shared also by: Kaufmann, *Sefer Shoftim*, pp. 226–227. In Boling's opinion (*Judges*, p. 208), on the basis of the architecture of the houses in that period, in which there were three rooms built on three sides of a court, it could be understood that Jephthah did expect to meet an animal when he entered his home. For an illustration of this, see *ibid.*, photograph no. c 8.

[55] Moore, *Judges*, p. 299; Burney, *The Book of Judges*, pp. 319–320; A. R. W. Green, *The Role of Human Sacrifice in the Ancient Near East* (American Schools of Oriental Research Dissertation Series, I), Missoula 1975, p. 162; Bal, *Death and Dissymmetry*, p. 45; Webb, *The Book of the Judges*, p. 64; Soggin, *Judges*, p. 215. In Exum's opinion (*Tragedy and Biblical Narrative*, p. 164, n. 8), on the basis of 1 Sam 18:6 and Exod 15:20, he expected a woman to come out to meet him. In Klein's opinion (*The Triumph of Irony in the Book of Judges*, pp. 91–93), Jephthah did not know that the Bible prohibited human sacrifice, and he was influenced by cultic outlooks of his period. This corresponds to Klein's opinion on the fact that he has no father and is ignorant of his people's history and the nature of its faith. She emphasizes that Jephthah lost his daughter because of his ignorance. On human sacrifice in the ancient East and in the Bible, see: G. C. Heider *The Cult of Molek: A Reassessment* (JSOTsup, 43) Sheffield 1985, pp. 94–222; J. Day, *Molech: A God of Human Sacrifice in the Old Testament* (University of Cambridge Oriental Publications, 41), Cambridge 1989. R. de Vaux, *Studies in Old Testament Sacrifice*, Cardiff 1964, pp. 53–90. On human sacrifice in the Bible, see: Green, *The Role of Human Sacrifice in the Ancient Near East*, pp. 161–187. On the opposition to human sacrifice in the Bible, see: Lev 18:21; 20:1–5; Deut 12:29–31; 18:10; 2 Kings 3:27; 2 Kings 16:3; 17:17; 21:6; 23:10; Mic 6:6–7; Jer 7:31; 19:5; 32:35; Ezek 16:20–21; 20:25–26; 23:37–39; Ps 106:36–38. The objection to human sacrifice appears in the account of the Sacrifice of Isaac (Gen 22) and also in the obligation to redeem the human firstborn, Exod 13:2, 12–13; 22:28; 34:30; Num 18:15. For a discussion of this matter, see: Burney, *The Book of Judges*, pp. 329–331; Green, *The Role of Human Sacrifice in the Ancient Near East*, pp. 161–169. According to Soggin (*Judges*, p. 218), the Jephthah's daughter account shows that the early Israelite religion has much in common with the religions of Canaan and the Ancient East. Indeed, this subject is mentioned frequently in the Bible, although it is impossible to know the scope of the phenomenon. I do not agree with de Vaux's assertion (*Studies in Old Testament Sacrifice*, pp. 65–66) that the author of the Jephthah account does not censure Jephthah's act, and that Jephthah is presented as a religious man. In opposition to his approach, see: Green, *The Role of Human Sacrifice in the Ancient Near East*, p. 163. The object of the account is to present Jephthah negatively, and this single case cannot lead to conclusions on the early Israelite religion. Martin (*The Book of Judges*, p. 145) considers that human sacrifice in this period was not widespread in Israel.

[56] The possibility that Jephthah intended the sacrifice to be someone for whose life he did not care and who was not of his family is unlikely, since human sacrifice was generally one of the children of the person making the sacrifice. Similarly, see: Martin, *The Book of Judges*, p. 145.

intend to sacrifice his daughter. Yet, the wording of the vow does not correspond to the sacrifice of an animal. If so, how is Jephthah's vow to be understood?

Since the meaning of his words is not that he will sacrifice an animal, but his reaction to the sight of his daughter coming out to meet him shows that this was not his intention either, perhaps the possibility to be selected is that he did not mean what he said. Possibly, Jephthah did mean to sacrifice an animal, but he expressed himself with wording that indicates precisely a person coming out of his house. What is the meaning of Jephthah's defective wording and what caused it? The wording of Jephthah's vow shows that he had in mind his personal success in the war and his desire for the people's recognition of his success. Therefore, even though he intended to speak of the sacrifice of an animal, what he actually said expressed his concern: "Then whoever comes out of the door of my house to meet me when I return victorious from the Ammonites" (v. 31). In Jephthah's mind's eye, he already thought of his return home and in his mind, he already saw the people cheering him as they cheer victors returning from war.[57] Thus, we will understand the meaning of the expression: "comes out . . . to meet me when I return victorious". If he was referring here merely to a sacrifice, Jephthah could have used another wording, which would lead him to make the choicest sacrifice. However, Jephthah's words introduced the subject of the homage that he hoped to receive among those greeting him on his return home as victor. Ironically, Jephthah's failure is also in that he destines precisely the first person who comes out to meet him for sacrifice.[58]

Jephthah's wording also intimates that his main concern is the desire for recognition of his greatness on his return as victor: "out of the door of *my house* to *meet me* when *I return* victorious" (v. 31). In Jephthah's wording, the use of the first person singular stands out; this usage shows that he is going to fight a national war, but it is only a means to achieve a desired personal status. We already saw this motivation at the time of Jephthah's commissioning by the elders. He received the commission in conditions allowing his personal advancement, and he agreed to head the people only if his condi-

---

[57] See for instance: Exod 15:20; 1 Sam 18:6 ff.

[58] See Klein (*The Triumph of Irony in the Book of Judges*, p. 96), who considers that the Bible is intentionally ambiguous on the question of whether Jephthah meant to sacrifice a human being or not.

tions were realized; there is no evidence that the national plight was of concern to him. Comparison of his words in the singular reveals Jephthah's personal motives, just as Gideon's use of the plural shows his feelings of solidarity for the plight of his people.[59]

Jephthah's personal interests also emerge clearly in the description of fulfilment of the vow and particularly in his dialogue with his daughter after he returns home from the war against the Ammonites:

> When Jephthah arrived at his home in Mizpah,
> there was his daughter coming out to meet him, with timbrel
>   and dance!
> She was an only child; he had no other son or daughter (v. 34).

After the short report of Jephthah's victory, it is recounted that Jephthah returns to his home in Mizpah. This detail is surprising since apparently his home was in the Tob country (v. 5). The indication that Jephthah's home is in Mizpah brings the reader back to 11:11: "and Jephthah spoke all his words before the LORD at *Mizpah*". He stood at this point after he was commissioned by the elders, and after he showed that his main object in his war against the Ammonites was to make a name for himself. Now we hear that his home is in Mizpah, apparently after the elders took him from the Tob country. However, when he returns from the war to his home in Mizpah— a transition that reflects the new recognition of his status by the elders—Jephthah expects to see how the elders and the people relate to him after he has successfully carried out his mission.[60]

---

[59] In Bal's opinion (*Death and Dissymmetry*, p. 45) Jephthah expressed his vow in such a way because he did not think that he was a hero and he did not expect to be victorious, and it is for this reason that he made a vow. She considers that the vow is Jephthah's failure. In Exum's opinion (*Tragedy and Biblical Narrative*, pp. 48–49), however, there is ambiguity in the account; it is possible that he is divinely inspired when he makes a vow, and in this case censure of God is to be seen. Or possibly he is not divinely inspired. She points out (*ibid.*, p. 164, n. 7) a similar ambiguity in the Gideon account when, after the spirit of the LORD clothed him, he expresses doubt as to whether God will help him to conquer Midian (6:34–35). In Trible's opinion ("The Daughter of Jephthah", pp. 97, 100, 104) the vow is a result of Jephthah's lack of faith in God and his attempt to force God to help him.

[60] However, in Burney's opinion (*The Book of Judges*, p. 300), this problem is resolved if we assume that there are two sources here that disagree on the question of whether Jephthah is from the Tob country, as stated in 11:1–11, or from Mizpah, as stated in 11:30–31, 34 ff. This explanation ignores the fact that the account deals with Jephthah's status. Initially he was expelled, and subsequently, when the elders of Gilead asked him to deliver Israel, his status changes, and then it may be assumed that he returns to his "inheritance" in Mizpah. In a different

The scene that meets Jephthah's eyes is very different from his expectations: "there was his daughter coming out to meet him, with timbrel and dance!

She was an only child; he had no other son or daughter".[61] Jephthah returns home, but not to enjoy his achievements. Instead, a dreadful personal tragedy befalls him. Before the war he vowed: "Then whoever comes out of the door of my house to meet me when I return victorious . . . be the LORD's and shall be offered by me as a burnt offering" (v. 31), and now the first person who comes out to meet him is his daughter. It was common in that period for women to come out to meet the victor in war on his return (Exod 15:19–21; 1 Sam 18:6–7). However, the description of how she comes out to meet him with timbrels, dances and rejoicing is very ironic, since this expression of joy is accompanied by a tremendous tragedy for both Jephthah and his daughter. The verse emphasizes this by repetition: (1) "She was an only child"; (2) "he had no other son or daughter".[62] This information clearly shows the severity of the tragedy. Firstly, she comes out alone, so the vow can only apply to her, and secondly, she is his only daughter and therefore the loss is total.

This is one aspect of the complex tragedy studied by most of the commentators. There is another aspect that has not been considered. Jephthah's daughter comes out to meet him with timbrels and dances, and this is the reception that he expects, but he hoped that the Israelite masses would come out to meet him. Yet his daughter alone came out to meet him. The words ורק היא יחידה (lit.: "she is the only one") can also be read with what was said previously: והנה בתו יצאת לקראתו בתפים ובמחלות ורק היא יחידה ("there was his daugh-

---

perspective, Klein (*The Triumph of Irony in the Book of Judges*, p. 88) explained that the name Mizpah shows the irony that Jephthah does not anticipate (מצפה from the root צפה—to look, to watch, to anticipate), i.e. does not take care when he makes the vow. She notes that the emphasis in the account on the place "Mizpah" is not for historical but for literary needs.

[61] The text should have read ממנה here. The same is true in Josh 1:7. In the Masorah, both these versions are indicated as סבירין.

[62] The expression ורק היא יחידה recalls a similar situation when Abraham goes to bind his only son, Gen 22:2. On the connection and the difference between the account of the binding and the account of Jephthah's daughter, see: Klein, *The Triumph of Irony in the Book of Judges*, p. 95; Webb, *The Book of the Judges*, p. 228, n. 59 and an additional bibliography in the matter there; Trible, "The Daughter of Jephthah", p. 101; Zakovitch, *Through the Looking Glass: Reflection Stories in the Bible*, pp. 72–74.

ter coming out to meet him, with timbrel and dance! She is the only one"). Namely, apart from his daughter nobody else came out to meet him. This is another personal tragedy for Jephthah. He went out to war against the Ammonites with the aim of receiving status in the eyes of the people, and he is appointed head of the elders of Gilead, but in fact the people do not come out to meet him, do not welcome him as a victorious leader. He moved his home to Mizpah and now he returns there, to the place from which he had been expelled, expecting to be acclaimed, but nobody thought to welcome him and to accord him prestige. The greeting with timbrels and dances is designed to show the situation to which Jephthah hoped to return; however, he did not hope for his daughter but for the masses. For Jephthah, this is a tragedy since it was for this that he went out to war.

The combination of the two tragedies further intensifies Jephthah's difficult situation. Jephthah returns to Mizpah in order to receive the long desired recognition. However, not only is there no improvement in his personal situation, or enhanced status in the eyes of the people, but he also loses what he possessed. He desired to be accepted by the people and on his return not only did this not happen, but he also loses his only daughter; he loses the only person who "was *coming out to meet him*" (vv. 31, 34).

Jephthah's personal motives in his war against the Ammonites appear very acutely precisely in his dialogue with his daughter when she comes out to meet him:

> "On seeing her, he rent his clothes and said,
> "Alas, daughter! You have brought me low; you have become my troubler!
> For I have opened my mouth to the LORD and I cannot retract" (v. 35).

The irony in the situation reaches its climax at this point. When Jephthah returns home and sees his daughter coming out to meet him with timbrels and dances he should be glad and content. Instead, he tears his garments. She came out to meet him in order to exalt him, but his vow made this a tragedy.

Jephthah's words to his daughter show just how self-centred he is: (ויאמר אהה בתי הכרע הכרעתני ואת היית בעכרי) "Alas, daughter! You have brought me low; you have become my troubler!" The word אהה ("alas") is an exclamation that expresses Jephthah's distress. The meaning of the root כרע is to go down on one's knees, and figuratively, its meaning here is to "crush", to "break". Repetition of the root expresses the excessiveness in the matter.[63] Jephthah expresses a feeling of depression and disaster, but he points an accusing finger at his daughter, "You have brought me low". He further blames her: "you have become my troubler!" Jephthah blames his daughter for coming out to meet him, and it does not occur to him that he alone is to blame for having made such a vow.[64] He transfers the blame to her instead of seeing his own shortcomings because of his egocentric worldview, and the inclusion of the dialogue in the account serves to present Jephthah's character.

Jephthah's egocentricity does not allow him to see his daughter's tragedy either. He sees only his own calamity: "You have *brought me low*; you have become *my troubler*!" Jephthah's calamity is tremendous, but his daughter's tragedy is no less, and yet he does not relate to this.[65] She came out to meet him in order to honour and gladden him, but he announces to her immediately that because of this he will sacrifice her.[66] In this situation, certainly it is expected that the father will see his daughter's sorrow, but Jephthah does not show any sign of being aware of it. The object of the passage is to illustrate the extreme extent of his egocentricity, in that he cannot even see his daughter's sorrow.[67]

---

[63] The intense significance of this verb can be learnt from its use in other contexts, in all the appearances of the root in the Biblical narrative: Gen 34:30; Josh 6:18; 7:25; 1 Sam 14:29: 1 Kings 18:17–18.

[64] See: Exum, "Murder They Wrote", p. 21.

[65] Similarly, see: Trible, "The Daughter of Jephthah", pp. 101–102.

[66] M. Garsiel (*Biblical Names*, pp. 105–106) and Klein (*The Triumph of Irony in the Book of Judges*, p. 94) consider that Jephthah's name is an etymological legend of opening his mouth in his vow to God: "For *I have opened* my mouth to the LORD . . . *you have opened* your mouth to the LORD" (vv. 35–36). Although the root פצה is used in the account and not the root פתח, Garsiel showed that the authors of the Bible used these two verbs indiscriminately. Above we studied the role of the meaning of the names Gideon, Jerubbaal and Abimelech in shaping of the account. The meanings of these names correspond to a central point in the action of the protagonists, and accordingly, Jephthah's vow also occupies a significant place in understanding the meaning of the Jephthah account. Similarly, see also Exum, *Tragedy and Biblical Narrative*, p. 48. The name יפתח is perhaps a short form of the name יפתח-אל ("Iphtahel") that appears in Josh 19:14. On the meaning of the name "Jephthah" as a keyword in the account, in which speech is the leitmotif, see also: Marais, *Representation in Old Testament Narrative Texts*, pp. 119–120. In Webb's opinion (*The Book of Judges*, pp. 73–76), dialogue is a central motif, which connects all the parts of the account, determines its structure and expresses its meaning. Polzin also formulated his analysis of the account around this motif (*Moses and the Deuteronomist*, pp. 176–181).

[67] On this matter, see also: Webb, *The Book of the Judges*, p. 67.

Jephthah does not try to find a solution to his tragic situation. When Saul curses anyone who eats during his war against the Philistines, and it transpires that his son Jonathan ate honey, he is prepared to execute his son (1 Sam 14:24–27, 43–44). However, the people cry out against this and save Jonathan from the death sentence (1 Sam 14:45). In the Jephthah story there is no initiative by a third party or by Jephthah to save Jephthah's daughter. The reason that Jephthah indicates for performing the vow is his undertaking to God: "For *I have opened my mouth* to the LORD and *I cannot* retract".[68] Again it appears in this sentence that what motivates Jephthah is his own interest: since God helped him he is obligated and he cannot retract his vow.

Jephthah's egocentricity is expressed clearly in his daughter's response:

> She said to him, "My father, if you have opened your mouth to the LORD, do to me according to what has gone out of your mouth, now that the LORD has given you vengeance against your enemies, the Ammonites.
> And she said to her father, "Let this thing be done for me: let me be for two months, and I will go with my companions and lament upon the hills and there bewail my maidenhood, my companions and I" (vv. 36–37).

Jephthah's daughter replies using the same words as her father: "if you have opened your mouth to the LORD, do to me according to what has gone out of your mouth" (v. 36). Jephthah's daughter also places the focus on her father and completely suppresses her own opinion or wishes. According to her words as well, Jephthah's alleged reason is sufficient cause to sacrifice her. She completely effaces herself before her father. In this she further shows the extent of Jephthah's egocentricity: "now that the LORD has given you vengeance against your enemies, the Ammonites" (v. 36).[69] In the words of Jephthah's

---

[68] On the significance of a vow and the power of words, and on the motif of speech and its function throughout the account, see: Exum, *Tragedy and Biblical Narrative*, pp. 60–65. On the vow in the Bible and in Ugarit, see: S. B. Parker, "The Vow in Ugaritic and Israelite Narrative", *Ugarit-Forschungen* 11 (1979), pp. 493–500.

[69] Therefore the daughter's lack of reaction is not to be seen as an expression of women's status in the Biblical Patriarchal period, as maintained by Exum ("Murder They Wrote", pp. 31–32), but shaping of a secondary character in the account in order to shed light on the personality of Jephthah, the protagonist of the account.

daughter, it again appears that the war fought by Jephthah is his
private war, and God helped him to take vengeance on Jephthah's
enemies.[70]

The ability of Jephthah's daughter to see the situation from her
father's viewpoint poignantly underscores her father's failure to relate to
his daughter's pain and sorrow. This is expressed in her next words:

> And she said to her father, "Let this thing be done for me: let me be
> for two months, and I will go with my companions and lament upon
> the hills and there bewail my maidenhood, my companions and I".
> "Go", he said and sent her away for two months. (vv. 37–38₁).

After Jephthah's daughter expresses her willingness to sacrifice herself for her father's benefit (v. 36), there appears to be a pause in
the dialogue, as shown by the fact that immediately afterwards she
continues to speak, and nonetheless the Biblical text commences:
"And she said to her father". This formula of ויאמר . . . ויאמר . . . ("She
said . . . and she said") indicates that Jephthah's daughter paused
between her words.[71] The object of this pause is to indicate an expectation that Jephthah will answer his daughter at this point. His answer
could have been an attempt to find a loophole in the vow to save
his daughter, and particularly after she showed such great self-sacrifice
for his benefit. The reader expects, at the very least, that Jephthah
will now express his pain and sorrow over his daughter's fate, perhaps by words of consolation and persuasion. However, the silence
here is deafening, Jephthah does not even relate to her words. This
emphasis on Jephthah's silence shows his indifference to his daughter's
sorrow, and the very extreme dimensions of his egocentricity.

Jephthah's silence obliges his daughter to go on to ask her father
to postpone performance of the vow for two months in order to
allow her to lament her maidenhood. This request, coming after
Jephthah's silence, points to a minimum course that Jephthah could
have suggested on his own initiative to his daughter. However, he
does not do even this. Jephthah's daughter sees her father's ego-

---

[70] Burney (*The Book of Judges*, p. 300) was misled by this expression and failed to
discern the rhetoric of these verses, which present Jephthah's personal motives in
the context of the people's war. On the basis of this verse, Burney thought that it
should be understood that Jephthah had a personal quarrel with the Ammonites.

[71] On the meaning of the structure ויאמר . . . ויאמר, see: M. Shiloah,
"ויאמר . . . ויאמר", ספר קורנגרין, Tel-Aviv 1964, pp. 251–276.

centric viewpoint, but he does not reciprocate her understanding. It is she who sacrifices herself for his benefit, and she has to make a small request from him, to postpone performance of the vow by two months to allow her to lament her disaster.

Jephthah's response to his daughter's request continues to be indifference and lack of consideration. All that he has to say to her, in response to her tragic request, is one word: "go" (v. 38). More than Jephthah's daughter's self-sacrifice, the tragedy here is Jephthah's complete disregard for his daughter's sorrow. He does not express any sympathy for his daughter and immediately, it is written: "and sent her away for two months". He sends her to weep, but he does not show any feeling. He yields to her request, but not only does he not seek a solution, he also does not even give her more time to grieve.

His insensitivity to her sorrow is emphasized by tacit expressions of her pain vis-à-vis her fate. Jephthah's daughter asks: ואלכה וירדתי על ההרים (lit. "I will go and descend upon the hills", v. 37). In this request there are two strange aspects: firstly the expression וירדתי על ההרים is odd.[72] Secondly, after it is already said ואלכה ("and I will go"), the verb וירדתי ("and I will descend") is superfluous. The expression "I will go down upon the hills" does not reflect a topographical situation, but in the mouth of Jephthah's daughter it expresses precisely her feeling—a feeling of going under.[73]

Jephthah's daughter is going to die and her last request is to bewail her situation: "and I will go with my companions and lament upon the hills and there bewail my maidenhood, my companions and I" (v. 37). Jephthah's daughter laments, but she does not lament alone, Israelite maidens lament with her. This situation highlights Jephthah's indifference; he does not lament with her. The difficult situation of Jephthah's daughter, in which her companions also participate, as opposed to Jephthah's apathy, is highlighted through the repetition in carrying out of her request: "So she departed, she and her companions, and bewailed her maidenhood on the mountains" (v. 38).

---

[72] Many explanations have been put forward in relation to this problem. The Aramaic version is: ואתנניד על טוריא, i.e. "I will wander upon the hills"; רדת is from the root רוד. This is also the meaning in Jer 2:31. Similarly, Burney (*The Book of Judges*, p. 323) adopts the amended version: וירדתי in the sense of going back and forward. Rashi considers that ירד is with the meaning of lament, as in Isa 15:3; Ps 55:3. For another explanation, see: Römer, "Why Would the Deuteronomists Tell about the Sacrifice of Jephthah's Daughter?", p. 37.

[73] Similarly, see also: Bal, *Death and Dissymmetry*, p. 48.

After two month's Jephthah's daughter returns to her father: "After two months' time, she returned to her father, and he did to her as he had vowed" (v. 39).[74] However, at this stage too, he does not express any feelings towards his daughter. After two months she could have decided not to return, but she returns to her father out of loyalty.[75] However, he does not express any fatherly or human feeling towards her. The verse continues to describe the tragedy of Jephthah's daughter: "She had never known a man".[76] The narrator again seeks to emphasize the extent of the daughter's sacrifice, in that she had not yet had time to realize her identity. However, again it is the narrator who expresses this, while Jephthah's silence in relation to his daughter is glaring.

The account ends with four days of mourning for Jephthah's daughter by the daughters of Israel, and the statement that these days of mourning were observed yearly:[77] "So it became a custom

---

[74] The simple meaning is that Jephthah offered her up as a burnt offering, and this was what was understood by the Rabbinical sages (see for instance: BT Ta'anit 4a) and early exegesis. See: Rashi on Ta'anit 4a; Nachmanides on Lev 27:29. R. Abraham Ibn Ezra (cited in Nachmanides, *ibid.*) and Kimchi in his father's name considered that he did not kill her but sanctified her and she dwelt in a kind of convent without marrying. Several commentators adopted this interpretation, inter alia: Gersonides, Abravanel. This interpretation was also adopted in Christian exegesis. See: Moore, *Judges*, p. 304. In addition to the fact that this interpretation does not coincide with the literal Biblical meaning, Green (*The Role of Human Sacrifice in the Ancient Near East*, p. 162) is correct in saying that we do not find in the Bible that an unmarried woman is holier than a married woman. On Ibn Ezra's interpretation, see: U. Simon, "Peshat Exegesis of Biblical Historiography: Historicism, Dogmatism, and Medievalism", M. Kogan, B. L. Eichler, J. H. Tigay (eds.), *Tehillah le-Moshe: Biblical and Judaic Studies in Honor of Moshe Greenberg* Winona Lake 1997, pp. 197–198. In Römer's opinion ("Why Would the Deuteronomists Tell about the Sacrifice of Jephthah's Daughter?", pp. 27–38), it is not conceivable that the Jephthah's daughter account is Deuteronomistic since this school was strongly opposed to sacrifice of children. Römer therefore concludes that this passage was introduced by a post-Deuteronomistic editor in the Hellenistic period. The purpose of the introduction of this passage, in his opinion, is to show that there are also tragic works in classical Jewish literature, just as there are in classical Greek literature. Apart from the fact that there is absolutely no basis for this hypothesis, Römer's research premise is problematic. Römer assumes that the outlook expressed in the text must correspond to the author's outlook. However, this assumption is incorrect and the account may well be intended to present the author's criticism of Jephthah's character and actions.

[75] Bal (*Death and Dissymmetry*, p. 50) considers that Jephthah's daughter had no choice since in her unmarried status, she was under her father's control.

[76] On the meaning of this expression, see: Bal, *Death and Dissymmetry*, pp. 48–51.

[77] The expressions of the heavy mourning by the maidens of Israel emerge from the comparison to the similar style in 2 Chr 35:25: "And Jeremiah lamented for

in Israel for four days every year the daughters of Israel would go
out to lament the daughter of Jephthah the Gileadite" (vv. 40₄–41).
The ending of the Jephthah account with this statement again underscores the great tragedy of Jephthah's daughter: all the daughters of
Israel mourned her fate, but her father does not show any sign of
expressing mourning and grief. In order to emphasize this, the mourning customs are indicated immediately after it is stated decisively and
dryly of Jephthah: "she returned to her father, and he did to her
as he had vowed" (v. 39). The fact that four days of mourning were
accepted as a binding and permanent custom (ותהי חק)[78] and were
observed מימים ימימה—"every year" highlights even more her father's
indifference to the matter.[79]

Now it is possible to understand why the account of Jephthah's
vow is interpolated in the account of the war in the alternating struc-

---

Josiah; and all the singing men and singing women spoke of Josiah in their lamentations, unto this day; and they made them an ordinance in Israel; and, behold,
they are written in the lamentations".

[78] The verb ותהי is in the feminine form whereas the noun חק is masculine.
According to Gesenius (*Hebrew Grammar*, 122), this is perhaps an example of the use
of the feminine form in order to express the neuter. Ps 69:11 is to be understood
in this way. It is also possible that the verb ותהי refers to the wailing in the previous verse, as interpreted by Elitzur, *Sefer Shoftim*, p. 131. Trible ("The Daughter
of Jephthah", p. 106) considers that the verb ותהי refers to Jephthah's daughter.
However, it is difficult to accept the meaning that Jephthah's daughter became an
ordinance in Israel. It is also possible that, as in many places in the Bible, there
is no agreement between masculine and feminine. In Moore's opinion (*Judges*,
p. 303), the sentence ותהי חק בישראל belongs to the next verse, and the end of the
verse should come after the word איש. Also: Soggin, *Judges*, p. 214; R. Joseph Kara.

[79] This intention of the mourning descriptions conflicts with the hypothesis that
the account of the mourning is originally an etiological account related to some
type of cult. In this sense see: Burney, *The Book of Judges*, pp. 332–334; Moore,
Judges, p. 305; F. F. Hvidberg, *Weeping and Laughter in the Old Testament: A Study of
Canaanite-Israelite Religion*, Leiden 1962, pp. 103–105, for an additional bibliography,
see there. In opposition to this point of view, see: Trible, "The Daughter of Jephthah",
p. 115, n. 53; Webb, *The Book of the Judges*, p. 229, n. 67; Boling, *Judges*, p. 210.
Klein (*The Triumph of Irony in the Book of Judges*, p. 92) rightly notes that the object
of the account is not to explain the tradition, but to censure it. Indeed, in the
Aramaic version the passage ends (v. 39) as follows: "And it is a decree in Israel
that a man will not sacrifice a son or a daughter, as Jephthah the Gileadite did,
who did not ask Phineas the High Priest, and had he asked Phineas he would have
redeemed her". The fact that mourning was made a binding custom around this
event for four days every year and that it was observed, as the verse attests, "every
year" negates the opinion that the vow imposed on Jephthah's daughter was that
she would not marry. It is unlikely that there would have been such great mourning because Jephthah's daughter was not allowed to marry and have children. (In
his commentary to Lev 27:29, Nachmanides uses this argument to negate Ibn Ezra's
conjecture that Jephthah dedicated his daughter to God).

ture indicated above. The narrator wished to explain Jephthah's personal motivation in the war as reflected in the account of his vow. The interpolation of the two accounts shows that, as in the account of his vow, so in the war against the Ammonites Jephthah's only desire was to make a name for himself. Jephthah's vow exposes what really concerned him before he went out to fight: "then whoever comes out of the door of my house to meet me when I return victorious" (v. 31). When Jephthah went out to fight he was not thinking of the people's good or the people's fate, but of the acclaim that he would receive for the deliverance when he returned in peace from the war.

His personal victory so blinded him that he could not distinguish that in his wording he would lead to the downfall of anyone coming to meet him. As is the way of egocentrics, he did not consider the good of others. It was his daughter who paid the price.

Ironically, Jephthah goes out to a national war in order to further personal interests. The result is the opposite. He indeed saved the people and solved the national problem, but he paid a heavy personal price. The national plane does not interest him, but it is precisely on this plane that he is successful. On the other hand, it is precisely on the personal plane, which is his main interest, that he fails. Jephthah saw in his mind's eye the people acclaiming him and coming out to meet him on his return, but when he returned not only was there no one to acclaim him and welcome him, but he sacrificed to his egocentricity his only daughter, who alone came to welcome and acclaim him.[80] The contrast between his victory in war and his personal tragedy is expressed through the use of the root שוב. Jephthah vows: "then whoever comes out of the door of my house to meet me when I return (= בשובי) victorious (= בשלום)" (v. 31). Jephthah indeed returns victorious, but it is his daughter who comes out to meet him and he decrees that he cannot retract (לשוב) his vow: "For I have opened my mouth to the LORD and I cannot retract (= לשוב)" (v. 35).[81] At this stage of the account, Jephthah

---

[80] Jephthah has one daughter whom he kills. This is in contrast to the minor judges who had many children, as pointed out by Exum, "The Center Cannot Hold", p. 421. Despite certain similarities between Jephthah and the minor judges, this difference underscores the great tragedy in the Jephthah account.

[81] Exum, *Tragedy and Biblical Narrative*, p. 52. The fact that he cannot retract his vow corresponds to the law in Num 30:3; Deut 23:22–23. The warning against

vanquishes the enemy at a heavy personal price. At the beginning of the account, the internal problem between Jephthah and the elders of Gilead was resolved because of the national problem.

Now it clear why the account of the war is not described in detail in the Jephthah account. This is the shortest war account in the Book of Judges. The brevity of the description of the war highlights the interpolated account of Jephthah's daughter, and indicates that it is not Jephthah's victory that is the main subject here, but Jephthah's motives.

There is very similar wording to Jephthah's vow in Israel's war against the King of Arad. Numbers 21:1–3 refers to the Kind of Arad who fought against Israel and in the first campaign of the war he took Israelite captives (21:1). Before the second campaign initiated by Israel against Arad, they vow that if God delivers Arad into their hands they will utterly destroy the cities conquered. A comparison of the two vows shows the linguistic similarity between them:

Numbers, 21:2–3	Judges 11:30–31
"*Then* Israel *made a vow to the* LORD *and said, If you will indeed give* (נתן תתן) this people into our hands, then we will utterly destroy their towns. The LORD listened to the voice of Israel, and handed over the Canaanites".	"*And* Jephthah *made a vow to the* LORD, *and said, If you will indeed give* (נתן תתן) the Ammonites into my hand, then whoever comes out of the doors of my house to meet me, when I return victorious"

Why does Jephthah's vow not have a good result in the way that Israel's vow does in the conquest of Arad? The answer to this question lies in the difference between the vows. Israel vow to God that they will destroy the cities that they conquer. Israel make a vow in order to win the war. Jephthah, however, does not speak of sacrifice at the national level, but of a personal sacrifice that he wishes to make to God. The difference between the two similar situations underscores Jephthah's egocentric attitude that is expressed in his

---

performing vows and even making vows recurs in the Wisdom Literature, Eccl 8:3–4. However, as already noted, in the case of Saul, who cursed anyone who ate, and who therefore sentenced his son to death, the people redeemed Jonathan (1 Sam 14:24–45).

vow. Unlike Israel in their war against Arad, who together destroy
the cities that were conquered, Jephthah does not vow on behalf of
the people, and it is not the people that will make the offering to
God; the motive is not national but personal. Jephthah wants the
victory for himself and therefore he wants the vow to be his personal
vow: "whoever comes out of the door of my house to meet me when
I return victorious from the Ammonites shall be the LORD's and shall
be offered by me as a burnt offering". (v. 31).[82]

It is interesting that in the Gideon account a description of the
confrontation with the men of Succoth and of Penuel is also interpolated in the description of the battle against the Midianites, and
the two descriptions alternate in the same way as the structure of
the account of Jephthah's war against the Ammonites and the account
of Jephthah's daughter. The following schema illustrates the similarity between the two structures:

The account of Jephthah's war against Ammon and the account of Jephthah's daughter	The account of Gideon's pursuit of Midian and the confrontations with the men of Succoth and of Penuel
Deployment for war (11:29) Jephthah's vow (30–31)	Gideon's pursuit of the Midianites (8:4) Gideon asks for the support of Succoth and of Penuel (vv. 5–9)
Jephthah's war against the Ammonites (vv. 32–33)	The continued pursuit and the capture of the Midianite kings (vv. 10–13).
Carrying out of Jephthah's vow (vv. 34–40)	Gideon's revenge in Succoth and in Penuel (vv. 14–17)
Jephthah's war against the Ephraimites (12:1–7)	Gideon executes the Midianite kings (vv. 18–21)

---

[82] On this point too, the idea emerges that the vow reflects principally Jephthah's
egocentricity and not his manipulation of God, as asserted by Trible, "The Daughter
of Jephthah", pp. 96–97. Webb (*The Book of the Judges*, pp. 64–65), however, does
not blame Jephthah so harshly. He explains Jephthah's vow as insecurity deriving
from the fact that God had not appeared to him as He had to Gideon, for instance,
and the vow is his attempt to receive some kind of divine confirmation of his success. Jephthah is the tool used by God to vanquish Ammon, but he does not know
this. Webb disagrees with Trible, who considers that Jephthah acts out of lack of
confidence in God, and thinks that Jephthah here is trying to bring God to work
for him. Similarly also, Jacobs considers that Jephthah makes a vow since he did
not receive any positive reaction from God. J. Jacobs, "The Story of Jephthah",
M.D. diss., Ramat Gan, 1998, p. 50 (Hebrew). However, the narrative explicitly

In both cases the narrator alternated between the two accounts. In both the Gideon and the Jephthah accounts, a story of internal tragedy is contained within the account of the judge's war against an outside enemy, in both cases, the internal account sheds light on the motives of the deliverer in his war against the enemy.

It is Jephthah's egocentricity that led to his failure. Jephthah's motivation in his vow was to "persuade" God to help him. Above, we argued that Jephthah intended to sacrifice an animal, but his eagerness for recognition of his achievements by those welcoming him led him to utter a sentence that he did not mean but which expressed his inner desire: "whoever comes out . . . to meet me when I return victorious" (v. 31). This unfortunate utterance of Jephthah contrasts sharply with the elaborate rhetoric that he demonstrates in his speech to the Ammonite king, in which his arguments are presented in a structured and convincing manner.[83] The difference between the consummate speech and the unfortunate vow following immediately after lies in the circumstances. The object of Jephthah's speech is to show his suitability for the role of deliverer and acceptance of his leadership by God. When Jephthah acts out of good motives what he says is perfect; when he acts out of negative motives, and focus on his personal interest, instead of thinking of the national situation, he fails. The contrast between his rhetorical skill in his speech and between the vow shows that as long as he is speaking for the sake of the people he succeeds; when he speaks for himself he fails. This failure, expressed in Jephthah's wording, and causing personal harm, will also lead to Jephthah's failure on the national plane,[84] as will be discussed in the next section.

---

states that the spirit of God was upon Jephthah (11:29). Further, Jacobs gives examples of judges who received a positive confirmation from God (*ibid.*, n. 19), but he does not indicate Ehud who did not receive such a confirmation. Roberts considers that the passage does not censure the sacrifice of Jephthah's daughter since in his opinion the source of this passage is from a local tradition of the Transjordan, where, as for the Moabites and the Gileadites, it was customary to sacrifice one's children. Roberts, *Content and Form Within the Jephthah Narrative*, pp. 112–115. In this matter he bases himself on the research of J. A. Hackett, "Religious Traditions in Israelite Transjordan", P. D. Miller, P. D. Hanson and S. D. McBride (eds.), *Ancient Israelite Religion: Essays in Honor of Frank Moore Cross*, Philadelphia 1987, pp. 131–134.

[83] See: Boling, *Judges*, p. 207; L. J. M. Claassens, "Notes on Characterization in the Jephthah Narrative", *JNSL* 22 (1996), p. 113.

[84] Since Jephthah's vow is a negative element, I agree with Zakovitch (*Through the Looking Glass*, p. 95) that Jephthah was victorious in the war not because of the vow, but because the spirit of the LORD came upon him, and that he was victorious

6. Jephthah's Confrontation with the Ephraimites (12:1–7)

We saw above that the main subject of the account is not Jephthah's victory over the Ammonites but the presentation of the personal motivations in his actions. The Jephthah account does not conclude with the victory over the enemy as do the Ehud and Deborah accounts. Its conclusion rather resembles the end of the Gideon account.[85] Rather than ending with the victory stage, both these accounts go on to describe the subsequent deeds of the judges.

After Jephthah's victory, the tribe of Ephraim complains that he did not call on them to participate in the war: "The men of Ephraim mustered and crossed the Jordan to Zaphon. They said to Jephthah, Why did you cross over to fight against the Ammonites, and did not call us to go with you? We'll burn your house down over you!" (12:1). This complaint recalls the similar complaint made by the Ephraimites to Gideon (8:1). However, the words addressed by the Ephraimites to Jephthah are more serious than those addressed to Gideon. Their complaint against Jephthah also contains a threat: "We'll burn your house down over you!" Despite this difference, Jephthah's harsh response to the Ephraimites is very marked, and the different reactions to the two similar situations illustrate the difference between the two judges.

Against one sentence of the Ephraimites, Jephthah's answer extends over five verses. Jephthah acts very highhandedly towards Ephraim. However, he first rebukes them:

> Jephthah said to them, "I and my people were in a bitter conflict with the Ammonites; and I summoned you, but you did not save me from

---

in the war despite the vow. Trible ("The Daughter of Jephthah", p. 97) however, considers that the linguistic connection between אם נתון תתן את בני עמון בידי "If you will give the Ammonites into my hand" and ויתנם ה' בידו "and the LORD gave them into his hand" proves that he was victorious thanks to the vow. She also adds that without the vow the spirit of the LORD would have helped him. However, it is not clear how she can know this!

[85] There is no basis to the opinion that the account of the confrontation with the Ephraimites is a late addition, as indicated by Moore, *Judges*, p. 306. Burney (*The Book of Judges*, p. 302) emphasizes that the transition from the account of Jephthah's daughter to the account of Jephthah's confrontation with the Ephraimites is not smooth; he therefore considers that the account of the confrontation is from another source. However, he failed to notice the shared principal meaning of the two passages, both of which stress Jephthah's egocentricity.

them. When I saw that you did not save me, I risked my life and advanced against the Ammonites; and the LORD delivered them into my hands. Why have you come here now to fight against me?" (11:2–3).

In the parallel situation, Gideon accepted the words of the Ephraimites, and in his rhetorically well constructed answer he praised them for their deed, while detracting from the value of his own deeds, thus averting a confrontation within Israel (8:2–3). This is not the case with Jephthah. He makes harsh accusations against Ephraim, indicating that they did not answer his calls and did not come to help in the war against the Ammonites. In his words, he emphasizes his own deeds. Moreover, his wording implies that all that occurred was on the personal level. The war against the Ammonites was his personal war: איש ריב[86] הייתי אני ועמי ובני עמון מאוד ("I and my people").[87] Jephthah's call to Ephraim was for them to assist him: "I summoned you, but you did not save *me* from them". According to Jephthah, he went out himself to fight Ammon because they did not assist him: "When I saw that you did not save me, I risked my life and advanced against the Ammonites" (v. 3). Jephthah says that his achievements are because God helped him: "and the LORD delivered them into my hands" (v. 3). However, when he describes Ephraim's criticism of him, the emphasis is again on their personal confrontation with him: "Why have you come here now to fight against me?" Again Jephthah reveals the egocentric motives in his actions against Ammon and now against Ephraim.[88] In a like situation, Gideon's main concern is the good of the people and therefore he praises the deeds of Ephraim to the detriment of the credit due to him (8:2–3).[89]

In both cases, the deed in question is capturing the fords of the Jordan (7:24; 12:5). However, there is a considerable difference between the two cases. In the Gideon account, the Ephraimites took

---

[86] On the meaning of the word ריב in the context of a legal proceeding, see: J. Limburg, "The Root *rib* and the Prophetic Lawsuit Speeches", pp. 289–304, in particular pp. 298–299.

[87] Jephthah's words contain a double emphasis on himself in the expression "הייתי אני". The English language has no parallel construction to reflect Jephthah's emphasis on self in this sentence.

[88] Therefore, it is incorrect to see Jephthah's individualistic wording as insignificant; he is not in fact is speaking on behalf of the Gileadites, as asserted by Moore, *Judges*, p. 307.

[89] Webb (*The Book of the Judges*, pp. 70–73) tends either to justify Jephthah's actions, or to see in them an inevitable response.

the fords of the Jordan in order to capture the Midianite princes Oreb and Zeeb there (7:24). In the parallel account, however, Jephthah takes the fords in order to capture the tribe of Ephraim. The taking of the fords in the Gideon account is in order to overcome the enemy, whereas Jephthah takes the same action in order to kill Israelites.[90]

In Jephthah's negotiations with the elders of Gilead, he managed to force them to accept his position and to appoint him head over all the inhabitants of Gilead, and he agreed to deliver the people. In his negotiations with Ephraim, he does not attempt to prevent an internal confrontation, and he goes out to a civil war. Again he is not prepared to "lose" in negotiations. However, while in the first negotiations his success led him to fight against the Ammonites, his "success" in the second negotiations led him to fight against an Israelite tribe.[91]

The confrontation between Gideon and Ephraim was avoided thanks to Gideon's words. In contrast, Jephthah wages a grievous war against the Ephraimites with brutal results:

> (4) And Jephthah gathered all the men of Gilead and fought the Ephraimites. The men of Gilead defeated the Ephraimites; for they had said, "You are fugitives from Ephraim, Gilead in the heart of Ephraim and in the heart of Manasseh".
>
> (5) The Gileadites held the fords of the Jordan against the Ephraimites. And when any fugitive from Ephraim said, "Let me cross", the men of Gilead would say to him, "Are you an Ephraimite?"; if he said "No,"
>
> (6) they would say to him, "Then say shibboleth"; but he would say "sibboleth", not being able to pronounce it correctly. Thereupon they would seize him and slay him by the fords of the Jordan. Forty-two thousand Ephraimites fell at that time (12:4–6).

Let us now examine whose argument was justified, Jephthah's or Ephraim's. Ephraim claimed that Jephthah did not call them to fight against Ammon, while Jephthah claimed that he did call them but that they did not come. Which of the two arguments is true? Did Jephthah call them and they did not come as he claimed, or did he

---

[90] For a structural analysis of the accounts dealing with the taking of the Jordan in the Book of Judges, 3:27–29; 7:24–8:3; 12:1–6, see: Jobling, *The Sense of Biblical Narrative*, pp. 110–116. For a comparison between Jephthah's confrontation with the Ephraimites and Gideon's confrontation with them, see: Zakovitch, *Through the Looking Glass*, pp. 39–40.

[91] Compare: Exum, *Tragedy and Biblical Narrative*, pp. 56–57.

not call them at all, as they claimed? There is no answer to this in the account. It is strange that the Bible does not indicate who is to blame, since the two opposite claims here caused a civil war. Suppressing of the information as to what really happened and what caused the present situation is certainly intentional. It seems that the Bible deliberately sought not to determine this question in order to show that the answer is irrelevant. The account does not focus on the question of who caused the present situation, so that we will pay attention only to the present situation, and the reader will judge the conduct of the sides only according to the circumstances related. From this viewpoint, the present description undoubtedly points an accusing finger at Jephthah's egocentric conduct.

At the stage of the verbal dispute, we already saw that the Bible details Jephthah's lengthy answer against the short claim of the Ephraimites. This fact in itself shows that Jephthah is the important factor in worsening of the situation. After Jephthah's answer we could have expected Ephraim to continue their arguments in response, and perhaps a verbal solution of the problem. However, Jephthah does not wait for a response from the Ephraimites and immediately goes out to war against them.[92] The fact that he does not wait to hear the answer contrasts with the negotiations that he conducted with the Ammonites. With the enemy Jephthah was prepared to talk and even to hear their position. With the Ephraimites, however, he is not prepared to hear their position and immediately he goes out to murder thousands of them.

Why did Jephthah fight Ephraim? It does not seem that this was out of self-defence despite their threat: "We'll burn your house down over you!" (12:1), since there is no evidence in the passage of military organization of Ephraim, and the broad scope of Jephthah's activity does not attest to defensive actions but to offensive actions. Jephthah wages war against them because of the very fact that they came to him with claims. The offence to Jephthah's honour and status is what motivated him to wage war.

Another reason for Jephthah's irrelevant motives is evident in the unclear sentence of the men of Gilead: "You are fugitives from Ephraim, Gilead in the heart of Ephraim and in the heart of Manasseh" (v. 4).

---

[92] Contrary to Boling's opinion (*Judges*, p. 212) that Jephthah takes care of internal problems in the same way that he handled the Ammonite problem, firstly by diplomacy.

It is difficult to understand the exact meaning of this argument,[93] but it appears from the sentence that this refers here to a previous dispute in which Ephraim, Manasseh and Gilead were involved. The Bible does not explain the background to this dispute, and again it seems that this is intentional. The background to the dispute is not developed, so that attention will be paid to Jephthah's wish for greatness, which led to tribal disputes that degenerated into civil war.[94]

The story does not expand on the military confrontation between the tribes, in which Jephthah's triumphs over Ephraim: "The men of Gilead defeated the Ephraimites" (v. 4), and it goes immediately to describe in detail Jephthah's cruelty at the stage of the flight of the Ephraimites. Jephthah takes the fords of the Jordan in order to capture the Ephraimites who are fleeing from Gilead to regain Ephraimite territory. At this stage, Jephthah could have allowed them to escape, but he employs great ingenuity and great cruelty in order to wipe out all the survivors of the tribe of Ephraim. The defeated Ephraimites try to flee, and at the fords of the Jordan they try to conceal their identity.[95] Jephthah however reveals their identity when he takes advantage of the inability of the Ephraimites to pronounce the letter *shin*, which they pronounce as *sin*.[96] Anyone who failed the test was slaughtered: "Thereupon they would seize him and slay him by the fords of the Jordan" (v. 6).

---

[93] On the meaning of the sentence, see: Burney (*The Book of Judges*, p. 327); Kaufmann, *Sefer Shoftim*, p. 232.

[94] On this point too, Klein explains that the confrontation between Jephthah and the Ephraimites indicates the need to study and understand the question of the alliance, see: Klein, *The Triumph of Irony in the Book of Judges*, p. 98. However, as already indicated, the main subject of the account is not the background to the dispute, but the egocentric character of Jephthah, who is concerned with his status even at the expense of others.

[95] Willesen maintains that the meaning of the word *'efrātî* cannot be "from the tribe of Ephraim", since nobody would answer the question "are you *'efrātî*" in the affirmative. F. Willesen, "The *'efrātî* of the Shibboleth Incident", *VT* 8 (1958), pp. 97–98. In his opinion, the meaning of *'efrātî* is anyone who came from Efrata in the tribe of Judah. Therefore, if someone answered this question in the affirmative, he could continue on his way. Only someone who answered in the negative was put to the "sibboleth" test.

[96] The matter of "shibboleth"—"shibboleth" has been discussed extensively in the literature, both as regards the meaning of the word and the different dialects in Israel. See, for instance: E. A. Speiser, "The Shiboleth Incident (Judges 12:6)", *BASOR* 85 (1942), pp. 10–13; R. Marcus "The Word *šibbolet* Again", *BASOR* 87 (1942), p. 39. See also Gaster, *Myth, Legend and Custom in the Old Testament*, p. 433. For a further bibliography on the subject, see: Soggin, *Judges*, p. 219.

Jephthah's cruelty against helpless people, who merely seek to flee for their lives, is shocking, and greatly stressed in the account. Jephthah's war against the Ammonites is recounted in far less detail than his war against the Ephraimites. The emphasis in the two descriptions is on Jephthah's personal motives and, therefore, they belong to one structure, as we saw above. Jephthah is motivated in his war against Ammon by the wish for status and honour. In this case, he delivers the people but it is not for the people's good. In Jephthah's confrontation with Ephraim, the concern is the undermining of Jephthah's status, and therefore he wages a merciless war against them. When his interest conflicts with the good of the people, Jephthah does not hesitate. He goes into combat against those whom he delivered shortly before, and slaughters them mercilessly.[97]

Jephthah's egocentricity was very prominent in his sacrifice of his daughter on the altar of his success against the enemy. He then fought his people because they offended him. He *sacrificed* his daughter up as a burnt offering; he *slaughtered* Ephraim at the fords of the Jordan (12:6).[98]

In the account of Jephthah's confrontation with the Ephraimites the word אמר (said) is repeated frequently. The episode commences when the Ephraimites said to Jephthah that he had not called them: "They *said* to Jephthah, Why did you cross . . ." (v. 1). In response Jephthah lays the blame on them: "Jephthah *said* to them" (v. 2). The real cause of the confrontation is: "for they had *said*, You are fugitives from Ephraim, Gilead in the heart of Ephraim and in the heart of Manasseh" (v. 4). The use of the verb אמר also recurs in the description of Jephthah's cruelty: "And when any fugitive from Ephraim *said*, 'Let me cross', the men of Gilead would *say* to him, 'Are you an Ephraimite?'; if he said 'No', they would *say* to him, 'Then *say* shibboleth'; but he would *say* 'sibboleth' (vv. 5–6). The fact that the war between Jephthah and Ephraim commenced with a verbal

---

[97] The thematic unity between this episode and the preceding events in the account negate the claim that Jephthah's conflict with the Ephraimites is connected only loosely to the Jephthah account. See, for instance: Boling, *Judges*, p. 213. Likewise, his opinion (*ibid.*, p. 214) that ultimately Jephthah is presented as a positive judge, the best since Othniel, is implausible. On the other hand, Dewitt's opinion (*The Jephthah Traditions*, pp. 205 ff., 246 ff.) that the five units of the Jephthah account are in a chiastic structure, with Jephthah's negotiations with the Ammonite king at the centre, is very forced.

[98] See also Exum, *Tragedy and Biblical Narrative*, pp. 53–54.

argument and degenerated into such extensive and grievous propor-
tions is designed to show that it could have been averted with
correct leadership by Jephthah, had he not been absorbed by his
personal status.

The tragic termination of the war shows Jephthah's entire leadership
in a negative light: "Forty-two thousand Ephraimites fell at that time"
(v. 6). This great number of men killed by Jephthah establishes
Jephthah's entire leadership as a disaster. Ultimately, Jephthah did
not bring deliverance to the people but a massive disaster, due to
the fact that he acted for himself and not for his people.[99]

The conclusion of the account also indicates Jephthah's absolute
failure: "Jephthah judged Israel six years. Then Jephthah the Gileadite
died and he was buried in one of the towns of Gilead" (v. 7). This
conclusion differs from the other conclusions of the judge accounts.

---

[99] In Webb's opinion (*The Book of the Judges*, pp. 73–76), the meaning of the
account is a criticism of Jephthah's attempt to establish his relationship with God
along the same lines that he manages his relations with men. He made the relations with God political through the vow. The tendency to introduce politics into
religion occurs, according to Webb, both at the personal and the national level.
The result is tragedy. Brettler insisted that all the judges in the Book of Judges are
presented as anti-heroes apart from Othniel. Brettler, "The Book of Judges: Literature
as Politics", pp. 395–418. In his opinion, the explanation is that all the accounts
must be read as an allegory designed to present a contrast between Othniel, from
the tribe of Judah, who is exemplary, and the other judges, from the other northern tribes, who are shown to be blemished either politically and/or religiously. This
idea is also the intention of the first part of the book (1:1–2:10) and the last part
(chaps. 17–21). The historical setting for the writing of this polemical composition
is before the Davidic kingdom. Indeed, pro-Judah outlooks clearly appear in the
first part of the book, Judges 1:1–2:10, and in the opinion of many, also in the
account of the concubine at Gibeah. However, there is no trace of this outlook in
the judge accounts. Firstly, Ehud and Deborah are presented positively. Secondly,
in all the accounts the matter of the tribe of Judah does not appear at all (except
for 15:10–13). The Othniel account is the only account in which the protagonist
is from the tribe of Judah, and indeed, there is no criticism of him in this short
account. However, it is difficult to accept that all the judge accounts are in contrast to this short account, in which there is no expansion in relation to the character of Othniel. If Brettler's assumption were correct, we would find extensive
expansion of a positive description of Othniel, and it is doubtful whether the author
would have dedicated such a great part of his book to the other tribes in contrast.
Jacobs, ("The Story of Jephthah", p. 64) considers that the account does not intend
to present Jephthah negatively, but to show the disastrous results of the appointment of a deliverer not commissioned by God. Since Jephthah was not chosen by
God, he therefore made a vow, and this led to his failure. It should be noted, however, that the account presents Jephthah in a negative light, in his motives to deliver
the people, by his vow, and finally in the account of his war against the Ephraimites.
Moreover, God did not appoint Jephthah initially, but He agreed to his appointment *de facto* after his negotiations with the Ammonite king, as shown above.

The other accounts indicate at the end years of peace following the judge's deliverance (3:11; 3:30; 5:31; 8:28). The Jephthah account does not end thus, because Jephthah's leadership was a failure even in his lifetime. He himself violated the "peace" of the people when he slaughtered the tribe of Ephraim. In the other accounts the period of peace in wake of the judge was a long period of forty years (or eighty years after Ehud), attesting to the stability that came in wake of the judge's actions. The use of the typological number forty is certainly designed to indicate that the judge brought peace to the people for a whole generation, symbolized by the number forty. Jephthah's leadership, however, was short-lived—six years only.[100] In contrast to the other accounts, which ended with years of peace following the deliverance by the judge, the Jephthah account ends with the report of Jephthah's death and burial: "Then Jephthah the Gileadite died and he was buried in one of the towns of Gilead" (v. 7). The other accounts do not generally end with such a statement. The deaths of Othniel and Deborah are not mentioned, and the report of Ehud's death comes in the Deborah account to explain the circumstances of the people's return to doing evil in the eyes of the LORD. Gideon's death is also mentioned in order to explain why

---

[100] Contrary to the opinion of the scholars (in this matter see, for instance: Moore, *Judges*, p. 309; Soggin, *Judges*, p. 206), who see in the indication of Jephthah's six years a typical element of the minor judges. Based on the fact that the Jephthah account does not end with forty years of peace as in the other judge accounts, but with indication of six years of his leadership and the place of his burial, Noth (*The Deuteronomistic History*[2], pp. 69–70) concluded that Jephthah was included in the list of the minor judges and was also part of the deliverer accounts. In his opinion, the judge-deliverer accounts and the list of the minor judges were independent and were merged because Jephthah was in both the lists. This opinion was accepted by many scholars. See, for instance: Soggin, *Judges*, pp. 207; Boling, *Judges*, p. 189. In opposition to this theory, see: A. J. Hauser, "The 'Minor Judges'—A Re-evaluation", *JBL* 94 (1975), pp. 176 ff.; K. W. Whitelam, *The Just King: Monarchial Judicial Authority in Ancient Israel* (JSOTsup, 12), Sheffield 1979, pp. 62–63. This theory is based entirely on the fact that the Jephthah account does not end in the same way as the other judge-deliverer accounts. Scholars explained this deviation in terms of redaction of the book, and in this context they did not pay attention to the aim of the account, which is to present Jephthah's failure, and the fact that the absence of forty years of peace are a result of this failure. Currently, there is a tendency to see the difference between the major judges and the minor judges as a literary difference and not a functional difference. See: Hauser, "The 'Minor Judges'—A Re-evaluation"; E. T. Mullen, "The 'Minor Judges': Some Literary and Historical Considerations", *CBQ* 44 (1982), pp. 185–201; Malamat, *History of Biblical Israel*, pp. 100–101; Whitelam, *The Just King*, pp. 61–69; Ishida, "The Leaders of the Tribal Leagues 'Israel' in the Pre-Monarchic Period", pp. 514 ff.; Exum, "The Center Cannot Hold", p. 421.

the people again turned to idolatry (8:33). The ending of the account
with the report of Jephthah's death is designed to express the idea
that whereas the other judges acted well, and the evil commenced
only after their lifetimes, Jephthah's life is to be evaluated negatively.

The Jephthah and the Samson accounts are the only judge accounts
in which the judge's burial is reported. The difference between these
two reports again underscores the negative evaluation of Jephthah.
Samson worked throughout his life alone and without any aid or
cooperation. However, on his death he received recognition with his
honourable burial by his brothers and his father's house in his father's
tomb: "His brothers and all his family came down and took him
and brought him up and buried him between Zorah and Eshtaol in
the tomb of his father Manoah". (16:31). In contrast, Jephthah
throughout his leadership aspired to receive recognition, but was
buried without any indication of who buried him and in which city
of Gilead he was buried; he was buried alone, unaccompanied, and
without indication of a specific place: ויקבר בערי נלעד (lit. "He was
was buried in the towns of Gilead").[101]

7. The Meaning of the Jephthah Account

In light of the recurrent pattern of events until the time of Jephthah,
God decided to change the habitual framework. In the introduction
to the Jephthah account God indicates that He will no longer deliver
Israel through a charismatic deliverer. This intention shows that God
has despaired of the judge leadership pattern and intimates the possibility of another kind of leadership that will lead to stability in worship of God. God continues to refuse to send a deliverer to save Israel
from the Ammonite oppressor, even after the people has completely
forsaken idolatry and returned completely to worship of God.

Since God does not send a deliverer, the princes of Gilead must
resolve the leadership problem themselves, without divine assistance.
However, they cannot find among themselves a man prepared to lead
the people into war against Ammon. In their plight they ask Jephthah,

---

[101] Kimchi and Kara interpreted "in the towns of Gilead" as "in one of the
towns of Gilead". This is the Masoretic Text. Another version is reflected in the
Septuagint: ויקבר בעירו בנלעד. "And he was buried in his town in Gilead". Similarly,
Josephus: Jewish Antiquities, vol. 5, vii, 12 (p. 123) relates: "he died and was buried
at his native place of Sebee (= Mizpah), in the land of Gilead".

who in the past had been driven out of his father's home, to return to Gilead and to deliver the people. Jephthah's expulsion from his home affects his considerations and decisions decisively in the account. Already at the stage of commissioning, he rebukes the elders for this and is not prepared to assume office unless he is appointed head over all the inhabitants of Gilead. He is not prepared to accept only a military commission as proposed to him by the elders of Gilead. From the beginning of the encounter with Jephthah, he is seen to be exploiting the people's plight in order to further his personal interests and to receive an honoured status among the men of Gilead.

Alongside this attribute, Jephthah demonstrates his belief that his future victory over Ammon depends on God's will and assistance. This viewpoint is further emphasized in the negotiations that he conducts with the king of Ammon. These negotiations do not solve the problem peaceably, and are included in the account because they underscore Jephthah's belief that Israel's victories are none other than God's victories. This belief expressed by Jephthah leads God to change His plan and to accept Jephthah as *de facto* deliverer because of the potential latent in his strong faith in God.

However, despite the potential latent in his viewpoint that his practical success is a result of divine assistance, Jephthah will fail completely, because of his obsession with his status and honour.[102] Jephthah wins the war against the Ammonites, and he indeed believes that this achievement is the result of divine providence. However, interpolated in the war account is the tragic account of the sacrifice of his daughter as execution of his vow. The account of Jephthah's vow shows his extreme egocentricity, both through the wording of the vow, and in that Jephthah is concerned only by the price that he pays and not by his daughter's tragedy. He shows no feeling at all for his daughter. The account greatly underscores Jephthah's personal tragedy and the personal price that he pays and plays down his military achievement. This is in accordance with his priorities, but above all, it expresses the shortcoming in the attention paid to personal considerations. The Bible presents a leader who exploited a national situation in order to further personal interests. The result is that

---

[102] In contrast to the opinion that Jephthah is presented as a positive antithesis to the negative character of Abimelech. See: Soggin, *Judges*, p. 208. It is clear that the account presents Jephthah in a negative light, even though he clearly does not reach Abimelech's level of failure and corruption. On the parallel between the two figures, see below.

alongside the success at the national level, precisely at the personal level his achievements are nonexistent. On the contrary, he makes a terrible personal sacrifice.

Jephthah's war against the Ephraimites illustrates the result of the conflict of personal interests with national interests. Jephthah wages this war in order to uphold his honour and his status. Since the tribe of Ephraim did not pay him the respect due to him, he wages an all-out, merciless war against them. The object of this account is to show the danger inherent in a leader who is guided by his personal interests. When the leader is concerned mainly by his personal good, ultimately the two interests are liable to conflict and the people is liable to pay the price of the leader's preference of his own good over the people's good. If we compare Jephthah's deliverance of the people from Ammon with the civil war that he wages against Ephraim, not only does this show Jephthah as not being on a par with the other deliverers in the book, who saved Israel from its enemies, but he is seen to be closer to Israel's oppressors in the judge accounts.

Jephthah's character is presented as a contrast to Gideon's character. Gideon and Jephthah are the only judges who are called "man of valour". This epithet comes in both cases in the context of their selection as deliverers (6:12; 11:1). Gideon is an inhabitant of an established city that is fighting against nomads; Jephthah lives as a nomad, an exile, and fights against an established people. Gideon is the son of an important family and Jephthah is on the margins of society. Gideon is estranged from his fellow citizens because of his destruction of the altar of the Baal and because he assumes the role of deliverer, whereas Jephthah returns to his city after his expulsion in order to accept the office of deliverer. Gideon underrates his personal worth and has reservations about accepting the office of deliverer (6:15). He receives the commission because of the solidarity that he demonstrates with his people's plight (6:14). Jephthah accepts the office willingly if he is accorded a higher status (11:4–11). Gideon acts because of his national motivation, Jephthah acts on account of personal motives. Jephthah and Gideon are confronted by the Ephraimites. Gideon prevents worsening of the situation by playing down his own worth. Jephthah, in contrast, wages war on them because they dishonoured him. Throughout the account, Jephthah always blames others: the elders (11:7), the Ammonite king (11:27), his daughter (11:35) and the Ephraimites (12:2–3). Gideon uses diplomacy with the Ephraimites and thus avoids confrontation. Jephthah wages war against his people, although he demonstrates his diplomatic ability in the negotiations with the Ammonite king.[103]

Jephthah is presented more as a figure parallel to Abimelech. Abimelech is the son of a concubine, and Jephthah is the son of a harlot. Jephthah was driven out by his brothers, and Abimelech kills his brothers. Both seek to receive from the heads of the tribe or the city a status of head, Jephthah through pressure and Abimelech by savage means. Abimelech uses "worthless and reckless" fellows (9:4) and Jephthah uses "vain" men (11:3). Jephthah is a marginal personality whose leadership was supposed to restore him to the consensus. Abimelech undergoes the inverse process: he goes out of the house of his father, the leader, and criminally destroys it. Both kill members of their family because they are self-centred and aspire to greatness. Abimelech kills his brothers in order to achieve the status of king; Jephthah kills his daughter on the altar of his ambition for greatness and is impervious to her pain. Gideon also clashes with his family, but not in a personal context; on the contrary, he comes out in support of God and against the Baal. The egocentricity of both the leaders leads to their downfall. A woman throws an upper millstone on Abimelech's head; the fact that his daughter comes out to meet him symbolizes Jephthah's failure. The egocentricity of both the leaders causes the destruction of their families. Abimelech kills his brothers and on his death all of Gideon's family is wiped out, except for Jotham; Jephthah kills his only daughter. Notwithstanding, there is a tremendous difference between Abimelech and Jephthah. Even though both are driven by personal motives and even kill their compatriots, Abimelech does not bring any benefit to his people. Jephthah, however, delivers his people from the Ammonite oppressor. Jephthah believes in his God, Abimelech does not relate to God at all.[104]

Jephthah's personality shows the figure of a leader who believes totally in the God of Israel. Notwithstanding, he brings a colossal disaster on the people since he is absorbed by his personal good instead of the good of the people. An egocentric leader, acting for himself instead of for his people, even though fully believing in God, is doomed to disaster and failure.

---

[103] On the analogy between Gideon and Jephthah, see: Klein, *The Triumph of Irony in the Book of Judges*, p. 89; Garsiel, "Models of Analogy and Sets of Comparison in the Bible", pp. 42–43; O'Connell, *The Rhetoric of the Book of Judges*, pp. 202–203.

[104] On the relation between Jephthah and Abimelech, see: Klein, *The Triumph of Irony in the Book of Judges*, pp. 83–84; Exum, "The Center Cannot Hold", pp. 420–421.

IDEOLOGY IN THE HISTORICAL CONTEXT

In the introduction to this study, I discussed the difficulty of determining the historical setting of the Book of Judges. In the body of the work, I focused on a literary analysis, and on uncovering the ideology at the basis of the Gideon, Abimelech and Jephthah accounts. While it is not clear to what extent the actual accounts are historical, the motivation in writing accounts dealing clearly with the subject of leadership involves of necessity a concrete historical situation, and these accounts certainly constituted a way of relating to this situation. The next few pages will summarize the ideology of the accounts discussed in this book, with an attempt to make a conjecture as regards the historical reality from which the accounts derived; this reality will provide the most appropriate context for completing our understanding of the Gideon, Abimelech and Jephthah accounts.

The most salient historical anchor in these accounts is the anti-monarchic outlook that appears principally in Gideon's words in chapter 8, v. 23. Scholars disagree as to the period in which this ideology existed. Wellhausen considers that Gideon indeed ruled, and that the verses expressing his opposition to the monarchy are a late addition (together with 1 Sam 8:7; 10:19; 12:12) which replaced the report of Gideon's acceptance of the kingship.[1] In Wellhausen's opinion, the anti-monarchic outlook dates from the exilic period when the monarchy no longer existed. However, the pro-monarchic outlook presented for instance in 1 Sam 9:16, belongs to the monarchic period of David and Solomon, that led to the situation of "Judah and Israel dwelt safely, every man under his vine and under his fig-tree".[2] Many scholars strongly oppose the opinion that the anti-monarchism dates from after the destruction of the Temple. In texts clearly related to the Second Temple Period there is no indication

---

[1] Wellhausen, *Prolegomena to the History of Ancient Israel*, p. 239 n. 1; *Die Composition des Hexateuchs*, pp. 226–227.

[2] Wellhausen, *Die Composition des Hexateuchs*, pp. 239, 254–256.

of anti-monarchism. On the contrary, in the Second Temple Period
there is a yearning for the restoring of the Davidic monarchy.[3]

There are two further possibilities as to the period of the anti-
monarchic outlook. Either this outlook in the Book of Judges in general and in Gideon's words in particular is from the monarchic period
or from the pre-monarchic period. Several suppositions were raised
in relation to the first possibility. According to Budde, the anti-monarchism is contemporaneous with the destruction of Samaria and in
keeping with Hosea's outlook (e.g.: 8:4; 13:9–11).[4] A modification of
this view is presented by Moore, who considers that vv. 22–23 belong
to a late layer of E, and the anti-monarchism reflects the period of
anarchy between the time of Jeroboam son of Nabat and the destruction of Samaria.[5] One of the main arguments of this approach is
the contradiction that scholars find between Gideon's opposition to
the monarchy and the assumption appearing in the Abimelech account
that Gideon had some royal authority that was passed on to his
descendants (9:2). However, such a conclusion cannot be drawn from
this source, since we must take into account the possibility that
Abimelech's words there are a strategy to have himself made king.
Moreover, in our analysis of the Abimelech account we saw that
Abimelech's character is the antithesis of that of his father Gideon,
and therefore his words concerning the monarchy are simply the
opposite of his father's intention.[6] Crüseman, who strongly disagrees
with the opinion that the anti-monarchism dates from after the
destruction of the Temple, also considers that the criticism presented
in Gideon's words could not have been made before Israel had expe-
rience of the monarchy. In his opinion, the anti-monarchism dates
from the early monarchic period, in Solomon's time.[7]

---

[3] Crüsemann, *Der Widerstand gegen das Königtum*, pp. 42–54; Kaufmann, *The Religion of Israel*, pp. 263–265.

[4] Budde, *Das Buch der Richter*, pp. 66–67; Budde, *Die Bucher Richter und Samuel*, pp. 184–186. However, it is doubtful whether Hosea rejects kingship, see e.g. J. L. Mays, *Hosea, A Commentary* (OTL), London 1969, p. 117.

[5] Moore, *Judges*, pp. 229–230; Burney, *The Book of Judges*, pp. 183–184, 235. In Martin's opinion (*The Book of Judges*, p. 108) the request and the refusal to rule do not reflect a historic reality but are a late theological addition of the Deuteronomist designed to present a contrast with the character and acts of Abimelech.

[6] Buber, *Kingship of God*, pp. 61–62.

[7] Crüsemann, *Der Widerstand gegen das Königtum*, pp. 42–54. In opposition to Crüsemann's opinion see: B. Uffenheimer, *Early Prophecy in Israel* (trans. D. Louvish), Jerusalem 1999, p. 230.

In Buber's opinion Gideon's words reflect the pre-monarchic period and express opposition to the monarchy before it was instituted, out of an ideological conception that the kingship of man contradicts the kingship of God.[8] This opinion was shared by many scholars, and is a prevalent opinion today.[9] Noth holds that this anecdote reflects the attitude among the tribes of Israel before the establishment of the monarchy. He asserts that only an anti-monarchic attitude during this period can explain the fact that the monarchy was established so late in comparison with the world around Israel. Noth states: "The exclusive committal of the association of the Israelite tribes to its God and to His will here had its effect on their history, and the particularity of Israel thus appears as historical fact".[10]

Noth's claim that the background to the Gideon, Abimelech and Jephthah accounts is in the pre-monarchic period and that this period must be seen as the time of creation of the work, does not negate the possibility that in later periods this work was used to attack the monarchic institution. Nor does it negate the possibility that in later periods the material was edited and new material was added. It is even possible that these accounts were written at a stage later than the establishment of the monarchy. The argument put forward here is that this composition reflects in the best possible manner the period prior to establishment of the monarchy. These accounts apparently constituted part of an extensive polemic on the advantages and disadvantages of the monarchy, in the framework of the public debate that arose after the desire to change the form of government came up on the public Israelite agenda.[11] Scholars indeed learnt from this book about Israelite society, the structure of the regime, the nature of the relations between the tribes.[12] In my view, a specific ideology

---

[8] Buber, *Kingship of God*, pp. 59–66.

[9] See Noth, *The History of Israel*, pp. 164–165; Bright, *A History of Israel*, pp. 173, 175; Kaufmann, *The Religion of Israel*, pp. 262–266; Uffenheimer, *Early Prophecy in Israel*, pp. 206–217; Weinfeld, "Zion and Jerusalem as Religious and Political Capital: Ideology and Utopia", pp. 87–88; Malamat, *History of Biblical Israel*, pp. 122–123; A. D. H. Mayes, *Judges* (Old Testament Guides), Sheffield 1985, p. 37; Weisman, "Charismatic Leaders in the Era of the Judges", p. 410; Boling, *Judges*, p. 35.

[10] Noth, *The History of Israel*, p. 165.

[11] For the relationship of the Book of Judges with the institution of monarchy, see also: G. von Rad, *Old Testament Theology*, I, *The Theology of Israel's Historical Traditions* (D. M. G. Stalker), Edinburgh and London 1962, pp. 332–333.

[12] Herrmann, *A History of Israel*, pp. 112–127; Reviv, "The Government of Shechem in the El-Amarna Period and in the Days of Abimelech", pp. 252–257. Uffenheimer, *Early Prophecy in Israel*, pp. 217–230. According to Hackett the centrality of women

is reflected in this book on the subject of the regime, in a period of change and political instability in the tribes of Israel.[13]

The change of the form of government is a very significant event in the daily life of the people and such a change certainly cannot be passed over in silence without any controversy. The Book of Judges, which contains texts reflecting reservations about the monarchy, and contrasting texts praising the monarchy,[14] reflects a reasonable picture of a pre-monarchic period and the difficult transition between the forms of government; it also allows a look at the certainly complex polemic around this undisputedly historic change.

The Book of Judges maintains historic authenticity in another aspect of Israel's leadership in the pre-monarchic period. The pre-monarchic period is identified in the Bible itself as ימי השופטים (the period of the Judges), and the protagonists of the period are judges (see: 2 Sam 7:11; 2 Kings 23:22; Ruth 1:1; 1 Chr 17:6, 10). However, historians insist that the established leadership of the people in the

---

in the book is possible since the period under discussion is an unstable transition period, and therefore women could fulfil leadership functions. J. A. Hackett, "Women's Studies and the Hebrew Bible", R. E. Friedman and H. G. M. Williamson (eds.), *The Future of Biblical Studies: The Hebrew Scriptures* (Semeia Studies), Atlanta 1987, p. 156.

[13] It may be assumed that as in other books, in cases where the text was written in a period later than its setting, anachronisms were naturally created. The assumption in the research is that an author cannot completely conceal his own period. If the book had been written after the time of David and Solomon or during this period, signs of the period could have been expected. For instance, we could have expected that Jerusalem would occupy a central place in the book, or that there would be an impression of importance in mention of Jerusalem. Yet, in the entire book of Judges Jerusalem does not play any role, and no importance is attributed in its mention. Jerusalem is mentioned twice in the book. In an anecdote in chapter 1, v. 8, the children of Judah conquered Jerusalem, but it is not related that they settled the city. On the contrary, it seems that they had no motivation to do so, or that they did not have the ability to do so, and therefore they set the city on fire, apparently without taking possession of it. In the same chapter, in verse 21 it is related that the children of Benjamin could not conquer the city from the Jebusites. Once more Jerusalem is mentioned, incidentally, in the account of the concubine of Gibeah in chapter 19, vv. 10–12. Again in this source the city is a Jebusite city, and the Levite refuses to enter it because it is a gentile city and he prefers to lodge in Gibeah. It is unlikely that the king's city, Jerusalem, would not have received a central place if the book had been written after the institution of the monarchy and the building of the royal palace and the Temple there. This argument is particularly true in light of the claim in the research that the Book of Judges is a pro-Davidic polemic against Benjamin or Ephraim. See: Brettler, "The Book of Judges: Literature as Politics", pp. 399–418; M. Sweeney, "David Polemics in the Book of Judges", *VT* 47 (1997), 517–529. This opinion has been already suggested by Boling, *Judges*, p. 185.

[14] Buber, *Kingship of God*, pp. 66–84.

pre-monarchic period was by the elders and not by the judges. The Book of Judges describes a reality in which patriarchal leadership of the elders could not cope with the political and military challenges posed by Israel's neighbours, and in the context of this total failure, a new kind of leader arose: charismatic judges. These judges rose sporadically according to the historic circumstances, and did not create a governmental continuity and stability. In times of peace, the Judges gave way to the authority of the traditional leadership of the elders.[15] The emergence of the charismatic judges and the erosion in the status of the elders created the conditions for institution of the monarchy in Israel.[16] In line with this, it seems that the Book of Judges came only to show the transition between the leadership of the elders and the institution of the monarchy. This transition was not instantaneous or smooth. The Book of Judges describes the failure of the traditional leadership of the elders, who were replaced by the charismatic leaders, who were also able to create religious and political stability, and the latter paved the way for institution of the monarchy.

The literary reading that I have presented in this work supports the argument that the historical setting at the basis of the Book of Judges is the pre-monarchic period. The reading that we presented can give a better basis for determining the historical setting. Generally, scholars related to the historical questions in relation to specific data in which the historical subject emerges more prominently, such as Gideon's opposition to the monarchy, discussed above. I wish to establish the historical setting of the accounts not from one statement or another, but based on the overall analysis of the accounts, and based on the comprehensive meaning and the message of these accounts.

The book initially presents the schematic structure of all the deliverance accounts recurring in the book (2:11–23). This framework contains four stages: transgression, punishment, lament and deliverance. This historiosophic summary of the period of the judges at the beginning of the book is exceptional in the Bible.[17] On reading this

---

[15] Weisman, "Charismatic Leaders in the Era of the Judges", p. 407. Reviv, "Types of Leadership in the Period of the Judges", 204–221.

[16] H. Reviv, "Elders and 'Saviors'", *Oriens Antiquus* 16 (1977), pp. 201–204; Weisman, "Charismatic Leaders in the Era of the Judges", pp. 399–411, esp. 406–407.

[17] The ascribing of this historiosophic summary to the Deuteronomistic redactor, who is responsible for the redaction of the books of the early Prophets and the book of Deuteronomy, underscores the uniqueness of the summary in the Book of Judges in particular.

summary at the beginning of the Book of Judges, it is understood
that the judge-deliverer model will be short-lived and will not solve
the religious problems, which are the main concern of the book, or the
political and military problems. Before reading even one account the
reader knows that he or she must examine not only what each judge
did, to what extent he succeeded and how, but also every judge's
failure to bring about stability. The reader knows that he or she
must study the disadvantages of the judge-deliverer leadership model,
and must anticipate an alternative model that is not mentioned in
the introduction.

In reading of the first three accounts in the book, the Othniel,
Ehud and Deborah accounts, the reader does not conceive of an
alternative to the model described. The reader also does not blame
the actual judge for the deterioration that occurred only after his death.
There is a drastic change in the fourth account, which is also the
account at the centre of the book, the Gideon account. Towards the
end of this account, the people ask Gideon to rule over them. Now
the tension increases and it seems that the leadership problem is
about to be solved, since the reader already knows in advance that the
judge model will not last. However, it immediately emerges that
there is no solution. Gideon rejects the proposal and accompanies the
refusal with a very powerful theological reason.

In the Abimelech account, which follows on the Gideon account,
the anti-monarchism is further reinforced. This account presents the
tremendous disasters occurring as a result of an inappropriate attitude
towards the monarchy. Abimelech in his craving to be ruler comes
to power through acts of savage murder in cooperation with the
men of Shechem who avail themselves of the opportunity to make
a profit in exchange for their support of Abimelech.

A reading of the Gideon and Abimelech accounts convinces the
reader that the monarchic model is not the desired leadership form
both with respect to the principle emerging from Gideon's words
and as regards the problematic reality of the monarchy as it appears
in the Abimelech account.

Following negation of the monarchic institution, the reader must
anticipate a different model. However since there is no new, different
model, the reader returns to the two models already known. One
institution is the patriarchal institution and the other is the charismatic
judge-deliverer model. Notwithstanding their drawbacks, the two possibilities are reconsidered. The long introduction to the Jephthah

account once more negates these two governmental alternatives (10.6 16). In this introduction God decisively expresses His unwillingness to again send a judge-deliverer since the people did not show that they were prepared to remain loyal to God over time, and went astray again and again (10:11–14). In the Jephthah account, God gives Israel another chance and agrees *de facto* to Jephthah's appointment as deliverer. Jephthah, however, brings a disaster on the people because he is unsuited to the role, and thus further criticism of the Judge-deliverer model is added. In this introduction, the helplessness of the elders that emerges is extremely pronounced. They are unable to do battle against the Ammonite enemy, nor are they able to persuade any of their number to take the initiative; hence the possibility of returning to this model is also negated.

After exposure to scathing criticism of the monarchy, the reader also learns that it is impossible to return to the models that had accompanied the people since they first took possession of the land. From further reading of the Book of Judges and the Book of Samuel, it will become clear, nonetheless, that the people is in a process of transition to monarchic rule. What then is the role of the Gideon, Abimelech and Jephthah accounts, which constitute a considerable part of this process?

The conclusion ultimately derived from these accounts is that one should not seek a positive or negative, a desirable or undesirable governmental model, but should consider the advantages and disadvantages of each type of regime. Above all one must consider the characteristics desirable in the leader of the people rather than the type of government. The three accounts, the Gideon, Abimelech and Jephthah accounts, focus on the human facets of the leaders, and present a set of considerations in selection of a leader and the risks inherent in this selection. Therefore, these three accounts are connected by the motif of a decision of the people in selecting the leader. After Gideon is chosen by God as deliverer and he delivers the people from their enemies the people ask him to institutionalize his leadership and to rule over them. Abimelech was chosen by the men of Shechem to rule, and Jotham's main criticism is against this unfortunate choice. Jephthah was chosen by the elders of Gilead to be head over them. The three accounts are the only ones in the book in which the motif of selection of the leader by the people appears. Hence this reinforces the conclusion that these accounts, that present the considerations for selection of the leader, were written for a public facing

such a decision, and with the intention of giving this public parameters to evaluate the suitability of a candidate for leadership.

The focus of these accounts on considerations in favour of and
against the monarchy is well in keeping with a reality in which there
is no king, and in which the possibility of replacing the existing
regime with a monarchic regime arises. If the monarchy had already
existed at the time of the first drafting of these books, one would
have expected works expressing support or opposition of the monarchy.
A discussion of the advantages and disadvantages reflects a reality
in which the monarchy did not exist, and the aim of the writer is
to set out considerations for and against. The fact that the Gideon
account deals intensively with the parameters to be used for selecting
a leader may derive from a situation in which there is a possibility
of choosing the leader and the question is who to choose. There is
almost no point in dealing with such a matter when the monarchy
already exists and is already handed down from father to son, with
a limited possibility for the people to be involved in appointment of
the king.

These three accounts differ from the first three accounts—the
Othniel, Ehud and Deborah accounts, and from the historiosophic
model at the beginning of the book. Unlike the first three accounts
that focus on the story of the deliverance, in the three accounts discussed in this work the personal, family and psychological aspects of
the protagonists are discussed extensively. The personal aspect in the
three accounts is manifest in a similar way, although they differ
greatly from each other, in that these three judges are the only judges
who fight against their own people in order to gain status or honour for themselves. The three accounts are also connected in that they
do not have a good end. Gideon fights against the men of Succoth
and of Penuel and even brings the people back to idol worship. In
the Abimelech and Jephthah accounts, there is no report of years of
quiet at the end of the account and they open with a cruel civil war.

The Gideon account is a long and complex account and presents
different facets of Gideon's personality and the changes in his characteristics and his behaviour. In this account, the reader reveals a
judge who has important leadership characteristics but accompanied
by inappropriate characteristics. Gideon at the beginning of the story
doubts God and His deliverance, and in a long process of transition
from doubts to faith gradually he becomes a man who trusts in His
God. Once Gideon's faith is well established, a second process com-

mences of transition from altruistic actions that he carries out for
his people and his God to selfish actions where the concern is for
his status and his honour. Through presentation of Gideon's change-
able personality, first on the spiritual plane and then on the personal plane, the account shows the two main parameters by which
a leader's suitability must be measured. A suitable leader is one who
believes in and acts in the name of God, and one who has concern
only for the good of the people.

Abimelech is Gideon's son and by virtue of this he wishes to rule.
There are many similarities between Abimelech and his father, but
also significant differences. Abimelech inherited the wish to rule from
his father, but in his father this inclination existed alongside national
motives and willingness for self-sacrifice for the sake of the people.
In the son, however, only the wish to rule appears. In relation to
the second parameter, the leader's attitude towards God, Abimelech's
attitude is unique in the Bible. Abimelech does not turn to God,
does not express any belief in God, but he is not presented as having
betrayed God or as not going in the way of God. Abimelech has
no attitude whatsoever towards God or towards any other god. This
fact underscores Abimelech's extreme egocentricity. The account
shows the disaster befalling the people when the leader, in cooperation with self-seeking agents, exploits the people and the status of
ruler for personal gain.

In the Jephthah account again a more complex picture of the
leader figure appears. Unlike Gideon, Jephthah from the outset
appears as trying to exploit the national situation for his personal
benefit. However, unlike Gideon who at the beginning of the account
doubts God, Jephthah expresses firm belief in God and in the view
that man's victory is God's victory. The Jephthah account shows
that despite Jephthah's piety, his self-interested motives bring a disaster
down on him and on the people. Only the leader who combines a
correct perception in relation to God with willingness to act for the
people without personal requests is a suitable leader.

Abimelech is presented as someone who has only negative attributes; in Jephthah there is good and bad. Abimelech is a king, Jephthah
is a judge. Both act out of personal aims and both bring a disaster
down on the people. One seeks support from the heads of the tribe
and the other demands to be appointed head over the town. Jephthah
applies pressure, in that if he does not receive what he wants he
will not agree to deliver the people; Abimelech acts with cunning

and cruelty. Jephthah is the son of a harlot, and Abimelech the son of a concubine. Jephthah begins as a man on the fringes of society and finds a way to return to established society; Abimelech goes through a reverse process, he comes from Gideon's house, kills his family and becomes a criminal. A woman is responsible for Abimelech's downfall; when Jephthah's daughter comes out to meet him, this brings about Jephthah's downfall. The accounts do not deal with the question of whether a king or a judge is preferable, they do not negate the monarchy and do not prefer the judge. Their aim is to indicate that egocentricity is dangerous.

In Jephthah's account, it seems that only Jephthah can save the people from their plight. Nonetheless, the account shows that also in these circumstances a man whose concern is for his personal aspirations must not be appointed as head over the people. This principle is correct also when there seem to be attenuating circumstances. Jephthah's egocentricity is the result of discrimination, of humiliating treatment that he suffered. There is a kind of social justice in Jephthah's return to a high-ranking status. However, even in these circumstances, the Jephthah account determines decisively that a leader who acts for himself and not for his people is not suited to be head over the people.

BIBLIOGRAPHY

S. Abramsky, "Abimelech's Leadership—King, Chief and Ruler", A Even-Shoshan et al. (eds.), *The Book of Siwan: A Collection of Studies and Essays in Memory of the Late Jerusalem Publisher Shalom Siwan*, Jerusalem 1979, pp. 163–176 (Hebrew) Abravanel = Rabbi Don Isaac ben Judah Abravanel (1437–1508), *Piruš ʿal neviʾim rišonim*, Jerusalem 1957

Y. Aharoni, *The Land of the Bible: A Historical Geography*[2] (trans. A. F. Reiney), London 1979

S. Aḥituv, "הנלעד מהר ויצפר ישב (Judges 7:3)", *Beer-Sheva* 15 (2002), pp. *20–*23 (Hebrew)

W. F. Albright, *Yahweh and the Gods of Canaan: A Historical Analysis of Two Contrasting Faiths*, Winona Lake 1968

R. Alter, *The Art of Biblical Narrative*, New York 1981

A. Altman, "The Development of the Office of 'Judge' in Pre-Monarchic Israel", *Proceedings of the Seventh World Congress of Jewish Studies* 7, 2 (1981), pp. 11–21 (Hebrew)

———, "העיר בעלי in the Bible", S. Ettinger et al. (eds.), *Milet: Everyman's University Studies in Jewish History and Culture*, II, Tel-Aviv 1985, pp. 5–33 (Hebrew, English summery, p. V)

Y. Amit, "The Dual Causality Principle and Its Effects on Biblical Literature", *VT* 37 (1987), pp. 385–400

———, *The Book of Judges: The Art of Editing* (Biblical Interpretation Series, 38, trans. J. Chipman), Leiden 1999

———, *Judges, Introduction and Commentary* (Mikra Leysraʾel), Tel Aviv and Jerusalem 1999 (Hebrew)

E. Assis, "Chiasmus in Biblical Narrative: Rhetoric of Characterization", *Prooftexts* 22 (2003), pp. 273–304

———, *The Literary Structure of the Conquest Narrative in the Book of Joshua (Chs. 1–11) and its Meaning*, Ph.D. Diss. Bar-Ilan University, Ramat-Gan 1999 (published by Magness Press under the title: *From Moses to Joshua and from the Miraculous to the Ordinary: A Literary Analysis of the Conquest Narrative in the Book of Joshua*, Jerusalem 2005)

———, "'How Long are You Slack to Go to Possess the Land' (Jos. xviii 3): Ideal and Reality in the Distribution Descriptions in Joshua xiii–xix", *VT* 53 (2003), pp. 1–25

———, "The Meaning of Samson's Birth Account (Judg 13)", *Shnaton: An Annual for Biblical and Ancient Near Eastern Studies* 15 (2004) (in press)

A. G. Auld, "Gideon. Hacking an the Heart of the Old Testament", *VT* 39 (1989), pp. 257–267

N. Avigad, "'The Governor of the city' Bulla", H. Geva (ed.), *Ancient Jerusalem Revealed*, Jerusalem 1994, pp. 138–140

———, "On 'A Second Bulla of a Sar Hāʾir", *Qadmoniot* 11 (1978), p. 34 (Hebrew)

Avraham ben Shlomo = Rabbi Avraham ben Shlomo, *Piruš ʿal neviʾim rišonim: Yehoshua, Shoftim* (Rabbi Joseph Kapach edition) Kiryat Ono 1999

M. M. Bakhtin, *The Dialogic Imagination: Four Essays*, ed. M. Holquist, trans. C. Emerson and M. Holquist (University of Texas Press Slavic Series, 1), Austin 1981

M. Bal, *Death and Dissymmetry: The Politics of Coherence in the Book of Judges*, Chicago and London 1988

G. Barkay, "A Second 'Governor of the City Bulla", H. Geva (ed.), *Ancient Jerusalem Revealed*, Jerusalem 1994, pp. 141–144

J. R. Bartlett, "The Conquest of Sihon's Kingdom: A Literary Re-Examination", *JBL* 97 (1978), pp. 347–351

——, "The Use of the Word ראש as a Title in the Old Testament", *VT* 19 (1969), pp. 1–10

J. Barton, *Reading the Old Testament: Method in Biblical Study*², London 1996

A. Berlin, *Poetics and Interpretation of Biblical Narrative* (Bible and Literature Series, 9), Sheffield 1983

E. Bertheau, *Das Buch der Richter und Ruth* (Kurzgefasstes exegetisches Handbuch zum Alten Testament), Leipzig 1883

W. Bluedorn, *Yahweh Versus Baalism: A Theological Reading of the Gideon-Abimelech Narrative* (JSOTsup, 329), Sheffield 2001

F. M. T. Böhl, 'Wortspiele im Alten Testament', *JPOS* 6 (1926), pp. 196–212

R. G. Boling, *Judges* (AB), New-York 1975

——, "'And Who Is *Š-K-M?*' (Judges IX 28)", *VT* 13 (1963), pp. 479–482

T. A. Boogaart, "Stone for Stone: Retribution in the Story of Abimelech and Shechem", *JSOT* 32 (1985), pp. 45–56

A. J. Brawer, "וישר אבימלך על ישראל' [= And Abimelech ruled over Israel]'", *Beit Mikra*, 16 (1963), pp. 120–121 (Hebrew)

M. Z. Brettler, "The Book of Judges: Literature as Politics", *JBL* 108 (1989), pp. 395–418

——, *The Book of Judges* (Old Testament Readings), London and New York 2002

J. Bright, *A History of Israel*², London 1972

W. Brueggemann, "Social Criticism and Social Vision in the Deuteronomic Formula of the Judges", J. Jeremias and L. Perlitt (eds.), *Die Botschaft und die Boten: Festschrift für Hans Walter Wolff zum 70 Geburtstag*, Neukrichen 1981, pp. 101–114

——, "Of the Same Flesh and Bone (Gn 2:23a)", *CBQ* 32 (1970), pp. 532–542

M. Buber, *Kingship of God* (trans. R. Scheimann), London 1967

D. K. Budde, *Das Buch der Richter* (KHAT), Leipzig und Tübingen 1897

——, *Die Bucher Richter und Samuel, ihre Quellen und ihr Aufbau*, Giessen 1890

C. F. Burney, *The Book of Judges*, London 1918

U. Cassuto, *The Goddess Anat: Canaanite Epics of the Patriarchal Age* (trans. I. Abrahams), Jerusalem 1971

L. J. M. Claassens, "Notes on Characterization in the Jephthah Narrative", *JNSL* 22 (1996) 107–115

R. E. Clements, "Baal-Berith of Shechem", *JSS* 13 (1968), pp. 21–32

G. A. Cooke, *The Book of Judges* (The Cambridge Bible for Schools and Colleges), Cambridge 1918

F. M. Cross, *Canaanite Myth and Hebrew Epic: Essays in the History of the Religion of Israel*, Cambridge Mass. 1973

A. D. Crown, "A Reinterpretation of Judges IX in the Light of its Humour", *Abr-Nahrain* 3 (1961–62), pp. 90–98

F. Crüsemann, *Der Widerstand gegen das Königtum* (Wissenschaftliche Monographien zum Alten und Neuen Testament, 49, Neukrichen Vluyn: Neukrichenre Verlag, 1978

J. A. Cuddon, *Dictionary of Literary Terms and Literary Theory*³, London 1991.

D. Daube, "Gideon's Few", *JJS* 7 (1956), pp. 155–161

——, "'One From Among Your Brethren Shall You Set King Over You'", *JBL* 90 (1971), pp. 480–481

G. H. Davies, "Judges VIII 22–23", *VT* 13 (1963), pp. 151–157

P. Davies, *In Search of 'Ancient Israel'* (JSOTsup, 148), Sheffield 1992

J. Day, "Asherah", *ABD*, vol. 1, 1992, pp. 483–487

——, *Molech: A God of Human Sacrifice in the Old Testament* (University of Cambridge Oriental Publications, 41), Cambridge 1989

R. de Vaux, *Studies in Old Testament Sacrifice*, Cardiff 1964

——, *The Early History of Israel* (trans. D. Smith), Philadelphia 1978

D. S. Dewitt, *The Jephthah Traditions: A Rhetorical and Literary Study in the Deuteronomistic History*, Diss., Andrews University 1987

J. Dishon, "Gideon and the Beginnings of Monarchy in Israel", *Tarbiz* 41 (1972), pp. 255–268 (Hebrew)

G. R. Driver, "Problems in Judges Newly Discussed", *The Annual of Leeds University Oriental Society*, IV (1962–1963), pp. 6–25

S. R. Driver, *An Introduction to the Literature of the Old Testament*, Edinburgh 1913

E. Eising, "*chayil*", *Theological Dictionary of the Old Testament*, IV, Grand Rapids 1980, pp. 348–355

O. Eissfeldt, *The Old Testament, An Introduction* (trans. P. R. Ackroyd), Oxford 1974

Y. Elitzur, *Sefer Shoftim* (Daat Mikra), Jerusalem 1976

J. A. Emerton, "A Consideration of Some Alleged Meanings of ידע in Hebrew", *JSS* 15,2 (1970), pp. 145–180

———, "Gideon and Jerubbaal", *JTS* NS 27 (1976), pp. 289–312

———, '"The Second Bull" in Judges 6, 25–28', *Eretz Israel* 14 (1978), pp. 52*–55*

J. C. Exum, "The Center Cannot Hold: Thematic and Textual Instabilities in Judges", *CBQ* 52 (1990), pp. 410–431

———, "Feminist Criticism: Whose Interests Are Being Served?", G. A. Yee (ed.), *Judges and Method: New Approaches in Biblical Studies*, Minneapolis 1995, pp. 65–90

———, *Tragedy and Biblical Narrative: Arrows of the Almighty*, Cambridge 1992

———, "Murder They Wrote: Ideology and the Manipulation of Female Presence in Biblical Narrative", *USQR* 43 (1989), pp. 19–39

C. Feigenboim, *The Story of Gideon*, M.A. diss., Bar Ilan University 1989

F. C. Fensham, "Salt as Curse in the Old Testament and the Ancient Near East", *BA* XXV (1962), pp. 48–50

———, 'The Numeral Seventy in the Old Testament and the Family of Jerubbaal, Ahab, Panammuwa and Athirat', *PEQ* 109 (1977), pp. 113–115

I. Finkelstein and N. A. Silberman, *The Bible Unearthed: Archaeology's New Vision of Ancient Israel and the Origin of Its Sacred Texts*, New York 2001

E. Firmage, "Zoology", *ABD*, vol. 6, New York 1992, pp. 1119–1167

J. Fleishman, "Legality of the expulsion of Jephthah (Judges 11:1–11)", *Diné Israel: An Annual of Jewish Law, Past and Present* 18 (1995–6), pp. 61–80

G. Fohrer, *Introduction to the Old Testament* (Trans. D. Green), London 1970

J. P. Fokkelman, "Structural Remarks on Judges 9 and 19", M. Fishbane and E. Tov (eds.), *"Sha'rei Talmon": Studies in the Bible, Qumran and the Ancient Near East Presented to Shmaryahu Talmon*, Winona Lake 1992, pp. 33–46

T. C. Foote, "The Ephod", *JBL* 21 (1902), pp. 1–47

V. Fritz, "Abimelech und Sichem in Jdc. IX", *VT* 32 (1982), pp. 129–144

M. Garsiel, *Biblical Names: A Literary Study of Midrashic Derivations and Puns* (trans. P. Hackett), Ramat-Gan 1991

———, "Homiletic Name-Derivations as a Literary Device in the Gideon Narrative: Judges VI–VIII", *VT* 43 (1993), pp. 302–317

———, "Models of Analogy and Sets of Comparison in the Bible: With Specific Reference to Judges and Samuel", S. Ettinger et al. (eds.), *Milet: Everyman's University Studies in Jewish History and Culture*, II, Tel-Aviv 1985, pp. 35–48 (Hebrew, English summary, pp. VI–VII).

T. H. Gaster, *Myth, Legend and Custom in the Old Testament: A Comparative Study with Chapters from Sir James G Frazer's Folklore in the Old Testament*, New York 1969

G. E. Gerbrandt, *Kingship According to the Deuteronomistic History* (SBL Dissertation Series, 87), Atlanta 1986

Gersonides = Rabbi Levi ben Gershom (1248–1344), Commentary in *Mikra'ot Gedolot*

Gesenius' Hebrew Grammar (second English edition by A. E. Cowley), Oxford 1910

S. Geviratz, "Jericho and Shechem: A Religio-Literary Aspect of City Destruction", *VT* 13 (1963), pp. 52–62

H. Gilad, "Diplomacy and Strategy in Two Wars with Ammon", *Beit Mikra*, 58 (1974), pp. 416–418 (Hebrew, English summary p. 454)

D. W. Gooding, "The Composition of the Book of Judges", *Eretz Israel* 16 (1982), pp. 70–79

C. Gray, *The Politics of the Arts in Britain*, London 2000

J. Gray, *Joshua, Judges Ruth* (NCB), Grand Rapids 1967

A. R. W. Green, *The Role of Human Sacrifice in the Ancient Near East* (American Schools of Oriental Research Dissertation Series, I), Missoula 1975

M. Greenberg, "The Hebrew Oath Particle *hay/hē*", *JBL* 76 (1957), pp. 34–39

F. E. Greenspahn, "The Theology of the Framework of Judges", *VT* 36 (1986), pp. 385–396

O. Grether, "Die Bezeichnung 'Richter' für die charismatischen Helden der vorstaatlichen Zeit", *ZAW* 57 (1939), pp. 110–121

K. R. R. Gros Louis, "The Book of Judges", K. R. R. Gros Louis, J. S. Ackerman and T. S. Warshaw (eds.), *Literary Interpretations of Biblical Narratives*, Nashville and New York, pp. 141–162

P. D. Guest, "Can Judges Survive Without Sources?: Challenging the Consensus", *JSOT* 78 (1998), pp. 43–61

A. Guillaume, "A Note on *'happar hassenī'*, Judges VI. 25, 26, 28", *JTS* 50 (1949), pp. 52–53

D. M. Gunn, "The 'Battle Report': Oral or Scribal Convention?", *JBL* 93 (1974), pp. 513–518

N. Habel, "The Form and Significance of the Call Narrative", *ZAW* 77 (1965), pp. 297–323

J. A. Hackett, "Religious Traditions in Israelite Transjordan", P. D. Miller, P. D. Hanson and S. D. McBride (eds.), *Ancient Israelite Religion: Essays in Honor of Frank Moore Cross*, Philadelphia 1987, pp. 125–136

——, "Women's Studies and the Hebrew Bible", R. E. Friedman and H. G. M. Williamson (eds.), *The Future of Biblical Studies: The Hebrew Scriptures* (Semeia Studies), Atlanta 1987, pp. 141–164

B. Halpern, "The Rise of Abimelek Ben-Jerubbaal", *Hebrew Annual Review* 2 (1978), pp. 79–100

M. Haran, "The Ephod According to Biblical Sources", *Tarbiz* 24 (1955), pp. 380–391 (Hebrew, Eng. Summary: pp. II–III)

——, "Shechem Studies", *Zion* 38 (1973), pp. 1–31 (Hebrew, English Summary p. I)

A. J. Hauser, "The 'Minor Judges'—A Re-evaluation", *JBL* 94 (1975), pp. 190–200

G. C. Heider, *The Cult of Molek: A Reassessment* (JSOTsup, 43) Sheffield 1985

R. L. Heller, "The Disappearing Deity and the Wages of Sin: The Theology of Divine Retribution in the Books of Judges," *Berkeley at Yale* 1 (1999), pp. 10–13

S. Herrmann, *A History of Israel in Old Testament Times* (trans. J. Bowden), London 1975

R. S. Hess, "The Dead Sea Scrolls and Higher Criticism of the Hebrew Bible: The Case of 4QJud^a", S. E. Porter and C. A. Evans (eds.), *The Scrolls and the Scriptures: Qumran after Fifty Years*, (JSOPsup, 26) Sheffield 1997, pp. 122–000

J.-M. Husser, *Dreams and Dream Narratives in the Ancient World* (trans. J. M. Munro, The Biblical Seminar, 63), Sheffield 1999

F. F. Hvidberg, *Weeping and Laughter in the Old Testament: A Study of Canaanite-Israelite Religion*, Leiden 1962

Ibn Ganah = Abulwalid Merwan Ibn Ganah, *Sepher Haschoraschim* (The Book of Roots), Berlin 1896

Ibn Kaspi = Joseph Ibn Kaspi (1279–1340), Commentary in *Mikra'ot Gedolot*

Isaiah di Trani = Isaiah di Trani (13th century?), Commentary in *Mikra'ot Gedolot*

T. Ishida, "The Leaders of the Tribal Leagues 'Israel' in the Pre-Monarchic Period", *RB* 80 (1973), pp. 514–530

J. Jacobs, "The Story of Jephthah", M.D. diss., Bar-Ilan University, Ramat Gan 1998 (Hebrew)

J. G. Janzen, "A Certain Woman in the Rhetoric of Judges 9", *JSOT* 38 (1987), pp. 33–37

D. Jobling, "Structuralist Criticism: The Text's World of Meaning", G. A. (ed.), Yee *Judges and Method: New Approaches in Biblical Studies*, Minneapolis 1995, pp. 91–118
——, *The Sense of Biblical Narrative: Structural Analyses in the Hebrew Bible*, II (JSOTsup, 39), Sheffield 1986

Josephus: Jewish Antiquities, vol. 5, H. St. J. Thackery and R. Marcus (ed. and trans.), London and Cambridge Mass. 1934

Kara = Joseph ben Simon Kara (11th century), Commentary in *Mikra'ot Gedolot*

A. Kariv, *The Seven Pillars of the Bible: Essays of Biblical People and Biblical Ideas*, Tel Aviv 1971 (Hebrew).

Y. Kaufmann, *Sefer Yehoshua*, Jerusalem 1976[5] (1956[1], Hebrew)
——, *The Religion of Israel: From Its Beginnings to the Babylonian Exile* (trans. and abridged by M. Greenberg), Chicago 1960
——, *Sefer Shoftim*, Jerusalem 1961 (Hebrew)

Kimchi = Rabbi David Kimchi, ?1060–?1235, Commentary in *Mikra'ot Gedolot*
——, *Sefer HaShorashim* (= The Book of Roots), Berolini 1847

L. R. Klein, *The Triumph of Irony in the Book of Judges* (Bible and Literature Series, 14), Sheffield: The Almond Press, 1988

A. Lemaire, in *Les inscriptions hébraïques I, Les ostraca*, Paris 1977
——, "La tablette Ougaritique alphabétique UF 29, 826 replacée dans son contexte", *UF* 30 (1998), pp. 461–465

N. P. Lemche, *Early Israel: Anthropological and Historical Studies on the Israelite Society Before Monarchy* (SVT, 37), Leiden 1985
——, *The Israelites in History and Tradition* (Library of Ancient Israel), London and Louisville 1998

T. J. Lewis, "The Identity and Function of El/Baal Berith", *JBL* 115 (1996) 401–423

J. P. U. Lilley, "A Literary Appreciation of the Book of Judges", *Tyndale Bulletin* 18 (1967), pp. 94–102

J. Limburg, "The Root *rib* and the Prophetic Lawsuit Speeches", *JBL* 88 (1969), pp. 289–304

B. Lindars, "Jotham's Fable—A New Form-Critical Analysis", *JTS* 24 (1973), 355–366
——, "Gideon and Kingship", *JTS* 16 (1965), pp. 315–326
——, "Deborah's Song: Women in the Old Testament", *Bulletin of the John Rylands University Library of Manchester* 65, 2 (1983), pp. 158–175

S. E. Loewenstamm, "The LORD Shall Rule Over You (Judges VIII 23)", *Tarbiz* 41 (1971–2), pp. 444–445 (Hebrew, Eng. Summary p. V)

A. B. Lord, *The Singer of Tales*, Cambridge, Mass. 1960

A. Malamat, "השופט המושיע כמנהיג בתקופת השופטים", *Types of Leadership in the Biblical Period*, Jerusalem 1973, pp. 11–25
——, "The War of Gideon and Midian", ed. J. Liver, *The Military History of the Land of Israel in Biblical Times*, Jerusalem 1964, pp. 110–123 (Hebrew)
——, *History of Biblical Israel: Major Problems and Minor Issues* (Culture and History of the Ancient Near East, vol. 7), Leiden 2001
——, "The Punishment of Succoth and Pennuel by Gideon in Light of Ancient Near Eastern Treaties", C. Cohen, A. Hurvitz and S. M. Paul (eds.), *Sefer Moshe: The Moshe Weinfeld Jubilee Volume: Studies in the Bible and the Ancient Near East, Qumran and Post-Biblical Judaism*, Winona Lake 2004, pp. 69–71

E. Maly, "The Jotham Fable—Anti-monarchical?", *CBQ* 22 (1960), pp. 299–305

J. Marais, *Representation in Old Testament Narrative Texts* (Biblical Interpretation, 36), Leiden, Boston and Köln 1998

R. Marcus "The Word *šibbolet* Again", *BASOR* 87 (1942), p. 39

D. Marcus, "The Bargaining between Jephthah and the Elders (Judges 11:1–11)", *JANES* 19 (1989), pp. 95–100

——, "The Legal Dispute Between Jephthah and the Elders", *Hebrew Annual Review* 12 (1990) 105–114

B. Margalit, "The Episode of the Fleece (Judges 6:36–40) in Light of the Ugaritic", *SHNATON—An Annual for Biblical and Ancient Near Eastern Studies* V–VI (1981–2), pp. LX–LXII

J. D. Martin, *The Book of Judges* (CBC), Cambridge 1975

A. D. H. Mayes, *The Story of Israel Between Settlement and Exile: A Redactional Study of the Deuteronomistic History*, London 1983

——, *Israel in the Period of the Judges* (Studies in Biblical Theology, 29), London 1974

J. L. Mays, *Hosea, A Commentary* (OTL), London 1969

J. L. McKenzie, "The Elders in the Old Testament", *Biblica* 40 (1959), pp. 522–540

D. A. Mckenzie, "The Judge of Israel", *VT* 17 (1967), pp. 118–121

P. E. McMillion, *Judges 6–8 and the Study of Premonarchial Israel*, Diss., Vanderbilt University 1985

Mekilta de-Rabbi Ishmael = Mekilta de-Rabbi Ishmael (trans. and edited J. Z. Lauterbach), vol. 1, Philadelphia 1933

I. Mendelsohn, "The Disinheritance of Jephthah in the Light of Paragraph 27 of the Lipit-Ishtar Code", *IEJ* 4 (1954), pp. 116–119

G. E. Mendenhall, "The Census Lists of Numbers 1 and 26", *JBL* 77 (1958), pp. 52–66

——, *The Tenth Generation: The Origins of the Biblical Tradition*, Baltimore and London 1973

A. Mez, "Nachnal Ri. 7:5, 6", *ZAW* 21 (1901), pp. 198–200

Midrash Rabbah, Genesis = Midrash Rabbah, Genesis, vol. I–II, trans. H. Freedman, London and Bournemouth 1951

Midrash Rabbah, Leviticus = Midrash Rabbah, Leviticus, vol. IV, trans. H. Freedman, London 1939

Midrash Seder 'Olam Rabba (Dov Ber Ratner ed.), Wilna 1894–1897

Mikra'ot Gedolot 'Haketer', A Revised and Augmented Scientific Edition of 'Mikra'ot Gedolot' Based on the Aleppo Codex and Early Medieval MSS, Joshua, Judges, M. Cohen (ed.), Ramat-Gan 1992. Contains commentaries of Rashi, David Kimchi, Joseph ben Simon Kara, Rabbi Levi ben Gershom (Gersonides), Joseph Ibn Kaspi, Isaiah di Trani

J. M. Miller and J. H. Hayes, *A History of Ancient Israel and Judah*, Philadelphia 1986

G. F. Moore, *Judges* (ICC), Edinburgh 1895

W. L. Moran, "A Study of the Deuteronomic History", *Biblica* 46 (1965), pp. 223–228

E. T. Mullen, "The 'Minor Judges': Some Literary and Historical Considerations", *CBQ* 44 (1982), pp. 185–201

R. Murfin and S. M. Ray, *The Bedford Glossary of Critical and Literary Terms*, Boston and New York 1997

N. Na'aman, "Migdal-Shechem and the 'House of El-berith'", *Zion* 51 (1986), pp. 259–280 (Hebrew, English Summary p. IX)

E. Nielsen, *Shechem, A Triditio-Historical Investigation*[2], Copenhagen 1959.

M. Noth, *The History of Israel*[2], London 1960.

——, *The Deuteronomistic History*[2] (JSOTSup, 15), Sheffield 1991.

M. A. O'Brien, *The Deuteronomistic History Hypothesis: A Reassessment* (Orbis Biblicus et Orientalis), Göttingen 1989

——, "Judges and the Deuteronomistic History", S. L. McKenzie and M. P. Graham (eds.), *The History of Israel's Traditions: The Heritage of Martin Noth* (JSOTsup, 182), Sheffield 1994, pp. 235–259

R. H. O'Connell, *The Rhetoric of the Book of Judges*, Leiden 1996

U. Oldenburg, *The Conflict Between El and Baʾal in Canaanite Religion*, Leiden 1969

G. Del Olmo Lete and J. Sanmartín, *A Dictionary of the Ugaritic Language in the Alphabetic Tradition*, I–II (trans. W. G. E. Watson), Leiden 2003

A. L. Oppenheim, *The Interpretations of Dreams in the Ancient Near East* (Transactions of the American Philosophical Society, 46, 3), Philadelphia 1956

——, "The Shadow of the King", *BASOR* 107 (1947), pp. 7–11

S. B. Parker, "The Vow in Ugaritic and Israelite Narrative", *Ugarit-Forschungen* 11 (1979), pp. 493–500

J. Pedersen, *Israel, Its Life and Culture*, I–II, London and Copenhagen 1926

F. Polak, *Biblical Narrative: Aspects of Art and Design* (The Biblical Encyclopaedia Library, XI), Jerusalem 1994 (Hebrew)

R. Polzin, *Moses and the Deuteronomist: A Literary Study of the Deuteronomic History*, New York: The Seabury Press, 1980

M. A. Powell, *The Bible and Modern Literary Criticism: A Critical Assessment and Annotated Bibliography*, New-York, New York and London 1992

J. B. Pritchard, *The Ancient Near East in Pictures Relating to the Old Testament*, New Jersey 1954

Rashi (acronym of Rabbi Solomon ben Isaac, [1040–1105]) Commentary in *Mikra'ot Gedolot*

J. Reider, "Etymological Studies: ‏ידע‎ or ‏ידע‎ and ‏רעע‎", *JBL* 66 (1947), pp. 315–317

H. G. Reventlow, *Liturgie und Prophetisches Ich bei Jeremia*, Gütersloh 1963

H. Reviv, "Types of Leadership in the Period of the Judges", *Beer-Sheva: Annual Studies in Bible, Ancient Israel and Ancient near East* 1 (1973), pp. 204–221 (Hebrew, English summary, pp. 233–234)

——, "Two Notes to Judges VIII, 4–17", *Tarbiz* 38 (1969), pp. 309–317 (Hebrew, Eng. Summary p. I)

——, "The Government of Shechem in the El-Amarna Period and in the Days of Abimelech", *IEJ* 16 (1966), pp. 252–257

——, *From Clan to Monarchy: Israel in Biblical Period²*, Jerusalem 1989, pp. 77–86 (Hebrew)

——, "Elders and 'Saviors'", *Oriens Antiquus* 16 (1977), pp. 201–204

W. Richter, "Die Überlieferungen um Jephtah: Ri. 10:17–12:6", *Biblica* 47 (1966), pp. 485–556

——, *Traditionsgeschichtliche Untersuchungen zum Richterbuch* (Bonner Biblische Beiträge, 18), Bonn 1966

——, *Die Bearbeitungen des "Retterbuches" in der deuteronomischen Epoche* (Bonner Biblische Beiträge, 21), Bonn 1964

S. P. Roberts, *Content and Form Within the Jephthah Narrative: A Literary-Historical Investigation*, Diss, The Southern Baptist Theological Seminary 1991

A. Rofé, *"The Book of Balaam" (Numbers 22:2–24:25): A study in Methods of Criticism and the History of Biblical Literature and Religion*, Jerusalem 1979 (Hebrew)

——, "The Belief in Angels in the Bible and in Early Israel", Ph.D. The Hebrew University of Jerusalem, Jerusalem 1979

T. C. Römer, "Why Would the Deuteronomists Tell about the Sacrifice of Jephthah's Daughter?" *JSOT* 77 (1998) 27–38

H. N. Rösel, "Jephtah und das Problem der Richter", *Biblica* 61 (1980), pp. 251–255

M. Rosenberg, "The Šofʿtim in the Bible", *Eretz Israel* 12 (1975), pp. 86*–77*

W. Rudolph, 'Textkritische Anmerkungen zum Richterbuch', J. Fück (ed.), *Festschrift Otto Eissfeldt zum 60 Geburtstag*, Halle 1947, pp. 199–212

T. J. Schneider, *Judges* (Berit Olam), Collegeville 2000

I. L. Seeligmann, "Menschliches Heldentum und Göttliche Hilfe—Die doppelte Kausalität im alttestamentlichen Geschichtsdenken", *TZ* 19 (1963), pp. 385–411

M. Z. Segal, "Studies in the Book of Judges", *Tarbiz* 2 (1930), pp. 1–32

K. Seybold, "melek", *Theological Dictionary of the Old Testament*, VIII, trans. D. W. Stott, Grand Rapids and Cambridge 1997, pp. 352–374

J. T. Shipley, *Dictionary of World Dictionary*, Totowa 1966

Sifra on Leviticus = *Sifra on Leviticus*, Venice edition 1545 (repr. Jerusalem 1971)

C. A. Simpson, *The Composition of the Book of Judges*, Oxford 1957

U. Simon, "The Parable of Jotham (Judges IX, 8–15): The Parable, Its Application and Their Narrative Framework", *Tarbiz* 34 (1964), pp. 1–34 (Hebrew, English Summary, pp. I–II)

——, "Peshat Exegesis of Biblical Historiography: Historicism, Dogmatism, and Medievalism", M. Kogan, B. L. Eichler, J. H. Tigay (eds.), *Tehillah le-Moshe: Biblical and Judaic Studies in Honor of Moshe Greenberg*, Winona Lake 1997, 171*–203* (Hebrew, English abstract p. 323)

——, *Reading Prophetic Narratives* (The Biblical Encyclopedia Library, 15), Jerusalem and Ramat-Gan 1997 (Hebrew)

J. Skinner, *Genesis* (ICC), Edinburgh 1910

J. A. Soggin, "The Migdal Temple, Migdal šᵉkem Judg 9 and the Artifact on Ebal", M. Augustin and K. D. Schunk (eds.), *Wünschet Jerusalem Frieden: Collected Communications of the XIIth Congress of the International Organization for the Study of the Old Testament, Jerusalem 1986*, Framkfurt am Main 1988, pp. 115–119

——, *Judges, A Commentary* (OTL), London 1981

E. A. Speiser, "The Shiboleth Incident (Judges 12:6)", *BASOR* 85 (1942), pp. 10–13

N. Steinberg, "Social Scientific Criticism", G. A. Yee (ed.), *Judges and Method: New Approaches in Biblical Studies*, Minneapolis 1995, pp. 45–64

M. Sternberg, *The Poetics of Biblical Narrative: Ideological Literature and the Drama of Reading*, Bloomington 1987

M. Sweeney, "David Polemics in the Book of Judges", *VT* 47 (1997), 517–529

M. Shiloah, "ויאמר . . . ויאמר קורנגרין", ספר קורנגרין Tel-Aviv 1964, pp. 251–276

A. Tal (Rosenthal), "צליל לחם שעורים", Y. Bahat et al. (eds.), *heqer veiyun: Studies in Judaism*, Haifa 1976, pp. 103–106 (Hebrew, Eng. Summary p. XII)

S. Talmon, "The Presentation of Synchronicity and Simultaneity in Biblical Narrative", J. Heinemann and S. Werses (eds.), *Studies in Hebrew Narrative Art throughout the Ages* (Scripta Hierosylimitana, 27), Jerusalem 1978, pp. 9–26

Tanhuma (Buber) = *Midrash Tanhuma* (S. Buber Recension), translated into English by J. T. Townsend, vol. 1, Hoboken 1989

Tanhuma = *Midrash Tanhuma-Yelammedenu* (The printed version), Warsaw 1879

J. P. Tanner, "The Gideon Narrative as the Focal Point of Judges", *Bibliothea Sacra* 149 (1992), pp. 146–161

T. L. Thompson, *Early History of the Israelite People: From the Written and Archaeological Sources* (Studies in the History of the Ancient Near East, IV), Leiden 1992

W. M. Timothy, "The Nature of Jephthah's Authority", *CBQ* 59 (1996), pp. 33–44

S. Tolkowsky, "Gideon's 300: Judges vii and viii", *JPOS* 5 (1925), pp. 69–74

J. Trebolle Barrera, 4QJudgᵃ, *DJD* XIV, Oxford 1995, pp. 161–164

——, "Textual Variations in 4QJudgᵃ and Editorial History of the Book of Judges", *Revue de Qumran* 54 (1989), pp. 229–245

P. Trible, "The Daughter of Jephthah: An Inhuman Sacrifice", *Text of Terror: Literary-Feminist Readings of Biblical Narratives*, Philadelphia 1984, pp. 93–115

B. Uffenheimer, *Early Prophecy in Israel* (trans. D. Louvish), Jerusalem 1999

B. Uspanski, *A Poetic of Composition: The Structure of the Artistic Text and Typology of a Compositional Form* (trans. V. Zavarin and S. Wittig), Berkley 1973

P. J. van Midden, "Gideon", J. W. Dyk, et al. (eds.), *The Rediscovery of the Hebrew Bible* Amsterdamse Cahiers voor Exegese van de Bijbel en zijn Tradities, Supplement Series 1), Maastricht 1999, pp. 51–67

J. Van Seters, *In Search of History: Historiography in the Ancient World and the Origins of Biblical History*, New Haven and London 1983

——, "The Conquest of Sihon's Kingdom: A Literary Examination", *JBL* 91 (1972), pp. 182–197

——, "Once Again—The Conquest of Sihon's Kingdom", *JBL* 99 (1980), pp. 117–119

G. von Rad, *Old Testament Theology*, I, *The Theology of Israel's Historical Traditions* (D. M. G. Stalker), Edinburgh and London 1962

——, "שלום in the OT", *Theological Dictionary of the New Testament*, vol. 2, Grand Rapids, pp. 402–406

N. M. Waldman, "The Imagery of Clothing, Covering, and Overpowering", *JANES* 19 (1989), pp. 161–170

B. G. Webb, *The Book of the Judges: An Integrated Reading* (JSOTsup, 46) Sheffield 1987

M. Weinfeld, "Zion and Jerusalem as Religious and Political Capital: Ideology and Utopia", R. E. Friedman (ed.), *The Poet and the Historian: Essays in Literary and Historical Biblical Criticism* (Harvard Semitic Studies), Chico 1983, pp. 75–115

Z. Weisman, "Charismatic Leaders in the Era of the Judges", *ZAW* 89 (1977), pp. 399–411

M. Weiss, "Einiges über die Bauformen des Erzählens in der Bibel", *VT* 13 (1963), pp. 456–475

J. Wellhausen, *Prolegomena to the History of Ancient Israel*, Cleveland and New York 1957

——, *Die Composition des Hexateuchs und der historischen Bücher des alten Testaments*, Berlin 1889

C. Westermann, *Basic Forms of Prophetic Speech* (trans. H. C. White), Cambridge and Louisville 1991

K. W. Whitelam, *The Just King: Monarchial Judicial Authority in Ancient Israel* (JSOTsup, 12), Sheffield 1979

C. F. Whitley, "The Sources of the Gideon Stories", *VT* 7 (1957), pp. 157–164

F. Willesen, "The *'efrātî* of the Shibboleth Incident", *VT* 8 (1958), pp. 97–98

J. G. Williams, "The Structure of Judges 2:6–16:31", *JSOT* 49 (1991), pp. 77–85

H. G. M. Williamson, "Isaiah 8:21 and a New Inscription from Ekron", *BAIAS* 18 (2000), pp. 51–55

C. W. Wolf, "Traces of Primitive Democracy in Ancient Israel", *JNES* 6 (1947), pp. 98–108

H. W. Wolff, "Kerygma of the Deuteronomic Historical Work", W. Brueggmann and H. W. Wolff (eds.), *The Vitality of the Old Testament Traditions*, Atlanta 1975, pp. 81–100

L. Wood, *Distressing Days of the Judges*, Grand Rapids 1975

G. E. Wright, *Shechem: The Biography of a Biblical City*, New York and Toronto 1965

M. Wüst, "Die Einschaltung in die Jiftachgeschichte Ri. 11:13–26", *Biblica* 56 (1975), pp. 464–479

Y. Yadin, *The Art of Warfare in Biblical Lands In Light of Archaeological Discovery* (trans. M. Pearlman), London 1963

G. A. Yee (ed.), *Judges and Method: New Approaches in Biblical Studies*, Minneapolis 1995

Y. Zakovitch, "אחת דבר אלוהים שתים זו שמעתי: 'מבעים דו-משמעיים בסיפורת המקראית'", לזכרו של פרופי מאיר ויס, Jerusalem 1999, pp. 21–68 (Hebrew) [= "One the Word of God Two I Heard This: Ambiguous Expressions in the Biblical Narrative, *In Memory of Prof. M. Weiss*]

——, "A Study of Precise and Partial Derivations in Biblical Etymology", *JSOT* 15 (1980), pp. 31–50

——, "יבדן = יפתח", *VT* 22 (1972), pp.

——, "Review on: A. Rofé, *The Book of Balaam* (Numbers 22:2–24:25): A study in Methods of Criticism and the History of Biblical Literature and Religion, Jerusalem 1979", *Kiryat Sefer* 54 (1979), pp. 785–789 (Hebrew)

——, "The Associative Arrangement of the Book of Judges and Its Use for the Recognition of Stages in Formation of the Book", A. Rofé and Y. Zakovitch and (eds.), *Isac Leo Seeligmann Volume: Essays on the Bible and Ancient World*, I, Jerusalem 1983, (Hebrew), pp. 161–183

——, "The Synonymous Word and the Synonymous Name in Name-Midrashim", *Shnaton: An Annual for Biblical and Ancient Near Eastern Studies* 2 (1977), 110–115 (Hebrew, Eng. Summary, p. xxviii)

——, "The Woman's Rights in the Biblical Law of Divorce", *The Jewish Law Annual* 4 (1981), pp. 28–46

——, "The Story of Yair and the Fiery Furnace: A Study of Pseudo-Philo Chapter 38", S. Japhet (ed.), *The Bible in Light of Its Interpreters: Sarah Kamin Memorial Volume*, Jerusalem 1994, pp. 141–156 (Hebrew)

——, *Through the Looking Glass: Reflection Stories in the Bible* (Hillal ben Haim Library), Tel Aviv 1995 (Hebrew)

——, "Assimilation in Biblical Narratives", J. H. Tigay (ed.), *Empirical Models for Biblical Criticism*, Philadelphia 1985, pp. 175–196

——, *The Pattern of Numerical Sequence Three-Four in the Bible*, Ph.D. Diss., The Hebrew University, 1977 (Hebrew)

——, *The Life of Samson (Judges 13–16): A Critical-Literary Analysis*, Jerusalem 1982 (Hebrew)

——, *The Concept of Miracle in the Bible* (The Broadcast University Library), Tel Aviv 1987

INDEX OF BIBLICAL REFERENCES

References from Judges 6–12 are listed only when referred to out of their immediate context

10:11–14	245	18:6–7	214
10:11–13	207	18:6ff.	212
10:11–12	2	22:9–23	124
10:11	183	24:14	62
10:13	201	26:10	68
10:17	201	29:4	68
11:1–12:7	1	31:4	102
11:1	29, 236		
11:3	237	*2 Samuel*	
11:7	236	2:4	51
11:27	236	3:7	112
11:35	236	3:8	62
12:1–6	228	5:1	136
12:2–3	236	5:3	51
12:4–6	3, 236	5:13	112
13–16	1, 127	6:20	137
13:1	17–18	7:11	242
13:22	38	9:8	62
13:23	38	11:21	170
14:6	51, 201	16:10	202
14:19	201	17:9	62
15:10–13	232	17:12	112
15:11	128, 190	19:12–13	136
15:14	51, 201	19:23	202
16:16	184	21:14	114
16:31	234	24:11–16	181
17–21	129, 232	24:17	39
17:5	107		
17:6	129	*1 Kings*	
19:10–12	242	2:10	114
		3:5	73
1 Samuel		8:54	63
1:24	37	10:1–10	137
7:3–4	181	10:12–14	137
8:7	145, 239	11:1–3	112
9:1	29	11:3	112
9:21	34	11:28	29
9:16	239	11:43	114
10:1	51	14:31	114
10:19	239	15:8	114
10:21–27	51	15:24	114
10:22	123	17:28	202
10:26	123	17:34	113
11:14–15	51	18:17–18	216
12:12	239	18:23–39	38
13:6	18	18:34–35	38
14:24–45	223	19:18	63
14:24–27	217	26:6	29
14:29	216		
14:33ff.	137	*2 Kings*	
14:43–44	217	1:15–16	39
14:45	217	3:13	202
15	124	11:1–16	141
15:13	51	15:20	29
17:43	62	19:7	39

SUPPLEMENTS TO VETUS TESTAMENTUM

64. HARLAND, P.J. *The Value of Human Life*. A Study of the Story of the Flood (Genesis 6-9). 1996. ISBN 90 04 10534 4

65. ROLAND PAGE JR., H. *The Myth of Cosmic Rebellion*. A Study of its Reflexes in Ugaritic and Biblical Literature. 1996. ISBN 90 04 10563 8

66. EMERTON, J.A. (ed.). *Congress Volume, Cambridge 1995*. 1997. ISBN 90 04 106871

67. JOOSTEN, J. *People and Land in the Holiness Code*. An Exegetical Study of the Ideational Framework of the Law in Leviticus 17–26. 1996. ISBN 90 04 10557 3

68. BEENTJES, P.C. *The Book of Ben Sira in Hebrew*. A Text Edition of all Extant Hebrew Manuscripts and a Synopsis of all Parallel Hebrew Ben Sira Texts. 1997. ISBN 90 04 10767 3

69. COOK, J. *The Septuagint of Proverbs – Jewish and/or Hellenistic Proverbs?* Concerning the Hellenistic Colouring of LXX Proverbs. 1997. ISBN 90 04 10879 3

70,1 BROYLES, G. and C. EVANS (eds.). *Writing and Reading the Scroll of Isaiah*. Studies of an Interpretive Tradition, I. 1997. ISBN 90 04 10936 6 (*Vol.* I); ISBN 90 04 11027 5 (*Set*)

70,2 BROYLES, G. and C. EVANS (eds.). *Writing and Reading the Scroll of Isaiah*. Studies of an Interpretive Tradition, II. 1997. ISBN 90 04 11026 7 (*Vol.* II); ISBN 90 04 11027 5 (*Set*)

71. KOOIJ, A. VAN DER. *The Oracle of Tyre*. The Septuagint of Isaiah 23 as Version and Vision. 1998. ISBN 90 04 11152 2

72. TOV, E. *The Greek and Hebrew Bible*. Collected Essays on the Septuagint. 1999. ISBN 90 04 11309 6

73. GARCÍA MARTÍNEZ, F. and NOORT, E. (eds.). *Perspectives in the Study of the Old Testament and Early Judaism*. A Symposium in honour of Adam S. van der Woude on the occasion of his 70th birthday. 1998. ISBN 90 04 11322 3

74. KASSIS, R.A. *The Book of Proverbs and Arabic Proverbial Works*. 1999. ISBN 90 04 11305 3

75. RÖSEL, H.N. *Von Josua bis Jojachin*. Untersuchungen zu den deuteronomistischen Geschichtsbüchern des Alten Testaments. 1999. ISBN 90 04 11355 5

76. RENZ, Th. *The Rhetorical Function of the Book of Ezekiel*. 1999. ISBN 90 04 11362 2

77. HARLAND, P.J. and HAYWARD, C.T.R. (eds.). *New Heaven and New Earth Prophecy and the Millenium*. Essays in Honour of Anthony Gelston. 1999. ISBN 90 04 10841 6

78. KRAŠOVEC, J. *Reward, Punishment, and Forgiveness*. The Thinking and Beliefs of Ancient Israel in the Light of Greek and Modern Views. 1999. ISBN 90 04 11443 2.

79. KOSSMANN, R. *Die Esthernovelle – Vom Erzählten zur Erzählung*. Studien zur Traditions- und Redaktionsgeschichte des Estherbuches. 2000. ISBN 90 04 11556 0.

80. LEMAIRE, A. and M. SÆBØ (eds.). *Congress Volume, Oslo 1998*. 2000. ISBN 90 04 11598 6.

81. GALIL, G. and M. WEINFELD (eds.). *Studies in Historical Geography and Biblical Historiography*. Presented to Zecharia Kallai. 2000. ISBN 90 04 11608 7

82. COLLINS, N.L. *The library in Alexandria and the Bible in Greek*. 2001. ISBN 90 04 11866 7

83,1 COLLINS, J.J. and P.W. FLINT (eds.). *The Book of Daniel*. Composition and Reception, I. 2001. ISBN 90 04 11675 3 (*Vol.* I); ISBN 90 04 12202 8 (*Set*).

83,2 COLLINS, J.J. and P.W. FLINT (eds.). *The Book of Daniel.* Composition and Reception, II. 2001. ISBN 90 04 12200 1 (*Vol* II); ISBN 90 04 12202 8 (*Set*)

84. COHEN, C.H.R. *Contextual Priority in Biblical Hebrew Philology.* An Application of the Held Method for Comparative Semitic Philology. 2001. ISBN 90 04 11670 2 (In preparation).

85. WAGENAAR, J.A. *Judgement and Salvation.* The Composition and Redaction of Micah 2-5. 2001. ISBN 90 04 11936 1

86. MCLAUGHLIN, J.L. *The* Marzēaḥ *in sthe Prophetic Literature.* References and Allusions in Light of the Extra-Biblical Evidence. 2001. ISBN 90 04 12006 8

87. WONG, K.L. *The Idea of Retribution in the Book of Ezekiel* 2001. ISBN 90 04 12256 7

88. BARRICK, W. Boyd *The King and the Cemeteries.* Toward a New Understanding of Josiah's Reform. 2002. ISBN 90 04 12171 4

89. FRANKEL, D. *The Murmuring Stories of the Priestly School.* A Retrieval of Ancient Sacerdotal Lore. 2002. ISBN 90 04 12368 7

90. FRYDRYCH, T. *Living under the Sun.* Examination of Proverbs and Qoheleth. 2002. ISBN 90 04 12315 6

91. KESSEL, J. *The Book of Haggai.* Prophecy and Society in Early Persian Yehud. 2002. ISBN 90 04 12368 7

92. LEMAIRE, A. (ed.). *Congress Volume, Basel 2001.* 2002. ISBN 90 04 12680 5

93. RENDTORFF, R. and R.A. KUGLER (eds.). *The Book of Leviticus.* Composition and Reception. 2003. ISBN 90 04 12634 1

94. PAUL, S.M., R.A. KRAFT, L.H. SCHIFFMAN and W.W. FIELDS (eds.). *Emanuel.* Studies in Hebrew Bible, Septuagint, and Dead Sea Scrolls in Honor of Emanuel Tov. 2003. ISBN 90 04 13007 1

95. VOS, J.C. DE. *Das Los Judas.* Über Entstehung und Ziele der Landbeschreibung in Josua 15. ISBN 90 04 12953 7

96. LEHNART, B. *Prophet und König im Nordreich Israel.* Studien zur sogenannten vorklassischen Prophetie im Nordreich Israel anhand der Samuel-, Elija- und Elischa-Überlieferungen. 2003. ISBN 90 04 13237 6

97. LO, A. *Job 28 as Rhetoric.* An Analysis of Job 28 in the Context of Job 22-31. 2003. ISBN 90 04 13320 8

98. TRUDINGER, P.L. *The Psalms of the Tamid Service.* A Liturgical Text from the Second Temple. 2004. ISBN 90 04 12968 5

99. FLINT, P.W. and P.D. MILLER, JR. (eds.) with the assistance of A. Brunell. *The Book of Psalms.* Composition and Reception. 2004. ISBN 90 04 13842 8

100. WEINFELD, M. *The Place of the Law in the Religion of Ancient Israel.* 2004. ISBN 90 04 13749 1

101. FLINT, P.W., J.C. VANDERKAM and E. TOV. (eds.) *Studies in the Hebrew Bible, Qumran, and the Septuagint.* Essays Presented to Eugene Ulrich on the Occasion of his Sixty-Fifth Birthday. 2004. ISBN 90 04 13738 6

102. MEER, M.N. VAN DER. *Formation and Reformulation.* The Redaction of the Book of Joshua in the Light of the Oldest Textual Witnesses. 2004. ISBN 90 04 13125 6

103. BERMAN, J.A. *Narrative Analogy in the Hebrew Bible.* Battle Stories and Their Equivalent Non-battle Narratives. 2004. ISBN 90 04 13119 1

104. KEULEN, P.S.F. VAN. *Two Versions of the Solomon Narrative.* An Inquiry into the Relationship between MT 1 Kgs. 2-11 and LXX 3 Reg. 2-11. 2004. ISBN 90 04 13895 1

105. MARX, A. *Les systèmes sacrificiels de l'Ancien Testament.* Forms et fonctions du culte sacrificiel à Yhwh. 2005. ISBN 90 04 14286 X

106. ASSIS, E. *Self-Interest or Communal Interest.* An Ideology of Leadership in the Gideon, Abimelech and Jephthah Narritives (Judg 6-12). 2005. ISBN 90 04 14354 8